BATAVIA PUBLIC LIBRARY DISTRICT

3 6173 00143 924

W9-CFJ-288

Timothy Mason
Ten Plays for Children

from the Repertory of
The Children's Theatre Company
of Minneapolis

WITHDRAWN

WITHDRAWN

TIMOTHY MASON
Ten Plays for Children

from the Repertory of
The Children's Theatre Company
of Minneapolis

YOUNG ACTORS SERIES

A Smith and Kraus Book

A Smith and Kraus Book
Published by Smith and Kraus, Inc.
PO Box 127, Lyme, NH 03768

Copyright ©1998 by Timothy Mason
All rights reserved
Manufactured in the United States of America
Cover and Text Design by Julia Hill

First Edition: March 1998
10 9 8 7 6 5 4 3 2 1

CAUTION: Professionals and amateurs are hereby warned that all plays and the excerpts from the musical scores thereto in this volume are fully protected under the copyright laws of the United States of America, and of all other contracting states of the Universal Copyright Convention. The sale or purchase of this volume does not constitute authorization to perform, read publicly, televise or adapt for television, film or adapt for motion pictures, record, broadcast, translate into other languages or reproduce the play wholly or in part, in any other manner, all such rights being strictly reserved. All inquiries regarding the plays in this volume should be addressed to International Creative Management, Inc., 40 West 57th Street, New York, NY 10019 (attention: Bridget Aschenberg).

The Adventures of Huckleberry Finn ©1981 by Timothy Mason.
Adventures of Tom Sawyer ©1976 by Timothy Mason.
African Tales: Kalulu and His Money Farm and Rumpelstiltskin ©1972 by Timothy Mason.
Aladdin and the Wonderful Lamp ©1977 by The Children's Theatre Company and School and Timothy Mason.
Kidnapped in London ©1970 by Timothy Mason.
Pinocchio ©1974 The Children's Theatre Company and School and Timothy Mason.
Treasure Island ©1975 by The Children's Theatre Company and School and Timothy Mason.
The Ukrainian Tales ©1974 by Timothy Mason.
Beauty and the Beast ©1978 by The Children's Theatre Company and School and Timothy Mason.
The Nightingale ©1974 by Timothy Mason.

The Library of Congress Cataloging-In-Publication Data

Mason, Timothy.
The Children's Theatre Company of Minneapolis: ten plays for children /
written and adapted by Timothy Mason. —1st ed.

p. cm. — (Young actors series)
Contents: The adventures of Huckleberry Finn — The adventures of Tom Sawyer — African tales — Pinocchio — Aladdin and the wonderful lamp — Treasure Island — Beauty and the beast — Ukrainian tales — Kidnapped in London — The Nightingale.

ISBN 1-57525-120-5

1. Children's plays, American—Minnesota—Minneapolis. [1. Plays.]
I. Children's Theatre Company (Minneapolis, Minn.) II. Title. III. Series.

PS3563.A799C48   1997
812'.54—dc21   97-17898
                  CIP
                  AC

CONTENTS

INTRODUCTION

Each of the plays in this anthology is an adaptation of a classic work of children's literature or folklore. Each was originally commissioned and produced by the remarkable Children's Theatre Company of Minneapolis, founded by John Clark Donahue in 1965.

One facet of the vision that shaped this company was a conviction that the greatest works of literature for the young maintain an undeniable, undying strength, no matter the era from which they may have sprung. The stories told by Robert Louis Stevenson, Hans Christian Andersen, and Mark Twain all speak to children today as clearly as they did when they were first written. They don't require doctoring to make them relevant or entertaining, any more than do the works of Homer or Aeschylus or Shakespeare.

There is no contemporary spin to any of these adaptations. These are not "Fractured Fairy Tales." I was nineteen years old when I wrote the first of them, and from that moment to the present day I have felt respect and a certain amount of awe to be in the presence of the masters who first told these stories. What I learned from them cannot be calculated. And, for hundreds of thousands of children who made up my audiences, these scripts have been an early introduction to the world of literature as well as a first glimpse of the transcendent, transforming world of the stage.

The Minneapolis Children's Theatre Company was and is unusual, in that it had relatively big budgets, big sets, and big casts. After the Moscow Central Children's Theatre, the Minneapolis CTC is probably the largest professional theatre for young audiences in the world. (This size was earned; the Company was not born with a silver spoon anywhere near it. The group was able to grow because it slowly taught the generous Twin Cities public that theatre for young people was an important part of its life and future.)

A few of the scripts here are modest in scale and production requirements (*The Nightingale, African Tales,* and *Ukrainian Tales*). Most of the other adaptations reflect the size of the company for which they were written: big sets, big casts. I want to emphasize, nonetheless, that all of the plays here have been subsequently produced successfully by small theatres, schools, and community groups. The imagination and resourcefulness of the director and producing group has made it possible again and again for these stories to be shared theatrically with a great many children. As the playwright involved, I have always allowed far greater liberties (in double casting, eliminating minor characters, and text-trimming) to those producing these plays than I would for anyone mounting my "grown-up" plays.

The Minneapolis Company always employed professional adult actors to play adult roles, and children to play children's roles. Here again, other groups have produced these plays successfully with all-child casts, and with all-adult casts. If the vision is clear and consistent, the plays seem to work, whatever the approach.

Plays have a life on the page, but they live more fully on the stage, so that's where I hope these plays end up. But whether you are a director, a producer, a teacher, or a reader, I extend to you an invitation to savor and share this decade of work with our most important audience, our children.

Timothy Mason
July 10, 1997

Kidnapped in London

Suggested by John Bennett's 19th century novel, *Master Skylark*

Kidnapped In London was first presented by
The Children's Theatre Company of Minneapolis on January 16, 1970.
Produced and directed by John Clark Donahue
Designed by Jon Barkla
With music composed by Roberta Carlson

Kidnapped In London was remounted by
The Children's Theatre Company in September, 1980.
Directed by Charles Nolte
Costume and set design by Tanya Moiseivitsch
Music by Steven Rydberg
Produced by John Clark Donahue

CHARACTERS *in order of appearance*

* Corin Marvell, A country boy, 11–13 years old, soprano voice
  Benjamin Marvell, His father (may double as a Player of Blackfriars)
  Nellie Marvell, His mother (may double as a Tavern Woman)
  Citizens, Sailors, and Tradesmen of London

THE PLAYERS OF BLACKFRIARS
* Diccon Burbage, The Master Player, 30s–40s
* Fan-Dan, An old actor
* Cuthbert Bogs, An actor
* Geoffrey Bile, The Master of Song, an older man
* Joseph Taylor, a little older than Corin, about 15 years old
  Boy Apprentices and Adult Actors

Two Rogues (may double as Players of Blackfriars)
Women and Serving Girls in the tavern
Peasant Man (may double as an actor)
Jailors, Prisoners (may double as actors)

* *Denotes principal speaking roles.*

Kidnapped in London has a running time of one hour, ten minutes.

SETTING
The Warwickshire countryside and London in the era of Elizabeth I, late 1590s.

The set resembles an open inn-yard theatre of Elizabethan London. A central platform has gallery space on either side. Each gallery has an upper and lower level. Upstage of the platform is a balcony and chamber space for the use of the Players. On the platform, which revolves, are posts hung with tapestried curtains. The costumes are period and the palette is of renaissance hues, gilding, greens, and earthy colors. Textures are velvet, homespun, silks, roughly hewn and elaborately carved.

NOTES ON THE PLAY
AND ITS ORIGINAL PRODUCTION

From the age of fifteen, I was virtually raised in and by a professional company of child and adult actors, as was the young protagonist of *Kidnapped In London*. Thus, on one level, the play speaks for myself and my "fellow-prisoners" in the exciting and sometimes harsh world of theatre. However, any interest which the play may hold is not limited to some elite circle of child-actors. My years of experience working with and for children (and, of course, my own childhood) have taught me that there is no creature more full of *yearning* than a young girl or boy. The gestures of childhood seem to be a reaching, grasping, sometimes almost envious striving for a world that lies waiting. For an audience of children, life on the stage becomes a metaphor for all of the yearnings that spell out the meaning of childhood.

The dialect, as it is printed in the script and as it was performed, is a conventional approximation of Elizabethan pronunciation. Although we can have no certain knowledge of what Shakespeare's English sounded like, some scholars feel that it resembled a modern Scottish brogue. This is the pattern that I followed.

The action and dialogue are, I believe, reasonably true to the period. Companies of child-players were very much in fashion (they are mentioned in *Hamlet,* Act II, Scene ii.) And, it was not uncommon for a promising-looking youngster to be literally kidnapped off the streets.

Timothy Mason, 1970

A FURTHER NOTE

The set for the 1980 revival described here was created by the legendary theatre designer, Tanya Moiseivitsch, who came up with an exquisite stylized suggestion of an Elizabethan playhouse. A much more modest design approach is perfectly acceptable, of course, since the essence of an Elizabethan stage is simply a platform with actors on it.

For information concerning the original score by Roberta Carlson, or the revival score by Steven M. Rydberg, contact The Children's Theatre Company of Minneapolis.

Kidnapped in London

SCENE I
Dusk in the Warwickshire Hills

Corin Marvell seated on a mound of hay. The boy is singing softly with the other sounds of dusk.

NELLIE MARVELL: *(Calling from Offstage.)* Cory. Whur beest thou? Come now. Tis gone bedtime, lad.

CORIN: *(Singing.)* To Mary, Queen, awakening
One bleak mid-winter morn,
Came like a falcon to its King
Fair Jesu to be born.
And though the wind was cold as stars,
And though the shadows, long,
When winter's cage flung wide its bars
The skylark found his song.
For spring awoke that very day
And warmed December's dawn,
To hear the skylark's gladsome lay
Like dew upon the lawn.

NELLIE: Now, I says, Cory.

CORIN: To Mary, Queen, awakening
One bleak mid-winter morn,
Came like a falcon to its King
Fair Jesu to be born.

NELLIE: *(Offstage.)* Cory!
(A frog croaks.)

CORIN: *(Laughing.)* Ssssh. Do na thou sing so, old toad. Tch, tch, tch, such a croak! List' to thy bird friend here. He hath more grace…

NELLIE: *(Offstage.)* Corin! I've ears ye know. I hear thee. Come in out o' that!

CORIN: *(Imitating Nellie.)* I've ears ye know, Corin. Lambs and she-goats, soft now. Sing low. Mother shall come wroth wi' thee. She hath ears, ye know. *(Yawn and stretch.)* Stars and bright things—do na shine so loud. Tis gone bedtime, don't ye see.

BENJAMIN MARVELL: *(Coming down to Corin.)* Sloth and folly, Nell. I'll have

no idler for a…Corin Marvell! I bid thee come, and come now, if thou
wouldst go wi' me morrow to London town.

CORIN: I' faith, Father, I was not idle. I was minding the flock, sir, with an
eye to that old ram, sir, do ye know the one, butting and jumping at
whiles, sir, and may I na' go wi' thee, Father, may I na'?

BENJAMIN: Minding the flock with a silly song, and a man might earn his
bread dancing in a motley jerkin if ye'd have thy way. Ah, Corin, shun
folly and do na let they head be turned. Come now to bed. We've a long
journey on the morrow. *(Benjamin goes into the house.)*

CORIN: *(To the hills.)* My sheep and billies, go quiet now to sleep. Mind ye
shun folly till I come back. I've a long journey on the morrow.

SCENE II
London!

*Tambourine bang! and lights up Downstage Center, where a jester pops out
from platform curtain. He jerks like a puppet on strings and beckons the
audience to follow him. Young girls dance by, dim shafts of light fall across
the stage to hint at people of the city gathered about in frozen motion.
Vendors slowly come to life, hawking their goods in a round.*

FIRST VENDOR: Red onions, buy my onions!

SECOND VENDOR: Fine laces for a lady!

THIRD VENDOR: Fresh mackerel, fresh mackerel!

FOURTH VENDOR: New oysters, new oysters!

*(Stage slowly begins moving into action as tradesmen, fine ladies and gentle-
men, chimney sweeps and others start crossing, calling out, dancing, acceler-
ating until it becomes a swirl of intoxicating song and activity. Sailors are
downstage left, unloading a barge. Corin enters, running. His parents follow, buying, haggling, but ill at ease in the big town. The boy stops, smells
the air, and looks about him as the Sailor begins to sing. Vendors bark in the
distance.)*

FIRST SAILOR: Cast her down easy, my hearty lads all,
Leave *Gabriel* behind.
For the goodliest mate that ever did sail
Sleeps now among the brine.
Full twenty and four at Whitsuntide,
Afore the moon did bleed.

Come into port on Michaelmas,
With only twenty-three.
There fast on deck stood gentle Dan,
Whilst we all hied to lee.
Come down, I cried, my Danly, dear,
Thou canst na' still the sea.
I'll hold the stays, sung darlin' Dan,
Aye, with me hands blood-red.
Tis but the wings of Gabriel,
A' beatin' 'bout my head.
Tell me lady, Marilee,
How she lost her Dan—
On the good ship *Gabriel*,
True as any man.
Came the morning, still the storm,
Danly, he was gone.
In the deep—some angel's wings,
A' driftin' with the foam.

(Small pause and quiet. Suddenly a Sailor throws Corin up in the air, and sets him on his shoulder.)

FIRST SAILOR: Whoy, lads, here be a piece o' baggage! Do we want it for to sail the briny deep?

SECOND SAILOR: Aye, that we do!

THIRD SAILOR: Need another hand!

SECOND SAILOR: I says, bring it along!

THIRD SAILOR: To Africa!

FIRST SAILOR: What, to Africa. To Ethiopia! Blackamoors!

SECOND SAILOR: Rings through their noses!

THIRD SAILOR: Bones…!

FIRST SAILOR: What say ye, boy? Will ye have a bit o' the sailor's life?

BENJAMIN: *(Approaching.)* Cory! Hie thee here!

CORIN: *(To Sailors as they set him down.)* Nay, sir. But thankee, sir. *(Runs to his parents.)*

NELLIE: *(Taking Corin in her arms.)* There's me stout son. Did yon rogue fright' thee?

CORIN: Nay, Mother. But didst thou hear him sing? Twas the beautifullest thing ever I list' to. I' faith, he was singing about islands and he said that might be I could go there…

(Tambourine, drum roll, horn and cymbal. The Players of Blackfriars enter

from Right and swirl across to Left Center, tumbling and waving swords and banners. The center platform turns, holding some actors, and the Citizens gather Downstage Left on the upper and lower levels, laughing and murmuring. Corin stands among those at the front of the crowd. In a matter of moments, the stage has become full. The Jester does a pantomime, and the Players sing.)

PLAYERS: The hunt is up, the hunt is up,

And it is well nigh day,

And Harry our King has gone a' hunting

To bring his deer to bay.

  The east is bright with morning light

And darkness it is fled.

The early horn wakes up the morn,

To leave its idle bed.

  The hunt is up, the hunt is up,

The dogs are running free.

The woods rejoice at the merry noise

Of hey, tan-ta-rah, ta-ree!

HERALD: *(Reading from a long scroll.)* Good, me citizens, hark ye well!

Today to 'Friars come ye all,

Where performed anon shall be

Most gay and witty comedie!

The Dame's Displeasure

Wherein a lady seeks to win

The attentions of two gentlemen.

(Fan-Dan and Geoffrey Bile do a comic pantomime: trying to win the favors of a maiden, with Joseph Taylor as the maiden. There is a great deal of interaction with the spectators throughout this scene. Burbage does a comic sword fight with Bile to finish the street presentation.)

FAN-DAN: *(Pointing to Corin.)* Here, Diccon, see how the bumpkin gapes!

BURBAGE: Why lad, thy mouth's so wide, could easy catch a cow! What? Hast thou no penny for the play? Take ye this one, then. *(Tosses Corin a coin.)* And, pray, shut thy mouth.

(In a friendly manner, Burbage taps Corin's mouth shut. The Spectators laugh; the Players sing and exit left. Corin turns to his parents, holding up the coin, but stops short when he hears his father.)

BENJAMIN: Such a pack o' rogues. Puttin' folly an' proud notions into silly heads. Cory. Nell. Come.

(Benjamin and Nell leave, Right. Corin stands, torn. He looks toward the

exiting Players, and then to his exiting parents. Looks at the coin and makes his decision. The boy runs after the actors. Two Sailors are kneeling beneath the gallery, Left. Corin scrambles up the backs of the sailors to pull himself onto the upper level and runs out Left.)

SCENE III
The Masque: "A Wedding in the Glade"

The afternoon's performance is nearly finished on the stage at the Blackfriars—the Center revolving platform. A Wedding in the Glade and the Epilogue remain. The audience stands about, holding up babies to see, eating, leaning on the railings. Corin stands among them. Actors holding arches of flowering branches stand at either side of Upstage Center. Other actors holding wreaths of evergreens and blossoms are at Downstage Left and Downstage Right. The Old Man of the Woods enters and stands Downstage Right Center. As he calls to various creatures, they enter in pairs from either side of the stage. Creatures are identified by mask: nymphs, unicorn, foxes, deer, birds.

OLD MAN OF THE WOODS: Come elves, sprites of earth and air,
Secret spirits, nymphs and bearded trolls;
Snow-crowned unicorns—hie thee here and there
With the Friends of Faerie to see married, merry souls.
Humbler creatures, too, I summon thee:
Little foxes, proud-head deer and fawn…
Any other? Aye, there's two-legg'd Greybeard—me!
Now a wedding dance dance ye on a crystal lawn.
(The creatures dance while Bride and Groom enter, Upstage Center, and stand framed by the flowering arch. Old Man hands each a wreath, and each crowns the other.)
OLD MAN: For in this holy grove beneath the bowers
Are wed in secret, King and Queen of May;
And in heart's secret place bloom secret flowers
To lighten Lord and Lady's secret way.
And who, dear friends, hath seen what no man dreams,
But you, dear friends, in whom this secret gleams.
(The Bride and Groom cross and stand with joined hands as the Old Man

stands behind them and slowly lifts his cape. His cape is lined in gold, and it forms a golden backdrop for the couple. As he does this, Burbage speaks.)

BURBAGE: When next with fire and smoke yon sun of wonder

By Ocean's lips devoured be, and put asunder

Are all our fancies—all our dreams, like dreams,

Forgot' and vanish'd—then shall grow till seems

Them waking visions, strange shapes of myst'ry and delight.

These our simple phantoms change, take flight,

And move men's souls. No longer one man's gesture,

Another's song, but alter'd so, a future

Age shall marvel, that sprung from these rough boards

A dance undying on ever-green greenswards.

(All join hands and dance a courtly masque, weaving in and out until finally Bride and Groom are framed at Center by all the creatures and flowers. They stand throwing rose petals at the audience as the lights fade.)

SCENE IV
Kidnapped!

The stage is empty, but for Corin. He picks up rose petals scattered by the Players, and lets them drift through his fingers. He is dazed.

CORIN: Oh. Twas good and…fine. I' faith, twas very good and fine… *(He does a few dance steps in imitation of what he has seen, then looks around and realizes that he is alone. He suddenly remembers that he has left his parents behind.)* Mother…My father…?

(Other persons drift across the stage. A man and woman walk by in conversation. Corin runs to them. He grabs the woman's arm and she whirls around.)

CORIN: Mother!…oh, mum, I…

(The woman pulls away gently and she and the man laugh as they exit.)

WOMAN: He thought I was his mother!

(Other people cross back and forth, adding to Corin's confusion and loneliness. People cross carrying baskets. An old man and two drunks pass by. An elegant lady carrying a rose crosses, accompanied by her servant. Corin gapes in awe; the elegant woman smiles and hands him the rose, then exits. Finally, Corin sits on the edge of the platform and, as one would whistle in the dark, he begins to sing.)

BURBAGE: Well?

(*Low murmuring from the crowd. Fan-Dan hands a mug to Corin. Corin starts to drink, stops, puts his finger in the ale and makes the sign of the cross on himself, then flicks ale at Burbage and throws the mug into Fan-Dan's face.*)

CORIN: Tis well?

(*He turns about, challenging them all. The crowd laughs and applauds.*)

BURBAGE: Now, don't ye see why it is I had to bring him. His name is Corin Marvell—and ain't he though. He's from the hills or so he says—but somewheres the country sun must have set fire to his tongue and the forest deer have taught him grace. "Tis well" what, Master Marvell? These are not they goats: Here be thy new colleagues of Blackfriars.

CORIN: I'd rather have me goats.

(*Burbage laughs. Varied reactions from the company to Cory's tongue.*)

MAUREEN: Oh, he's a beauty!

GEOFF: Fire? Oh, his tongue's on fire, sure.

FAN-DAN: Aye, and it's forked as well.

DICK: Goats! He can go back to his goats, I says.

LILY: But such a beauty!

(*Geoffrey Bile, the Singing Master, approaches.*)

BURBAGE: (*Silencing the crowd.*) Here, cuckoos! (*To Corin.*) So. Corin, is it? Well, my name is Geoffrey Bile, Master of Song and Light Aires. So. Hast thou a tongue, sweet? A mouth? Little teeth?

(*Corin breaks away, leaps over a bench. Joseph Taylor, a younger actor, has had his head in a bowl of pudding. Looking up, he sees that things have gotten rough with Corin. As Corin leaps, Joseph rises from his bench and quickly guides Corin to a Downstage Left table. Other stage action freezes. Lights focus on the two boys.*)

JOSEPH: Pay them no heed, Corin. They'll come fond of thee, ye know.

CORIN: Me mother and father are fond of me, too, and more, I dare say.

JOSEPH: Thy mother and father. Hast any brothers, Cory?

CORIN: Nay, nor sisters, neither.

JOSEPH: Well, Cory, thou hast no brother, and I have no mother, see? Then we'll be brothers, what Cory? (*Pokes him.*)

CORIN: (*Poking him back.*) First, brother, tell me thy name, brother, afore I make thy eye black, brother.

JOSEPH: (*Stepping back with dignity and bowing.*) I be Master Joseph Taylor, play-actor of Blackfriars. And ye, sir?

CORIN: (*Bowing very ineptly.*) Corin Marvell, the son of my father, sir, shepherd.

JOSEPH: Was that a bow, or are there ants in thy pants?

(Joseph pours ale for them both and they sit. Burbage has approached unnoticed and is listening.)

JOSEPH: Oh, Cory, I'll teach thee how to bow, and how to fence, and how to kiss a lady's hand and...

CORIN: To fence? With swords?

JOSEPH: With rapiers!

CORIN: Cowr!

JOSEPH: And with me, thou'lt be one of Bile's boys and sing till...

CORIN: Bile who?

JOSEPH: *(Laughs.)* Why, Geoffrey Bile, Cory. That one there. With the face like a prune what's been kept in a box overlong. *(Mimics the Singing Master.)* Tut, my cuckoo—Bile talks thus—Birdies, open thy mouths! *(Breaks off, laughing.)* Faith, Master Burbage will teach thee how to play-act and soon...

CORIN: Master Burbage! Nay, he hath stolt me away from me home and I hates him.

JOSEPH: Corin. Do na speak so about thy betters. I' truth, I have hated Diccon Burbage, at whiles. But some say that he is the best play-actor in all of England—some say, Cory, that he be the best play-actor ever was. So. Work hard and soon thou'lt perform with me, what Cory? Come brother, because a man's a low rogue is nothing against his acting.

(Burbage steps into the lights and grabs Joseph's hair in a grip meant to seem playful, but a bit too rough to be taken as such.)

BURBAGE: Upon my troth, Joey's right, boy. Now, aren't ye pleased Diccon Burbage is making a famous man of ye?

CORIN: Master Joey is very kind, sir, but I can na say I be pleased, sir, because of I'm not, sir, I'm not.

(Blackout.)

SCENE VI
Fan-Dan

Curtain is drawn shut at front of Center platform. Several boys are quietly talking and rehearsing at points Upstage. Fan-Dan and Corin are seated Downstage Center on stools, playing a hand game. Fan-Dan writes his name on his hands as the scene opens, then plays hide-and-seek with them, opening and closing his palms swiftly and moving them around. Corin tries to see what is written on them; makes guesses. Finally, Fan-Dan shows his hands to Cory.

FAN-DAN: That's it. Fan-Dan. Now you've got it. Me name. See? Fan-Danny. Well...? God's 'lid, boy! Gape and stretch! How do they call thee?

CORIN: Sir?

FAN-DAN: Thy name, Block. What do they call thee? *(Slaps his hands on his knees in a playful rhythm.)*

CORIN: They do na call me nothin', sir, because of I do na know *them*. *(Imitates slaps on his own knees.)*

FAN-DAN: Thy tongue's sharp anyways, Mister Nothin', if thy wit's not. But they'll know ye soon enough, and ye them, I trow. They're a lot, they are. I remember...

CORIN: Me mother an' father, they call me "Cory." But that's not me name, Christian.

FAN-DAN: Aye, they're a lot, sure. "Colley," did ye say?

CORIN: No.

FAN-DAN: Well, Colley, just you take me own name, if they ain't a lot.

CORIN: Robin, who's me cousin, says just "Cor" sometimes.

FAN-DAN: Well, Robin...

(Corin tries to correct him.)

FAN-DAN: When it was I come to London, 'twas not me name at all. Did I na tell thee just now that me name is Fan-Dan?

CORIN: Yes.

FAN-DAN: Well, Colley, that was not me name at all.

CORIN: What was it, then?

FAN-DAN: Hired out here at the Friars as 'prentice. Was not a bit older than ye are now, not a jot. And if they ain't a lot now, they were then, I'll tell you. "Foot it, Dan" they'd say, meaning to step it in the dance. I danced in those days, Colley-boy. "That's me Fan-Dan!" they'd say, "That's me pretty Danny-high-stepper." From the first day, that's what they called me, don't ye see.

CORIN: Sir, pray, what was thy name?

FAN-DAN: I do na know why they said it. But they're a lot. 'Twas not me name. Fan-Dan. I told them they had it all wrong but they just laughed and said it anyways. I' faith, it's not me name. Me name is John. John Fish. *(Corin takes the pen and scribbles on his hand. He briefly repeats the hand game, then holds his palm open to Fan-Dan.)*

CORIN: Corin Marvell, John. Pleased.

SCENE VII
Bile's Boys

(The quiet stage with Corin and Fan-Dan ending their game bursts into motion as Bile enters. Joseph runs on past Bile and catches a plumed cap that is thrown from the wings. Corin leaps up and rushes after, and suddenly the stage is filled with Bile's boys, shouting and playing keep-away with the cap—Bile in the Center of it all.)

BILE: *(Sputtering, using his stick on every boy within reach.)* Point and counter-point, cuckoo! Here, dreadful children. I loathe each and every one of ye. Little tarts, I'll do something to you. Oooo, such nasties. What? Would ye tread on my toe? That same toe which was once much talked about in some very high places?

(A boy treads on the toe, running.)

BILE: Ooohh! I shall put sharp things in thy shoes. I'll put cuckoo in sacks. You there, thou cast not tell a fugue from a fig! Here, I'll staccato you!

(He flails at the boys with his stick. Burbage enters. Bile straightens himself, mumbles, acts stern. Burbage laughs a bit, then becomes stern himself.)

BURBAGE: Peace, my little bucks!

(He throws his poniard into the stage floor. Instant silence. The boys group into choir positions quickly at Center—all but Corin, who sits on the floor, convulsed with laughter, pointing to Bile's wig that has slipped down around his shoulders.)

BURBAGE: Thou, Marvell, in particular had best heed me. Sir Geoffrey has told me...

BILE: Master of Song, cuckoo, and light aires...

BURBAGE: Bile here has told me that thou spendest thy weeks moping for thy mother like a lost dog.

CORIN: Not lost, sir, but stolen.

BURBAGE: Wretched ingrate. Don't you know that thou'rt Blackfriar's favorite? The whole town's mad for thee.

(The boys turn Upstage. Bile leads them in a soft madrigal, humming.)

CORIN: I was famous once. Famous wi' me mother an' father. Aye, famous.

BURBAGE: Listen, I do love thee. And I'll send thee home straightway, if only ye'll act for me a bit longer. In faith, thou wert born to it, lad. Thou must. Yes, Corin?

CORIN: If I must, sir.

BURBAGE: That's my marvel-throat! *(To Bile.)* Here, old prune-face, get these rogues out of here. And do please put that wig back on. Master Marvell!

Joey Taylor! I did na give thee leave to go. Dost think, Master Marvell, that because ye can turn a fancy note or two that thou canst play-act? Why, ye cannot even talk proper. Joey, show me that thou hast taught this boy to fence.

(*Joey and Corin take dueling swords and begin to fence. Cory does quite well, but Joey is obviously his better. Burbage shouts advice, encouragement. Joey scores a touch.*)

BURBAGE: *(To Corin.)* Come, give me thy weapon.

(*Burbage fences with Joseph. He outmasters him and Joey's sword falls to the floor.*)

BURBAGE: Well, no matter boys. Ye've done me proud and proud I am. Corin, I shall grant thee thy wish.

CORIN: What, Master Burbage, thou'lt let me go home?

BURBAGE: Nay, now I did na say that. Nay, I grant thee today the master's part in the revel of spring! Thou'lt take the part of the young shepherd. I' faith, should suit thee well!

SCENE VIII
Shepherd Masque: "A Tale of Spring"

Preparation transition: Boys are donning robes, getting into costume, practicing bits of song. Meanwhile Bile is clucking about, giving directions. Then Bile bustles the boys out to the stage. Lights down, and up again on a Chorus of boys on the upper level, and an Audience gathered before them. The Chorus sings while a tableau is enacted: Corin is the Shepherd, other boy actors play the Maiden, a Lamb, the Rival Suitor, and the Sun and the Moon. It is a simple tale of spring love, summer marriage, autumn sorrow. The audience responds vocally.

CHORUS: Two songs only does the lover sing:
One for summer, one for spring.
Let fail other seasons, other songs—
Tis not for these the lover longs.
Two voices stir within the heart:
One for dreams and one to part
The soul from dreaming. Pass them by—
Other voices—let them die.
(*Musical transition.*)

In a glade, on a day,
In the dreaming month of May
Lies our tale of love and lover—
Tale of spring, tale of summer.

CORIN: Fast alone the shepherd lives:
The nightingale small comfort gives
When even' falls and lambs do sleep.
And no one grieves to hear me weep.
One I know and her I'll woo,
And for her hand in marriage sue.
When even' falls and lamps will sleep,
I'll comfort know and no more weep.

BOY SOPRANO: In the shade, in the gloom,
Of the waking month of June
Lies our tale of love and lover—
Tale of spring, tale of summer.
(Courtship, marriage pantomime.)

CORIN: Summer came and I was wed,
And for a season round our bed
Did posies grow and myrtle bloom,
For joy that slept twixt Bride and Groom.
(As Corin speaks the following, the Rival Suitor steals the Bride.)

CORIN: The nightingale, never heeding
Flow'rs fall, burst and bleeding,
Sang a song of love's lost lover:
Tale of Spring, Tale of Summer.
(Panto: Corin draws dagger, stabs self, while audience calls to him not to do it. Flowers and laurels from the audience. Curtain call. Great cheering. Corin is borne away on the arms of the citizens. When the crowd has dispersed, we see that Burbage remains alone on the stage, his head sunk on his chest. Lights fade on him.)

SCENE IX
"Two Voices Stir Within the Heart"

Lights up on Burbage, alone. He drinks from a goblet.

BURBAGE: *(Sings.)* "Two voices stir within the heart—

One for dreams and one to part
The soul from dreaming…"

Nay, but from this one dream I would na fain be parted. He's the very spit o' meself, he is. What is it then, Burbage, twenty? Nay, thirty years since twas thou decked out in shepherd's garb for the revel of spring. My robes were not so fine as his, nor was our house as grand, for we had neither the Queen's grace nor even a queen. For a roof, we had the sky—them damn birds kept after droppin' on us. I recall me once how a dropping lit on little Jem's head. He just looked up, quick as ye please, and said "Are the angels fartin' stars, now?" For a crowd, we had the rag-taggle o' London, but they loved us—loved me, even then. Oh, twas a heady wine. Went straight to me head and it was all I ever wanted.

But this Corin, how, this Marvell that I found—him I do not understand. No rag-tag he plays for, but lords and high dames. They sigh and wring their hands and throw flowers, plenty. Who wouldn't, with him stepping pretty as ye please, speaking honey from out his throat? But once he's off, aye, the moment he steps down from the boards, it's all hills and billy-goats with him.

But come, Diccon, dost understand thyself? Ye knew the hills, once.

Aye. And I wonder, do the horses still sleep standin' up? And what of the Avon?

Fool, of course they do—been sleeping so since the seventh day. And the Avon—it flows. What might ye have done in the hills, Diccon, if ye'd had the chance?

I made me own hills right here on these boards, I did; *and* loud streams *and* prancing fillies, and ought else I wanted. Give the boy his chance, Diccon—his choice. Thou hast plenty other players—there's young Joe Taylor… But the boy's the very spit o' meself. I canna let him go. Oh, these voices…

(*Sings.*) Pass them by—other voices,
Let them die…

(*Corin enters and crosses, Burbage stops him, calls him over, and kneels to be at eye level with him.*)

BURBAGE: Cory, come here one time. Look at this piece of glass and tell me what thou seest.

CORIN: A goblet, Diccon. Tis thy goblet.

BURBAGE: Nay, but lad—look *in* the glass and what doest thou see?

CORIN: (*Understanding.*) Me own face, many times.

BURBAGE: Hast ever seen the sun, Cory?

CORIN: O' course I have.

BURBAGE: What? Canst thou look in the sun, then, boy? Is it not too hot for thine eyes?

CORIN: Well, aye sir, in faith it *is* too bright. I canna bear to see it. But when I turn like this, wi' both eyes tight shut, I can feel it warm inside 'em.

BURBAGE: Good. Now, look ye at Diccon Burbage's eyes.

CORIN: They're blue.

BURBAGE: Remember the glass, boy.

CORIN: Me own face, twice.

BURBAGE: Oh, Corin, if ever thou canst bear to open thine eyes to the sun, thou'lt see thine own face, gazing back.

(Lights slowly fade.)

SCENE X
The Warwickshire Hills

Corin's parents and a Peasant Man are in conversation as lights rise.

PEASANT: Lost? Far from it, nor dead neither! I' faith, I was there, see? Tis me custom, don't ye know, to go to London Town come Mayday. Soul o' man, nigh on ev'ry spring sinced I were a little nip I've made the journey, sure. I've kin there, don't ye know, in a big...

BENJAMIN: Come, man! Have done with chatter! If he be not dead, then what?

PEASANT: Dead? Far from it, nor lost neither!

NELLIE: Lord be praised! Then what then...

PEASANT: Why, thy son's famous, Ben. A play-actor, don't ye know.

NELLIE: No! Famous, Ben.

PEASANT: Sings like a very angel. Blackfriar's favorite, and the pet of all London.

NELLIE: Sings? What, did he sing then? We would sing together, at whiles, come Sabbath. I' faith, I taught him to sing, sure.

PEASANT: See, I was there meself. Tis my custom...

NELLIE: Oh, Ben. We must fetch our son.

BENJAMIN: Singing. Pet o' London. *(To Nell.)* Son? What son is that? In truth, I had a son. But this man here speaks of a play-actor what's got famous. Whose son is that? *(Speaking over Nell's lines.)* Had a son. Boy was good wi' the sheeps. But whose son is that? That's not Ben Marvell's son...

NELLIE: *(Over Ben's lines.)* *Our* son. He canna be happy where he is at. Our
son. Me own son.
(Blackout.)

SCENE XI
Escape

*Swan's Down Inn. Members of Blackfriars and others in the tavern are dic-
ing, drinking, talking, singing. The company is rowdy. Burbage is once again
dicing with Cuthbert Bogs. Corin and Joey are at a separate table.*

ACTOR: Come, Bile, what say ye to another round? *(Whistles for drinks.)*
BILE: *(Giggling, already a bit tipsy.)* Oh, my cuckoo. Twould na be seeming.
Still, my little nasties hath put me in ill humor. P'raps just one more.
ACTOR: That's me buckoo. What there—a jug of sack for Bile's nasties!
BILE: What *jug,* silly. A barrel-full, cuckoo!
LADY-FRIEND: Oh, Geoffrey, thou'rt too scandalous!
BILE: There comes a time, dear lady, when a man must drown discord. Here's
to harmony!
*(They drink, arms locked. Stage motion freezes. Lights focus on Corin and
Joseph.)*
JOSEPH: Nay! Run away, Cory? Thou canst not! Cuthbert Bogs there would
stop thee straightway.
CORIN: I care not a fig for Cuthbert Bogs, nor Diccon Burbage. I shall run!
JOSEPH: And wouldst thou leave me, as well?
CORIN: Joey, come with me!
(Flute softly plays "To Mary, Queen, Awakening.")
CORIN: Thou'd love the hills, I know it. There's no fencing, but there's fish-
ing. Fishes big as me, Joey; i' faith, bigger!
(Stage comes to life with Burbage's oath.)
BURBAGE: God's blood!
(Music and boys stop.)
BURBAGE: The bloody things canna always fall so!
*(The Company is hushed. Talking gradually resumes, then freezes again.
Again, soft music.)*
CORIN: The Warwickshire Hills in spring, Joey. And sometimes—there's a
special place by the river's edge, see—and sometimes I sit there and sing,
or, p'raps, just sit there... And once I found a bird there, Joey—just a little
snip of a bird—too young to be out and about by hisself. I tried to make

him go back to his nest, but he wouldn't, not him. So we just sang there, together, him and me—just sang. Oh, will ye na come, Joey? Will ye na?

JOSEPH: Nay, Corin, I will na. I canna, Cory. This is where I live, see? These people... This... I must live it. Must, brother. Tis very pretty to sing with a bird, Cory, I do na say it's not. But to sing for people—real persons, Cory—now that's something different altogether. It changeth them somehows, if ye know what I mean. But I expect ye don't, what Cory? That's something ye've to learn for thyself.

(Music stops, stage action resumes.)

BURBAGE: A plague on the dice! Bogs, if ye do not play me true, I swear I shall play thee on the end of my dagger.

BOGS: I canna answer for thy own ill fortune, sweetheart.

(Stage freeze. Music again.)

CORIN: Then thou will na come with me?

JOSEPH: Nay, I will na.

CORIN: Will ye not even help me to escape?

JOSEPH: Aye, Cory, I shall...but sadly, Corin.

(Crowd begins to move in slow motion.)

JOSEPH: I'll see to Master Bogs, there, whilst ye leave. Fare ye well, Marvell.

CORIN: Good-bye, Joey.

(Music stops. Stage action is up to normal tempo. Joseph swaggers by Bogs and Burbage.)

JOSEPH: Why, Cuthbert Bogs, thou'rt a sight tonight—indeed thou art. *(Joseph knocks Bogs's mug.)* Oh, look. Ye've spilled thy ale all down thy hose. Tut, tut.

(Bogs rises, angrily brushing off the ale that Joseph spilled down his front. Bogs sees Cory making for the door.)

BOGS: Marvell!

(Burbage leaps to chase Corin, but is blocked by Joseph.)

BURBAGE: Fool!

(Burbage strikes Joseph. Crowd in chaos. Joseph rises from the floor and struggles with Burbage.)

JOSEPH: Cory, run!

(Burbage draws his poniard and wounds Joseph in the struggle. Corin runs back into the fray, places himself between Burbage and Joseph, and strikes Burbage.)

CORIN: Do na touch him again, thou rogue!

(Burbage sinks onto a bench, his hands covering his face. Silence; then a sudden rush, as the crowd gathers around the wounded boy. Corin is holding Joseph as the lights go out.)

SCENE XII
Prison

A dimly lit prison. Gaping holes with bars and shreds of men behind them. Men chained to pillars; men lying about in chains; men breathing heavily. A dirge of low moans. A heavy door opens; a shaft of white light pierces the gloom. The Jailor ushers Corin in and points the way. Corin comes before Diccon Burbage, chained.

BURBAGE: How is it with the boy?

CORIN: He'll mend.

BURBAGE: Thank God. And thank God ye came. Ye must hate me so; why came ye?

CORIN: Ye sent for me and I came. If ye've naught else to say, I'll leave again. Good-bye.

BURBAGE: Nay, Corin, dearheart. Do na leave just yet. I do na seek thy forgiveness, lad. I could not ask it. But I do have somewhat to tell thee.
(Jeers, moans, rattlings from neighboring cells.)

BURBAGE: Be still, dogs! *(In anguish, over the prisoner's jeers.)* I set thee free, Corin. I am 'prisoned now for a time, as I have prisoned thee. I am bound and thou canst go…to thy house… I was mad, Corin, the dice made me so, I swear it. I did love thee, lad; doest truly hate me? Say thou dost not hate Diccon Burbage, Corin, please.

JAILOR: Move it, block. Time to go.

BURBAGE: Oh, Corin, dost remember when I found thee? Thou wert singing. Thou'rt no more bound to sing, but I feign would hear thee once more.

CORIN: *(After some hesitation.)* I'll sing for thee, Diccon.
To Mary, Queen, awakening,
One bleak mid-winter morn,
Came, like a falcon to its King,
Fair Jesu to be born.
(Prisoners shout for quiet.)

JAILOR: Here, be still!

CORIN: And though the wind was cold as stars,
And though the shadows, long,
When winter's cage flung wide its bars
The skylark found its song.
(Silence now in the prison. Faces are peering out at the boy.)

CORIN: For spring awoke that very day

And warmed December's dawn,
To hear the skylark's gladsome lay,
Like dew upon the lawn.
To Mary, Queen, awakening,
One bleak mid-winter morn,
Came, like a falcon to its King,
Fair Jesu to be born.
(Silence. Corin looks about him in wonder.)

PRISONER: …mea culpa, mea culpa, mea maxima culpa. Ideo precor beatam Mariam…

JAILOR: *(Finally.)* Time's good and up, sirs.

BURBAGE: My Marvell…

CORIN: I must be going, Master Burbage.
(Corin quickly kisses Burbage's hand on the bars and leaves.)

PRISONER: …et te, Pater, orare pro me ad Dominum nostrum.
(Fade.)

SCENE XIII
Freedom

Corin is alone on the stage of Blackfriars. The Center platform curtains are closed behind him. He is rummaging through his old leather bag, and pulls out his old shepherd's clothes. He stands, looking at them. One of the child-actors rushes past, half-in, half-out of his costume. He shouts to Corin.

BOY: Hurry, Cory! They're about to start! Get dressed, man!

CORIN: *(Shouts after him, but the boy is gone before he's through.)* Nay, Barry! I'm na coming at all. I'm leaving! I be free! *(To himself, alone again.)* I be free. *(Pulls on his old sheepskin cloak.)* Goin' home. To me home.
(Fan-Dan enters, carrying a deer-head mask.)

FAN-DAN: Time, gentlemen, please, Time! *(Sees Corin.)* Colley! Will ye foot it, kindly! Move, sir!

CORIN: Nay, Fan-Dan. I'm leavin' now, see? Goin' home to the hills.

FAN-DAN: *(Stops.)* Oh. I see. Well, good-bye then.

CORIN: Good-bye.

FAN-DAN: But Colley, will ye remember to step high today in the dance. Be high-stepper, Colley, not like some old cow, what?

CORIN: But Fan-Dan, I'm not…

FAN-DAN: I know, faith, I know ye can do it. I've seen ye. High-stepper like old Fan-Danny, that's it. Foot it, now! *(Fan-Dan exits.)*
(Corin drops the clothes in his hands; stands, lost in reverie. An intense white light rises on him. He does a bow, looks up, shuts his eyes, opens them, looks up again, smiles.)

CORIN: If ever thou canst bear to open thine eyes and look at the sun…
(Joseph Taylor enters, his wound bound.)

JOSEPH: Come, Cory, what did Burbage say?

CORIN: He freed me. He said that I am no more bound to sing. He said that I may go home. To the hills.

JOSEPH: Then, brother, I bid thee farewell and wish thee all godspeed.
(Bows formally. Corin lifts him up again.)

CORIN: Nay, I shall na go. Now I am free, I would na be so. I canna go home, for this be my home. We'll be brothers a bit longer, what friend?
(They look at each other in silence, then laugh. Lights out. Lights up again immediately to reveal the Company in tableau on the turning Center platform. It stops as all face Center. An audience is gathered to either side of the stage on upper and lower levels. This is the conclusion of the afternoon's performance. Corin speaks the epilogue.)

CORIN: Believe me when I say,
God makes with man a happy jest:
The Fool—he knows the way,
And the tawny bird who left his nest
Sings now a shining lay.
And you who watch are now twice-blest:
You hear the song. Now walk the way.
(Bows.)
(A shower of rose petals; the audience cheers; the lights fade out.)

END OF PLAY

African Tales:
Kalulu and His Money Farm and Rumpelstiltskin

African Tales: Kalulu and His Money Farm and Rumpelstiltskin
was commissioned and first presented by
The Children's Theatre Company
and School of Minneapolis, Minnesota.

Music Composed by Roberta Carlson
Directed and Choreographed by Myron Johnson

CHARACTERS

African Tales

* Narrator
* Ju Ju Man

Kalulu and His Money Farm

* The King
  Giraffe
  Monkey
  Lion
  Zebra
  Warthog
* Kalulu, the Rabbit (doubles as Ju Ju Man)
* Mrs. Kalulu
* Turtle (may double as one of the other animals)

Rumpelstiltskin

* The King
  The Miller
* The Miller's Daughter
  First Father
  Singing Daughter
  Second Father
  Dancing Daughter
  Third Father
  Short Daughter
* Rumpelstiltskin (doubles as Ju Ju Man)
  Villagers, Queen's Men (doubling with the Fathers and
  Daughters)

Denotes principal roles.

African Tales is told primarily by the use of African masks and African dance. The age of the actors is not important; their ability to dance with large colorful masks is. There are a few Swahili words throughout this text; in the original production the dancers were tutored by an African student who taught them many more Swahili phrases.

African Tales has a running time of an hour and ten minutes.

For information concerning the original score by Roberta Carlson, contact The Children's Theatre Company of Minneapolis.

African Tales

PRESHOW

Drumming. Company performs a physical warm-up as Narrator addresses the audience.

NARRATOR: My friends and I are here to tell you a story.
  Two stories, really.
  We're going to tell our stories with drums and dancing
  and big masks and big costumes.
  And these people here are your storytellers.
  But in order to dance and drum and wear big masks
  they must "warm themselves up" beforehand.
  They have to get their muscles and bones
  and bodies and minds all working together.
  These young people have been practicing a long time
  in order to tell these two stories in a special way.

  You know, everyone has his own way of telling stories.
  You have your way; I have mine.
  Maybe your parents have their own way of telling you stories.
  And somebody's father who lives in China
  has *his* way of telling a story.
  Or somebody who lives in France, in Norway…
  People tell stories, you know, all over the world.
  Everybody likes a good story.
  Everyone has his own way of telling it.

  Today we're going to tell you our stories in something like the
  way they might be told if you and I lived in Africa.
  When you hear the storytellers speak on stage—
  the actors and actresses speak on stage—
  you probably won't be able to understand what they're saying. [That is,
  unless you speak Swahili, which is one of the languages of Africa.]

  And Swahili is the language that these people are going to use
  in the stories that you are going to hear today.

But don't worry about that.
Because I'll be here and I'll tell you what they're saying,
so you'll understand in English what they're saying in Swahili.

Between the two stories that we're telling today, we'll take a little
break and I'll teach you some Swahili words and a Swahili song.

(Warm-up ends.)

Now the actors and actresses are going backstage.
They will put on their makeup
and put on their big masks and big costumes.

In a moment or two the stories will begin.

PROLOGUE

NARRATOR: I'm going to tell you something about Africa.

In some parts of Africa,
all the children know exactly what their favorite time of day is.
It comes toward evening
when they gather with their fathers and mothers
and sisters and brothers
around a big open fire.
The fire crackles
and sends sparks up into the night sky,
and the shadows move among the trees.

And all the children wait—
wait very quietly—
because pretty soon one man will stand
up from the circle around the fire
and will begin to tell them stories:
wonderful, magical stories.

The first story that we're going to tell you today is called
"Kalulu and His Money Farm,"
and it's about a bragging rabbit
who promises to grow an impossible crop.

The second of the two stories is one that you already know.

It is called "Rumpelstiltskin,"
and it's really a German tale,
but today we're going to tell it as if you and I lived in Africa.

In Africa,
and it is evening,
and we are all gathered
around a big, open fire,
waiting very quietly
for the story to begin…

KALULU AND HIS MONEY FARM

A woman sings a lullaby, continuing under narrative.

NARRATOR: There was once a time—
    a dreaming, magical time—
    when everything was like every other thing.
    Men looked like trees,
    and trees were not so very different from men.
    Animals spoke to each other
    and to the men and women and children who were their friends.
    Even heaven was closer to the earth—
    as close as the roof of your house.
    And everybody lived a dream with everybody else.

    (Ju Ju Man enters.)

    There was a magic man
    who brought the sky down on his shoulders
    and wore it like a ribbon.
    A magic man
    who danced and sang
    and told his people magic stories
    and listened to the grass.
    A magic man
    who loved the jungle beasts
    and danced with them at dusk.
    At dusk,
    when the shadows of the trees are long,

Ju Ju—
the magic man—
danced with the animals
and told his magic stories.

(Animals enter and dance.)

Ju Ju
and the animals of the jungle
danced the night back into its own dark home
so that the morning sun came
and lived with them again.
This is a very special morning for them all
because the King has arrived.

(King sings chant; Others respond. After chant. King addresses the Animals in Swahili.)

I'll tell you what he's saying
The King is saying,

"Hello, my friends;
it is spring.
The earth was thirsty
and the rains gave it something to drink.
Now the earth is hungry.
You must feed it.
I will give you seeds and you must plant them.
And when it is harvest time
you must bring the crops that you have grown
back to me."

NARRATOR: So the King called each animal to him, one by one.

"Giraffe, your neck is long;
you bring coconuts from the tops of the trees.

"Monkey," said the King, "you grow beans."

"Lion, some corn, if you please."

"Zebra, you grow bananas which are nice and yellow."

"Warthog, bring me peanuts."

Then the King said, "Kalulu!"

But no one in the jungle answered him.

"Kalulu!" he said again.
"Where is that rabbit?! It's a very bad thing to make an important person wait for a rabbit!"

And the King began to shake all over, he was so angry.

Just then, a rabbit appeared in the clearing.
He didn't seem to be in a big hurry,
even though he was late.
His name was Kalulu.
And Kalulu never hurried for anyone.

"Kalulu." said the King, "you're late!
Grow me some yams and bring them back at harvest time."

"Yams?" said Kalulu. "I don't even like yams."

"What?!" said the King.

(King in Swahili: "What?!")

"What?!" said the animals of the jungle.

(Animals in Swahili: "What?!" one after another.)

"Money—that's 'what,'" said Kalulu.
"I'll grow you some money
in my special money garden.
Just give me some gold
and I will plant it for you."

"Impossible!" said the King.

But Kalulu said, "It is not impossible;
not if you know the secret.
And *I* know the secret…"
[Now, the King was very tall, but he was not very smart. He was beginning to be interested in a crop that would grow money.]
"…Just give me lots of gold; that's all I need."

Well, the King believed the bragging rabbit

and gave him a bag of gold.
And wasn't Kalulu pleased with himself!

"But remember," said the King,
"bring your crop at harvest time with the others."

And Kalulu hurried home to tell his wife the good news.

NARRATOR: Mrs. Kalulu wondered why her husband was so late coming
home.

(Kalulu shouts "Sungura!")

Kalulu knew that his wife would be very happy.
She always said Kalulu didn't make enough money.

(Kalulu: "Sungura!")

He didn't make *any* money.

(Mrs. Kalulu: "Moombaza.")

"Where did you get all that money?"

"I'll tell you," said Kalulu.
And Kalulu told her.
"It happened like this:
the King gave me a bag of gold.
He thinks I'm going to plant it
and grow a money farm.
Can you believe that?
Of course, I have to give it back in a year,
but now we can buy
all the things we ever wanted…"

(Mrs. Kalulu cuts him off with a gesture.)

"What's wrong?" said Kalulu.

"What are you going to do
when you have to pay back the King?"

"We'll think about that later.
Let's go to the market!"

NARRATOR: The market was a wonderful place, if you had the money.
But nobody in the jungle had any money.
Business was always slow in the market.

But then came Kalulu and his wife.
And even though they knew better,
there they were with all the King's money
and there were all the things they ever wanted.
And they began to buy.
They bought and they bought.
And then they bought some more.

They bought pineapples from the Warthog
and bells from the Giraffe.
They bought jewels from the Monkey
and rings and beads
and bracelets and bangles.
They bought bananas from the Lion
and new clothes from the Zebra.

They bought things a rabbit would never need.

They bought so much, they could hardly hop.

NARRATOR: The year passed quickly.
Spring grew into summer
and all the seeds of the earth grew ripe.
And the earth was very happy.

Finally, it was harvest time.
All the beasts of the jungle
brought their crops to the King.
And they were happy too.

The Warthog was happy because it was a good year for peanuts.
The Lion was happy because the corn was tall.
The Zebra's bananas were nice and yellow.
The Monkey was happy because her beans were just right.
The Giraffe brought coconuts, and she was happy too.

But Kalulu wasn't too happy.
He didn't know what to do.

"Kalulu," said the King,
"where is my crop of money?"

"Well," said Kalulu,
"you've got to understand,
money is a very slow-growing crop."

"Maybe," said the King,
"but next year my money had better be ready."

So the King waited for a whole year...

But the next year, it was the same story.

"It was a bad year for money," said Kalulu.
"These things take time."

"Time?!" said the King.
"I'll give you some time in my rabbit stew!
One more year, Kalulu."

But of course it was no different the next year.

"Not yet," said Kalulu.
"You have to wait a little longer."

"Wait?!" said the King.
"I've waited long enough!
Warthog—you go *with* Kalulu to his money farm.
See that he brings his crop back to me."

NARRATOR: Now Kalulu was really worried.
   What was he going to do?
   He didn't have any money tree in any money garden.

   But suddenly, he got an idea.

   "Warthog," he said,
   "I forgot my spear in the hall of the King.
   I better go back and get it.
   There might be hunters in the jungle.
   You wait here...."

   Now, Warthog was a hungry sort of fellow,
   and this looked like a good time for a meal.

He looked around for something to eat.
And just as he was about to pick some berries,
Kalulu yelled out:
"Hunters!
Hunters!
There's a fat warthog!
Let's shoot him
and spear him
and have him for supper!
Quick!
This way!
There he went!
Catch him!"

The Warthog didn't want to be anybody's supper,
so he ran away as fast as he could.

And Kalulu laughed
and laughed
and laughed.

The King said,
"Kalulu!
Where is the Warthog?
And where is my money?"

"There were hunters in the jungle,"
said Kalulu.
"I fought them off,
but Warthog ran away."

"Oh. Well…
Lion—you're a brave one!
You go with Kalulu to his money farm."

Kalulu was so scared he didn't know what to do.

But he told the Lion that it was a long way to his money farm
and finally the Lion grew very tired.

"Oh, Lion, why don't you take a rest?
Anyway, I forgot my shovel at the King's hall.
We'll need it to dig up all the gold."

Now, this Lion was a tired old lion anyway,
so he just curled up
and went to sleep as fast as you please.

NARRATOR: Kalulu was so frightened, he didn't watch where he was going.
He tripped over a big something in the grass.
But he was in luck.
It was an antelope horn.
Kalulu ran back to the sleeping Lion,
put the horn to his ear,
and blew as hard as he could.

"Run!" said Kalulu.
"It's right behind you!
This way! Hurry!
Look out! It's catching up!
Closer and closer!
Just don't look back!
Oh, oh—there it goes again! And again! And again!"

And the Lion ran all the way back to the King's hall.

"What's going on?" said the King.

"Oh," said Kalulu, "it was nothing.
I don't know what frightened the Lion so much,
but he sure was scared!"

"Shame on you, Lion!" said the King.

Now the King thought to himself:
Warthog, who was an honest fellow, ran away.
Lion, who was known for his courage, turned out to be a coward.

"I know! Turtle! Come here!"

And the oldest turtle in the world walked in the door.

"Turtle! You're a sensible fellow.
Make Kalulu lead you to his money farm.
See that he harvests his crop
and bring it to me.
Now, hurry!"

"I said, *Hurry!*"

NARRATOR: "Say, Turtle, old friend...

I seem to have forgotten my spear.
I'll just run back and get it."

"Oh, no,"
said the Turtle,
"Don't worry about that.
You can use mine if you want."

"Thanks," said Kalulu.

"Oh, no!"
said Kalulu,
"I really *am* a fool!
I forgot my shovel to dig up all the money.
I'm afraid I'll have to go back and get it."

"Well,"
said the Turtle,
"we *are* in luck!
I have my shovel right here."

"What was that?!"
said Kalulu.
"There are evil spirits in this jungle!
I'm going back for my magic charms."

"Oh, no,"
said the Turtle,
"I've got lots of nice charms
right here around my neck."

"Yours don't work!
You do what you want!
I'm going!"

And the Turtle wondered
what he would tell the King
about Kalulu's money farm.

NARRATOR: So Kalulu ran all the way home,
jumped in his house, and shouted to his wife,
"Help me! Hide me!

They know I cheated!"

"About the money farm?"

"Yes! Yes!
Hide me somewhere!"

"Where? How?
Here? There's nowhere!"

(Mrs. Kalulu has an idea.)

"I know! Pretend that you're my *baby!*

I'll pull out all your fur, so that you look just like a baby rabbit."

"Ouch! Ouch!"

"Now, you hush up! You brought this on yourself!"

And she pulled out all his fur
and took him and laid him on a blanket.

Just then, there was a knock on the door.

"Hello?"

"The King wants Kalulu!"
said the Lion.
"Where is he?"

"He's not here.
Maybe he's harvesting the crop on his money farm.
Only Baby and I are home.
Aren't we, Baby?"

"Baby comes with us!
We'll hold him hostage until Kalulu returns with his money crop."

"Oh, no!
You can't take my baby!
He's...

(Mrs. Kalulu suddenly has an idea.)

sick!

And he might die!
Won't you, Baby?"

(Lion gestures.)

"Baby comes with us!"

NARRATOR: But when they arrived at the King's hall
and brought the baby before the King—
sure enough!—
Baby was dead.
At least, that's how it *looked*.
Its eyes were closed,
its body was stretched out,
and its little paws hung down limp.

(Mrs. Kalulu wails.)

"My baby! My baby!" cried Mrs. Kalulu.
"You've killed my baby and now he's dead!"

The Giraffe said, "There, there…"
and did what she could.

(More wailing.)

The Warthog tried everything he could think of
and so did the Zebra…

(More wailing.)

…but nothing would help.

Even the Lion said, "I'm sorry."

The King said, "I'm *so* sorry.
Take this bag of gold.
I know it's not much when your baby is dead, but please take it.
I insist."

So Mrs. Kalulu took the bag of gold,
and Warthog and Lion took up Kalulu,
and together they all went home.

Kalulu was groaning
and shivering in his nakedness.
"I'm cured of boasting and bragging and cheating.
I promise never to do it again!"

And when Kalulu had grown a new fur coat—
longer, thicker, and glossier than ever—
he took the bag of money
and laid it before the King.

The good King was happy,
but no happier than Kalulu,
who had learned
that lies bring only troubles
and worries
and a sore hide!

(Reprise of King's chant and Animal response.)

RUMPELSTILTSKIN

NARRATOR: The Ju Ju Man knows everything.
    He knows every story that anybody ever told anybody else.
    He even knows a story that you know by heart.
    Only when he tells it, it is different.
    It is magic.

    It is the story of Rumpelstiltskin
    and it begins like this…

    (Villagers and King enter with chant/response "ku-me-pam-ba-zu-ka.")

    Once upon a time,
    there was a little kingdom,
    where mothers and fathers
    and sisters and brothers
    lived and worked and played
    and blew their noses
    and went to bed at night.
    So it really was like the place where you live,
    or where anybody ever lived,
    even though it was a long time ago.

    The only thing wrong with this little kingdom was its King.

    The King didn't have a Queen.
    And he was lonely.
    Of course,
    it was mostly the King's own fault,
    because he always said
    that no ordinary girl
    could become his Queen.

    "She must be extraordinary!"

    And since there were a lot of very nice
    but very ordinary girls
    living in the kingdom,
    the King lived alone.

    Still, he never gave up trying to find an extraordinary girl.

So, the King called the fathers of his little kingdom together
and said,
"I want someone to be my Queen.
But not just anyone, mind you.
The girl I marry must be extraordinary!
Tomorrow,
fathers must bring their daughters before me,
to show me what extraordinary things they can do.
And remember—
you fathers with just ordinary daughters—
you keep them at home!"

NARRATOR: Now *every* daughter is extraordinary—
at least to her father.
So every father went home
very excited
thinking that his little girl
was sure to be the next Queen.

That is,
every father but one.

The Miller was a little discouraged
when he went home
because he just had to admit
that his daughter was a bit
on the ordinary side.
"In fact,"
he thought,
"she must be
the most ordinary girl
who ever lived!"

Now, the Miller's Daughter was very nice—it wasn't that.
She was just a bit ordinary, that's all.
When she ground grain in a big earthen pot…
it was just an ordinary sort of grinding in the usual sort of pot.
Nothing special ever.
And when she spun thread on her spinning wheel…
it was the most ordinary sort of spinning.
Even her conversation was a bit dull.

"Look, Father," she would say,
maybe two or three times a day.
"See how the sunlight strikes the thread I'm spinning.
It almost looks like gold!"

"Who cares?" said the Miller.
"Now, if it really *were* gold,
that would be extraordinary!
You had better think of something good by tomorrow
if you ever want to become the Queen."

NARRATOR: But the next day came
and the Miller's Daughter couldn't think of a thing
out of the ordinary,
and neither could the Miller.
So they just waited,
very quietly,
while the other fathers proudly presented their daughters
to the King.

One father's daughter could sing.
(Daughter sings very poorly.)
"Ordinary!"
said the King.
"Go home!"

Another daughter could dance.
(Daughter steps forward and prepares.)
First she got herself all ready.
(Daughter dances awkwardly and finally stubs her toe.)
But the whole kingdom fell asleep,
it was so ordinary.

And one girl
could sing, dance, laugh,
play musical instruments,
whistle, cook, weave, sew and knit.
*(Daughter demonstrates talent. Finally, King stands
beside her.)*
But she was too short.

So the King said,

"Doesn't anybody have a daughter
who can do something
out of the ordinary
and isn't too short besides?"

"My daughter..." said the Miller.

"What?" said the King

"My daughter...
isn't *short*...
and besides...

(*A sudden idea.*)

...she can spin straw into gold!"

"Extraordinary!" said the King

"Spin straw into *what?!*" said the Miller's Daughter.

"Gold!"
said the King
"Come right this way!"

NARRATOR: The Miller...
wished that he hadn't said a thing.

The Miller's Daughter...
wished that she were somewhere else—quick.

The King...
was a little suspicious.

"Bring in the straw!" he said.
"Miller's Daughter—
you must spin all this straw into gold by morning."

"I can't!" said the Miller's Daughter.

"Can't what?!"

"I can't...wait till morning!"

"If you succeed, you will be my Queen.
But if you've been lying to me, you will die."

The Miller's Daughter picked up a handful of straw
and tried to spin it.
But the straw turned into straw.
She didn't know what to do.

Just then, she heard a noise.

(Rapping.)

"Mice?" said the Miller's Daughter.

(Rapping.)

But it was so loud.
"I must be imagining things."

(Rapping and Rumpelstiltskin enters.)

"Oh!"
And it was the strangest little man she had ever seen.

"Who are you?" she said.

"Never mind that now.
What you need is some gold."

"How did you know?"

"Never mind that now.
If I spin all this straw into gold,
what will you give me?"

"Well. I have this little ring…

"Does it sparkle? I'll take it!"

And the little man
sat down at the spinning wheel
and began to spin.

(Lights fade to Blackout.)

NARRATOR: And all the long night through
    the little man
    spun all the straw
    in the room

into gold
while the Miller's Daughter slept.

(Lights rise.)

And in the morning,
on the spinning room floor,
there were piles of gold coins.

But the little man was gone.

And the Miller's Daughter was very happy.

(King and Villagers enter.)

"You *are* extraordinary!" said the King.
"Now bring in more straw!"

The Miller's Daughter could hardly believe her ears!
More straw…
and more straw…
and still *more* straw!

(King and Villagers exit.)

Now there was more straw than ever before.
The door was locked,
and she was all alone.

But not for long.

(Rumpelstiltskin enters.)

"What am I going to do?" said the Miller's Daughter.

"What will you give me tonight?"

"I don't have much left,
but you can have my necklace if you want it."

"Is it made of ivory? I'll take it!"

And once again,
the little man sat down
and began to spin the straw into gold.

(Lights fade to Blackout.)

And once again,
the Miller's Daughter fell fast asleep
and slept the long night through
while the funny little man
spun straw into gold.

NARRATOR: At dawn the Miller's Daughter awoke
to find piles of gold coins everywhere.

(Lights rise.)

But the little man had disappeared.

The Miller's Daughter was so happy,
she rushed to show the King her gold.

(King and Villagers enter.)

But that wasn't good enough for him.
He wanted still *more* gold.

(King and Villagers exit.)

The poor girl didn't know what to do.
She waited for the little man,
but he never came.

(Miller's Daughter calls in Swahili.)

"Little man!" she called.
But no one answered.

(Another call.)

"Little man! Help me!"

(A third call.)

And finally she began to cry.

(She cries. Rumpelstiltskin enters.)

"What will you give me
if I spin all your straw into gold?"

But the Miller's Daughter had nothing left to give.

"If I spin all your straw into gold,
the King will marry you
and make you his queen.
Give me your first-born child!"

"What?!" said the Miller's Daughter.
"I could never do that!"

"Alright," said the little man,
"then I'll just go…!"

"No! Wait!"

The Miller's Daughter had no choice.
She promised to give the crooked little man
her first-born child.

(Lights fade to Blackout.)

And for the third time,
the crooked little man sat down at the spinning wheel
and spun gold coins out of straw
while the Miller's Daughter slept
and dreamt of a glorious morning.

NARRATOR: It was a glorious morning.
The sun was singing in the sky
when the King and his people came to see
the Miller's extraordinary daughter.

"You have done a wonderful thing,"
said the King.
"Will you consent to be my queen?"

The Miller's Daughter said, "I will."

The people danced for joy,
and the King and the Miller's Daughter danced for love,
and the sun sang in the sky for a glorious morning.

They were married that very day,
and the Miller's Daughter became the new Queen.

Time passed.
Men and women and children lived
and worked
and played
and listened to the sound of wings
above their heads.

Time passed.
The earth grew full
and round
and lovely,
and the trees made a sound like wings.

Time passed.
The new queen gave birth
to a beautiful baby boy,
and the kingdom was filled
with the laughter of a baby
and with the sound of wings.

NARRATOR: The Queen loved her baby very much.
Often, she would sit alone with him in her room
and play and tell stories and laugh.
She laughed so much
that she forgot all about
the crooked little man who spun the straw into gold.

But one day, when the Queen was laughing with her baby
and telling him stories,
the crooked little man came back.
(A rapping precedes Rumpelstiltskin's entrance.)

"Now!" said the little man.

"Who are you?" said the Queen. "Go away!"
And she held her baby tightly.

"Now!" said the little man. "I've come for my reward!"

"What do you mean?"

"You promised! You promised! Your first-born child!"

"No!" said the Queen. "I'll give you anything!
Gold, jewels, anything you want!"

"I want your baby, to keep me company deep in the forest."

And the Queen, who loved her baby very much, began to cry.
(She cries.)

"Stop!" said the little man. "You promised!"

But the Queen couldn't stop crying.

"Stop!" said the little man.
"You can keep your baby *if* you guess my name!
I'll give you three guesses on three nights."

So the Queen made her three guesses:

"Are you Sadele?"

"No!" said the little man.

"Are you Umpudu?"

"No!" said the little man.

"Fogo?"

"Wrong!
Two more nights to guess my name
and then—
the baby is mine!"

NARRATOR: The Queen called three of her men…

(Men enter.)

…and said to them:
"There is a crooked little man
who lives deep in the forest.
He's about as tall as a spinning wheel.
Search for him,
and find out what his name is.
Go!"

(Search.)

But the crooked man of the forest
was hard to find.
He was everywhere,
and he was nowhere.

(Search continues unsuccessfully.)

All the next day,
the Queen tried to think of every name
that ever was
between the sun and the earth.

But the sun went down
and the crooked little man appeared
out of nowhere,
and the Queen still couldn't think of the right one.

(Rumpelstiltskin enters.)

"What's my name?" he said.

"Are you called Juma?"

"No!"

"Is your name Jaha?"

"Of course not!"

"Could you possibly be called Jahi?"

"Never!" said the little man.
"No one knows my name,
and no one ever will!
One more night, foolish Queen!"

(Rumpelstiltskin exits. Men enter. Another search.)

The Queen's men searched through the deepest forests.
and further—
into the darkest jungles.
They searched high and low.
They looked everywhere for the little man.
But he was nowhere to be found.

NARRATOR: Finally,
in the deepest, darkest, nastiest part of the most hidden forest,
they found a little clearing.

And in the clearing,
sitting on a stump,
they saw the strangest, crooked little man that ever was.

(Rumpelstiltskin sings.)

And the crooked little man was so pleased with his trick,
that he told his secret name to the forest...

(Song continues, ending with a shout: "Rumpelstiltskin!")

And the men ran back to tell the Queen the news.

(Men approach Queen and bow to her.)

"What have you learned?" said the Queen.

"Rumpelstiltskin is his name!"

(Men exit. Queen smiles.)

"Rumpelstiltskin!"

And that night
the crooked little man returned for the third time.

(Rumpelstiltskin enters.)

"My name! My name! Do you know it?"

"Your name isn't Abasi, is it?
Abdalla? Abdi? Abdu? Abudu?
Fogo? Haji? Hamisi? Hamasud?
Rumpelstiltskin?!"

And the crooked little man went mad with rage.
He shook his fist at the Queen,
and pounded the floor,
and he was never seen again.

He made so much noise
that the King came to see what was wrong.

The Queen looked at her King,
and decided to tell him the truth.
She told him how she had never spun straw into gold,
and all about the little man named Rumpelstiltskin.
But none of it mattered to the King,
because he had finally learned
that his Queen *was* truly extraordinary.

(Reprise of wedding song and dance. Curtain.)

END OF PLAY

Carlo Collodi's
Pinocchio

Pinocchio was created for and first performed by The Children's Theatre
Company and School of Minneapolis, Minnesota.
The play premiered September 29, 1974.

Music Composed by Hiram Titus
Produced by John Clark Donahue
Directed by John Clark Donahue and Gene Davis Buck
Scenic Design by Dahl Delu
Costume Design by Rae Marie Pekas
Lighting Design by Robert S. Hutchings, Jr.

CHARACTERS

* Geppetto
* Pinocchio, 11–14 years old
* The Fox
* The Cat
* Lampwick, about 14 years old
* Coachman
* Pigacci
  Blue Fairy
  Innkeeper
  Townspeople, Boys and Girls

Denotes principal roles.

This show was the premiere production in the newly built Children's Theatre of Minneapolis in 1974. As such, it was presented on an epic scale, with a vast cast and elaborate settings. Since then, however, it has been produced by community theatres and schools around the country, presumably with smaller casts and more modest stagings.

Pinocchio has a running time of one hour and forty-five minutes, including intermission.

For information concerning the original score by Hiram Titus, contact The Children's Theatre Company of Minneapolis.

Pinocchio

ACT I
SCENE I

Overture. Painted show curtain with separate overlay that reads: "Pinocchio. The Story of a Puppet." Near end of overture, curtain rises to reveal empty Italian street. It is the middle of the night; shops and apartment widows are shuttered, fruit and flower stands are covered with canvas. An old, white-haired man, Geppetto, wanders in, wearing a long, tattered coat.

GEPPETTO: *(A sigh.)* Ahhh, Geppetto. Why don't you go home to bed, huh? Everybody else is sleeping—sleeping in their little warm beds. Mamas… papas…little boys…little girls; sleeping and dreaming. Or just sleeping and snoring, I don't know. *(He yawns.)* Ahhh—it's so blue. Everything's so blue. It's the moon, Geppetto. It's the moon. *(He takes a small piece of wood from his pocket and a whittling knife.)* So. Whadda you gonna make next, old woodcarver? Huh? You got your wood, you got you knife—whadda you gonna make? A whistle? Geppetto, you got sixteen wooden whistles already; you don't need no more. *(He gives the whistle he took out from his pocket a little tweet. He is about to put it away, then stops himself.)* Wait a minute. *(He blows on the whistle, louder.)* Hey! Hey! Is anybody awake? *(Another blow.)* Anybody wanna talk to Geppetto? *(More blows and Hey's! The shuttered windows of a second-floor apartment Upstage Right fly open to reveal Signora Bonaventura in nightcap and gown.)*

SIGNORA BONAVENTURA: Hey! Hey! Who's that?!

GEPPETTO: Buona notte, Signora Bonaventura; how are you?

SIGNORA BONAVENTURA: Geppetto! Is that you?

GEPPETTO: *(A bit sheepish.)* Si; it's me.

SIGNORA BONAVENTURA: *(Speaking to someone in her house.)* It's that Geppetto. *(To Geppetto.)* Geppetto! Why don't you shut up that noise and go home to bed! *(She bangs the shutters closed.)*

GEPPETTO: *(Turning away and walking Downstage.)* Good, Geppetto. That's real good. *(A sigh.)* Oh, if only I could *make* something…if only I could make something so people would look at me and say, "There's Geppetto! He's the man who *made* something!" And even after I went away, they'd

look at what I made and say, "Now, *there's* Geppetto! *That's* who he was."
If only I could…

BLUE FAIRY: *(Appearing beside him, or voice only.)* Why don't you make a puppet, Geppetto?

GEPPETTO: *(A little laugh.)* The moon…it's so blue… *(Slight pause. An idea.)*
Sure! Sure—a puppet!
(Blue Fairy laughs warmly.)

GEPPETTO: Why not? A little face…ears…

BLUE FAIRY: A puppet as big as a boy!

GEPPETTO: *(Becoming excited.)* No! No—a puppet as big as a boy! *(Slight pause.)*
Signora! *(He blows on his whistle and runs toward Signora Bonaventura's
window.)* Signora Bonaventura!

SIGNORA BONAVENTURA: *(Opening her window; disgusted.)* What is it?!

GEPPETTO: Listen to this: I'm gonna make a puppet!

SIGNORA BONAVENTURA: Well, listen to this: "I'm gonna make you wet!" *(She
takes a bucket of water and pours it over Geppetto's head, then slams the
shutters again.)*

GEPPETTO: *(Walking Downstage again.)* Sure…why not? A puppet as big as a
real boy!

BLUE FAIRY: A real boy!

GEPPETTO: A real boy!

BLUE FAIRY: A *real* boy!

GEPPETTO: A real boy!

*(Blue Fairy disappears. Geppetto starts Offstage but is met by an old Woman,
wearing a blue shawl and slowly pushing a wheelbarrow that holds a very
large piece of wood.)*

GEPPETTO: Oh! Pardone, signora; you frightened me. I didn't know anyone
else was awake tonight but me.
(Woman continues slowly walking across the stage, silent.)

GEPPETTO: I couldn't sleep, see? So I took a walk. Maybe you're out for a walk
too, eh? The moon—it's real blue tonight, ain't it?
*(Woman stops, takes the wood from the wheelbarrow and gives it to
Geppetto. She turns away and continues on.)*

GEPPETTO: Firewood? Is this for me? Uh, signora—do I owe you any money?
Cause if I do, I ain't got none. But tomorrow I can…
(The Woman is gone. To himself, gazing excitedly at the wood in his arms.)

GEPPETTO: …tomorrow I can…I can make something! Tomorrow I can make
something *wonderful!*

(Exit Geppetto. Distant cries of people awakening, roosters crowing, light of dawn rises on the street.)

SCENE II

The street is soon filled with people and bustling activity. Nine ragged boys: Allesandro, Tomasso, Miguel, Vittorio, Luigi, Giovanni, Massemo, Sergio, Leonardo. Two caribiniere: Alfredo and Alonzo. A fishmonger: Signor Bertolucci. A fruit and flower vendor: Irma. Various townspeople including Signora Bonaventura and her daughter Lucia. A "Drum and Leather Salesman"—the Coachman—who stands Stage Left at the back of a wooden cart; the front of the cart is Offstage and we occasionally hear the braying of the donkey which pulls it. A very foxlike man, the Fox, and a very catty woman, Cat, are mingling with the crowd, but we are not much aware of them, or their peculiar features, until later. An older, rough-looking boy— Lampwick—slouches about, wearing a felt hat.

IRMA: *(Calling over chatter and music.)* Frutta e fiore! Dio mio! Rosse, rosse! Dove sono? Ma per chi erano quelle rose rosse? Frutta e fiore!
(The Boys see Geppetto carrying his block of wood, Stage Left; they run to him.)

TOMASSO: Hey! It's Geppetto!

MIGUEL: Buon giorno, Geppetto!

SERGIO: Hey, Geppetto—what's that you got there?

GEPPETTO: *(As Boys swarm around him.)* Buon giorno! Hello, boys! Did you all work real hard in school yesterday?
(Boys groan.)

GEPPETTO: Oh, I know *you* did, Vittorio; you study so hard you fall asleep, eh?
(Boys laugh at Vittorio.)

GEPPETTO: And that teacher of yours—Signor Bellini, eh?
(Boys sneer and echo the name.)

GEPPETTO: He makes you study your knuckles with his ruler, eh?
(Boys rap their own knuckles with their hands and hop in mock pain.)

GEPPETTO: So—where you boys going, eh?

ALLESANDRO: To the rides!

GIOVANNI: To the *donkey* rides!
(Boys pretend they are donkeys, laughing and braying. One bumps Geppetto and nearly knocks the wood out of his arms.)

LUIGI: Say, Geppetto, what are you going to do with that wood? Make some whistles out of it?

(Boys laugh.)

LEONARDO: No, it's a log for his fire; ain't that right, Geppetto?

ALLESANDRO: Si! Geppetto's gonna cook a snail for his supper!

LEONARDO: *(Snatching the log from Geppetto.)* Let's see it! *(Leonardo stands up on a stool and holds it away from Geppetto, then tosses it over Geppetto's head to Allesandro, starting a game of "keep-away.")*

GEPPETTO: Allesandro! Give me that!

ALLESANDRO: What's it for?

GEPPETTO: It's...it's for...a puppet.

BOYS: *(Variously.)* A puppet?!

(Boys laugh and continue game of "keep-away." Geppetto calls after them and runs accidentally into Signora Bonaventura.)

SIGNORA BONAVENTURA: Buon giorno, Geppetto. Cold, ain't it?

GEPPETTO: *(Distracted.)* What? Oh, buon giorno. My log, Signora Bonaventura.

SIGNORA BONAVENTURA: You know my daughter Lucia, don't you?

GEPPETTO: *(Paying little attention.)* Oh, yeah, sure, I know Lucia. Hi, Lucia.

SIGNORA BONAVENTURA: *(Poking Lucia.)* Lucia!

(Lucia curtseys to Geppetto.)

GEPPETTO: *(To Signora and Lucia.)* Good-bye.

(Running after the Boys again. Signora, offended, exits with Lucia.)

GEPPETTO: Sergio! You're a nice boy; now give it here!

(Boys run about and toss the log from one to the other with great glee and chatter. Geppetto finally gets the log and holds it above his head as the Boys surround him, reaching for it. Lampwick, who has been smoking a cigar, gets log from Allesandro, who has snatched it away from Geppetto again. A kick sends the Boys toppling backwards into a heap on the ground.)

LAMPWICK: *(To Geppetto; a snarl.)* What's it for?

GEPPETTO: *(Politely.)* It's for a puppet.

LAMPWICK: A puppet, eh? *(Holding out his hand to Geppetto for a tip for rescuing the log.)* Two million lire!

GEPPETTO: *(Slight pause, then shakes Lampwick's hand.)* Grazie! *(Geppetto snatches the log from Lampwick.)*

LAMPWICK: *(Angrily throwing his hat to the ground.)* Hey!

(Again Geppetto is surrounded and the Boys and Geppetto play "keep-away" with great laughter and good humor. Alfredo and Alonzo, the caribiniere, appear and cross the square as Geppetto and Boys cease their raucous activity and politely bow. Alfredo and Alonzo are given a buttonhole flower from

Irma and exit again. Allesandro takes the log and holds it high, preparing to throw it to the others. He does so, Geppetto catches it, and they all fall down again in a merry heap.)

GEPPETTO: *(Laughing, catching his breath.)* Oh, you boys! You boys is rascals, but…I gotta go home! Arrivederci! Good-bye! Arrivederci!

(Geppetto starts off; Allesandro pulls his coattails.)

ALLESANDRO: Geppetto! Your house is that way!

(Geppetto stops, Boys laugh, and Geppetto walks Offstage Left as Boys wave good-bye and laugh affectionately. General street activity resumes for a moment. Fox and Cat appear from Stage Right and sneak up to fishmonger's stand. Stage action freezes as Cat grabs a fish and hands it to Fox. Action resumes suddenly.)

SIGNOR BERTOLUCCI: Hey! Who stole my fish! There they are! Stop! Thieves! Crooks!

(The stage is filled with chaotic running as Boys, Townspeople, Caribiniere pursue the Fox and Cat. At the height of the chase the street scene begins to disappear: carts and wagons are pulled Offstage as flats and scenic units for the next scene shift on and people gradually exit.)

SCENE III

Lights and scenery shift to evening in Geppetto's workshop. A large work-bench dominates the room; along the back wall is a fireplace and a mantel that holds an old clock. The blue rays of the moon shine through a window. Geppetto is working by the light of an oil lamp, finishing his creation: a fully-dressed puppet about the size of a ten-year-old boy. He knocks with his chisel here and there and dabs with a paintbrush.

GEPPETTO: *(Lifting puppet up from bench.)* Oh, you are gonna be the *one,* ain't you?! You gonna be the best puppet *ever!* Oops—not if you ain't got no ears, you ain't! *(Reaching for the paint.)* Geppetto, I'm saying to you, you gotta be more careful. *(Painting ears on the puppet's head, then speaking to it.)* Hello in there. Can you hear me talking to you? *(Responding in falsetto and manipulating head like a ventriloquist and dummy.)* "Si, Papa." This is you Papa talking to you. "I know, Papa." You gonna be a real good boy to you old Papa, ain't you? "No, Papa." *(He raps puppet on the head.)* Yes, you are. You are gonna walk… *(He moves puppet's legs and they walk together.)* …and run, too, eh? *(They run a few steps.)* And laugh and tell real good jokes and sing and dance and get rich and famous… *(He has the puppet take a deep bow.)* …and be a real good son to you old Papa! *(As he pulls puppet upRight again its head falls off onto the floor.)* Oh, no you ain't. Listen to me: talking to a piece of wood like it was somebody. *(He replaces the head and carries puppet back to workbench.)* You ain't gonna do none of them things. You just a puppet, ain't you? Just a puppet.

(Clock chimes three tones.)

GEPPETTO: Time for bed. Time for bed, my wood-head boy. *(Geppetto goes to his little cot in the Upstage corner to put on his nightshirt.)* Hey, what's you name, anyway? Giovanni? Ahhh, no, no—everybody's "Giovanni." *(An idea.)* Wait a minute. Hold still! I knew a man once; his name was— Pinocchio! That's right. His papa's name was Pinocchio. His mama's name was Pinocchio. His two brothers: Pinocchio, Pinocchio. His pretty little sister: Pinocchio. They all got put in prison, but they was real nice folks. *(He has finished dressing and moves back to workbench.)* Si! That's gonna be you: Pinocchio! I just wish you were a real… *(He stops himself; turns away.)* What am I saying? Good night, Geppetto; go to bed. *(He sneaks another look at the puppet.)* Oh, Pinocchio—what you look like that for, huh? You look like you sad. You look like you wish you were a real, live little boy. *(He hugs the puppet.)* Well, you ain't. Buona notte, Pinocchio. *(He goes to his cot and kneels.)* God bless my tools, God bless my bench, God bless my wig. *(He gets into bed.)* Buona notte, Pinocchio! *(He blows out lamp.)* Good night. *(He yawns.)* Good night, Kitty. Go to sleep.

(More yawns. Geppetto snores. A shaft of blue light hits the workbench.)

BLUE FAIRY: Pinocchio—you look so sad. You look like you wish you were a real, live little boy. Wish you were a live little boy. Wish you were alive…Pinocchio! Wake up!

(Pinocchio's arm flops down and hangs off side of bench.)

BLUE FAIRY: Pinocchio!

(Pinocchio's head rises up, followed by his torso. He sits on the bench and looks, woodenly, Left and Right.)

BLUE FAIRY: Pinocchio—who are you?

PINOCCHIO: Who…who…

BLUE FAIRY: Who are you?

PINOCCHIO: Pin…occhio. Pinocchio. I am…Pinocchio!

BLUE FAIRY: *(A warm laugh.)* Very good, Pinocchio. Now—who am I?

PINOCCHIO: Who…Blue…Blue…

BLUE FAIRY: You know me, Pinocchio. I am the Blue Fairy. And I will be your friend, always. Always.

PINOCCHIO: Buon...gi...orno.

BLUE FAIRY: *(Another laugh.)* You see? You already know so much. And I will always be your teacher, and your friend, if you will listen to me, and tell the truth—to me, and to yourself, and to your Papa...

PINOCCHIO: Papa!

(Geppetto stirs in his sleep.)

BLUE FAIRY: Yes, Pinocchio. Your Papa, who made you and who loves you and who wished to have a real, live little boy for his son...

PINOCCHIO: A real...live...boy?

BLUE FAIRY: Yes.

PINOCCHIO: Am *I* a...real boy?

BLUE FAIRY: No, Pinocchio. You are not a real little boy. You are made of wood. Geppetto made you out of wood. You are a puppet.

PINOCCHIO: *(With sorrow and disappointment.)* Not a...boy...

BLUE FAIRY: *(After a moment.)* Someday, Pinocchio—if you are honest, and if you work hard and love your Papa—I will make you this promise: Pinocchio, the puppet will die; and Pinocchio, the real boy, will be born.

PINOCCHIO: Be...born? The...truth?

BLUE FAIRY: *(Fading away.)* Good-bye, Pinocchio. I am with you when you need me. Love your Papa. Good-bye, Pinocchio. Good-bye...

(Pinocchio has risen to his feet to wave good-bye.)

PINOCCHIO: Good-bye! Good... *(Pinocchio looks down with wonder at his body: his hands, arms, legs. He turns his head and looks at the sleeping figure of Geppetto.)* Papa.

(Geppetto grunts in his sleep. Pinocchio kicks one foot, likes it, and kicks the other.)

PINOCCHIO: Papa! Look! *(Pinocchio kicks both feet and falls off the bench to the floor with a crash.)* Papa!

(Geppetto quickly awakens as Pinocchio lies motionless on the floor Downstage of the workbench. Geppetto quickly lights the lamp and cautiously gets out of bed.)

GEPPETTO: Who is that? Huh? Who is that? Kitty? What was that? *(He reaches the bench and notices that the puppet is not there.)* Pinocch...Pinocchio! Where did you go? *(He searches about the bench and as he moves Downstage he sees Pinocchio on the floor. He sets lamp down on bench and picks the puppet up to set it back in its place.)* Pinocchio! What are you doing down there, huh? You stay up on the bench where you Papa puts you, hear?

PINOCCHIO: Si, Papa.

GEPPETTO: *(Turning to go back to bed.)* That's better. *(Freezing in his tracks; looks back at motionless puppet, then shakes his head.)* Oh, Geppetto—you must still be dreaming. Go back to bed...

PINOCCHIO: *(Suddenly standing.)* Well, Papa—how was work today?
(Geppetto looks at puppet then recoils in terror, squeaking and mumbling in fear.)

PINOCCHIO: The Blue Fairy said, "Pinocchio, wake up!" And she said, someday, I'll be a real boy. Is it true, Papa?

GEPPETTO: *(Stammering.)* Blue...Fairy?

PINOCCHIO: Is it true?

GEPPETTO: *(To himself.)* Oh, yes...yes, it's true...all these dreams...they all coming true... *(To Pinocchio.)* You...you talk!

PINOCCHIO: What is..."talk?"

GEPPETTO: *(Pointing to his own quivering mouth.)* Talk...talk...I...I am...I am talking. Do you...walk, too?

PINOCCHIO: What is "walk?"

GEPPETTO: I...I show you. *(Geppetto begins an extremely exaggerated walk around the workbench.)* Like this.

PINOCCHIO: *(Jumping down to the floor.)* Like that?

GEPPETTO: Like this.
(Pinocchio imitates him and follows.)

PINOCCHIO: Like this?

GEPPETTO: Yes! Like that! That's right!
(Pinocchio enjoys walking and laughs. He picks up speed and is eventually chasing Geppetto around and around the bench. Pinocchio stops suddenly and points Stage Right.)

PINOCCHIO: Papa! Look!

GEPPETTO: *(Rushing from Stage Left.)* What is it?
(As he passes in front of Pinocchio, Pinocchio stretches out his leg to trip Geppetto. Geppetto sprawls on the floor as Pinocchio laughs and applauds himself.)

GEPPETTO: Ouch! Pinocchio! Pinocchio, that's not a good trick. That's a bad trick!
(Pinocchio's laughter turns into a yawn. Geppetto stares at Pinocchio.)

GEPPETTO: Geppetto, I'm asking you, what have you made? What have you made?

PINOCCHIO: Papa? What will I do?

GEPPETTO: *(Going to Pinocchio.)* The first thing you gonna do, Pinocchio, is lie down and go to bed. *(He helps Pinocchio back up onto the bench.)* My little wood-head… *(He embraces Pinocchio for a moment. He takes a paintcloth for a blanket and tucks it around Pinocchio as he wipes away a tear.)* And…and tomorrow you can go to school, just like the other boys, and learn your "ABCs" real good, and be a real good son to your old Papa. *(Taking the lamp from the bench.)* Good night…Pinocchio.

PINOCCHIO: Good night, Papa.

GEPPETTO: *(Turning toward his cot.)* "Papa!" *(He blows out the lamp.)* *(Blackout.)*

SCENE IV

Lights rise on Geppetto's workshop. A rainy morning. Pinocchio is alone, dressed in a little apron, sweeping the floor as he recites his "ABCs."

PINOCCHIO: A, B, C, D, E, F, G, H…H…H…A, B, C, D, E, F, G, H…H… *(Pinocchio stops his sweeping, looks about to see that he is alone, then up-ends the broom and tries to balance it on the end of his finger. After several balances, wobbles, and falls, the broom falls against the mantel, knocking the clock to the floor with a crash and release of springs.)*

GEPPETTO: *(Offstage.)* Pinocchio! I'm home!
(Pinocchio looks at the broken clock in dismay then fervently resumes sweeping the floor. Geppetto enters, clutching a small package; he is wet and shivering without his overcoat.)

PINOCCHIO: *(Rushing over to Geppetto.)* Papa! Papa! What comes after "H," Papa?

GEPPETTO: "I" comes after "H," you know *that!* But look, Pinocchio—you gonna learn your "ABCs" real good from now on. Look—a brand new spelling book!

PINOCCHIO: *(Hugging him.)* Oh, Papa! Now I can go to school just like all the other boys!

GEPPETTO: Sure you can, Pinocchio! To school!
(They dance happily for a moment.)

GEPPETTO: But, hey—Pinocchio—you ain't gonna go to school with an apron on, are you?
(Pinocchio removes his apron and sets it on the bench.)

PINOCCHIO: Papa, where is your coat? It's cold and rainy outside.

GEPPETTO: Oh, I don't know…it was, uh…too hot. But don't worry about

that, Pinocchio. It must be time for you to go to school, huh? Hey—
what time *is* it, Pinocchio?

PINOCCHIO: *(Suddenly hanging his head in shame.)* I don't know.

GEPPETTO: *(Thinking he's embarrassed due to ignorance.)* Oh, that's all right,
Pinocchio. I teach you to tell time… *(Geppetto turns toward the mantel
and sees no clock. He looks at the floor, crouches, and picks up shattered
pieces of the clock.)* Oh-oh. My old clock don't look too happy.
*(Slight pause as Geppetto looks at Pinocchio, waiting for an explanation.
Pinocchio offers none.)*

GEPPETTO: Do you think Kitty might have broke the clock, Pinocchio?

PINOCCHIO: *(A thought.)* Kitty? Kitty *might* have. Maybe Kitty was playing
and the clock fell down and broke, or… *(Pinocchio suddenly stops and
taps his nose twice.)*

GEPPETTO: What's the matter, Pinocchio? You nose itch?

PINOCCHIO: *(A slight pause.)* You know what, Papa?

GEPPETTO: No. What.

PINOCCHIO: It wasn't Kitty who done it.

GEPPETTO: Really?

PINOCCHIO: It was me. I seen the other boys; sometimes they balance a stick,
and I tried it, and I'm sorry, Papa. I wish I didn't.

GEPPETTO: *(Hugging Pinocchio.)* Pinocchio—if this was my favorite clock, I
don't care if it's broke. What's important is you didn't lie to me. You tell
me the truth. You know, Pinocchio—lies, they just keep on growing.
They ain't no good.
(The sound of schoolboys yelling in the street outside.)

GEPPETTO: But listen, the others boys is already on their way to school. You
go too, eh? Arrivederci.

PINOCCHIO: *(Starting off.)* Good bye, Papa!

GEPPETTO: Oh, Pinocchio—when you come home tonight, I'll have a nice
surprise for you.

PINOCCHIO: *(Waving.)* Arrivederci!

GEPPETTO: Ciao! *(Suddenly seeing spelling book on workbench.)* Pinocchio! You
forgot your spelling book!
(Pinocchio runs back, takes the book, and hugs Geppetto.)

PINOCCHIO: I love you, Papa!

GEPPETTO: Ciao!
(Pinocchio runs out. Geppetto sighs and turns proudly to audience.)

GEPPETTO: That's Pinocchio. I made him. He's my son!
(Music in. Workshop shifts out and Geppetto exits.)

SCENE V

Morning in the street. Enter Polo and Lorenzo through the arch: an Italian "Mutt and Jeff." Lorenzo carries playbills and Polo a bucket of paste and a billboard brush. They paste up a poster advertising "Pigacci's Puppet Theatre" on the wall, Center, and exit, but their brief scene is a cameo of slapstick, pratfalls, paste in the face, etc.—all accompanied by a steady flow of Italian epithets. Just before they leave, Lampwick appears under the arm of a sinister man in a large black cape: Coachman.

COACHMAN: So, Lampwick, I'll be back here one week from today. And I'll meet you at the Inn of the Red Lobster.

LAMPWICK: Sure. The Inn of the Red Lobster.

COACHMAN: And Lampwick—for every boy you bring me, I'll give you a single gold piece, eh? Lampwick—I got a whole bag of gold pieces, eh?

LAMPWICK: Sure.

COACHMAN: Arrivederci.

LAMPWICK: *(Exiting Stage Right.)* Ciao…Papa.

COACHMAN: *(With a chuckle, exiting Stage Left.)* Ciao!
(Polo and Lorenzo exit Upstage and Pinocchio appears at top of stairs Stage Right, alone, apprehensive, and excited. He stands for a moment, looking about. Miguel and Sergio run past him toward Center.)

PINOCCHIO: *(To Boys.)* Buon giorno!
(They pay no attention.)

PINOCCHIO: Boys! Hello!
(They pause for a moment and look at him.)

PINOCCHIO: I'm going to school.
(Boys turn away and rush up to read the poster.)

PINOCCHIO: Are you?
(Signora Bonaventura and Lucia bustle past Pinocchio.)

PINOCCHIO: Buon giorno.

SIGNORA BONAVENTURA: *(Without really looking.)* Buon giorno.

PINOCCHIO: Please, Signora, could you tell me the way to the school?

SIGNORA BONAVENTURA: *(Halting and cheerfully explaining.)* Sure. You go down this street here, and you turn left at… *(She does a double take at Pinocchio.)* All right, that's it! Lucia—we going to you grandmama's for a good long rest! *(Dragging Lucia quickly Stage Left and Off.)* A puppet is talking to me in a street! That's enough, that's all, I mean it, Lucia, we going to you grandmama's…

PINOCCHIO: But Signora…

> *(Pinocchio stands alone for a moment. The rest of the Boys rush on and past him, setting him spinning. They all converge on the poster with much talk and excited jabber. Pinocchio decides to try and see what they're all looking at but is buffeted about the edges of the crowd.)*

GIOVANNI: What does the sign say?

ALLESANDRO: It says: "Pigacci's Puppet Teatro. A Big Show. Puppets, Marionettes From Every Land."

TOMASSO: *(Continuing.)* "Stunts."

SERGIO: "Tricks."

VITTORIO: "And the Eating of Fire!"

> *(All Boys gasp.)*

LEONARDO: "Come One…"

ALL BOYS: "Come Everyone!"

ALLESANDRO: Hey—whadda you say we skip school and see this, eh?

> *(Boys all whoop in agreement and run past Pinocchio toward Stage Right and Off. Allesandro and little Massemo are the last ones to leave.)*

MASSEMO: *(Tugging at Allesandro.)* But what about school?

ALLESANDRO: I can go to school some other day. But *you* can go, Massemo, if you *want* to.

MASSEMO: *(Shaking his head emphatically.)* Un-unh! Un-unh!

> *(The Boys exit. Pinocchio, alone, moves up close to the poster and uses his spelling book in an attempt to read it. Enter Fox and Cat from Downstage Right.)*

CAT: *(Noticing Pinocchio.)* Jean-Claude! There's a puppet reading a sign…

FOX: *(A glance as they move Upstage and almost Off.)* I know, Pucci. I can see. I'm not blind. Now, don't interrupt. As I was… *(Fox screeches to a halt, looks at Pinocchio, grabs Cat.)* Pucci!

CAT: What?

FOX: There's a puppet reading a sign!

CAT: I know, Jean-Claude; that's what I *told* you: I said, "There's a puppet…"

FOX: *(Clapping his hand over Cat's mouth.)* Pucci! Now, you listen to me. This is it. We gonna make lots of money with this one. So you shut up you face! *(Releasing Cat and strolling toward Pinocchio; sweetly.)* Buon giorno!

PINOCCHIO: *(Looking up from his book.)* Buon giorno.

CAT: My mother in heaven! It talks!

FOX: *(After a quick angry glare at Cat.)* Please allow me to introduce my dear friend and companion along life's weary road: Puccinella.

CAT: *(A bow.)* Buon giorno.

FOX: And my humble self, your humble servant, Jean-Claude Batiste.

PINOCCHIO: Please, Signor, can you tell me what this sign says because I don't know how to read but I'm going to school to learn how?

CAT: *(Moving closer to Fox and Pinocchio.)* Ohhh, Jean-Claude; ain't that *sweet?*

FOX: *(A sneer at Cat.)* Sign? What it says? Well, now…it's a very *big* sign, as you can see. And on it, I see the name of my dear friend: Signor Pigacci. *(To Cat.)* You remember old Pigacci, now *don't* you, Pucci.

CAT: No.

FOX: No doubt you do, uh-huh, good! *(He pushes Cat down to the ground. Sweetly, to Pinocchio.)* And on this sign it says: "Wanted: A Puppet That Can Walk and Talk But Doesn't Have No Strings. For Signor Pigacci's Big Puppet Teatro. Fame and Fortune Guaranteed!" So you see, little one, whadda you need to learn how to read for when you're gonna be rich; you're gonna be famous!

PINOCCHIO: What's "rich?"

FOX: *(A second's silence, then forced laugh.)* Ah-ha-ha-ha! *(To Cat.)* He makes a little joke! *(To Pinocchio.)* That was very clever! I beg your pardon, I don't yet have the pleasure of your name.

PINOCCHIO: Pinocchio.

FOX: *(Putting his arm around Pinocchio.)* Well, then…Pinocchio…shall we go?

PINOCCHIO: Go? Where?

CAT: Yeah, Jean-Claude, where we going? I'm hungry and I…

FOX: *(Releasing Pinocchio and grabbing Cat's nose.)* Listen, whisker-lips!
(Cat reacts in pain as Fox turns back to Pinocchio.)

FOX: Why, we're going to Pigacci's Big Puppet Teatro! Oh, Signor Pigacci, he just gonna love you! And by tonight, he'll put you in his show and then you'll be famous; everyone will know your name: "Pinocchio—The Famous Puppet!"

PINOCCHIO: Oh, no! I can't. Papa sold his coat and bought this spelling book and I've gotta go to school!

FOX: Just think of how proud your papa will be, Pinocchio!

PINOCCHIO: *(Starting to walk away from Fox.)* Oh, I don't know.

FOX: *(Quickly blocking Pinocchio's path.)* Pinocchio—with the money you make, you could buy your papa *two* new coats.

PINOCCHIO: New coats?

CAT: With the money you make, you could buy your papa *ten* new coats!
(A glare from Fox; Cat quickly corrects herself.)

CAT: *Four* new coats!

FOX: So, then—we are agreed, yes? *(Gesturing for Cat to take Pinocchio's Right arm.)* Pucci?

CAT: Mmmmyeeesss! Agreed!

FOX: *(Offering his arm to Pinocchio.)* Pinocchio?

PINOCCHIO: Well, maybe…

FOX: *(Quickly.)* Good! Let's go!

(Arm in arm the three promenade about the street and head Offstage Right. Cat lags behind, spying a rope along the proscenium wall.)

CAT: Mmmmm—curious!

(Cat picks rope up and tugs. Show curtain falls rapidly as Cat rushes Offstage.)

SCENE VI

The moment the show curtain touches the floor, three Boys scurry out from beneath it, followed by a giant of a man with a long, black beard: Pigacci. Pigacci chases the frightened Boys with a slapstick.

PIGACCI: Hey, you! Get outta here! Two hunnert lire or you don't see nothin', you got that in you dumb heads?! Go on!

(He slaps one last little Boy with slapstick and Boy rushes Off. Pigacci turns away and suddenly notices the audience waiting for the puppet show to begin. He stands very awkwardly, hiding the slapstick behind his back.)

PIGACCI: Ha, ha. Boys. Ha, ha.

(An urgent growl Upstage.)

PIGACCI: Hey, Lampwick! Shut up back there, eh? *(With a false smile, to audience.)* So, anyways…ladies and gentlemen, gentlemen and ladies, and all you little bambini with you little feets and you little shoes on…Hello! This is Pigacci, and this is a *big show!* We got for you puppets… *(He imitates a hand puppet talking with one hand, first in falsetto.)* Hello. *(Then a deep bass.)* Good bye. *(Resuming his normal voice.)* We got for you marionettes… *(He hangs his arms and legs in the angular stance of a marionette. Falsetto again.)* Harlequino! *(Normal again.)* We got…we got for you all *kinds* of things! And *me*, Pigacci, I run the *whole* show! How do you like *that* for special, eh? So, anyways, get ready in you seats. Maestro, get ready…

(Orchestra begins to tune up. Pigacci calls Upstage through curtain.)

PIGACCI: Lampwick! Get ready back there! *(With a grand gesture to audience.)* We gonna begin—*now!*

(Music. Show curtain rises to reveal the puppet theatre from backstage. Lampwick is on a high wooden platform above the puppet stage, operating

a marionette; Pigacci quickly climbs the ladder to join him. We can see the puppet theatre audience Upstage, watching. The marionette show is a simple, classic commedia tale: Harlequino, Columbina, Pantelone. Above the music and laughter and applause from the audience we hear bits of dialogue delivered by Lampwick and Pigacci.)

LAMPWICK: *(As Harlequino.)* Columbina! Come here quick!

PIGACCI: *(As Columbina.)* Don't touch me! Don't touch me!

LAMPWICK: Kiss me on the cheek!

PIGACCI: Don't tell my Papa.

LAMPWICK: Marry me!

PIGACCI: *(As Pantelone.)* What? Is that *you* with my daughter? *(As Columbina.)* Quick! Hit him with your stick! *(As Pantelone.)* Ouch! Don't! *(As Columbina.)* Hit him with your stick! *(As Pantelone.)* Ouch! Don't!

LAMPWICK: *(As Harlequino.)* Kiss, kiss, kiss!

PIGACCI: *(As Pantelone.)* Help, help, help!

LAMPWICK: *(As Harlequino.)* Love, love, love!

(Music swells and marionettes bow to applause and a few coins tossed up on the stage. Puppet stage curtain drops and marionettes collapse in a heap on the stage as Lampwick and Pigacci drop the strings.)

PIGACCI: *(Descending the ladder.)* All right, Lampwick—you go out there and pick up the money. I'm going over here to sit down and rest.

(Lampwick exits Upstage and Pigacci sits at table Stage Right. Fox and Cat appear from the shadows Stage Left, followed by Pinocchio who has a black cloth draped over him. Pigacci slumps, exhausted and drinks from a bottle, but when he sees Fox and Cat he quickly stands.)

PIGACCI: Oh, no! Not you two again! No, no—no more money; that's it!

FOX: It was a marvelous show, Pigacci, oh, *simply* marvelous!

PIGACCI: *(After a moment of puzzled silence.)* You liked it?

CAT: We *loved* it, Pigacci—simply *loved* it!

PIGACCI: *(A smile of pride.)* So you liked it, huh?

CAT: *Loved* it. Of course, there were *some* things…

FOX: *(Obviously rehearsed.)* Pucci! Don't you dare!

PIGACCI: What? Now, now—what was you gonna say?

CAT: Nothing. It was a marvelous show. Simply marvelous.

FOX: *(Nodding his head.)* Marvelous. *(After a slight pause.)* What Pucci is trying to say is…

CAT: Don't, Jean-Claude; it's not important.

PIGACCI: *(Losing his patience.)* What! What!

FOX: Oh, nothing.

CAT: What *you* need is something *new,* Pigacci. Something fresh…

FOX: Puppets on strings, Pigacci; now that's *sweet,* but…

CAT: *(Shaking his head.)* Same old thing.

FOX: *(In agreement.)* Same…old…thing.

PIGACCI: *(Menacingly.)* Whadda you mean, "same old thing?!"

> *(Lampwick re-enters from puppet stage.)*

FOX: It's got no…*class,* Pigacci.

CAT: *(Shaking his head.)* No class!

PIGACCI: "Class?' Say, listen… *(He walks in a friendly way to Fox and Cat and puts his arms around them,.)* I'll give you some "class"… *(Roughly picking them up by their lapels.)* …right on you nose! Hey, Lampwick! Come here! We gonna take care of two real "classy" people!

FOX: *(Squeaking rapidly.)* No! Wait, wait, wait! What if you had a puppet that could walk and talk but didn't have no strings?

PIGACCI: "No strings?!" Well, what if I had a Fox and a Cat without no tails, huh? *(Lampwick steps forward with a small knife and waves it threateningly. Pinocchio, still draped by cloth, walks Downstage Center toward them.)*

PINOCCHIO: Please, Signor Pigacci! These are my friends; they gonna make me rich!

PIGACCI: *(Dropping Fox and Cat.)* What's *this?*

> *(Pigacci steps up to Pinocchio, removes the cloth.)*

PINOCCHIO: *(Offering his hand.)* Pleased to meet you.

PIGACCI: *(Grabbing Lampwick for protection, stepping away.)* My mother in heaven—it talks!

FOX AND CAT: *(In unison; haughty.)* And it walks, *too!*

FOX: Well, Pigacci, we can see that you ain't interested.

CAT: Got no class.

FOX: No class! *(Taking Pinocchio gently by the arm and heading Stage Left.)* Come along, Pinocchio. We'll find someone who can appreciate your talents.

> *(Cat throws cloth over Pinocchio's head and the three begin to exit.)*

PIGACCI: Wait a minute, wait a minute! Come on back here. How much do want for this here thing?

FOX: *(A gasp.)* "Want?"

CAT: *(A gasp.)* "Want!"

FOX: Pinocchio! Pucci! I think we're being insulted! Let's go.

PIGACCI: *(Just as they reach exit.)* Listen! I'll give you six gold pieces that's it!

CAT: Ten!

PIGACCI: Eight!

FOX: Twelve!

PIGACCI: Sold!

> *(Lampwick tosses coin bag to Pigacci, who tosses it to Fox.)*

FOX: *(Quickly.)* Arrivederci, Pinocchio. *(Pushing Cat quickly out; to Pigacci.)* Pucci loved the show…

PIGACCI: Out, out, out, out!

> *(Fox and Cat are gone. Pigacci goes to Pinocchio, picks him up, carries him Stage Right and sets him up on the table.)*

PIGACCI: Well, Lampwick, let's see what we bought here. *(He pulls the cloth Off Pinocchio.)* All right, Pinocchio—watch this.

> *(Pigacci swings his arms like a marionette; Pinocchio imitates.)*

PIGACCI: Hey, that's pretty good, little one!

> *(Pigacci gives Pinocchio a little pat on the cheek; Pinocchio "imitates" with a rough slap to Pigacci's cheek.)*

PIGACCI: Hey! *(Pigacci curbs his anger. A chuckle.)* I'm gonna teach you lots of things, just listen to me. You gonna be in the show tonight! You gonna be a big star! Now listen to me: my name is Pigacci. Now say that: "Pigacci."

PINOCCHIO: *(Intentionally mispronouncing.)* Pig-a-ggi.

PIGACCI: No, no, no, no! That's "Pigacci," eh? "acci, acci, acci!"

PINOCCHIO: God bless you.

> *(Lampwick and Pinocchio laugh.)*

PIGACCI: *(A growl.)* You some sort of smart one, or something? Now *say* it: "Pigacci! Pigacci!"

> *(Pinocchio and Lampwick join Pigacci in the chant. Music in.)*

PIGACCI, PINOCCHIO, LAMPWICK: Pigacci! Pigacci! Pigacci! Pigacci!

> *(Music grows louder as chant continues and lights fade. Show curtain quickly falls.)*

SCENE VII

> *The music continues but the chanted "Pigacci" becomes a crowd chant of "Pinocchio! Pinocchio!" Show curtain rises up and down repeatedly as we see Pinocchio, in a grand brocaded costume and plumed hat, bowing to puppet theatre audience chanting, applauding, and showering the stage with gold coins. The action freezes and music strikes a single chord as we hear Geppetto in the distance, with a plaintive call: "Pinocchio! Pinocchio!" Music and action resumes and the show curtain remains up as puppet stage curtain*

drops. Pinocchio turns and swaggers down from the stage as Lampwick gets up from the table to gather the coins.

PINOCCHIO: *(Arrogantly.)* Well, Lampwick, old boy—how did I do today? *(Pinocchio pokes Lampwick in the stomach.)*

LAMPWICK: Listen, Sticks—you don't talk to me like that, you unnerstand? *(Lampwick shoves Pinocchio back.)*

PINOCCHIO: Well, why *shouldn't* I? *You* ain't nobody! Nobody comes here to see *you.* They come here to see *me.* I'm the one!

LAMPWICK: Oh, yeah? Well, one of these days, Pinocchio, you gonna be *real* sorry!
(Lampwick exits Upstage. Pinocchio watches him exit, pretending not to care about the warning. An intense blue light suddenly fills the Backstage area of the puppet theatre.)

BLUE FAIRY: Well, Pinocchio—"old boy"—what did you learn in school today?

PINOCCHIO: *(Startled; looking about.)* School? But I don't go to school…

BLUE FAIRY: Do you still remember your Papa, Pinocchio? Do you still remember Geppetto?

PINOCCHIO: Of *course* I do!

BLUE FAIRY: Now do you know who I am?

PINOCCHIO: *(With guilt.)* The Blue Fairy.

BLUE FAIRY: Why didn't you obey your Papa, Pinocchio? Why didn't you go to school?

PINOCCHIO: *(Thinking fast.)* Papa said…he said…"Pinocchio, you can go to school, but first get rich and famous!" Cause…cause he wanted a new coat…that's what he told me.
(To Pinocchio's great astonishment, his nose grows several inches in length.)

BLUE FAIRY: Your Papa wanted you to come here?

PINOCCHIO: *(Panicked; feeling his nose.)* Yes! Yes, he did! He said, "If you don't get rich, you're gonna be sorry." He really did!
(Pinocchio's nose grows longer still.)

BLUE FAIRY: Pinocchio! If you are honest…

PINOCCHIO: I *am* honest!

BLUE FAIRY: …and if you work hard, and love your Papa…

PINOCCHIO: Papa!

BLUE FAIRY: …Pinocchio, the puppet, will die. And Pinocchio, the real boy, will be born.

PINOCCHIO: But I *do* love my Papa!

BLUE FAIRY: *Do* you, Pinocchio? Geppetto is looking for you right now… looking everywhere. When you didn't come home, you broke his heart. You broke his heart, Pinocchio.

PINOCCHIO: I didn't mean it! I didn't mean it! And you know what? Geppetto never told me to come here; I just came. And now I'm sorry and I'll go home to my Papa right now. I promise. But my nose…my nose… *(Pinocchio's nose suddenly shrinks back to its normal length.)*

BLUE FAIRY: Remember, Pinocchio. You have one more chance to prove yourself. Good-bye, Pinocchio. Good-bye.

PINOCCHIO: *(Calling.)* I promise! I promise!
(The sound of a drunken Pigacci, laughing Offstage.)

PINOCCHIO: I gotta go home to my Papa!
(Pinocchio exits Stage Left as Pigacci appears from Stage Right and stumbles to the table. He has a bottle and pours liquor into two glasses.)

PIGACCI: *(Calling to wherever Pinocchio might be.)* Ah, Pinocchio, old boy— you're getting better every day! The people, they love you! We gonna make lots of money together: you and me. *(A toast.)* Here's to you and me, Pinocchio! *(Pigacci empties one glass in a single swallow. He takes the other glass.)* Here's to our success—yours and mine! *(Pigacci empties that as well.)*

PINOCCHIO: *(In regular dress, a knapsack on a stick over his shoulder.)* I'm leaving, Signor Pigacci. Ciao.

PIGACCI: *(Rising suddenly.)* "Leaving?! *Ciao?!"* What are you talking?

PINOCCHIO: *(Heading Stage Left.)* I'm going home to my Papa. I promised.

PIGACCI: *(Rushing over and grabbing Pinocchio.)* Papa, Shmapa! You gonna stay right here! *Nobody* leaves Pigacci! *(Calling over his shoulder.)* Hey, Lampwick—get in here! *(Dragging Pinocchio over to table and picking up a piece of wood from a basket.)* Hey, little one—see this here little piece of wood? It used to be a little puppet.
(Pigacci breaks the piece of wood over his knee with a monstrous roar, followed by a maniacal laugh. Lampwick enters.)

PIGACCI: What took you so long, dumb one? *(Pigacci slaps Lampwick.)* The puppet here wants to go home to his Papa. *(Pigacci laughs and hands Lampwick a coil of rope.)* Well, you tie him up good and tight! Nobody leaves Pigacci!
(Lampwick drags Pinocchio to ladder Stage Left and ties him up as Pigacci sits down again and resumes drinking from the bottle.)

PINOCCHIO: Please, Lampwick, don't! I want to go home to my Papa! I want to start all over!

LAMPWICK: *(Striking Pinocchio across the face.)* Aw, shut up, Pinocchio!

PIGACCI: *(Reaching affectionately for Lampwick.)* See? Little Lampwick knows what's good for him, eh?

LAMPWICK: *(Walking over to Pigacci.)* Sure, sure…

PIGACCI: *(Violently hurling Lampwick over the table.)* He knows he wouldn't get no place without Pigacci! Ain't that right?!
(Pigacci releases Lampwick who holds his arm in pain and withdraws Upstage Center. Pigacci takes another long swig from the bottle and begins to swoon.)

PIGACCI: Ain't gonna get no place…without…Pigacci… *(Pigacci's head falls to the table in a drunken stupor.)*

LAMPWICK: *(Muttering.)* Why, you miserable…

PINOCCHIO: *(Pitifully.)* Please, Lampwick. I want to go home.
(Lampwick urgently signals for silence by pressing his finger to his lips, then quickly unties Pinocchio.)

LAMPWICK: Shut up, Pinocchio; I wouldn't care if you was firewood. *(Over his shoulder, to Pigacci.)* "Nobody leaves Pigacci," huh? We'll see about that.

PINOCCHIO: *(Not understanding.)* Lampwick! What…

LAMPWICK: *(A fierce whisper.)* Shut up, Sticks!
(Pinocchio is free. Lampwick silently motions for him to get up on the puppet stage. As Pinocchio does so, Lampwick sneaks over to the sleeping Pigacci and carefully ties one end of the rope to Pigacci's leg and the other end to the leg of the table. When the task is completed, Lampwick stands and gives Pigacci a kick.)

LAMPWICK: Hey! Pigacci! Wake up!

PIGACCI: *(Semiconscious.)* Wha…? Oh, shut up and let me sleep!

LAMPWICK: *(A loud command.)* Hey! I said get up off you face, meathead!
(Another kick, and Pigacci quickly awakens with anger.)

PIGACCI: Whadda you say to me?!

LAMPWICK: I said, you face needs a rest, O Great Thick One! *(Another kick.)*

PIGACCI: *(Rising; roaring.)* I'll get you…

LAMPWICK: *(Running quickly Upstage, grabbing Pinocchio.)* Quick, Pinocchio!
(Pigacci reaches the end of the rope and falls to the floor with a scream of rage as Lampwick and Pinocchio escape beneath the curtain of the puppet stage. Lights quickly fade and show curtain falls.)

SCENE VIII

Dim light rises in front of show curtain. Music. Thunder and wind. Lampwick and Pinocchio scramble out from beneath the curtain.

LAMPWICK: Quick, Pinocchio—this way!

PINOCCHIO: No, Lampwick! I can't! I gotta go home to my Papa! I promised!

LAMPWICK: You come with me and I'm telling you, you'll have a real good time!

PINOCCHIO: Come where?

LAMPWICK: To the Inn of the Red Lobster. It's all set up already, Pinocchio. There's a man there; he's waiting for me and he'll take us for a ride, Pinocchio—to a magic island.

PINOCCHIO: But, Lampwick...I *promised!*

(A stooped old Woman in a blue shawl, pushing a wheelbarrow, appears and slowly moves across the stage.)

LAMPWICK: Oh. So maybe you don't think I ever did you no favors, is that it?

PINOCCHIO: Oh, no, Lampwick! You're my best friend!

LAMPWICK: Aw, you don't have to say nothin' like that. So long, Sticks!

(Lampwick exits Stage Right. Pinocchio is Left alone, torn with decision. He sees Woman approaching from Stage Left toward him and is frightened.)

PINOCCHIO: *(Running after Lampwick.)* Wait, Lampwick! Wait for me!

(Pinocchio exits. After a moment, Geppetto appears from Stage Left, carrying a lantern.)

GEPPETTO: *(Calling over the thunder and wind.)* Pinocchio! Pinocchio! *(Rushing up to Woman.)* Pardoni, Signora. Have you seen my little boy? His name is Pinocchio. He must be lost, because he never came back. *(The Woman silently continues on her way.)*

GEPPETTO: Signora? *(Geppetto turns and exits the way he entered.)* Pinocchio! Pinocchio!

(Lights fade to Blackout.)

SCENE IX

Show curtain rises and lights reveal the Inn of the Red Lobster. A single booth sits Center. Innkeeper wiping Off the table. From Upstage appear Fox, Cat, and the Coachman.

COACHMAN: *(To Innkeeper.)* A table for me and my new...associates. Quickly!

INNKEEPER: Immediately, Signor. Will this do?

(Innkeeper gestures to booth before them. Coachman waves Innkeeper away. Coachman, Fox, and Cat all look under table for spies and then stand upRight again.)

COACHMAN: Sit down.

(They sit. Fox and Cat are extremely nervous. Fox swaggeringly tosses a little bag of gold onto the table. Coachman sets a bag twelve times larger on the table.)

COACHMAN: Good. Now we can talk business, eh? Signore—my business is...joy! Joy and happiness for little ones! Ain't that sweet?

CAT: That is *so sweet!* Ain't that sweet, Jean-Claude?

FOX: Sweet...

COACHMAN: Shut up and listen!

(Fox and Cat freeze, nervously.)

COACHMAN: There is an island, not far offshore...*my* island...Paradise Island! A little bit of heaven-on-earth for little boys! *(Lowering his voice.)* We ride to the harbor tonight. For every boy you bring me, I'll give you twenty pieces of gold, and when they get there...

(He draws Fox and Cat very near to him and mutters. Fox and Cat put their hands over their ears and scream.)

CAT: Meeeeeeoooooww...!

FOX: *(Hoarse whisper.)* No...No...!

COACHMAN: *(A sinister laugh.)* The skin of a donkey brings a good price, don't you think? *(Another sinister laugh.)*

PINOCCHIO: *(Suddenly appearing behind Coachman with Lampwick.)* Hello.

(Coachman, Fox, Cat are silent; stunned. Pinocchio sits beside Fox.)

PINOCCHIO: I didn't think I'd ever see *you* again. Or anybody. You know what?

FOX: No. What?

PINOCCHIO: That Signor Pigacci—he's a bad man!

FOX & CAT: *(Feigned astonishment.)* Noooo!

PINOCCHIO: But my friend Lampwick, he helped me to get away. And now I'm going home to my Papa.

(Coachman has been examining Pinocchio incredulously, then turns to Lampwick.)

COACHMAN: Lampwick—we meet again, eh? You're just in time! *And* you brought a little friend...just like you said you would.

(Coachman covertly passes a small bag of gold to Lampwick. To Pinocchio.) Well, my little friend, what is your name?

PINOCCHIO: Pinocchio. What's yours?

COACHMAN: *(Clears his throat.)* Ah...umm...well, to tell the truth...my little friends usually just call me "Papa." *(A loud command toward Offstage.)* Innkeep! Bring these boys something good and sweet and lots of it!

FOX: *(Ingratiatingly.)* We *discovered* Pinocchio—Pucci and I.

CAT: It was us who found him.

COACHMAN: Pucci, Jean-Claude—perhaps you would be good enough to give your seats to my young friends! They must be weary.
(Fox and Cat scramble to their feet and move behind the benches.)

FOX: *(Fussing over Pinocchio.)* Oh, of course! Silly not to think of it. Sorry. There you go. Comfortable?

COACHMAN: *(Undertone, to Fox, as Lampwick and Pinocchio situate themselves.)* Shut up! *(To Pinocchio.)* So, Pinocchio—you look like a bright one. A shame, though, that you...well, you *are* only a...forgive me...a puppet, eh?

PINOCCHIO: But I *am* gonna be a real boy. Soon! The Blue Fairy said...

COACHMAN: *(Interrupting.)* The Blue...*what?*

PINOCCHIO: The Blue Fairy.

COACHMAN: *(Humoring him.)* Well, Pinocchio...all right...what did she say?

PINOCCHIO: She said if I work hard and go to school and...

COACHMAN: "School," huh? Well, you do what you like, but...but I wonder how much this, uh, little "Fairy" of yours knows about *real* boys. *(With a friendly glance at Lampwick.)* Eh? Your good friend here, Candlestick—he's a real boy; I'll bet he knows all about school, don't you, my boy?

LAMPWICK: Sure. Sure. It's no good, Pinocchio. It's no good.

FOX & CAT: *(Adding their two-cents worth.)* No good. Un-unh. It's no good.

COACHMAN: But, whatever little Pinocchio wants...of course, he's only a puppet...
(Fox, Cat, and Lampwick laugh in agreement. Coachman puts an arm around Pinocchio.)

COACHMAN: Oh, Pinocchio. Ohhhh. Well, I *do* hope you'll call me "Papa"...

PINOCCHIO: But you ain't my papa!

COACHMAN: *(Not hearing Pinocchio's protest.)* I just happen to be taking a whole lot of little boys tonight to a place where boys... *(A thought.)* ...a place where puppets who wasn't real boys turn into real boys, just like that! No work, no school...

LAMPWICK: *(Excited.)* No school?! Where is it?

COACHMAN: Where is it? Oh, Dampwick, Dampwick, Dampwick—it's an island! A lovely little island! And it's called…it's called…"The Island of…*Real* Boys!" *You'd* like to be a real boy, wouldn't you, Pinocchio?

PINOCCHIO: Oh, yes! Yes, I would!

COACHMAN: But you have to make up your mind right now if you want to come with me. Because my coach is just *full* of boys, just waiting to leave for the harbor. And we leave *now! Tonight!*

LAMPWICK: *(Standing.)* I'll go!

COACHMAN: And you, Pinocchio?

PINOCCHIO: *(After a brief pause.)* Papa said, "Work—it's a *good* thing."

LAMPWICK: *(Scoffing.)* Huh—you think so?

COACHMAN: And right you *are,* Pinocchio, right you *are!* Good-bye! Work hard! Come on, Lampwick. *(Coachman pushes Lampwick Downstage and out of booth; he places a fatherly arm around Lampwick's shoulder and gestures hypnotically as he speaks, exhorting Lampwick to imagine the Utopia ahead.)* We've got a ride ahead of us…twenty little donkeys will take us to the sea… a ferry-ride in the darkness…and then…*joy* Lampwick! My business is joy! *(Shoving a cigar into Lampwick's mouth.)* Have a cigar. *(Fox and Cat have cautiously crept Downstage behind Coachman, hoping to get in on some of the action.)*

COACHMAN: Pucci. Jean-Claude. We won't be needing your services after all. Good-bye. *(To Lampwick again.)* Happiness…good times, Lampwick! *(Suddenly turning back and seeing Pinocchio sitting, watching.)*

COACHMAN: Oh, I forgot… *(With great mock sorrow.)* …our little friend Pinocchio won't be coming with us. Too bad.
(Starting Offstage Left with Lampwick.)

COACHMAN: Good-bye, then; good-bye! Come along, Lampwick!

PINOCCHIO: Wait!
(Coachman and Lampwick freeze and slowly turn to Pinocchio.)

PINOCCHIO: I want to go with you…to the coach. I'll say good-bye there.

COACHMAN: Is that all right with you, Lampwick?

LAMPWICK: Well…

PINOCCHIO: I really *do* want to go! And then I'll go straight home.
(Coachman stands silent for a moment, then spreads his caped arms wide to Pinocchio with a sinister grin.)

COACHMAN: Ohhhhh, Pinocchio…!
(Pinocchio rushes to Coachman, who lifts him up onto his shoulder.)

COACHMAN: And you *will* call me "Papa," won't you?
(Music. Coachman, Pinocchio, and Lampwick quickly sweep Offstage Left. Cat and Fox remain, sitting down dejectedly at the table. Blackout.)

SCENE X

Dim light rises on a fog-shrouded coach; Boys hanging, scrambling and running on and around it. Lampwick, Coachman, and Pinocchio run Onstage from Left. Coachman sets Pinocchio down and moves Upstage to check on the donkey team which, through the darkness and fog, we hear braying. Boys greet Lampwick and look with derision at Pinocchio.

LUIGI: Hey, everybody! Look at *this* one—it's made of wood!

LAMPWICK: *(Snickering.)* Yeah, it's a puppet and it thinks it's a boy!
   (Chorus of laughter from Boys.)

PINOCCHIO: *(Nervously, to one of the Boys.)* Hello. What's your name?

BOYS: *(In unison, mocking falsetto.)* "What's your name?"

COACHMAN: *(Herding Boys up onto coach.)* Silenzio, boys! Silence! The donkeys are harnessed; the coach is ready. Paradise Island awaits! Come on, boys; let's go!

PINOCCHIO: Lampwick! Wait!

LAMPWICK: Whadda you want now, Pinocchio?

PINOCCHIO: *(Slight pause.)* Nothing. Good-bye, Lampwick.

LAMPWICK: *(Turning to mount coach.)* Yeah—good-bye, Sticks.
   (Coachman approaches Pinocchio.)

COACHMAN: Pinocchio—the time has come for us to say "good-bye."
   (Coachman reaches out his hand in farewell, but when Pinocchio reaches to shake it, Coachman withdraws it with a nasty laugh.)

COACHMAN: Good-bye! Hahahahaha! *(With a flourish of his cape, Coachman turns away to mount the coach.)*

PINOCCHIO: Wait!

COACHMAN: *(Freezes.)* "Wait" *what?*

PINOCCHIO: *(A slight pause.)* Wait…Papa!

(Music. With a sinister laugh Coachman leaps back down and runs to Pinocchio. He envelopes Pinocchio in his cape and leads him through the fog in a stylized dance, drawing from within his cape various candies to tempt him. As Pinocchio reaches for each object of his desire, Coachman tosses them up to the Boys on the coach. Finally, Coachman leaves Pinocchio and jumps onto the coach, which heads Upstage Right, grabs the reins, and the ride begins. Music crescendos and the coach bumps and sways through the fog, Boys shouting, Pinocchio running behind. Running with all his might, Pinocchio finally catches up to the coach and Lampwick reaches down from the back of the coach, grabs Pinocchio's arms, and pulls him on board.

Thunder, lightning, donkeys screaming, Boys shouting, Coachman laughing, and fog swirling and music rises to a frenzied rhythm and show curtain quickly descends.)

Intermission

ACT II
SCENE I

Music. Show curtain rises to reveal "Paradise Island"—a series of ramps, stairways, booths, carnival banners, pennants, carnival rides in the distance Upstage. Boys with luggage stand in tableau, looking out at the departing ferryboat. A low, repeated fog horn. Boys wave, shouting "Arrivederci! Ciao!" etc.

BOYS: *(Turning away and investigating environment.)* Stop pushing! Are we here? Luigi, wake up! What time is it? Hey, what's up there? I said, "Don't push!" I'm hungry. Hey, Tomasso, look at this!

COACHMAN: *(Appearing at top of stairs Stage Right.)* Boys! Boys! Silenzio! Give me your attention for one moment, and then you'll never have to pay attention again in your little lives!
(Boys cheer.)

COACHMAN: Good! Welcome...to Paradise!

BOYS: Ahhhhh!

COACHMAN: Are we all here? Where's the wooden one? *(Calling Offstage.)* Guido!

LAMPWICK: Pinocchio? Who needs Pinocchio! Let's go!

COACHMAN: Why, Lampwick—*we* need Pinocchio just like we need *you!* To have a good time. To have a real good time.

GUIDO: *(A clownlike servant; carrying Pinocchio in.)* Papa—the wooden one is a little slow in the legs.
(Boys laugh.)

PINOCCHIO: Don't talk to *me*, Signor Guido. *You* a little slow in the *head!*
(Boys laugh and cheer Pinocchio. Guido is unamused, however, and swings Pinocchio out over the pit while forcing a laugh.)

COACHMAN: Don't you worry about a thing, Guido.
(Guido sets Pinocchio down and Pinocchio goes to the Coachman.)

COACHMAN: We'll speed Pinocchio up; just you wait, Pinocchio, we'll speed you up good. *(Coachman lifts Pinocchio up onto his shoulder.)* So. Boys! Welcome to the Island of Boys, where anything you want to do, that's what you do!
(Boys cheer.)

COACHMAN: And wherever you want to go, that's where you go!
(Another cheer.)

COACHMAN: And whatever you've had enough of, you can get some more!

BOYS: More!

COACHMAN: More!

BOYS: More!

PINOCCHIO: *(Trailing behind.)* More!

(All laugh at Pinocchio. When the laughter dies out, little Luigi steps up to Coachman.)

LUIGI: But...when does the boat come back to get us?

(Silence. Double takes by Coachman, Guido, and the second helper: Filipo.)

COACHMAN: *(Astonished, with disbelief.)* "Boat? Come back?"

FILIPO: Say—what kind of a boy *is* this?!

COACHMAN: But Luigi, Luigi...you're in *Paradise!* You don't think about boats coming back to get you in Paradise...

LUIGI: *(On the verge of tears.)* But...I wanna...

COACHMAN: *(Mimicking him with a vicious whine.)* "But I wanna go home!" Maybe *all* of you boys want to go home; is that it?! *(To Guido.)* Guido! Get that boat back here! Somehow, I don't care how you do it, but these boys want to go home!

(Boys murmur among themselves indecisively.)

COACHMAN: All right, let's settle this. How many want to go home right now?

(Silence. Luigi sniffles a bit.)

GUIDO: No one, Papa.

COACHMAN: And how many want to stay with me in Paradise for ever and ever?

(Silence again, then Lampwick steps forward boldly.)

LAMPWICK: *I* do!

(Lampwick looks around for support from the others. When none comes, he starts shoving Boys forward.)

BOYS: *(Variously.)* I do. I do. I do, too. I'll stay. We do. Forever!

PINOCCHIO: *(Again a bit behind the others.)* I do! I do!

COACHMAN: Good. I'll remember that. So. Let's not waste any more time. First—Guido will give you lots and lots of tickets to buy anything you want. And what do we got? I'll tell you: We got ice cream, we got candy, we got rides, we got games, we got cigars you can smoke, we got punch 'em up, we got knock 'em down, we got biting, we got pinching, we got anything you want to do when you feel mean. We got sabers and swords and fudge of all sorts; we got dicers and slicers and beaters and rammers. Everything is yours, and *we never stop!* Get your tickets, boys—let's go! *(The orgy begins. Boys rush every which way. Guido tosses strips of tickets into the crowd like streamers; Boys madly grab them.)*

GUIDO: Tickets here! Get your tickets now! Get 'em while they last!

FILIPO: *(With armfuls of assorted candy.)* Candy! We got candy here! If it's sweet, we got it! If it's sticky, we got it! If it gets all over your clothes, we got it! That's right, boys; form a line!

GUIDO: *(Appearing with a huge book of tattoo patterns.)* Tattoos! Tattoo needles! Be a tattooed man, just like me!

(He opens his shirt and shows his arms, revealing solid tattoos. One Boy looks at them, turns out to audience with wide eyes, beats his breast with desire.)

GUIDO: Put a dancing lady on your belly! Wrap a snake around your arm! Carve an anchor on your shoulder! Be a man! One little prick, and you're fixed for life!

(Filipo reappears with a "picture box"—a hand-cranked peep show which resembles an old-fashioned box camera.)

FILIPO: Pictures! Special pictures! Get your peeks while they last! Peek-a-boos for little boys. See things your mother never told you about. One at a time, one at a time. Put your eye up to the hole, son.

COACHMAN: *(Carrying buckets of ice cream.)* Ice cream! Ice cream! Ice cream by the bucketful! Eat it! Eat some more! Put it in your mouth! Put it in your hair! Put it on your foot! And the first boy who eats a whole bucket, gets another bucket!

GUIDO: Tickets! You need more tickets! Get your tickets here! Whadda you need? You need more!

(Filipo appears at top of stairs Stage Right behind Coachman carrying an effigy of the Boys' schoolteacher, which dangles by strings from a pole.)

COACHMAN: Attenzione! Attenzione! Signor Bellini!

(Boys hoot and jeer.)

COACHMAN: You got your teacher where you want him! See Bellini walk the gangplank!

(Boys cheer.)

FILIPO: *(Falsetto.)* Mercy! Mercy!

COACHMAN: No mercy for you! Walk down the gangplank and fall into the sea to meet the killer whale!

(Filipo has effigy walk the gangplank which leads Upstage Right and then drops it over the edge into the sea. Boys are strangely unenthused, not quite sure how they feel. Coachman turns to them again.)

COACHMAN: Hahahaha—Boys! This way. This way to the rides! Be the first to ride a ride! This way to the rides!

(Coachman herds Boys Stage Left and Off. Guido and Filipo get brooms from Offstage and start to sweep up the mess. The sound of Boys laughing

and cheering and the calliope music of carnival rides in the distance. After a little while, and after Guido and Filipo are finished sweeping and off, Tomasso and Allesandro enter.)

TOMASSO: How...how do you like it so far?

ALLESANDRO: I like it. I like it. I could do this forever, couldn't you?

TOMASSO: What? Oh. Yeah. I could do this forever.

(Both Boys suddenly rush Upstage and get sick over the edge of the platform. Other Boys soon enter, sputtering over their cigars, ice cream on their faces, none of them looking well and all generally moaning.)

COACHMAN: (Re-entering, surveying the scene, laughing.) Boys! What's wrong? Aren't you having a good time?

(A few feeble moans of "Yes.")

COACHMAN: Maybe you'd like some more ice cream?

(Several desperate "Nos!")

COACHMAN: Well, listen. I got just the thing to fix you up good. (He holds up a large jug which has donkey ears attached to its sides.) It's called the special "Magic Donkey Juice." One little drink of this, and you'll be strong like a donkey! Miguel, do you want to try some?

(Miguel steps forward and Coachman pours some into his mouth. Miguel instantly perks up in a weird, goofy fashion, his legs somewhat out of control, kicking and prancing like a donkey's.)

COACHMAN: One little drink of this, and you can eat some more of everything!

(Other Boys crowd around Coachman and drink from the jug he holds; as they are each rejuvenated, they head back off Upstage Left and out for more fun.)

COACHMAN: Have some more, boys; it's good for you! That's it, Massemo!

(Only Lampwick and Pinocchio remain.)

COACHMAN: Lampwick—try some of this.

(Lampwick drinks, then stands up on his toes as if his feet were hooves; he starts Off.)

COACHMAN: Wooden one! Pinocchio! This will make you grow like you never thought you would! (Coachman tips the jug for Pinocchio, but nothing comes out. He raps on the bottom of the jug. It is empty.) Just lick a little off the edge, Pinocchio.

(Pinocchio runs his finger around the rim of the jug and then licks it. Coachman withdraws and Pinocchio rushes up to Lampwick before he exits.)

PINOCCHIO: Lampwick! Wait!

LAMPWICK: What is it now, Sticks?

PINOCCHIO: Nothing, I just… *(A slight pause. Not very genuine.)* I'm having a real good time, aren't you, Lampwick?

LAMPWICK: Sure am, Pinocchio! Have a cigar.

(He gives Pinocchio his cigar. Pinocchio puffs, coughs; Lampwick pounds him on his back.)

PINOCCHIO: *(Choking.)* Thanks, Lampwick. You're a real friend.

LAMPWICK: Of course I am! Now aren't you glad I talked you into coming? Huh?

PINOCCHIO: Sure. Only…

COACHMAN: *(Stepping out of the shadows.)* "Only"…*what,* Pinocchio?
(Pinocchio doesn't answer.)

COACHMAN: Come, Pinocchio—on this island you can say whatever you want…because nothing makes any difference anyway. Say it!

PINOCCHIO: Well…what do we do next?

COACHMAN: Tell him, Lampwick.

LAMPWICK: Whadda you mean? We just have more *fun;* that's what we do next!

PINOCCHIO: And then what?

LAMPWICK: *More* fun!

PINOCCHIO: And then?

LAMPWICK: *(Disgusted.)* Hey, what are you talking?!

COACHMAN: I think, dear Lampwick, that you don't know what our friend Pinocchio is talking about. But I do. I do. *(Coachman steps up to Pinocchio and puts his arm around his shoulder.)* You know, Pinocchio, a boy is a lot like a silly little donkey: He's stubborn, he wants to have a good time all the time, and he don't know what's good for him. But if that's the way boys are, that's the way they are. Let them *be* silly little donkeys if they want to!

PINOCCHIO: That's not what my Papa said. Papa said…

COACHMAN: *(An angry growl.)* Listen! *I'm* the Papa *here,* you understand?! *(Sweetly.)* So, Pinocchio—why don't you just have a good time, like the other boys. *(Increasing menace; he leaves Pinocchio and steps up near Upstage Right gangplank.)* Because there's no going back, Pinocchio! Beneath us is the sea, and in the sea lives the monster—the monster whale, Pinocchio—the killer whale! *(Flatly.)* Good-bye, boys. Have a good time, you hear?

LAMPWICK: Bye, Papa!

(Coachman exits Stage Right. Pinocchio watches him leave, then turns with great concern to Lampwick.)

PINOCCHIO: Lampwick! We shouldn't have come here to this place!

LAMPWICK: *(Shimmying; strangely intoxicated.)* What? And miss all the fun? Not *me!*

PINOCCHIO: I don't care. I want to go home to my Papa…my *real* papa!

LAMPWICK: Your Papa! *I* don't need no papa; I don't need nobody but *me!*

PINOCCHIO: But my Papa said, he said…

LAMPWICK: *(Mimicking.)* "He said…He said…He said…" I'm tired of hearing you say, "He-*Haw!*"

PINOCCHIO: What?

LAMPWICK: *(Spasms are stronger.)* You *Hee*-heard me! *Hee-Haw!*

PINOCCHIO: Lampwick!

LAMPWICK: What's the matter? *Hee-Haw! Hee-Haw! Hee-Haw! (Lampwick tosses his head like a donkey and his cap falls off, revealing two large donkey ears.)*

PINOCCHIO: Lampwick! Your ears!

LAMPWICK: *Hee*-huh? *Hee-Haw! (Lampwick reaches up and feels his ears; panicked he runs to the edge of the platform to peer at his reflection in the water below.)* My ears! *Hee-Haw!* Oh, no! No! *Hee-Haw!*
(Suddenly the air is filled with the braying of donkeys. Boys appear around the set, crawling on all fours, with the heads and tails and hooves of donkeys.)

PINOCCHIO: Lampwick! Look!

LAMPWICK: Help me, Pinocchio! What's happening to…*Hee-Haw! Hee-Haw!*
(Pinocchio runs back and forth, panicked at the sight of the helpless Boys. Coachman appears from Upstage Right and Guido and Filipo appear from Downstage Right and Upstage Left carrying pitchforks and nets, herding the donkeys and pulling them back off. Coachman conducts them, laughing maniacally and cracking his whip. Lampwick and Boys are eventually all herded Offstage and Coachman, Guido, and Filipo pursue Pinocchio. Pinocchio runs and is able to evade Guido and Filipo, causing them each to knock themselves out by rushing at him and hitting a part of the scenery. Coachman corners Pinocchio at the gangplank; Pinocchio is edged further and further back along the gangplank by Coachman, who cracks his whip.)

COACHMAN: There's no way out, Pinocchio! There's only the sea! The sea and the whale, Pinocchio—the monster whale! Jump, Pinocchio! Jump! Hahahahahahaha!
(Pinocchio falls backward off the gangplank and Coachman continues to laugh as lights fade quickly on the scene.)

SCENE II

Thick, underwater sounds in the absolute darkness. Through a scrim with dim, undulating water patterns, we catch a glimpse of Pinocchio falling through the water: spinning, descending slowly, spinning, falling. He finally hits the ocean floor. He looks about and lifts his hand up beside his mouth to call.

PINOCCHIO: *(Gurgling.)* Hello? Is anybody down here? Hello! Have you seen Geppetto?

(Low, ominous music. Upstage of Pinocchio we see a tiny glimmer of yellow light, which widens to reveal a huge eye opening behind Pinocchio and looking Right at him. Pinocchio sees it and tries to run away but is only able to run in place because of the water.)

PINOCCHIO: It's a big eye! It's the whale! It's the monster whale!

(The eye closes and music and sound effects suggest the whale opening its mouth and the ocean being sucked into it. As Pinocchio screams and runs we see him straining against the suction.)

PINOCCHIO: Help! The whale's going to swallow me! Help! Help! Help meeeeee!

(Pinocchio suddenly flies up off the ocean floor, across the dark stage, and out of sight. We hear the enormous sound of a gulp, another gulp, another gulp, a pause, a bubbly belch. Silence.)

SCENE III

We hear the gentle lapping of water, and dripping, reverberating as if in an enormous cave. Far Upstage we see the faint glow of a lantern, which draws nearer. As it does so, it illumines the set: The lantern is hanging on a tiny boat, which holds Geppetto. We are inside the belly of the whale: Huge bluish-red riblike membranes surround the stage and stretch Upstage to infinity. The distant sound of the whale's belch.

GEPPETTO: *(Listening.)* Thunder? No. No thunder here. No clouds. No sky. No days. No days in the belly of a whale. Only nights. Only one long night. *(He sits on a little stool, dejected.)* Oh, Pinocchio…where did you go? Where did you *go*, Pinocchio? *(He wipes away a tear.)* Ahh, Geppetto—how about something to eat? Whadda you gonna eat tonight, eh? How about…some fish? That sounds real good. Of course, I *could* have some fish, instead. Then again, I could have some fish. No, I've got it: some fish! *(Geppetto tosses a line over the Upstage side of his boat.)* Come on, fishy. Come to Geppetto. Come on. *(A big tug on the line.)* Hey! What's this pulling so hard… *(Another tug. Geppetto looks over the edge of the boat.)* Hey—this fish got hands! *(He reaches down and pulls a hand over the side.)* Hands and…arms! *(Two arms hook themselves over the side, Geppetto reaches over and pulls. Pinocchio flies into the boat, looks up, sees Geppetto.)*

PINOCCHIO: *(Holding out his arms.)* Papa!

GEPPETTO: Pinocchio!

(They embrace.)

GEPPETTO: Pinocchio! Oh, Pinocchio…I never thought…oh, Pinocchio!

PINOCCHIO: Papa—how did you get here?

GEPPETTO: Pinocchio, I look for you *everywhere*…where did you *go*, Pinocchio? Where did you *go*?

PINOCCHIO: Oh, Papa—I met these two friends and they took me to Pigacci's Puppet Theatre to get rich.

GEPPETTO: *I* went to the puppet show, but Signor Pigacci got real mad when I said your name, so I knowed you must have been there.

PINOCCHIO: Then Lampwick, he took me to the Inn of the Red Lobster.

GEPPETTO: You ain't gonna believe your old Papa, but I met these two people, and one of them looked a lot like a fox…

PINOCCHIO: The Fox and the Cat! They were there, too.

GEPPETTO: And they said, "Pinocchio? Pinocchio's gone away in a boat, across the sea."

PINOCCHIO: To Paradise Island, Papa. To the Island of Boys.

GEPPETTO: So I got *me* a boat, but this great big whale came and opened it's mouth and swallowed your Papa up—boat and all!

PINOCCHIO: To the Island of *Real* Boys, Papa. But they all turned into… into…

(Pinocchio turns away from Geppetto and the old man sees a donkey's tail growing from behind Pinocchio.)

GEPPETTO: Pinocchio! You got a tail! A donkey tail!

PINOCCHIO: *(Crying; hugging Geppetto.)* Oh, Papa!

GEPPETTO: *(Holding him close; patting his back.)* Oh, Pinocchio—that's all right…that's all right…at least now we are together. We can be together…before…we die…

PINOCCHIO: *(Lifting his head up.)* "Die?!" What do you mean, Papa? We gotta get *out* of here!

GEPPETTO: *(Standing and walking away, frustrated.)* We *can't* get out of here, Pinocchio; don't you know? It's hopeless! It's hopeless!

PINOCCHIO: But I can't let you die here, Papa!

GEPPETTO: Oh, warm your hands by the fire.

PINOCCHIO: *(His chin cupped in his hands, staring at the tiny fire on the floor before him.)* Oh, if only…if only there were… *(A pause. An idea.)* Papa! Papa—the fire!

GEPPETTO: *(Flatly; not paying attention.)* That's right, the fire.

(Pinocchio quickly grabs more wood and sets it on the fire.)

GEPPETTO: Pinocchio! Hey, Pinocchio—whadda you doing?

PINOCCHIO: Build up the fire, Papa! We'll make lots of smoke, and maybe the whale will sneeze!

GEPPETTO: *Sneeze?!* You crazy!

(Pinocchio pays no attention; he keeps breaking wood and tossing it on the pile.)

GEPPETTO: It *might* work…

PINOCCHIO: Help me, Papa!

GEPPETTO: Yes! Yes, we need more wood, don't we? *(Joining in, excited.)* Here…the stool, Pinocchio; put that on, we don't need it.

PINOCCHIO: And the fishing pole!

GEPPETTO: Look, Pinocchio! Smoke! It's working!

PINOCCHIO: Fan the fire, Papa!

(Geppetto uses his shawl to fan the fire. A great cloud of smoke rises and begins to fill the belly of the whale. The "walls" of the whale's belly begin to shudder and we hear the distant, increasing sound of a sneeze coming on.)

GEPPETTO: Listen!

(Pinocchio and Geppetto cock their heads and listen intently.)

PINOCCHIO: Papa! It's going to sneeze! Papa—the whale is going to sneeze us out!

GEPPETTO: *(Clutching Pinocchio close to him.)* Hold on to me, Pinocchio! Hold on! I can't swim! Hold on!

PINOCCHIO: Look out, Papa! Hold on tight!

(The sound has increased and mounted to one, gigantic sneeze. The raft quickly retreats Upstage as lights simultaneously blackout. Music swells and on the scrim we see flying patterns of swirling water and debris. The sound of violently rushing water and the indistinct cries of Pinocchio and Geppetto calling each other's names.)

SCENE IV

Through a scrim, lights rise on a blue, mist-filled grotto. A rocky shoreline stretches across most of the Downstage edge of the stage; a large, craggy rock stands isolated Upstage Left. From out of the swirling white-horses of dry-ice mist, a pair of hands appear over the shoreline ridge, followed by the rest of Pinocchio. He pulls himself up and over, stands and looks about for a moment, then quickly turns back to the ocean to help Geppetto.

PINOCCHIO: Papa! *(He pulls Geppetto up and over.)* Papa—it's land!

GEPPETTO: *(Stumbling over the ridge.)* Land!

PINOCCHIO: We're on land, Papa!

(Exhausted, they both collapse with their backs against the ridge, panting to catch their breaths.)

PINOCCHIO: Oh, Papa…I'm so sorry for everything, Papa…I wasn't good to you…I ran away from you, Papa, and…and I forgot about you…I forgot how good you were to me and…and I'm sorry, Papa…I'm so…tired… I'm so…tired… Papa…

(Pinocchio lets his head fall back against the shoreline and he lies there, motionless. Geppetto reaches over and touches Pinocchio's knee.)

GEPPETTO: "Sorry?" Oh, Pinocchio—I know you done all those things, and…and for a while I wished I did not make you, but…but then, you came to me, Pinocchio, and you saved my life. And you showed me you was a real…a real *son*, Pinocchio! *(Geppetto pats Pinocchio's knee and notices Pinocchio doesn't respond.)* Pinocchio? *(Geppetto anxiously moves closer to Pinocchio, lifts his arm; it drops down, lifelessly.)* Pinocchio! *(Geppetto stands and picks the lifeless body up in his arms and presses it close to him. An anguished cry.)* Oh, don't die, Pinocchio! I want you to live! Pinocchio, I want you alive! *(Sobbing.)* I want you to be alive!

(As Geppetto stands, weeping and rocking the body in his arms, a dazzling shaft of blue light strikes the Upstage rock. The Blue Fairy appears from out of the rock and floats over the waves toward Geppetto, who does not hear her.)

BLUE FAIRY: Geppetto. It's all over, Geppetto. You can take him home, now. You can take your boy home. Your *boy*, Geppetto. The story of the puppet is over. Good-bye, Geppetto. Good-bye, Pinocchio.

(Geppetto slowly carries Pinocchio Offstage Right. With a wave of her arms, Blue Fairy causes seashore to disappear and transform into the street of Geppetto's hometown.)

SCENE V

The village slowly materializes and freezes behind the scrim as Geppetto re-enters from stage right, trudging wearily Downstage of the scrim, carrying Pinocchio, whose chest and head rest Upstage against Geppetto. Geppetto reaches Center Stage and stops. He sinks slowly to the ground to rest, falling instantly asleep with Pinocchio lying across his lap. Music. A shaft of light on Pinocchio. Pinocchio stirs and rolls off Geppetto's lap and onto the ground. He lifts his head up to reveal the face of a real boy. Pinocchio looks at his hands, his body, feels his face with wonder and delight. He rushes to Geppetto and nudges him to awaken.

PINOCCHIO: Papa! Papa!

 (Geppetto awakens, rises to his feet with a start, then sees Pinocchio and faints immediately.)

PINOCCHIO: Papa!

 (Pinocchio lifts Geppetto back up onto his feet. Geppetto looks in awe at Pinocchio.)

GEPPETTO: *(Holding out his arms.)* Pinocchio!

PINOCCHIO: *(Running into Geppetto's arms.)* Papa! I'm a boy! I'm a boy!

GEPPETTO: *(Laughing and twirling him around in his arms.)* You're a boy!

 (Music swells. Scrim rises and Pinocchio and Geppetto dance merrily through the street. The Cast assembles gradually and join Geppetto and Pinocchio in their celebration and taking their bows. Suddenly Pinocchio runs Downstage, out of the scene, and gestures for the show curtain to descend. It does, with the overlay which reads: "Pinocchio. The Story of a Puppet." Pinocchio quickly reads the sign, shakes his head "No" to the audience. With a piece of chalk he quickly strikes out the word: "Puppet" and with gusto writes the word "Boy" over it. He bows to the audience. Show curtain flies out to reveal full cast; Pinocchio joins Geppetto and Blue Fairy for final cast bow. Show curtain in.)

END OF PLAY

Hans Christian Andersen's
The Nightingale

Directed and Choreographed by Myron Johnson
Music Composed by Steven M. Rydberg
Scenic Design by Don Yunker
Costume Design by David Draper
Lighting Design by Jon Baker

CHARACTERS

**Narrator
*I-Ming, a wild old woman/Witch of the Burning Cave/Death
 Young Man
*Li-Ching, Young Man's Bride/The Nightingale
*The Emperor of China
 Imperial High, High Lord Chamberlain
 Glorious General of the Imperial Armies
 Little Pin-Won, 7–10 years old
*Woo-Ling, in her mid- to late-teens
 Other Members of the Court
 The Emperor of Japan
*The Mechanical Nightingale

** *Denotes speaking role.*
 * *Denotes principal roles.*

The story of *The Nightingale,* and the *Proverb* which precedes it, are told through narration and dance, in a style inspired by the work of the Peking Opera. The set is minimal: fabrics, screens, pastel colors.

The Nightingale has a running time of about an hour.

For information concerning the original score by Steven M. Rydberg, contact The Children's Theatre Company of Minneapolis.

The Proverb

The Narrator ceremoniously assumes his or her position.

NARRATOR: Good friends: I say to you "Hello."

I am the teller of stories, and in the great and ancient land of China, people tell stories by what they wear, and by the color of their painted faces, and most important, by the way they move.

In the stories I am telling you today, the actors will say very little with their voices, but very much with their feet and legs and arms, and with their little hands.

When they do speak, they will speak their own language—the lovely language of the Chinese.

I will tell you today two stories.
One is about the great and ancient land of China…
and a little tiny bird.
The other story is small and simple,
but it will show you how people tell stories with their
bodies, and your imagination.

It is about an old woman
in an old boat,
on the great river,
Yang Tze.
(As the Narrator speaks, I-Ming appears, steering a boat on a river.)
NARRATOR: There was once
a wild old woman
who steered a wild old boat
on the river, Yang Tze.
She was a smart one,
and her name was
I-Ming.
(A proud Young Man appears on the river bank.)
NARRATOR: Do you see this young man?
He has just married a wife

and he acts like he had
the river Yang Tze in his pocket.
He doesn't, though.
Oh no.
(A Shy Young Bride appears.)
Do you see the young man's wife?
She is very lovely.
Just so.

Ah, the young man wishes to cross
the great river, Yang Tze,
with his bride. He asks I-Ming
how much he has to pay.

Nothing! said I-Ming.
You pay nothing, if
you truly love your bride.
The young man said, Of course I love her.
I just married her.
Now quickly drive us across the river.

You'll never forget her? said the old woman.

Quickly! I have no time to waste!

And in his haste, the young man set forth
across the river Yang Tze.
He had not gone far
before he realized that
something was missing.

YOUNG MAN: Li-Ching!

NARRATOR: His lovely wife! Oh no…
    (I-Ming paddles the boat to shore.)
    Wife, he said, get in the boat!
    Cast off now, hurry!

NARRATOR: Are you sure? said I-Ming.

Cast off! I know what I am doing!

and he forgot the old woman behind.
Why aren't we getting anywhere? said the young man.

Because I am on the shore, said I-Ming.
Pick up the paddle!
(The young man paddles back to shore.)
This time
the young man made sure
that both the old woman
and his bride
were safely on board. I'll cast off!
he said.
(I-Ming paddles Off with Li-Ching, leaving the young man on shore.)
NARRATOR: But that wasn't right either.
The young man cried,
Come back! Come back!
But I-Ming brought the young man's bride
to the other side of the river.

Come back! cried the young man.

But I-Ming said, Oh no.
I'm sorry. You told me you love your bride
but you forgot
what was important. Now
your bride stands there,
and you stand where you stand,
and the great river Yang Tze
is between you. Good-bye. Good-bye.

And the moral, good friends?
I will tell you. Do
not be in such a hurry to
get there,
that you forget
why you went.
Listen
now to the story
of the nightingale. It
may help you.

The Nightingale

NARRATOR: Listen closely!
  This is a story which needs to be heard.
  Watch carefully!
  These are things which must be seen.
  Listen, and watch!
  *(Throughout, the actor/dancers move screens and fabrics and, with the music
  and their movements, enact the story which the Narrator relates.)*
  In the ancient land of China,
  there lived an Emperor
  whose kingdom touched the sea.
  The flowers of the Emperor's gardens
  wore tiny silver bells,
  which tinkled softly for all times
  and forever. Beyond the gardens,
  there was a deep and lovely forest.
  And in the branches of these trees
  there lived a Nightingale.

  The Emperor lived
  in the most beautiful palace in the world.
  It was made all of porcelain,
  and was so delicate,
  it could only be touched
  with the greatest of care.
  The members of the Emperor's court
  lived in the palace, too,
  and they were all very happy to be there.

  Only now and then
  did a strange and lovely song
  come from the trees
  as far as the palace window.
  But most of the people in the palace
  were too important to notice it.

  Like the Imperial High, High

Lord Chamberlain. He was very high.
He was so high, that when
anyone of a lower rank dared
to speak to him
or to ask him a question,
he would only answer
'P'
which doesn't mean a thing
but which is high,
believe me.

Then there was the Glorious
General of the Imperial Armies.
He was very old,
and so he was very, very important.

But the most wonderful man in China
was the Emperor, himself.

And so, the Emperor
and his court lived quite
happily in their porcelain palace.
But none of them knew
about the wonderful nightingale,
whose song was for the trees.

Travelers from all over the world
visited the Emperor's land,
and many books were written
about the ancient land of china.
One day the Lord Chamberlain brought
a new book to the Emperor.
Gracious Emperor, he said.
Here is a gift
from the Emperor of Japan.
It tells all about
your glorious realm.
(While the Emperor and the Chamberlain examine the book, a small boy,
Pin Won, enters and plays, not too reverently.)

NARRATOR: Little Pin Won,
    the Emperor's sister-son,
    played the ancient Chinese game
    of hide-and-seek.

    The Japanese book praised
    the Emperor's palace made of porcelain,
    and the flowers with their bells of silver.
    "But the nightingale," it said,
    "Is better than anything."

    The Emperor suddenly sat up very straight
    and called the Imperial High, High
    Lord Chamberlain. "This book speaks
    of a wonderful bird called
    the nightingale.
    Why didn't you ever tell me about it?"
    And the Emperor said that if
    the Lord Chamberlain brought the nightingale
    to sing in the palace,
    he wouldn't have to be trampled on
    after supper.

    "Trampled on?"

    The High Lord Chamberlain had never
    heard of the nightingale,
    but he had been trampled on
    and he didn't care for it.
    So he read,
    and he read, and he
    read.

    The book said that
    the nightingale is daughter
    to the Witch of the Burning Cave.
    "That's a clue. I must ask
    the Glorious General
    if he knows what to do!"

(The Chamberlain goes to the General, who is pursuing his hobby.)
NARRATOR: The Glorious General painted pictures
    when he had the chance.

    "Read this!" said the Lord Chamberlain.
    "The lovely nightingale is daughter
    to the Witch of the Burning Cave."
    She will know
    where to find the nightingale.
    (The lovely Woo Ling happens by.)
    "Woo Ling will bring us there!"

    "You can lead us to the Witch
    of the Burning Cave. She knows
    all things."
    And they were so frightened,
    they even took me.
    (The Chamberlain and the General grab the Narrator and Woo Ling and
    set off on their journey.)
NARRATOR: The Witch of the Burning Cave
    was really the Wisest
    of all creatures. She
    was as old as the earth itself.

    "I sleep in the garden of death,"
    she said. "Who awakens me?"
    (A dance sequence, in which the Witch of the Burning Cave "interrogates"
    the cowering Chamberlain and the elderly General and the lovely Woo Ling.)
NARRATOR: The Witch of the Burning Cave
    chose to tell Woo Ling
    how to find the nightingale's
    secret home.

    And together,
    they set out to find the nightingale.
    They heard many sounds of the forest
    along the way.

    "Listen!" said the General,

"What tone! The nightingale
is marvelous indeed."

"Glorious General," said Woo Ling,
"That was a pig.
But marvelous, yes. You are
so right."

"Mmmm," said the General.
"What a lovely song!"

"Good sir, that is a cow.
But I agree, it is lovely.
Come along with me."

"Pretty. Very pretty."

"Frogs, good sir.
But you may hear the nightingale
soon. Listen!"
*(And suddenly we can see the Nightingale, and hear her lovely song. She
dances.)*
NARRATOR: "Don't frighten
the nightingale," said Woo Ling.
"We must be gentle."

And they took the nightingale
away from the trees
to sing for the Emperor
in his porcelain palace.

The Emperor said, "We will hear
the song of the nightingale."
(Nightingale music, she dances.)
The Emperor had never heard such lovely singing.

"Dear little bird," he said,
"Stay with me always.
I will hear your song
at the hour of my death."

The General bowed low
before the nightingale,
and so did the Lord Chamberlain.
And so did the ladies of the court.
Everyone in the Emperor's court
loved the little bird,
but none so much
as the Emperor,
himself.

Days passed, and months,
and the Emperor's palace was filled
with the nightingale's many songs.
She sang for the whole court,
once at dawn
and once at dusk,
all days, and every day.
The more she sang,
the sweeter seemed her songs
to the Emperor of China
and his court.
But the nightingale could not be happy
in a palace made of porcelain.
Her song was for the trees.
(Music, dance, shifting seasons.)
NARRATOR: One day everything changed—
the mighty Emperor of Japan
came to visit.
(Grand entrance of the Emperor of Japan and his Courtiers.)
The Emperor of Japan brought a marvelous gift.
(Entrance of the Mechanical Nightingale.)
It was a mechanical nightingale,
and it could sing one
of the real nightingale's songs.
The members of the court thought
it was prettier to look at
than the real nightingale.
"We are pleased with your gift,"
said the Emperor. "Let us
hear it sing."

When they wound it up again,
it sang the same sweet song.

And no matter how many
times they wound it up,
it still sang the
same mechanical song.

"What a remarkable machine!
It looks so real! Now
we must hear both birds
sing together."

The nightingale cried, "No!"

And the Emperor had to command
the living bird
to sing
with the mechanical bird.

The nightingale grew frightened.
Her song was for the trees,
and to the trees
she slipped quietly away.

But no one noticed, not even the Emperor.
They were too interested
in the mechanical bird
to care.
Only Woo Ling saw what happened.

"My Emperor,"
she said.
"The bird is gone!"

"The nightingale?
No matter," said the Emperor,
"We have got the better bird.
Pay no mind
to the ungrateful nightingale."

Days passed,
and months,
and the mechanical nightingale
still played on.
It could only sing one song,
and so the people
of the Emperor's court
came to know it by heart.
(Throughout the following, action to suit.)
NARRATOR: Sometimes it even seemed
they knew it too well.

Sometimes it got in the way.

Sometimes it was even dangerous.

And sometimes they wished
it would just stop singing
and go away.

But a mechanical bird
is not like a living creature
that sings with its own breath.
And finally the day came
when something went wrong
inside the mechanical nightingale.
It jerked,
and lost its artificial feather,
and finally
the music stopped.
The mechanical bird was broken.

Just at that moment,
Little Pin Won ran in to say,
"The Emperor's very sick."

"The Emperor's dying!"
said the Lord Chamberlain.

"The Emperor's dead?" said the General.

And they all rushed off
to see the Emperor
whom they loved
very much.
(Death enters.)
NARRATOR: But Death arrived before them.
Death had come
for the Emperor,
and the eyes of Death were cold.

Death came
to show the Emperor
what he had done wrong,
and what he had done right.
Death brought all memories,
and the eyes of Death were cold.
(We see all memories, all evil actions, all good actions.)
NARRATOR: Death brought
the Emperor's good deeds
and his bad deeds.
Some of the faces
were kind and gentle.
Some were hideous
and cruel.
But the eyes of Death were cold.

"No!" cried the Emperor.
"I never knew all this.
Music!
Sound music
that I may not hear
what they are saying.
Precious bird,
sing!
Sing!"

But the mechanical bird could not
help the Emperor.
It was only a machine—
a broken machine.

Death
took the Emperor
by the hand
and led him away.
Evil deeds,
mistakes,
false promises,
forgotten friendships.
Death brought all this
to the Emperor,
and the eyes of Death were cold.

NARRATOR: "This is your sickness,"
said Death.
"You forgot
what was truly important—
a true heart
and a gentle voice.
Have you forgotten
the nightingale?"
said Death.
"She sang for you.
She brought tears
to your eyes,
but you forgot
the nightingale
and her song,
and so you lost her!"

But suddenly
through the palace window
came the living song
of the nightingale.
She had heard the cries of Death
and the moaning
of her dear Emperor.
The nightingale's bright wings
hurt the eyes of Death.
The nightingale's song

brought to Death
a longing
for Death's own garden,
and like a cold, gray mist
Death passed
out of the palace.

Like a man waking from a deep sleep
the Emperor sat up in his bed.
The Emperor saw the nightingale
whom he had forgotten.
The Emperor saw the living bird
whose song saved him from Death.

"Dear bird," he said,
"You have driven away
Death itself.
How can I repay you?"

"You have already rewarded me,"
said the nightingale.
"There are tears
in your eyes."

The Emperor said,
"You must stay with me always."
But the nightingale answered,
"I cannot live
in your palace.
But let me come and go
as I wish.
Then I will sing to you—
to make you happy
and to make you thoughtful, too.
For I love your heart
more than your crown."

But outside the Emperor's chambers
there was only sorrow
and sighing.

"Any news of the Emperor?"

"No, no news."

"Anything at all?"

"Nothing at all."

"Can you tell us how he is?"

"I can tell you nothing."

The members of the court
had heard the shrieking
and the cries.
They had heard the sound
of Death dancing,
and they knew
their Emperor could not live.

They remembered
his gentle ways
and the sound of
his laughter at nightfall.
But they could do nothing.
Their Emperor was dying.

But no!
There was the nightingale,
whom they had missed
for so long,
and with her was...
the Emperor!
He was not dead,
he was laughing.
It was a miracle.

The Emperor told them all
how the nightingale

had saved him
from Death.
And he told them, too,
the lesson he had learned.
He caught Pin Won
in his arms,
and soon the whole court
was laughing with him.

"Do not be deceived,"
he said,
"By glitter and show.
A true voice
and a gentle heart
are all
you will ever need."

Dance now!

Dance for
the Emperor's nightingale!
(Music, dance, curtain.)

END OF PLAY

The Ukrainian Tales
The Fat Cat &
The Chatterbox

Directed and Choreographed by Myron Johnson
Music by Hiram Titus
Set Design by Gene Davis Buck
Costumes and Masks by David F. Draper
Lighting Design by Jon Baker

CHARACTERS
The Fat Cat & The Chatterbox

    ** Narrator
    * Evas/Mouse, 8–12 years old
    * Tusya/Fox
    * Tomas/Pan Kotsky
    * Master Player/Bear
    Members of the Troupe playing:
      The Boar
      The Porcupine
      Yuri, a Rabbit
      Guri, a Rabbit
    Townspeople

** *Denotes speaking role.*
 * *Denotes principal role.*

These two tales are told in narration and dance, with only ad-lib interjections by the dancers speaking *Ukrainian.* The original production employed a mix of adults and children; the ages of the characters are left to the director's wishes.

The set is minimal, reflecting the simple, brightly painted flats which a group of traveling players might carry with them from place to place.

Ukrainian Tales has a running time of a little over an hour.

For information concerning the original score by Hiram Titus, contact The Children's Theatre Company of Minneapolis.

Ukrainian Tales

A Gypsy Wagon rolls on; Villagers greet the Gypsies. The Gypsy Players begin setting up their stage, with one of their troupe, Tusya, chattering and scolding. The Blind Bandura Player emerges with a small boy, Evas, on his shoulders. The Bandurist taps his way with a stick.

BANDURIST: *(In Ukrainian.)* Hurry now, everybody! Lift up the banners! Put on your costumes! Hurry!
(He sets Evas down. Evas leads Bandurist Downstage to his position, where he sits.)

BANDURIST: *(In English.)* This is my friend, Evas. Give the people good health, Evas.

EVAS: *(In Ukrainian.)* Good health to you.

BANDURIST: That's good. Now get out of here!
(Evas runs back up to the wagon, out of sight.)

BANDURIST: So. These are the skommadai—the play-actors of the Ukraine, who travel from village to village throughout all this land—and do you know why? To tell stories. Yes. It's true. Tusya! Stop your mouth from running so fast!
(She continues.)

BANDURIST: *(In Ukrainian.)* Tusya! Be quiet!
(She stops talking, bows sheepishly, smiles.)

TUSYA: *(Pointing to herself.)* Tusya. *(She bows again and runs to the wagon.)*

BANDURIST: You met already Evas. Well that's his mama, who talks so much your ears will fall off—dear Tusya. As the will of God would have it, she married a quiet man. Tomas! Where are you?
(Tomas is half-into his Cat costume. He runs Downstage.)

TOMAS: *(In Ukrainian, bowing briefly.)* Good morning, old man. *(He runs back up.)*

BANDURIST: Good morning to you, Tomas. A good thing for him he's got no secrets. With a wife like that, they wouldn't last. So where was I? You met Evas, you met his mama and papa, you'll soon meet the play-actors of the skommadai when they play out their play—oh, yes. There's me. I'm an old man. That's all. My eyes don't work anymore, so now I see with my heart—and do you know? That's plenty. And then I sing of what I see. I am the teller of stories—the Bandurist, and this… *(He feels for his bandura.)* Evas!

(Instantly Evas is there with the bandura. Evas is now dressed as the Mouse. Bandurist takes bandura.)

BANDURIST: …And this is my bandura.

(Soft bandura music.)

BANDURIST: Thank you, Evas.

EVAS: *(In Ukrainian.)* You are welcome.

(He begins to sit down behind the Bandurist's shoulder. Tusya runs down to Evas, boxes him on the ears, and sends him up to the wagon. She remains with Bandurist.)

TUSYA: Evas, tch, tch, tch, tch.

BANDURIST: Tusya, do you want something?

(She shakes her head "no.")

BANDURIST: Tusya, are you shaking your head at a blind man?

(She shakes her head "yes," then "no," then "yes.")

BANDURIST: For God's sake, woman, will you speak?

TUSYA: *(In Ukrainian.)* No.

BANDURIST: Good. Then I can go on. *(To the audience.)* The forests of the Ukraine are very deep and oh so dark. Creatures live in them who have not seen God's good sky since the world was changed. And so, these village people…

(Tusya shakes Bandurist's arm.)

BANDURIST: What is it, Tusya?

(Tusya whispers into Bandurist's ear.)

BANDURIST: Tusya wants you all to know that she is the most important lady in the play.

(Tusya shakes him again.)

BANDURIST: And that her husband, Tomas, plays the most important man.

(Tusya shakes him again.)

BANDURIST: Who is a cat.

(The Master Player approaches the Bandurist and whispers in his ear. He is dressed as a Bear.)

BANDURIST: And this old bear wants you to know that he is the Master Player of this skommadai, and that their play is great and famous. And that donations will be accepted. And I want everybody to know that if everybody doesn't stop talking to me and get ready, I will tell no stories today! *(In Ukrainian, to Bear and Tusya.)* I mean it!

(They run up to wagon, out of sight. Pause. Bandurist stands.)

BANDURIST: Meanwhile, the borsch was ready, the table was laid, and the animals looked for places to hide. The Boar hid himself under the table, all but his tail. The Bear climbed into an oak tree, and the Porcupine hid in a bush beneath the tree. The twin Rabbits sat very still, and pretended they were stones.

Yuri told Guri to stop all that loud breathing. The Boar had an itch that he tried not to scratch. The Bear was afraid of heights, so he closed his eyes and held on tight.

The Porcupine sneezed...twice...and then, all was quiet.

(Pan Kotsky and Fox enter, carrying their spoons.)

BANDURIST: Now, there were very few things which could make old Pan Kotsky move, but one of them was the sight of food.

(Pan Kotsky, suddenly excited, drops the Fox's arm, jumps onto the table, and does a little dance of joy amid the food.)

BANDURIST: "Mi-ow-er!"

(The animals whisper in Ukrainian.)

BANDURIST: Pan Kotsky ate and ate and ate, while all the animals hid. Finally, Pan Kotsky had eaten his fill. Mrs. Fox untied his bib, and Pan Kotsky stretched out on the table for a snooze.

Just then, the Boar had such a terrible itch, he couldn't help scratching it. Scratch, scratch, scratch. But Pan Kotsky thought it was a mouse! And if everyone will hold still, I'll tell you what happened next: Pan Kotsky jumped right on top of the Boar. The Boar jumped up and ran smack into a tree. The Bear jumped out of the tree and landed on the Porcupine. The Porcupine jumped up and tripped over the Rabbits, and the Rabbits hopped away as fast as ever they could. Now...is everybody ready? Go!

(Pan Kotsky jumps on Boar; Boar runs into tree; Bear falls out of tree, lands on Porcupine; Porcupine trips over Rabbits; Rabbits and other animals run Off.)

Poor Pan Kotsky didn't know what had happened. So he sat shaking with fright up in the tree, while the Fox begged him to come down. For supper, of course. And he did that.

(Pan Kotsky and the Fox leave. The other animals poke their noses out from trees, bushes.)

BANDURIST: And that's how a fat old Cat came to be known as the fiercest animal in all Ukraine.

(The actors emerge from the trees, taking off their masks. They shout and do a spirited circle dance, passing a tambourine for coins thrown on.)

BANDURIST: That, dear ones, is the story of Pan Kotsky, the Fat Cat. But do you know what happened to Pan Kotsky and his nice wife *after* that?

Nothing. They just went on. I think maybe Pan Kotsky lived forever, and his little wife opened a bakery in the forest. Thank you! That's all! Good-bye!

(Villagers throwing coins. The players should clearly bring their coins to the Master Player. Perhaps the Master Player singles out Tomas: snaps his fingers and calls Tomas to him, Tomas turns over a few coins he has picked up, Master Player shakes his finger at him.)

BANDURIST: These people...these people. Hey. This is a secret: I love them. And this is another secret: I'm going to play a joke on them.

(The people slow down into some other time-scale.)

BANDURIST: What do you think would happen if something came into the simple lives of these people—to make things not so simple anymore? Huh? Something like a lot of money, for example—something like...a bag of gold... *(He pulls a large bag of gold from his tunic.)* Don't be surprised at me...I told you, I am the teller of stories, and anything is possible with me. Now, this is the bait. We'll just see which fish will bite, huh?

(Villagers and actors come to life. Bandurist throws the bag. All slow down again, except Tomas who sees the bag of gold and goes to it in real time. He picks it up, thinks better of it, and puts it down again.)

BANDURIST: I think, dear ones, that we have caught a fish.

(Stage comes alive again. Actors pack up, villagers wave good-bye. Tomas keeping his eye on the gold all the time.)

BANDURIST: It is time now for us to leave this village, and travel on through the forests. But how do you suppose Tomas will keep his chatterbox wife from finding out about the gold? You see the master player there? *(Bandurist points him out.)* He's the boss here. He gets to take all the money, and no one is allowed to hold anything back. So if our Tomas wants to hide his gold, he'll have to think of something—quick. Well...we shall see, let's just wait and see. Good-bye! Evas! Come help me to the wagon!

(Evas comes, takes Bandurist's arm, leads him to his place on the wagon. As the wagon leaves, Tomas lingers behind. Evas hides behind a tree to watch his father. When the last of the villagers is gone, Tomas approaches the bag of gold, picks it up, takes out a coin and bites it, drops it back into the bag and runs off with the gold. Evas come out from behind the tree, and runs after him. Lights out.)

(Lights up on the wagon traveling Left to Right. The gypsies have been traveling—it is apparent—for hours. Tomas and Evas are walking together, talking. The Bandurist rides above them, listening.)

BANDURIST: It is a long and weary road to the next village, but Tomas seems especially worried. Listen, and I'll tell you what he's saying: "Evas, your mama's a good mama, but she just can't keep a secret. If she finds out about the gold, she'll tell everyone, and the Master Player will take the gold away from us!"

"Well, papa, she better not find out then, am I right, papa?" "Evas, you are your papa's son!" *(Bandurist laughs.)*

And so, Tomas thought up a plan. He decided to fool Tusya, and fool her and fool her, until Tusya made such a fool of *herself*, that no one would believe her—even if she *did* chatter about the gold. And this is how he did it: "Evas! There are some bagels in the wagon. Get a bunch of them, and bring them to my bed. Wait, Evas! I'm not finished. There's some fish, too, and a big string of sausages. Bring the bagels, the fish, and the sausages to my bed, but don't let no one see you! Quick now!" *(As Bandurist.)* Fish? Sausages? Bagels? Keep your eye on those two. I think they're about to set a trap. *(In Ukrainian.)* Good night. *(In English.)* Good night. *(In Ukrainian.)* Good night. *(In English.)*

The lonely band is sleeping.

The trees and leaves are sleeping.

But the eyes of birds are open…

The eyes of birds, and mine.

That old song again, it's in my ears tonight. Me? I never sleep, or hardly. But I think tonight maybe someone else is having trouble getting to sleep…Bagels? *(He laughs.)*

(The band has settled into their beds—all except Tusya.)

TOMAS: *(From his blanket.)* Tusya!

(Tusya gets under the blanket, chattering. Isn't comfortable, turns over. Gets out of bed, picks up the blanket and shakes it out, exposing Tomas in his nightshirt. She gets back into bed, settles down, and appears to fall asleep. Tomas quietly gets out of bed with his bagels, tiptoes two steps.)

TUSYA: *Tomas!*

(Tomas jumps, throwing the bagels into the air. He returns to bed, grumbling. Tomas waits for Tusya to fall asleep. We see the Bandurist light a lantern from another part of the stage. Tomas gets out of bed, tiptoes, gets down on his hands and knees trying to find the bagels in the darkness. He crawls away from the sleepers, bumps into a pair of knees. They are Tusya's.)

TUSYA: Tomas…

(Tomas looks up at her, smiles, turns around—still on his hands and knees—and crawls back to his bed, with Tusya following. They both get into bed, the Bandurist laughing softly. Tusya begins to snore. Tomas gets up, looks at her.)

TOMAS: Tusya?

(She snores louder.)

TOMAS: Tusya!

(She turns over, snoring louder still. Tomas takes bagels, fish and goes to where Evas is sleeping. Taps Evas who jumps out of bed with a coil of sausages. Evas holds a lantern for Tomas, while he hangs bagels from the branches of a tree. Tomas and Evas take the rest of their things [fish and sausages] and continue on into the woods, out of sight. Bandurist laughs. A sudden gust of wind blows his lantern out.)

(Morning. The wagon and the troupe are just moving Off as the lights rise. Tomas lingers behind. The Bandurist is hidden, but visible to the audience.)

TOMAS: *(Calling after the wagon.)* Tusya! *(In Ukrainian.)* Wait a minute!

BANDURIST: *(As Tomas.)* "Tusya! Wait!"

(Tusya comes back.)

BANDURIST: "What are you doing, we've got no bread for today, got no food, Tusya, what do you think? Don't you love your husband? Are you going to let your son go hungry?" *(As Tusya.)* "Tomas! I bake bread for you every day!" *(As Tomas.)* "Why bake bread when it's growing on the trees?"

(Slight pause. Tusya looks at her husband.)

BANDURIST: *(As Tusya.)* "I see. Tomas, you're making a *joke* with me. Oh, you funny boy!"

(Tusya begins to laugh wildly. She thinks her husband is such a joker. She laughs till she walks into a tree. She stops laughing.)

BANDURIST: *(As Tusya.)* "Tomas. There's bagels growing on this tree." *(As Tomas.)* "Well pick them, Tusya!"

(She looks at Tomas, hesitates, and then begins picking the bagels gingerly.)

TUSYA: *(In Ukrainian.)* But, Tomas…

BANDURIST: *(As Tomas.)* "And don't forget to gather the fish for supper!" *(As Tusya.)* "Fish! You don't *gather* fish! You *catch* fish! Gather fish, indeed!"

(She kicks some leaves with her toe, stoops over and comes up with a string of fish.)

TUSYA: *(In Ukrainian.)* Fish.

BANDURIST: *(In English.)* Fish.

TUSYA: *(In Ukrainian.)* Fish.

TOMAS: *(In Ukrainian.)* Fish.

BANDURIST: *(As Tomas.)* "And sausages, too—don't forget the sausages!"

TUSYA: *(In Ukrainian.)* No. No, no, no, no, no.

BANDURIST: *(As Tusya.)* "No, Tomas. Stop *right* there. The next thing, you're going to tell me it rains sausages from out of heaven and I'm not going to...to...

(Sausages begin raining on Tusya. Evas, hidden behind the tree, throws them over, one by one.)

TUSYA: *(Totally bewildered to the point of anger.)* Oooooooooooooo... *(She is holding the six bagels and the string of fish, and she begins picking up the sausages as they come over.)*

TOMAS: Tusya?

BANDURIST: "Tusya? There's one more thing. We're rich."

(Tomas takes bag of gold from his tunic.)

BANDURIST: "A bird dropped this bag of gold in my lap. This morning, I think. But don't you tell a soul, *not one soul!*

TUSYA: B...b...b...b...b...b

BANDURIST: *(As Tusya.)* "A bird? Bag? Gold? A bird bag? A rich bird? A b...bag of...*Gold!*"

TUSYA: Oh, Tomas!

TOMAS: Shhhhhh!

(Puts his hand over her mouth. She immediately becomes furtive.)

BANDURIST: "Shhhhhh! Tusya, if you tell any *body*, the Master Player will find out and we'll lose it all. Do you understand?" *(As Tusya.)* "Tomas! You know *me*. I won't breathe..."

(Tomas claps his hand over her mouth and pushes her Off after the wagon. She struggles to breathe. With his head, he gives the high sign to Evas, and covers her eyes with his other hand. Evas drops out of the tree, sausages in each of his hands.)

BANDURIST: *(As Tomas.)* "There's the Master Player now! Shhh! Oh, don't look, it's terrible! Look! Oh, don't look. It's terrible! He's being beaten...you won't believe it...a string of sausages has dropped from the sky and is beating him. Mercilessly." *(Bandurist laughs at this turn of the joke. But then...)*

(Evas sees the Bandurist in his hiding place, runs and begins to beat him—gently—with the sausages. The Bandurist is, for once, surprised.)

BANDURIST: Ouch! Ow! Ouch! Stop it! Ouch! This isn't part of it! Don't, ouch!

TOMAS: *(In Ukrainian.)* Tusya, let's go!

(They exit, following the wagon.)

BANDURIST: Evas! *(Slight pause. Then, Bandurist begins to laugh.)* I deserve it. It's my own joke and I deserve it. Now poor Tusya thinks that bagels grow on trees, fish come out of bushes, and she even thinks that a string of sausages attacked our Master Player. Who do you think would believe her now if she said she found a bag of gold? I wouldn't. Would you? *(He laughs.)*

(Evas runs after the wagon. Lights change. Master Player approaches Tomas.)

BANDURIST: "Tomas!" said the Master Player. "Come here!"

(Tomas approaches.)

BANDURIST: "I order you to bring me the bag of gold that you have found!" *(As Tomas.)* "Gold, sir? What gold?" *(As Master Player.)* "Your wife says you have found a bag of gold. Now bring it here!"

TUSYA: *(In Ukrainian.)* No, Tomas. Really I didn't…

BANDURIST: *(As Tomas.)* "My wife? My wife?! What doesn't my wife say? Ask her yourself!"

MASTER PLAYER: Tusya?

BANDURIST: *(As Tusya.)* Well, yes sir, I'm afraid I must confess that, yes, we did have the good fortune to come across a bag of gold—not a large bag, of course, just a small one, the sort of bag you might mistake for a dead mouse on the road or a leaf of spinach which someone might have carelessly dropped or let fall to the ground, perhaps as a secret message for a sweetheart, *I* don't know, it could have been any one of a number of things, but *you* know what I mean."

(Everyone on stage goes, "Oh, God!" in Ukrainian.)

BANDURIST: *(As Tusya.)* Oh, you want to know *where* we found it? Well, I didn't actually do the finding, it was my husband, Tomas—he's such a good man, and so intelligent and perky and, *you* know, finding things— bags, little sacks, my goodness, what that man doesn't find. Why, just this morning he found some bagels growing in a tree, and fish in some bushes, and sausages raining down from heaven…

MASTER PLAYER: *(In Ukrainian.)* Bagels? Sausages?

BANDURIST: *(As Tusya.)* Yes, I said bagels, it's remarkable, isn't it, but there you have it, a whole string of bagels growing from a tree. *Yes*, I'm sure. I remember because—well, how could I forget it—it was just before, if you will pardon me, sir, just before you were chased through the camp by a string of sausages and beaten by them quite severely—I was so sorry to hear about it, are you feeling better now?

MASTER PLAYER: *(Roars.)* Roooooooar!

(The troupe all laugh.)

BANDURIST: *(As Master Player.)* Be careful what you say, woman! What you need is a good lashing to keep you from making up such stories!

TOMAS: *(In Ukrainian.)* Please, sir.

BANDURIST: *(As Tomas.)* Please sir, don't be angry—my wife, sir. She's...well, not quite right, if you know what I mean... *(He taps his head significantly.)*

MASTER PLAYER: *(In Ukrainian.)* Nonsense!

BANDURIST: *(As Master Player.)* Not quite right? Sir, you wife is a lunatic! *(All laugh.)*

MASTER PLAYER: *(In Ukrainian.)* Players! Set up the play!

(Villagers begin to arrive, the players begin to set up the play, laughing, dancing. All slow down and quiet down while Tomas and Tusya move Downstage together.)

TUSYA: *(In Ukrainian.)* Oh, Tomas, how could you?

(Tusya begins to sniffle. Tomas hugs her, comforts her. He gives her a little kiss, Evas tugs at her skirt, she laughs and picks Evas up—"Oooof!" too heavy. She sets him down, laughs again, and the three of them rejoin the others. Normal time.)

(The Bandurist, during the above, has come down to address the audience.)

BANDURIST: And so, Tomas got to keep his bag of gold and no one was the wiser. Tusya promised not to be such a chatterbox anymore, but...if you got to talk, you got to talk. And me? I promise I'll play no more jokes on anyone for a long time to come...at least, two or three days. And now, the players of the skomoroki wish you...good health,. and long life...and many happy stories! Farewell! Good health! Farewell! *(All dance.)*

END OF PLAY

Robert Louis Stevenson's
Treasure Island

Produced and Directed by John Clark Donahue
Music Composed by Hiram Titus
Scenic Design by Dahl Delu
Costume Design by Gene Davis Buck
Lighting Design by Jon Baker

THE CHARACTERS

In order of appearance:

* Jim Hawkins, 12–14 years old
  Blind Pew
  Billy Bones
  Mrs. Hawkins, Jim's mother
* Dr. Livesey
  Emlyn Jenkins
  Emlyn's Friend
  Emlyn's 2nd Friend
  Black Dog
  Dirk
  John Dancer
* Squire Trelawney
* Long John Silver
* Captain Smollett
  O'Brien
* Israel Hands
  Redcliff
  George Merry
  Tom Morgan
  Dick
  Rogers
  Hunter
  Redruth
* Benn Gunn
* Voice Of Older Jim Hawkins

* *Denotes principal roles.*

THE SETTING

In its original production, this adaptation of *Treasure Island* received the benefits of the considerable facilities at the Minneapolis Children's Theatre Company, for which it was written. The sets, designed by Dahl Delu, were in a grand and romantic-naturalistic style. They comprised four basic set locales: the *Admiral Benbow*, a naturalistic cut-away of an old English country inn on the western coast near Bristol; the *Hispaniola*, a fairly complete two-masted schooner of the period; the *Island*, which through the use of soft hanging trees and vines and a blue "sea-scrim" beyond, was capable of depicting four different island locations; the *Stockade,* one of the four island locales, with a log fortress and out, beyond the sea-scrim, a small model of the *Hispaniola* at anchor in the bay.

Within these four main locales, two other set locations were made possible through the use of an Act Curtain Scrim. This was painted with a crude map of Treasure Island (Flint's map), and served as the pre-set, as well as being brought in during some of the Jim Hawkins's narrative voice-overs. For the Captain's Cabin scene (Act I, Scene VII), the Act Curtain was lowered, a wagon setting of the captain's cabin was rolled in Upstage of it, and the scrim was burned through, revealing the cabin in a "framed" view. For the death of Israel Hands (Act II, Scene IV), the same technique was employed. The Act Curtain scrim came in during Jim Hawkins's narrative voice-over, and then was burned through to reveal an enlarged detail of the deck of the *Hispaniola,* with the center mast from which Israel falls into the sea (onto a gymnastics mat) prominent.

Obviously, not every producing company will be able to provide such elaborate settings for this play. However, this adaptation of *Treasure Island* has been quite successfully produced by small community theatres and others throughout the United States. These notes on the setting are only intended to provide a rough image of the play as it was originally conceived and produced.

Treasure Island has a running time of one hour fifty minutes, including intermission.

For information concerning the original score by Hiram Titus, contact The Children's Theatre Company of Minneapolis.

Treasure Island

ACT I
SCENE I

*Night, the wind, the sea. The weathered signboard, "Admiral Benbow,"
creaking on its hinges above the tavern door. The inn is empty but for Jim
Hawkins polishing glasses behind the bar, and its warm and flickering light
makes it feel cozy and safe compared to the windswept cobble-toned street
outside.*

VOICE OF JIM HAWKINS: Although it's been years, I remember that night as if
it were yesterday. The wind was up—and the sea was high—and it was
bitterly cold for November. But my mother's inn, the Admiral Benbow,
had quite settled down for the evening. Our only lodger, Captain Bones,
seemed to be quiet for once, and kept to his room. I had nearly given up
hope we'd have any visitors at all when—without warning—my great
adventure began. Of course, I—Jim Hawkins—had no notion I was
starting out on my journey to Treasure Island.
*(We hear the tapping of a stick on the stones, and from the shadows see a
hunched figure, wrapped in a huge tattered sea-cloak and hood, slowly drawing near to the tavern, making his way with a stick. He taps, walks, stops,
and listens. He sniffs and cocks his blind head, as though he were smelling
something out—and then starts again. Inside, Jim notices the tapping, looks
up and listens. Blind Pew stops still. Jim goes back to polishing the glasses.
Then he hears the tapping a second time—Blind Pew has reached the tav-
ern door—and Jim leaves the bar, glass and cloth in hand, and walks to the
door. Just as he opens the door, Pew ducks into a shadow and Billy Bones
roars from upstairs.)*
BONES: Hawkins!
(Jim drops the glass and it shatters on the floor.)
JIM: Oh, bother the man!
BONES: Jim Hawkins!
JIM: Yessir, Cap'm Bones, sir. Straightaway, sir!
*(We hear a thin, high wail from the street which, if we knew it, serves Blind
Pew for laughter. Jim hears it and turns back to the door.)*
BONES: *Hawkins! Will you not stand to!*

JIM: *(Turning back into the tavern.)* Aye, sir. Coming, sir! *(Regarding the broken glass on the floor.)* Never mind the mess, Jim.

(Jim runs up the staircase and out of sight. The wind rises as Pew opens the tavern door a crack. Wisps of fog crawl in along the floor.)

PEW: So it's *"Captain"* Bones, is it? We'll give you "Captain" my mate—aye, we'll give you that and more.

(High-pitched wail again. Billy Bones appears on the staircase and clambers down into the taproom, followed by Jim Hawkins.)

BONES: Discipline, Jim!

(The tavern door shuts quickly and quietly. Pew feels his way on, into the darkness.)

BONES: Discipline! Now, if you had sailed along of Bones, you wouldn't o' stood there to be spoke to twice—not you. That was never the way with Cap'm Bones, nor the way of sich as sailed wif him. And you, wif yer paar Daddy dead and done wif, you got to laarn yer propers, don't you Jim? Fetch me a noggin o'rum, boy.

JIM: Yessir, Cap'm. Aye, sir.

(Jim fills a noggin of rum from the keg behind the bar. Bones suddenly stops dead still, facing the street door. Jim comes around to the Captain with the rum.)

JIM: Here it be, Cap'm.

(Bones does not respond.)

JIM: That'll be tuppence, Cap'm.

(Bones does not move.)

JIM: Cap'm *Bones*, sir?

BONES: *(Slowly, after a pause.)* What's here?

JIM: Sir?

BONES: What smells? I got a quare feelin' an' I don't like it. Somethin' rotten is here...or was. Quick, Jim! Step to the door and put yer head out!

(Jim hesitates.)

BONES: Do as yer told, boy!

(Jim runs to the door, opens it and looks out. The sound of the wind rises.)

BONES: Sing out if there's ought amiss, Jim!

(The wind. Jim finally closes the door.)

JIM: Nothin', Cap'm.

BONES: *(Furtive whisper.)* Are ye cartin', Jim? Not a soul?

JIM: Only Emlyn Jenkins, and he's making his way here to the Admiral Benbow, like as not.

BONES: None other, then? Not a man—listen to me, Jim—not a man wif no eyes in his head?

JIM: No *eyes?*

(Jim opens the door again and looks out. The wind.)

JIM: No, sir. Bless my soul, sir, there ain't.

BONES: Not even...Jim!

(Jim turns back inside, closing the door.)

BONES: Not even...a seafarin' man wif only one leg, Jim? There weren't none o'those out there, was there?

(Jim laughs.)

JIM: Oh, Cap'm! Beggin' your pardon, Cap'm, but you're a sight! One-legged men and men without no eyes, sir? I think you'll be wantin' your rum now, sir...

(Bones slowly begins to laugh.)

BONES: That's right, Jim. Ha haaaa! Sharp as a handspike, ain't you, and only a yard long!

(Claps Jim on the back and they both laugh.)

BONES: Jim knows there's nought to be afeard of, don't he? Anyways, I was just tryin' you out, lad—seein' what you was made on. Ha haaaa! Only...see my mark, Jim? *(Bones points to the long scar which runs down the side of his face.)* Not very pretty, is it. The hand what put it there don't move no more, Jim. And when there's evil lurkin' about, I feel it right here, Jim... *(Indicating his scar.)* My mark tells me.

(Mrs. Hawkins has been standing for a few moments past in the staircase door. She descends now and enters the taproom.)

MRS. HAWKINS: Tells you what, Mr. Bones? Tells you to pay up the three weeks food and lodgin' you owes me? Tells you to stop fillin' my boy Jim with outlandish stories, then, Mr. Bones? What does it tell you, uh?

BONES: Ahhhhh, Mrs. Hawkins, you are a wonder, you are. And so's yer fine, boy, here. A couple o'wonders, you is. Ha haaaa!

MRS. HAWKINS: The only wonder is I don't throw you out, Mr. Bones—Captain or no Captain. *(Moving to the door.)* Lor' bless me, there's a wind. Jim! What's all this mess here? Not another broke glass, Jim!

JIM: Yes, mum.

BONES: Not to worry, Mrs. Hawkins. When I gets my own back, you'll be took care of proper, you *and* yer fine lad here.

MRS. HAWKINS: I'd ruther be took care of now, Mr. Bones. I'd ruther you just paid for that drink what's in your hand already. Clear away the mess, Jim.

(Bones grumbles off into the public room and sits. Jim begins to pick up the broken glass. His mother watches him for a moment.)

MRS. HAWKINS: Jim…

JIM: *(Looking up.)* Mum?

MRS. HAWKINS: *(Suddenly moves to her son and hugs him.)* There now. Get busy. The good doctor'll be droppin' by tonight, or so he said.

JIM: Dr. Livesey!

MRS. HAWKINS: Who else?

JIM: Will he bring toffee?

MRS. HAWKINS: Never mind. And Jim…don't listen with more than half an ear to that old rogue. *(Indicating Bones.)* Cause half of what he says is made up out of his head, and the other half is the fault o' rum. Go on, now. *(She exits up the stairs.)*

BONES: *(Strident whisper.)* Jiiiim!

JIM: Cap'm Bones?

(As Jim approaches, Bones suddenly stands and grabs him by the shirt.)

BONES: It's my old seachest they're after, Jim.

JIM: Who?

BONES: They want what's inside it.

JIM: Who is it you're talking about, Cap'm?

BONES: Why, Flint's crew, of course! All old Cap'm Flint's crew, man and boy—all that's left. I was first mate, I was, old Flint's first mate, and I'm the only one as knows the place. Flint gave it me in Savannah, when he lay a'dyin'. That's why they're after me, don't you know, an' if they find me, they'll tip me the black spot, they will, they'll put the black spot on Billy Bones.

JIM: What's the black spot, Captain?

BONES: It means yer called for, matey. It's the summons.

JIM: *(After a slight pause.)* It's all nonsense, Cap'm. You're makin' it up out of your head!

(Dr. Livesey appears at the door of the Benbow and opens it unnoticed.)

BONES: *Damn you, boy!* You keep a civil tongue!

DR. LIVESEY: You, sir, would do well to mind your own advice. Let go that child.

JIM: Dr. Livesey!

DR. LIVESEY: Sir! Do as I say this instant!

BONES: *(Releasing Jim from his grasp.)* Yes sir, yer honor, sir. We was just havin' a bit of a chat, me and Jim, wasn't we? Just fancy stories, sir, yer honor, no harm in that, is there? Besides... *(With an evil glance at Jim.)* Jim here is too bright to believe a word of 'em. Ain't you, Jim

(Emlyn Jenkins arrives at the Inn door with a couple of cronies. These are locals, a bit drunk already.)

EMLYN: Evenin', Doctor Livesey. Hello, Jim. How's yer mum?

LIVESEY: Good evening, Emlyn.

ANOTHER MAN: *(Indicating Bones.)* Oh oh. *He's* here. Let's sit in here, what?

EMLYN: Couple o'noggins, Jim!

JIM: Right, Emlyn. *(Jim goes to fetch the rum.)*

LIVESEY: I doubt you need much more rum, Emlyn.

EMLYN: Only one more to steady me nerves, Doctor. I just had an awful fright.

MRS. HAWKINS: *(Appearing at the top of the staircase.)* Evening, Doctor. Jim, be quick an' fetch the Doctor what he wants.

LIVESEY: Nothing for me, Mrs. Hawkins. I'm waiting to hear what's happened to Emlyn Jenkins. It appears he's had "an awful fright."

EMLYN: And that I did, sir...that I did, Mrs. Hawkins. It *were* awful. Thanks, Jim.

(Emlyn takes the mug that Jim has offered him.)

LIVESEY: Well, come on, man. Tell us what it was and have done!

EMLYN: Well, sir, it was not a furlong from the Benbow...not a furlong from yer own front door, ma'm, sorry to say it. I was on my way along, when I sees this old bent chap, lurkin' like in the shadows. I says to meself, there's some old seafarin' gent what's lost his way...I took him for an old man, see? And then, I heard this noise. It was like he was pokin' at the stones with a stick or somethin'.

(Bones in the other room slowly rises, listening. Jim stops polishing the glass that he holds in his hand and listens closely.)

EMLYN: And then, I gets closer to him, see? And still he's scrapin' away at the stones and movin' at a snail's pace. And then, sir, the clouds moved away and the moon, it shone full in his face, and, beggin' yer pardon, ma'm, but this old man...he didn't have no eyes.

(Jim drops the glass and it shatters. Bones utters a cry and sinks into his chair. Within the space of a moment, the wind blows open the outside door and the tavern is filled with fog. Light changes, the figures in the Benbow become indistinct and slow moving: a vague tableau of figures surrounding Billy Bones, trying to revive him.)

SCENE II

Continuous with the above. During the following voice-over narration, there is a passage of time: The figures in the dimly lit Benbow slowly move out of sight leaving only Bones and Jim Hawkins in the inn.

VOICE OF JIM HAWKINS: Not the smallest wonder of that night was that my mother never scolded me for breaking not one, but two glasses in the course of the evening. She must have forgot to. For that was the beginning of the mysterious events which rid us at last of old Captain Bones, and started us off on our great adventure. As for Cap'm Bones, we finally managed to bring him around. But for days after, he never left his place in the taproom, and despite all our good efforts, never once left off his rum. So things passed, until one day, about nine o'clock of a bitter, foggy, frosty evening. I was just passing out the door when I saw someone drawing slowly near along the road...
(Jim Hawkins steps out of the Benbow and then ducks back into the Inn, standing apprehensively at the door. We hear the stick. Jim peeks back out the door.)

BLIND PEW: *(Just coming into sight.)* Will any kind friend inform a poor blind man, who has lost the precious sight of his eyes in the gracious defense of his native country—God bless King George!—where he may now be?

JIM: *(Taking a cautious step out of the tavern door.)* You are at the "Admiral Benbow," sir, Black Hill Cove.

PEW: I hear a voice, a young voice. Will you give me your hand, my kind young friend, and lead me in?
(Jim tentatively holds out his hand, and Pew grabs it like a vise and pulls Jim into the street with him.)

PEW: Now, boy, take me in to the Captain.

JIM: Sir, upon my word, I dare not!

PEW: Take me in or I'll break your arm.
(Pew bends Jim's arm back behind him. Jim cries out.)

JIM: Sir, it is for yourself I mean. The captain is not what he used to be. He sits with a drawn cutlass...

PEW: Come now, march! Lead me straight up to him, and when I'm in view, you say these words to him... *(Pew whisper's into Jim's ear.)* And if you don't, I'll do this.
(He jerks Jim's arm back and up. Jim stifles a cry. Pew pushes Jim before him into the inn. Bones does not see them until Jim speaks.)

JIM: Here's…a friend…for you, Bill.

(*Bones looks up, and an expression of sickness and terror comes over his face. He makes a movement to rise.*)

PEW: Now, Bill, sit where you are. If I can't see, I can still hear a finger stirring. Business is business. Hold out your left hand. Now, this dear child as I've took such a liking to, will take your left hand by the wrist and bring it near to my right.

(*Both Jim and Bones do as they're told. Pew passes something from the hollow of his hand into the palm of the captain's, which closes upon it instantly.*)

PEW: And now, that's done.

(*Pew turns and taps his way out. Bones and Jim remain motionless for a moment, Jim still holding Bone's wrist. Then Bones pulls back his hand, and looks into the palm.*)

BONES: Ten o'clock!

(*In a sudden, unsteady fury, Bones picks up the cutlass from the table and lurches to the door.*) Mister Pew…Come…Back… (*Bones screams and swings the cutlass aimlessly through the air, it strikes the "Admiral Benbow" signboard and notches it. Bones suddenly clutches at his heart, staggers back in the door, stands swaying for a moment and then, with a peculiar sound, falls from his whole height face foremost to the floor.*)

(*Jim stoops over the body for a moment and then runs to the staircase.*)

JIM: Mother! Come quick! It's Cap'm Bones!

(*Jim rushes back to the captain and kneels. Mrs. Hawkins appears for a moment in the door at the top of the stairs, then runs down into the room.*)

MRS. HAWKINS: What is it, then, Jim? Drunk?

JIM: No, mum. The Captain is dead.

MRS. HAWKINS: Dead!

(*Jim, with a great effort, turns Bones over on his back. Mrs. Hawkins lets out a brief scream.*)

JIM: It was the blind man. He called him "Mister Pew."

MRS. HAWKINS: He killed 'im?

JIM: No, mum. He put the black spot on him. They was pirates, mum, both of 'em—even Cap'm Bones. And there's others about—all of Captain Flint's men.

MRS. HAWKINS: The black spot? Pirates? God in heaven, boy, what are you talking about?

(*Jim suddenly remembers the black spot, kneels over the corpse, and unfolds Bones's hand. He peels off a black circle of paper and stands.*)

JIM: The black spot. It means you're called for. It must have been the fright killed him. The seachest! They're after his old seachest!

MRS. HAWKINS: Well, dead men or no, *I'm* after the three weeks food and lodgin' Mr. Bones owes me, and is not likely to pay now. If there's aught to be had in that seachest what's rightfully mine, I mean to take it, be there ever so many pirates. *(Starting for the staircase.)* Dear Lord, if only yer poor father was alive.

JIM: Mother! What time is it?

MRS. HAWKINS: Oh, the Lord gave me a stupid son. Nearly ten, I should imagine. What do you want to know such a thing for?

JIM: Because there's some writing on this here black spot. It says, "You have till ten o'clock!" Mother they're coming back for him, they're coming back for whatever it is he's got!

MRS. HAWKINS: *(As she turns and runs up the stairs and out the door.)* Get help, Jim! I'll fetch the seachest!

(Jim turns helplessly to the body and then to the outside door. He cautiously steps out and looks. No one. He goes back into the inn, and runs to the other outside door, opens it and looks out. Sees someone.)

JIM: Emlyn! Emlyn Jenkins!

(Emlyn pokes his head in the door.)

EMLYN: Hello, Jim, old man. How's yer mum?

JIM: Quick, Emlyn! You must ride to Doctor Livesey's, you must fetch help at once! Bone is dead. Pirates. Flint's men!

EMLYN: Flint! God help us!

JIM: Quickly, Emlyn! Fetch the Doctor! Fetch Squire Trelawney! Go on, man!

EMLYN: God help us! Pirates!

(We hear him running off down the cobble stones. From the staircase we hear a loud banging sound: It is Mrs. Hawkins dragging the seachest down the stairs.)

MRS. HAWKINS: Give us a hand, Jim!

(Jim runs to help her, together they pull the chest clattering down the stairs into the room.)

MRS. HAWKINS: It's locked, Jim.

JIM: Oh, mother, let's never mind it! The blind man will be back, mother, and he won't be alone!

MRS. HAWKINS: The key to it's on him, I'll wager. Go and see, Jim.

(Resignedly goes to the corpse, kneels by it.)

JIM: It's there, mother, round his neck.

MRS. HAWKINS: We have to get it off him…Who's to touch it I should like to know…

(*Jim reluctantly pulls at the string—Bones's head flops up. Jim breaks the string and brings the key to the chest.*)

JIM: There now. (*Opens the chest.*)

MRS. HAWKINS: (*Looking in.*) Where's all the money? It's mostly papers and things.

JIM: It's almost ten, mother! Hurry!

MRS. HAWKINS: Here's a bag. I'll show those rogues I'm an honest woman. I'll have what's owed to me and not a farthing over.

(*She begins picking through the bag of coins, pulling out one here and there and making a small pile of them. Jim goes to Right door, bolts it; the window, locks it; and the Left outside door, bolts it.*)

MRS. HAWKINS: One an' eight. One an' eight, fourpenny. One an' nine.

JIM: (*Furtive whisper.*) Mother! Listen!

(*She stops her counting and they both listen. The tapping of the blindman's stick, growing nearer. Pew at the door, Jim on the other side of it, not breathing. The door handle turns slowly. Locked. The handle is rattled. Locked. The tapping begins again and recedes.*)

JIM: Mother, for mercy's sake, take all of it and let's be going! (*Jim grabs a handful of the chest's contents.*)

MRS. HAWKINS: I'll not have a penny more than is due to me.

JIM: Well, take none of it then! Mother, they'll be back!

MRS. HAWKINS: None of it? What an idea! None of it, indeed.

(*She goes back to counting. Jim examines a packet of papers he's pulled from the chest.*)

JIM: Look what I've got here, mum.

(*Just then, we hear a low whistle some distance away, and the clock begins to strike ten.*)

MRS. HAWKINS: Oh, my Gawd.

JIM: it's them, mother!

MRS. HAWKINS: Well, I'll just have to take what I have.

JIM: (*Putting the packet of papers into his vest.*) And I'll take this to square the count. This way, mum. (*Jim unbolts the street door, peeks out.*) Now!

MRS. HAWKINS: Wait.

JIM: Now, mother! (*Jim takes her by the arm and urges her out into the street.*)

MRS. HAWKINS: (*Suddenly stopping.*) My dear, I'm afraid you'll have to take the money and run, because I'm going to faint.

JIM: Not now!

(She faints into his arms. Jim looks about him distractedly. The low whistle again, twice. Jim half-carries, half-drags his mother to the tree, Stage Left, and eases her down into the little ditch beneath the bridge. Then he too crawls down and hides there, although we can see his head peering out. Just then, we hear running footsteps and muttered speech. Four men come into view beneath the sign board—two of them supporting Blind Pew, one at each hand.)

PEW: Down with the door!

DIRK: It's open, Mister Pew.

PEW: *(Screeching.)* Well then, *in, in, in!*

(The three rush into the Benbow, leaving Pew standing in the street.)

BLACK DOG: Mr. Pew! Bones is dead!

PEW: Well search him, you dog! The rest of you aloft and get the chest!

JOHNNY: The chest is right here!

DIRK: Someone's been before us! It's been turned inside out!

PEW: Is it *in* there?

DIRK: The money's here.

PEW: *Damn* the money! Flint's map, I mean! Is the map in there?

DIRK: I don't see it nowheres.

PEW: Black Dog! Is it on Bones?

BLACK DOG: Bones's been overhauled a'ready. There's nothing left.

PEW: It's those people of the inn—it's that *boy!* I wish I had put his eyes out! They were here no time ago—they had the door bolted when I tried it. Scatter, lads, and find 'em! Rout the house out!

(The men ransack the inn, overturning furniture, kicking in doors, while Pew stands in the street and raves.)

PEW: Find them! Find that boy! You have your hands on thousands, you fools, and you hang a leg! They must be close by! You have your hands on it! Oh, shiver my soul! If I had eyes!

(One by one, the three men cease the search and file out into the street.)

DIRK: There's no one, Pew. They've made off.

PEW: Dogs! If you had the pluck of a weevil in a biscuit you'd find them!

BLACK DOG: Hang it, Pew, we've got the doubloons!

PEW: Curse the doubloons! It's the map!

JOHNNY: They might have hid the blessed thing. Take the doubloons and don't stand here squalling!

PEW: Squalling, is it? I'll give you a squall about your filthy head, John Dancer! *(Pew begins striking at them blindly with his stick.)*

JOHNNY: Ouch! I'll break your old neck, Pew, eyes or no eyes!

PEW: Cowards!

DIRK: Pew! I'm warning you!

BLACK DOG: Get the stick from him!

PEW: Cowards! Fools! I'm to lose my chance at fortunes because of you!

(*They struggle. Suddenly a series of frantic whistles from the distance. The men stop fighting and listen.*)

JOHNNY: There's Morgan! It's up, lads!

BLACK DOG: Someone's found us!

(*A pistol shot rings out.*)

BLACK DOG: Run!

DIRK: Run for it!

(*The three men scatter, abandoning Pew. The sound of horses galloping.*)

PEW: Wait! Don't leave me! Johnny, Black Dog, Dirk—you won't leave old Pew, mates—not poor Blind Pew! Come back!

(*Sound of horses closer.*)

PEW: Help me! (*Pew staggering aimlessly, frenzied. He runs and trips into the ditch where Jim and his mother are hiding, landing directly on Jim.*)

PEW: Help! Who's there? Help me!

(*Jim pushes Pew up and out of the ditch. Sound of galloping horses very loud.*)

PEW: (*Staggering up the street and out of sight, screeching.*) Alms! Alms for a blind man! Alms!

(*Loud horse whinny. Pew screams. Horse hooves come to a stop. Silence.*)

JIM: (*On his feet, looking up the street after Pew.*) Lord!

DR. LIVESEY: (*Offstage.*) The man is dead. Stone dead.

JIM: Oh, Doctor Livesey!

DR. LIVESEY: (*Entering and shouting back to others behind.*) Jenkins! Take my horse! (*To Jim.*) Hello, Hawkins. Terrible situation. I'm afraid I've killed a blind beggar. Ran right into my path.

JIM: It was no beggar, Doctor Livesey. It was Pew, the pirate, and he would've put my eyes out, and mother's... (*Suddenly remembering.*) Mother!

(*He turns to the ditch. Mrs. Hawkins, disgruntled and disheveled, is dusting herself off.*)

MRS. HAWKINS: Good evening, Doctor Livesey.

DR. LIVESEY: Mrs. Hawkins.

(*Squire Trelawney and Emlyn Jenkins, having cared for their horses, enter and gather round Jim and his mother.*)

DR. LIVESEY: You know Squire Trelawney, I believe?

MRS. HAWKINS: *(Brushing off her muddy clothes.)* We've never really had the pleasure, I'm afraid.

SQUIRE: Madam.

(They enter the Benbow.)

MRS. HAWKINS: Will you look! They've ruined everything! And Bones there still owes me for three weeks!

(The men look at each other and laugh.)

SQUIRE: Jenkins. Draw a thimbleful of rum for Mrs. Hawkins, there's a good man.

(Jenkins does so, Mrs. Hawkins sits apart.)

DR. LIVESEY: Now, Jim. Suppose you tell us what these rogues were after. What did they want with poor Bones here?

JIM: If I'm not mistaken, sir, it was *this*.

(Jim pulls the oilskin packet of papers from his vest. Livesey takes it.)

LIVESEY: If Jim is agreeable…?

(Jim nods. Livesey opens the packet and unrolls a small scroll.)

SQUIRE: A map, Livesey! It's Flint's map!

LIVESEY: You've heard of this Flint, then?

SQUIRE: Heard of him! He was the bloodthirstiest buccaneer that sailed. Blackbeard was a child to Flint.

LIVESEY: Well, I've heard of him myself. But what I want to know is this: Supposing what we hold here is some clue to where Flint buried his treasure, will that treasure amount to much?

SQUIRE: *Amount, sir!*

LIVESEY: Pray, keep your voice down!

SQUIRE: Amount, sir! It will amount to this: If we have the clue you talk about, I'll fit out a ship in Bristol dock and take you and Hawkins here, and Jenkins along, and we'll have that treasure if I search a year!

LIVESEY: Well, it's clearly the map of an island. *(Reading from the map.)* "Skeleton Island E.S.E. and by E. Ten feet. Tall tree, Spy-glass Shoulder, bearing a point to the N. of N.N.E."

SQUIRE: That's it, man! That's it! Livesey, tomorrow I start for Bristol. We'll have the best ship, sir, and the choicest crew in England. Hawkins shall come as cabin-boy. You'll make a famous cabinboy, Hawkins!

MRS. HAWKINS: My Jim?

SQUIRE: Famous, Mrs. Hawkins, famous!

LIVESEY: Trelawney! I'll go with you, and so will Jim. There's only one man I'm afraid of.

SQUIRE: And who's that? Name the dog, sir!

LIVESEY: It's you, sir, for you cannot hold your tongue. We are not the only men who know of this map. Those fellows who attacked the inn tonight...

(Livesey falls silent, looking beyond Jim and the Squire to the man who has just opened the tavern door. The other two see him looking and turn.)

MRS. HAWKINS: *(Faintly.)* Oh, my gracious...

LONG JOHN SILVER: Beg pardon if I'm interruptin'.

JIM: It's the one-legged man!

LIVESEY: Jim! I'm ashamed of you! This is the man that saved your life, and the life of your dear mother!

SILVER: No, sir. The lad's dead right. Count me legs any way you choose—there's only one of 'em.

JIM: Saved my life?

LIVESEY: It was he who told us you were under attack by pirates.

JIM: But I sent Emlyn Jenkins...

SQUIRE: Mr. Silver, here, got to us before Emlyn. He keeps a public house in Bristol, and he overheard these rogues planning the whole thing. If it hadn't been for Silver, we would have been too late. Silver, I want you to meet Hawkins. Jim Hawkins.

SILVER: Awwww, Jim. The pleasure is all mine, I'm sure. The pleasure is Long John Silver's entirely, Jim, en*tire*ly!

JIM: I...I'm sorry, Mr. Silver. I mistook you for somebody else. Thank you, sir.

SILVER: Ha haaa. There's a trump, gentlemen! This Hawkins is a trump, that's for sure. *(He tousles Jim's hair and cuffs him on the shoulder.)* Now, gentlemen. Did I hear talk of a seafarin' voyage, or did I not? Ha haa!

(The parrot on Silver's shoulder squawks and says, "Pieces of eight, pieces of eight!")

SILVER: There now, Cap'm Flint. Ha haaa! Gentlemen, meet Cap'm Flint...

(Curtain.)

SCENE III

Continuous with the above. Lights on Act Curtain scrim.

VOICE OF JIM HAWKINS: It was longer than the Squire imagined before we were ready for the sea, and that was too long for me altogether. I lived in a sea-dream all the while, and made of that island the most wonderful and changing of prospects. Sometimes it was thick with savages;

sometimes the island was full of dangerous animals; but in all my imag-
inings, I could foresee nothing so strange and tragic as our actual adventures. So the weeks passed on, until one fine morning, there came a letter
from the Squire in Bristol. "Dear Livesey," it read. "The ship is bought
and fitted…"

*(Act Curtain scrim is burned through to reveal the Squire on the deck of the
schooner. He is writing a letter in agitation.)*

SQUIRE: "The ship is bought and fitted. She's called the *Hispaniola* and she
lies at anchor, ready for sea. Everything, in fact, has gone off without a
hitch. Of course you remember this man, Silver, who did us the good
turn back at the Benbow. Well, I signed him on as cook.

(We see figures of men beginning to swarm about the deck.)

SQUIRE: Well, sir, I thought I had found only a cook, but it was a crew I had
discovered. Between Silver and myself, we got together a company of the
toughest old salts imaginable—not pretty to look at, but fellows of the
most indomitable spirit. Livesey—we are ready to sail! So—grab that
Hawkins fellow and come posthaste—do not lose an hour if you respect
me. Yours for treasure, John Trelawney."

*(Act Curtain scrim up, full ship in view. Livesey and Hawkins boarding
her.)*

LIVESEY: John Trelawney! I say, Trelawney!

SQUIRE: At your service, Livesey! Hawkins!

*(The Squire helps them aboard and laughs at Hawkins' wide-eyed, open-
mouthed wonderment.)*

SQUIRE: Hawkins, you look a perfect ninny.

JIM: Yes, sir.

SQUIRE: "Yes, sir!" he says. He *is* a ninny! We're *all* ninnies! What ho, men!
Ninnies coming aboard! I tell you, Livesey, I am more excited by the
prospect of the sea than all the treasure in the world! Hang the treasure!

LIVESEY: Keep your voice down, Trelawney! Goodness, man, you *are* a ninny
if you're that free with that particular word!

SQUIRE: Hmm, quite right, old man. Carried quite away. Never happen
again, sir. Although we've nothing to fear from these men, and it *was* a
capital notion, what Jim?

*(Jim has spotted Long John Silver coming aboard, bag over one shoulder,
parrot on the other. Jim runs to Silver.)*

JIM: Mister Silver, sir! Long John!

SILVER: Hawkins, bless my poor soul! Never a welcomer sight—I'd lay to that!

JIM: Will he talk again, sir?

SILVER: Who, then, Jim?

JIM: The bird!

SILVER: You mean Cap'm Flint here? Sure and he will, Jim—sure and he will…
(Captain Smollett has appeared on the deck above the two of them, looking grim and immaculate.)

SMOLLETT: You there, cook! You may go below, my man. Hands will want supper.

SILVER: Aye, aye, sir. Dooty is dooty. Jim. *(Silver touches his cap and disappears below.)*

SMOLLETT: Squire Trelawney, sir! I wish a word with you.

SQUIRE: I am always at the Captain's orders.

SMOLLETT: *(To Jim who, disappointed at Silver's forced departure, has run up to join Livesey and the Squire.)* Here, you ship's boy! Out o'that! Off with you to the cook and get some work.

JIM: *(After a glance at Livesey.)* Yes, sir, Captain. *(Moves off slowly, in time to hear Smollett's next remark.)*

SMOLLETT: *(To Livesey.)* I'll have no favorites on my ship.
(Jim looks and disappears.)

SQUIRE: Well, Captain Smollett—all's well, I hope—all shipshape and seaworthy?

SMOLLETT: No, sir—and I'd better speak plain. I don't like this voyage; I don't like the men; and I don't like what's happening on this ship. That's the short and sweet.

SQUIRE: *(Instantly angered.)* Really, sir? Well, possibly you don't like your employer either, is that it?

LIVESEY: Stay a bit, stay a bit! There's no need for harsh words. The Captain must explain himself. You say you don't like this voyage. Why?

SMOLLETT: I was engaged, sir, on what we call sealed orders, to sail this ship where this gentleman should bid me. So far so good. But now I discover that we are sailing for treasure—and who do I hear it from? My own hands! I don't call that fair, do you?

LIVESEY: No sir, I don't.

SMOLLETT: Now, I don't like treasure voyages on any account, and I don't like them above all when they are a badly kept secret. Is that understood?

SQUIRE: If you're suggesting for a moment that I have blabbed this thing about, I'll…

SMOLLETT: I'm suggesting nothing, sir. I'm telling you that every man Jack aboard this vessel knows that we are sailing for treasure, and knows the exact latitude and longitude of the island we sail for, sir!

SQUIRE: I never…Livesey…I swear I never…

LIVESEY: *(Seeing the approach of Israel Hands.)* One moment, Squire.

ISRAEL: Captain, sir. She stands ready. We await your orders to cast off.

SMOLLETT: Thank you. Go below and await them, then.

(Israel leaves.)

LIVESEY: What you're saying, in other words, is that you fear a mutiny?

SMOLLETT: If I were saying *that*, sir, I would not be standing here talking with you gentlemen. I would be in my own home, having tea. No—these men may well be honest, for all I know. I merely want to know if you gentleman are determined to go on this cruise.

SQUIRE: We are, sir, like iron!

SMOLLETT: Then sir, I want it known that I am Captain of this ship, and I want things done my way.

LIVESEY: And so they shall be, sir, and so it shall be known.

SQUIRE: *(An awkward aside to Livesey.)* Livesey, I don't like this man.

JIM: *(Who has been hiding and eavesdropping.)* Neither do I, Squire Trelawney. Let's have Long John Silver for captain!

LIVESEY: Jim Hawkins! For shame, boy!

SQUIRE: *(Trying to stifle a laugh.)* I say, Hawkins. That'll be enough out of you. *(Aside.)* "Neither do I" he says. "Neither do I."

SMOLLETT: Whether you like me or not, Hawkins, does not signify. But whether you can obey orders or choose to disobey them may well mean your life some day. Now, join the hands on deck. It looks as though we're going to go a-sailing. *(To the crew.)* Gentlemen! You may cast off!

(A great to-do. Music rises with casting-off theme. Commands are shouted, sailors climb the riggings, Jim runs to the ship's prow. Lights fade as the ship lurches—the actors lurching to create the illusion—and begins to move out of Bristol dock.)

SCENE IV

Morning lights rise on the schooner at sea. The crew moving lazily about their tasks in the scorching heat. Long John Silver has carried his stool and a sack-full of potatoes up onto the deck and sits not far from the apple barrel, peeling them with Jim. The Squire paces the upper deck, removing his clothing bit by bit, looking extremely uncomfortable with the heat. Captain Smollett stands, looking cool and immaculate, sighting with a brass telescope and sextant. Dr. Livesey sits at a small table on the upper deck and writes in a journal.

VOICE OF LIVESEY: "Morning of the 21st day. Entered tropical zones some-time during the night, according to Smollett. All progresses smoothly, and I believe even the Captain is coming to have some respect for this hardworking crew. John Silver, in particular, seems an amazing sort of fellow. He has a way of talking to each member of the crew, and doing everybody some kindness. To young Jim Hawkins he is especially good."
(Jim has disappeared head-foremost into the apple barrel. Silver comes up behind him and plays his legs like an accordion.)

SILVER: *(Shouting down into the barrel.)* Hawkins! Do you want an apple that bad, boy?

(Jim Rights himself and his head pops out of the barrel.)

JIM: Yes, sir! Do you want an apple, too, Long John?

SILVER: I wouldn't mind, Jim. But listen, boy. I heard tell of a poor sailor once who got lost in an apple-barrel just like that one!

JIM: No!

SILVER: Yes I did, Jim. This fellow, he were a pirate, Jim, a pirate. But he got what he deserved, didn't he.

JIM: How?

SILVER: Well, when he finally came out o'the barrel, some six months later, there weren't no difference twixt him and an apple tart, Jim, an apple tart this big…Ain't that right, Israel Hands?

ISRAEL: It's bloody hot, that's all I know.

VOICE OF LIVESEY: "It is a joy to see the friendship which has sprung up between the boy and this poor crippled seaman."

SQUIRE: I say! Livesey, old man! Is it hot enough for you?

LIVESEY: Quite.

(The Squire trips over his feet, comes close to falling overboard. The men laugh.)

SQUIRE: Hmm. Nearly fell in the water. Hmm.

VOICE OF LIVESEY: "Squire Trelawney continues to be rather tiresome. But good-hearted, through and through. He and the Captain, however, are still on the worst of terms."

SQUIRE: *(To Smollett.)* Come, sir. You'll have to admit that you were wrong, at least, about this *ship*, sir. Never in all my days have I…

SMOLLETT: I'll admit, Squire Trelawney, that I've taken a downright fancy to her. She'll lie a point nearer the wind than a man has a right to expect of his own married wife.

SQUIRE: There now. Didn't I tell you?

SMOLLETT: All the same, we're not home again and I don't like this cruise.

(The Squire turns away from Smollett in exasperated rage and addresses the thick air.)

SQUIRE: A trifle more of that man, and I shall explode!

(Lights slowly fade.)

SCENE V

Evening at sea. The lights of a dozen lanterns strung about the ship slowly rise.

ISRAEL: All hands! Ho there! Day's done! Grog, gentlemen! Grog!

(The men at their various tasks stop when Hands calls them, and cheer at the call for grog.)

THE MEN: Here, here! Cheers! Grog, sirs! Let go the ropes! Etc.

SMOLLETT: *(Interrupting their cheer in a huge voice.)* Mister Hands!

(The cheer fades apprehensively.)

SMOLLETT: Mister Hands, sir.

ISRAEL: Yessir, Cap'm?

SMOLLETT: *Double* grog for the gentlemen tonight, I should think.

(Great cheer from the men. They begin to drop out of the shrouds, climb up out of the hatches, lay down ropes and riggings and form a line by the grog barrel. Emlyn Jenkins presides at the barrel, ladling out the men's portions.)

EMLYN: The grog starts here, gentlemen! Form a queue. Orderly, now, gents…we mustn't rush things. There's yours, George. Hello, Redcliff, you're looking well. Dirk. Morgan…Mister Morgan! One moment *please.* From the look of it, you've not washed your hands. Step right to the end, Mister Morgan, and don't let me see you here until you're clean and tidy.

MORGAN: I'll shove your bloody head in, I will…

SILVER: Mister Morgan! I'm shocked at your language. Go below and wash, Morgan.

(Morgan moves off, muttering, with an evil glance at Emlyn.)

EMLYN: *(Still ladling out more drinks.)* That's better. Tst, tst, tst. A dirty man. A dirty-handed man.

SILVER: A song, Rogers! A sweet one, for a sweet evenin'. *(To the men.)* Pipe down, swabs! We'll have a song!

(Affirmative ad-libs from the men.)

ROGERS: *(Sings when the men fall silent.)*
> Make haste, make haste, my merry men all,
> Our good ship sails the morn.
> Oh say not so, my master dear,
> For I fear a deadly storm.
>
> Late yesterday eve I saw the new moon
> With the old moon in her arms
> And I fear, I fear, my master dear
> That we will come to harm.
>
> O long, long may the ladies sit
> With their fans held in their hands,
> O ere they see Sir Patrick Spens
> Come sailing to the land.
>
> Half over, half over to Aberdeen
> It's fifty fathoms deep.
> And there lies Sir Patrick Spens,
> With the Scots lords at his feet.

JIM: *(After a pause, in the hush that follows the song.)* Was beautiful, Billy.

DICK: Now, Long John, you tip us a stave!

MERRY: Livelier, livelier this time!

(Long John pipes a jig in the dim lantern light; stars begin to appear in the sky. One of the mates stands in the middle of the circle of men and dances a jig.)

SQUIRE: *(From the quarter deck, where he stands watching with Livesey.)* Hawkins—you join him, lad! Go on!

SEVERAL SAILORS: Hawkins! Put Hawkins in the ring!

(Jim is thrust into the middle. After a sheepish moment, he begins to follow the dancingman's step. The lantern lights begin to fade. The jig comes to an end. Jim is Left standing in the small pool of remaining light. Israel Hands appears behind him, crooks his arm around the boy's neck in a rough, but seemingly affectionate, embrace.)

ISRAEL: Ahh, you're a fine lad, Jim Hawkins! A fine lad, to be sure!

(Lights out.)

SCENE VI

The light of dawn rises over the decks of the schooner. There is a white mist surrounding the ship and crawling up over the decks. Captain Smollett stands aft, near the helmsman, who whistles a strain of the ballad of Sir Patrick Spens. Other than these two, the decks are deserted.

VOICE OF JIM HAWKINS: It was on the last day of our outward voyage that I made my terrible discovery. Everyone was in the bravest of spirits, because we were now so near to our goal. But because of an old apple barrel and my own disobedience, I learned that our goal was sudden and violent death, and that the lives of all honest men aboard depended upon me alone.

(Jim pops up out of the forecastle hatch, laughing. He notices the Captain watching him and his laugh stops. The Captain descends the stairs from the upper deck, looking at Jim, and then suddenly turns and disappears through the quarterdeck hatch into the Captain's cabins. Jim, as soon as the Captain is out of sight, moves to the apple barrel and leaps in.)

JIM: *(Popping up again, holding an apple.)* This one's rotten. *(Throws the rotten apple over the Upstage side of the deck. Ducks down into the barrel, and pops up again.) And* this one.

(Tosses the second apple, and then hears footsteps and voices coming up the forecastle hatch.)

JIM: That's Long John, that is. We'll give him a little surprise, won't we.

(As Long John Silver comes up into sight, talking with a young crewman, Jim slowly sinks back into the barrel.)

SILVER: *(To the young man, Dick.)* Now you look here, Dick: You're young, you are, but you're smart as paint. I seed that when I first set eyes on you, and I'll talk to you like a man. Now this ain't no bundle o'sticks we're after, Dick. This is treasure! *Flint's* treasure, man! Seven hundred thousands in gold, Dick...

DICK: Seven hundred thousands...

SILVER: Well, it ain't like pickin' the parson's pocket, you'll have to allow me that much.

DICK: I will, Mister Silver, and more! I'm with you, Mister Silver, and here's my hand on it!

SILVER: Agreed, then—you're with us, and a smart lad you are for it.

(Silver gives a low whistle and Israel Hands appears out of the hatch.)

SILVER: Israel—Dick's with us.

ISRAEL: Oh, I knew he'd come around. He's no fool, is Dick. But, look here—here's what I want to know: How much longer are we goin' to wait afore we strike? I've had enough o' Captain Smollett, *and* that boy I might tell you.

SILVER: Israel, your head ain't much account, nor ever was it. Now, here's what I say: We'll wait, and we'll wait, and then we'll wait some more! If I had my way, I'd have Captain Smollett sail us halfway back to England with the treasure safe on board before I struck.

ISRAEL: Well, I don't say you no, do I?

SILVER: *(Like a knife.)* No, and if you're smarter than I think you are, you won't start now, Israel Hands.

DICK: What you say is all right with me, Long John, but when we *do* strike, what do we do with 'em?

SILVER: Now that's what I calls business! Well, what would you think? Put 'em ashore, like maroons? That would have been England's way. Or cut 'em down like that much pork? That would have been Flint's way, or Billy Boneses.

ISRAEL: Billy was the man for that. "Dead men don't bite," says he. Well, he's dead now hisself, and he knows the long and short of it.

SILVER: Mark you—I'm an easy man. I'm quite the gentleman, normally—but this is serious. Dooty is dooty, mates. I give my vote—death. Wait is what I say, but when the time comes, death for 'em all!

DICK: John, you're a man!

SILVER: Only one thing I claim—I claims Trelawney. I'll wring his calf's head off his body with these hands. Dick! Jump up like a sweet lad and get me an apple, will you?

(Dick stands and moves to the apple barrel.)

ISRAEL: Fetch one for me, too, will you, Dick?

DICK: *Right.*

(Just as he is about to lean over the barrel, a cry from the forward hatch.)

THE WATCH: Land ho!

(Dick straightens and looks at the other two.)

SILVER: That's it, lads. *(Getting to his feet.)* Dooty is dooty.

(Suddenly there is a great rush of men across the deck, the crew tumbling up from the cabin and forecastle to see the island. In a moment, Jim's head appears out of the apple barrel, looks about, and then he leaps out and runs directly into Doctor Livesey. All action freezes.)

JIM: *(In the silence of the freeze.)* Doctor, let me speak. Get the Captain and the Squire down to the cabin, and then make some excuse to send for me. I have terrible news.

LIVESEY: *(Startled for a moment, then regains composure. In an artificially loud voice.)* That's right, Jim. I left my pipe lying on the Captain's table. I'd be obliged if you'd fetch it for me.

(Action on deck resumes.)

SILVER: *(From the forward part of the ship.)* Hawkins! Jim Hawkins! Come and see, lad! It's a fine sight, this island!

(Jim looks at Silver, then turns and runs down the officer's hatch. Silver stands staring after him as the lights quickly fade.)

SCENE VII

In the Captain's cabin. The Captain, the Squire, Livesey, Emlyn Jenkins, Hunter, and Redruth listening to Jim finish his story.

SMOLLETT: You're certain of all this, Jim?

JIM: I swear, Captain, I heard every word he said!

SQUIRE: Then, Captain Smollett, I owe you an apology. They had me fooled entirely.

LIVESEY: That's due to Silver. A very remarkable man.

SMOLLETT: He'd look remarkably well hanging from the gallows. But this is talk, it doesn't lead to anything. Gentlemen, I see three or four points, and I'll name them. We must go on, because we can't turn back. If I gave the word to turn about now, they would strike at once. Second point— we have time before us—at least until this treasure is found. Third point. There are some faithful men aboard. We can count on your own servants, I take it, Squire?

SQUIRE: Emlyn?

EMLYN: You can be certain o'that, sir!

SQUIRE: Redruth?

REDRUTH: We're with you, sir!

SQUIRE: Hunter?

HUNTER: Like iron, sir!

SMOLLETT: Good. That makes six men and a boy against their sixteen. Well, gentlemen, the best that I can say is not much, but there's no help for it till we know who else might be with us.

LIVESEY: Jim here can help us more than anyone. The men are not shy with him, and Jim is a noticing lad.

SMOLLETT: Hawkins, I put great faith in you.

JIM: Yes, sir, Captain Smollett. And Captain Smollett, sir. I'm sorry, I...

SMOLLETT: That's no use to us now, Jim. But I accept, with thanks. Well, gentlemen, there is an old stockade on this island, built by Flint himself. It's plainly marked on the map...

(Screech of parrot from behind the door. "Pieces of eight, Pieces of eight, Pieces of eight!" A knock.)

SMOLLETT: Come in, Mister Silver.

(Jim anxiously darts away from the door. The door opens and Silver puts his head in.)

SILVER: Beggin' your pardon, gentlemen. The mates has asked me to speak with you, sir. They wants permission to go ashore—stretch their legs if you like. Have a look around, that sort of thing. No harm in that now, is there?

(Slight pause.)

SMOLLETT: None whatsoever, Mister Silver. In fact, why don't you take Hawkins here with you.

JIM: Captain!

SILVER: Why, what's wrong, Jim? This here is a sweet spot, this island—a sweet spot for a lad to get ashore on.

JIM: Nothing's wrong, Long John. Only the Captain had ordered me to stay aboard for a day—as punishment—for eavesdropping.

SMOLLETT: I think we can forget that, Jim. This little talk we've had has done you good, I think. We'll come ashore later and meet you. For now, though, I want you to get some of the devil out of you on that island. Orders, Hawkins.

SILVER: Dooty is dooty, Jim. Why, you'll have a capital time. You'll swim, you'll climb trees... Why it makes me young again to think.

(Jim moves to Silver, and they leave, Silver still talking.)

SILVER: It's a pleasant thing to be young and have ten toes, Jim, and you may lay to that, Jim, you may lay to that.

(The door shuts behind them.)

SMOLLETT: *(Looking out the cabin window.)* Jenkins. Lower a boat and bring it around for us. We're going ashore.

(Curtain. Intermission.)

ACT II
SCENE I

A wooded stretch of shoreline and a grassy slope that rises up from the banks of the island. The ship is visible some distance out in the bay, i.e., a tiny model of the ship behind the ocean scrim. Suddenly, a great cry of startled island birds rising up through the trees. Then, Jim Hawkins comes running up the slope and into sight. He looks behind him.

SILVER: *(Offstage.)* Hawkins! Wait for me, lad! Give a hand to your old friend, Long John, won't you!
(Just as Silver comes up into view, Jim turns and darts off into the wood. Silver hobbles as fast as he can, then stops, looking off after Jim.)
SILVER: Hawkins! I'm surprised at you, my mate. Surprised, indeed.
(Tom Morgan appears up from the shore.)
SILVER: Morgan! That boy knows something or I'm mistaken.
MORGAN: What if he does? He'll know even more when I've got my hands around his dirty little neck, and that won't be long if I have my way.
SILVER: Oh, you'll have your way, my dear, and soon enough at that.
(Six more men come up the bank and join Silver and Morgan.)
SILVER: You men! Listen to me. We make for Flint's old stockade. It's not a mile from here, in a tight little clearing. We'll hole up there—plenty o'guns and plenty o'powder. From there, we can live like lords and make 'em sweat—until we find it!
(The men cheer.)
SILVER: That's the story! Let's off, then, lads.
(Lights fade, sound of bird cries.)

SCENE II

As the cries of birds rise and then fall, the lights come up on another part of the island; i.e., the tree drops track to a different arrangement and the model of the ship is no longer visible behind the scrim. Jim Hawkins runs into view, comes to a stop, and sinks panting onto a stump. He sits there for a moment, catching his breath. Then he looks up and notices how dark this part of the island is.

JIM: I don't like it here...

BENN GUNN: *(Unseen, from behind a tree.)* Cheese?

JIM: *(Leaping to his feet.)* What's that?

> *(Distant bird cries, sound of the ocean. Jim sits again, warily.)*

BENN GUNN: Any cheese?

JIM: *(On his feet again.)* Who is that? Come! I know you're there!

> *(Benn Gunn comes out from behind his tree, but is behind Jim's back and unnoticed by him.)*

GUNN: Cheese. I want cheese…

> *(Jim pulls the pistol out of his trousers and, holding it with both hands, turns in a slow circle.)*

JIM: All right, you—whatever it is you are. Come out o'that! Do you hear me? Come out this instant! Oh! *(Jim is startled to turn and find Benn Gunn standing before him.)* Stop, I say!

GUNN: Benn Gunn's not going anywhere. Benn Gunn hasn't gone anywhere for ever so long.

JIM: Who are you?

GUNN: I just told you. Benn Gunn. Do you have any cheese?

JIM: *(At a loss.)* Well, where did you come from?

GUNN: A good Christian home, and a pious mother. Do you have any cheese?

JIM: But how did you get *here*, sir!

GUNN: Marooned. Deserted. Abandoned. Three years ago.

JIM: Three years!

GUNN: They left me here to die three years ago, and I haven't talked to a man these three years. What do you call yourself, mate?

JIM: Jim.

GUNN: *(Pleased to hear a human name.)* Ahh, Jim. Jim. There's a name. Jim. For instance, you wouldn't think I had a pious mother, would you? To look at me?

JIM: Why…no, not in particular.

GUNN: Ahh, well, but I had. Remarkable pious. And I was a civil, pious boy, and could say my catechism that fast, as you couldn't tell one word from another. And here's what it come to…*Jim*. And it all began with breakin' church windows. Oh, it went further than that—my mother predicked it would—she predicked the whole thing, pious woman. I've thought it all out on this here lonely island, and I'm back on piety. Have you got any cheese?

JIM: Well…no.

GUNN: Many's the long night I've dreamed of cheese—toasted, mostly—and woke up again, and here I were.

JIM: If ever I can get on board again, you shall have all the cheese you want!

GUNN: If *ever,* you says. Why now, who's to stop you?

JIM: Flint's men.

GUNN: *(Instant scream.) What! What! Flint! What!*

JIM: *(Alarmed.)* Not Flint himself, Benn Gunn. Flint's dead. The ship's been taken over by some of Flint's men.

GUNN: Not a man…with one…leg?

JIM: Silver?

GUNN: *That's him! That's him! Silver!*

JIM: He's the ringleader for them all. I heard him.

GUNN: Listen to me, Jim, says I. I'm listenin', says you. All right. I got a little boat for you. I got a little boat you can use, Jim, and might be you could get your ship back from 'em, Jim, and might be you could even get some cheese, Jim, some cheese.

JIM: But Long John Silver's going to kill the Squire—I heard him. He's going to kill all of us and take the treasure for himself.

GUNN: *(The wrong word has been used in Benn Gunn's presence.)* The what? The *what,* did you say?

JIM: The *treasure,* Benn Gu…

(Gunn claps his hand over Jim's mouth.)

GUNN: Shhh! That's enough of *that,* Jim. Benn Gunn'll do what he can. No, no—you just remember what Benn Gunn told you. Look for the little boat beneath the white rock and Jim will save the ship, he will, Jim will save us all. The Squire, did you say?

JIM: Squire Trelawney.

GUNN: You just tell your Squire that Benn Gunn will do what he can—tell him that, Jim. Benn Gunn will do what he can, Jim, Benn Gunn will do what he can…

(The lights fade.)

SCENE III

Lights rise on one corner of a log stockade and the log-fence enclosure surrounding it. All is quiet and deserted. The stockade overlooks a large bay, and out in the bay we can see the tiny figure of the Hispaniola. *Then, the sound of rough voices, and startled birds. Silver emerges from the wood, Right, surrounded by his men. They stop and look at the stockade.*

SILVER: There now, lads. What did Long John Silver tell you? Pretty as a picture, ain't it, and right where old Cap'm Flint left it, ha haa!

MERRY: But what'll we do? What's the *plan*, Long John?

SILVER: What'll we do?! Why, we *take* the *stockade*, Mister Merry. Israel Hands is on board that ship, along with Tom O'Brien, and they'll keep a sharp eye on the Captain and the others, they will. And in the meanwhile, Mister Merry, that wretched boy is somewheres on this island— and as long as *he's* here, and *they're* on the ship, those gentlemen ain't going anywhere, Mister Merry. Not until they give us that blessed *map*, Mister Merry! Now *if* there ain't no more bright questions, Mister Merry, I suggest we make ourselves to home!

SEVERAL PIRATES: Aye! Aye, Long John!

(Silver and the others take three steps in the direction of the stockade and then stop short. Squire Trelawney slowly appears on the stockade roof, leaning over the side with a musket trained on the men below. Then, from around the Upstage corner of the fortress, we see Emlyn Jenkins appear with two pistols pointed at the pirates. At the same time, Doctor Livesey comes up from the Downstage corner of the stockade roof, musket aimed at the men; and Hunter and Redruth likewise. The pirates stand in dumb astonishment. Captain Smollett emerges from the stockade door, and coolly raises the Union Jack up the flagpole.)

SMOLLETT: Do you men want something?

(This serves to break the spell: Several pirates run back to the wood for cover.)

SILVER: *(In a rage, to the deserters.)* Swabs! Cowards! *(To Captain Smollett.)* Yes, sir, Captain Smollett. We do want something. We want that treasure, and we mean to have it.

SMOLLETT: And who might you be?

DICK: *(Defiant.)* That, sir, is Captain Long John Silver, sir.

SMOLLETT: "Captain" Silver? Don't know the man.

SILVER: These poor lads have chosen me Cap'm after you deserted 'em, sir. Now all I want is a word with you, sir—and your promise that you'll not fire on me…like the gentleman you are, sir.

SMOLLETT: My man, I have not the slightest desire to talk to you. If you wish to talk to me, you can come, that's all. If there's any treachery, it'll be on your side, and the Lord help you!

SILVER: Ha haa! A word from you's enough. I know a gentleman and you may lay to that! *(Silver advances to the stockade.)*

SMOLLETT: If you have anything to say, my man, you had better say it.

SILVER: Ah, right you are, Cap'm Smollett. Dooty is dooty, to be sure. You have a map. Now, I never meant you no harm, myself…

SMOLLETT: That won't do with me, Silver. We know exactly what you meant to do, but we don't care; for now, you see, you can't do it.

SILVER: *(Rage.)* And who's to say I can't?

SMOLLETT: *(Weary.)* Is this what you came to talk about?

SILVER: *(Recovering his composure.)* Ah, to be sure it ain't, Cap'm. You're right on that one. Here it is: You give us the map to get the treasure by, and stop pointing guns at poor innocent seamen—you do that, and we'll drop you at the nearest port, we will. Now that's handsome, that is— you'll have to agree on that!

SMOLLETT: *(Lighting his pipe.)* Is that all?

SILVER: *(Pause. Then, rage.)* Every last word, by thunder! Refuse that and you've seen the last of me but musket balls!

SMOLLETT: Very good. Now you'll hear me. If you come up, one by one and unarmed, I'll clap you all in irons and take you home for a fair trial in England. If you won't, as my name is Alexander Smollett, I'll see you to the devil.

(The pirates react variously.)

SMOLLETT: No? Well, those are the last good words you'll get from me, Silver—for in the name of heaven, I'll put a bullet in you when next we meet. Now get out. Bundle on out o'this, please, hand over hand and double quick!

(Silver jumps back, trips over his crutch and falls. The men in the stockade laugh.)

SILVER: *Laugh, by thunder, laugh!* *(He struggles to his feet.)* Here's what I think of you!

(He spits. One of Silver's young men, Rogers, steps forward.)

ROGERS: They've got us, Silver, can't you see that? Captain Smollett, sir—I'm with you…

(Silver pulls a pistol from his belt and shoots the man dead.)

SILVER: *(To his men, pistol in hand.)* Any others?

(Silence. Smollett taps out his pipe on his shoe.)

SILVER: Dick! Signal to the ship. Tell 'em to fire, Dick, tell 'em to fire! *(To the Captain and the men in the stockade.)* I'll see you dead and done!

(Dick runs to the Upstage edge of the bank, facing Upstage, and fires a pistol into the air as a signal to the ship. Silver scrambles for cover, along with the rest of the pirates.)

LIVESEY: *(To the Captain.)* Well done, man! Well done!

SMOLLETT: You, sir! Back to your post! Gentlemen! Take cover, please! Quick march!

(The men in the stockade do so, and Smollett himself hurries into the stockade door. The clearing is deserted for a moment. Just then, Jim Hawkins runs into the clearing from another direction, stops, and stands looking up at the Union Jack. Smollett bursts out of the stockade.)

SMOLLETT: Jim!

(Smollett grabs Jim and pulls him to the ground—just as we see a flash from the deck of the ship, i.e., the model behind the scrim. There is the crack of a distant explosion, followed by a sharp whistling sound and then a cannon ball lands inside the stockade fence.)

SMOLLETT: *(Half-rising from the ground and shouting up to the men.)* Doctor— you take the door. Squire Trelawney—you and Redruth, man the west side.

(From the ship, another flash, crack, and whistle, and a cannonball lands up of the stockade with a burst of sand and grass.)

SMOLLETT: Jenkins, my man. You take the east side of the enclosure—here. Hawkins, you and I will stand by to load and bear a hand. Ready now!

(A third flash and crack from the deck of the ship.)

SQUIRE: If you please, Captain, if I see anyone, am I to fire?

SMOLLETT: Well of course, man!

SQUIRE: Very well, then.

(The Squire takes aim and fires. His shot is returned by a volley of nine shots from the woods. Smollett flattens himself and Jim onto the ground.)

SMOLLETT: *(After a moment.)* Did you hit your man, sir?

SQUIRE: No, sir.

SMOLLETT: Well, there's something to be said for honesty. Come along, Hawkins!

(Smollett and Jim scramble into the stockade. Sudden onslaught of fire from the woods. The Captain's men return the fire: The fight is now in earnest. Some pirates run out of the wood and leap up onto the enclosure fence, only to be shot by muskets from the stockade roof. Emlyn Jenkins and Hunter move out of the stockade to take better aim with their muskets. Firing continues.)

EMLYN: *(Calling back to the stockade.)* Hawkins!

(Jim runs out of the stockade and fills Jenkins's musket. Jim runs back inside again. A pirate appears out of the wood and takes aim at Jenkins.)

LIVESEY: Jenkins! Watch yourself!

(Jenkins wheels about and fires at the pirate. The pirate falls. Immediately

another pirate appears with musket aimed at Jenkins from the opposite direction. Smollett rushes out of the stockade.)

SMOLLETT: Emlyn!

(The pirate fires and Jenkins falls. Smollett rushes to him, takes him in his arms and is attempting to drag him back to the stockade when the pirate fires again. Smollett falls. Jim is out of the stockade, tugging at both of the fallen men. The pirate runs at them, and Jim takes the musket from Emlyn Jenkins hands and swings it, butt end front, at the man's head. He falls. Smollett gets up on his knees.)

SMOLLETT: *(Calling up to the stockade.)* Out, lads! Out and fight 'em in the open!

(The men from the stockade rush out into the enclosure, firing. Hand-to-hand combat, in some cases. Jim takes up a pistol and joins in the fray. Silver occasionally darts into the periphery of the clearing, urging his men on, and then disappears. Finally, one of the pirates leaps onto the enclosure fence.)

PIRATE: *(Rallying the remaining pirates.)* At 'em! At 'em! All hands!

(The Pirate raises his cutlass above Jim's head and is about to bring it down when Hunter fires from another part of the enclosure and the pirate falls. The remaining pirates flee into the wood. Suddenly, all is still; the air is thick with smoke. After a moment, the stockade men gather around the fallen Jenkins.)

JIM: *(Falling on his knees by Emlyn.)* Emlyn!

EMLYN: Hello, Jim. How's yer mum? *(He dies.)*

LIVESEY: Cover him up, Mister Hunter.

(Hunter takes off his coat and lays it over Jenkins.)

JIM: Emlyn...

LIVESEY: He died a man, Jim.

SQUIRE: Six of them, by my count, Captain.

SMOLLETT: With the one man Silver himself dispatched, that leaves nine of them. Two on board ship, and seven in these woods. Nine against our seven.

JIM: *(Getting up, somewhat hysterical.)* We must stop them... We must! *(To the Captain.)* The man on the island!

LIVESEY: What are you talking about, boy?

JIM: Benn Gunn's boat!

SMOLLETT: Who?

JIM: Benn Gunn! He'll find you! I must go...! *(Jim leaps over the enclosure fence.)*

SQUIRE: Jim!

SMOLLETT: Hawkins! Come back at once! Orders, Hawkins!

(Jim hesitates for a moment, then turns and runs into the wood.)

SMOLLETT: You're a disobedient boy, Jim Hawkins! You're a disobedient…

(A pistol shot from the woods. Bird cries, then silence. Lights fade on the men, who stand looking into the wood. Act Curtain down.)

SCENE IV

Narrative voice-over accompanied by the wind and the crash of the sea.

VOICE OF JIM HAWKINS: Never in my life had I done so foolish a thing. I didn't stop running until I'd reached the east coast of Treasure Island, and there, just as Benn Gunn predicted, was a large white rock, and beneath it, a primitive handmade boat. I had no plan, save that I would find the ship and cut her cable. But once the tide caught me up, I could not even steer the tiny boat, and every minute I was swept further out to sea.

(The Act Curtain scrim begins to burn through, and we see Israel Hands and Tom O'Brien fighting on the deck of the Hispaniola.*)*

JIM: Suddenly, I heard the sound of drunken voices…

(Moonlight on the deck of the ship, Israel Hands dealing a blow to the side of Tom O'Brien's head. O'Brien staggers for a moment, then puts his hands around Israel's neck and squeezes. Israel does the same for Mr. O'Brien. They stand locked together.)

ISRAEL: Try this one, Tom O'Brien!

O'BRIEN: I took enough from you, Israel Hands!

ISRAEL: Oh, you ain't took near enough, Mister O'Brien!

(They struggle. Jim Hawkins appears, drenched to the skin, crawling up over the Upstage side of the upper deck. He stands shivering in the moonlight for a moment, watching the two pirates. Then he pulls one of the pistols from his trousers and aims it with both hands at the men. They do not see him.)

O'BRIEN: *(Choked.)* Swab!

(O'Brien makes choking noises and slowly sinks to the deck. Just as he is about to collapse, he lets go of Israel's neck, pulls a knife from his belt, and stabs Hands in the leg.)

ISRAEL: *(Cries out in pain.)* Ahhhh! This will do for you, O'Brien!

(Israel exerts a final effort, O'Brien drops to the deck. Israel slumps and sits panting with his back to Jim. Jim still has his pistol pointed at Hands.)

ISRAEL: *(In a quiet voice, without looking around.)* Welcome aboard, Hawkins.

(Jim jumps back with shock. Israel still doesn't turn.)

ISRAEL: Don't look so worried, Hawkins. Israel Hands has got eyes at the back of his head.

JIM: *(Still pointing the pistol.)* Are you much hurt?

ISRAEL: Not half so much as Tom O'Brien, there, and he's dead. Now where mought you have come from?

JIM: *(Mustering courage.)* I've come aboard to take possession of this ship, Mister Hands, and you'll please regard me as your captain until further notice.

ISRAEL: God save the King.

JIM: I mean what I say, Israel Hands!

ISRAEL: No doubt you do. *(He slowly turns and stands facing Jim.)* Now look you here. We've had about enough of this foolery, *Captain* Hawkins.

JIM: Don't take another step, Mister Hands!

ISRAEL: *(Taking another step toward Jim.)* Him as strikes first is my fancy— dead men don't bite, Hawkins...

JIM: Just one more step, Mister Hands, and I'll fire!

ISRAEL: So be it, amen.

> *(Israel takes a single step, Jim takes aim and fires. A dull click. Israel instantly flashes out a knife.)*

ISRAEL: My, what a fierce click! Seawater ain't good for pistols, Captain Hawkins. Makes 'em wet, like. And now, Captain Hawkins, we'll have us a little talk, we will.

> *(Hands, still standing beneath the upper deck, lunges toward Jim, catches his feet with one hand, and pulls them out from under him. Jim lands on his backside, but instantly rolls out of Israel's reach, crouches and leaps into the shrouds. Jim begins to climb, then stops and pulls a second pistol from his belt and re-primes it. Hands catches his breath for a moment, watches Jim climb. Then, he starts after him in silence, his knife clenched in his teeth. Jim edges up the shrouds. Suddenly, he looses his footing and his legs swing down. Hands slashes at them with his knife, but Jim pulls them up again, and swings around to a secure position. He now faces Hands, aiming his pistol down at him. Hands puts the knife between his teeth again and climbs another notch upward.)*

JIM: Stop there, Mister Hands, or I'll blow your brains out!

> *(Israel laughs.)*

JIM: *This* powder is *dry*, Mister Hands!

> *(Hands stops laughing. He looks over his shoulder to the sea beneath him. He looks back up at Jim.)*

ISRAEL: *(Taking the knife out of his teeth.)* Jim, lad. You're young, but you're smart as paint. I seed that from the first. We can still be mates, Jim, can't we?

JIM: Well, I suppose, but…

ISRAEL: Good!

(Instantly Hands draws back his hand and sends the knife flashing through the air. It catches Jim at the shoulder. At the same moment, Jim's pistol goes off and strikes Israel Hands. He falters for a moment, and then plunges down into the sea. Jim pulls the knife out of the mast as the lights fade.)

SCENE V

Dim lights on Act Curtain.

VOICE OF JIM HAWKINS: All throughout that dreadful night I labored to steer the ship away from its anchorage and into a hidden cove on the north side of the island. It was a huge task for a boy half the size of the helm itself, and I wonder now that I was able…what with the wound of the knife in my shoulder, and the memory of Israel Hands's fall into the sea. It was nearly dawn when I finally beached the *Hispaniola*. By that time, I hated the Treasure Island, and only wanted to see the faces of my dear friends.

(Lights of dawn rise on the stockade clearing. Jim stumbles on, stops before the stockade fence and stands, panting and exhausted.)

JIM: *(Breathless.)* Doctor Livesey! Captain Smollett! I'm back! Squire Trelawney? It's Jim Hawkins come back! *(Silence. Jim takes a couple of steps toward the stockade door.)* Hello! *(Silence. Jim takes another step toward the door.)* It's Jim Hawkins! I've saved the ship!

(Silence. Jim puts his head in the stockade door. Instantly, a terrible screech from within: "Pieces of eight, Pieces of eight, Pieces of eight!" Jim turns and runs in terror, Right around the stockade, stops. John Dancer emerging from the shadows of the Upstage Right corner of the stockade, blocking Jim's way. Dancer walks slowly forward, Jim backs away, turns and bolts Left, but as he passes the stockade door, Silver puts out his crutch and Jim flies sprawling over it to the ground. Silver comes out and stands over him.)

SILVER: So here's Jim Hawkins, shiver my timbers. Well, come—I take that friendly.

(Three other pirates emerge from the stockade—George Merry, Sam Redcliff, and Tom Morgan. Along with Dancer, they gather and stand above Jim.)

SILVER: It's a pleasant surprise for poor Long John, and you may lay to that.

JIM: Where are my friends?

SILVER: Friends? I don't reckon you've got many friends left on this here island, Jim… exceptin' Long John Silver, of course. What friends you had you lost, Jim, when you run off against orders. Redcliff—you heard Doctor Livesey. What was it the good doctor said about our Jim?

REDCLIFF: *(Stupidly.)* Wot?

SILVER: That's right, Redcliff. He said, "We don't know if he's alive or dead and we don't much care." Them's his words exactly Redcliff, what a memory you have, man. So, Jim, the long and short of it's this: You can't go back to your own lot, because of they won't have you; and, without you start a third ship's company all by yourself, which might be lonely, you'll have to join with Cap'm Silver.

JIM: So they are alive. And if they are no longer my friends, I deserve no better, for I deserted them.

SILVER: But what of you, lad?

JIM: Am I to choose, then?

SILVER: You are to choose and you may lay to that!

JIM: Then I have the right to know why you are here and why the others are not.

MORGAN: He'd be a lucky one as knowed that!

SILVER: *(To Morgan.)* And you, sir, will batten down your hatches until you're spoke to! *(To Jim.)* Late last night, Mister Hawkins, down came Doctor Livesey to our camp with a flag of truce. Says he: "Cap'm Silver, it's all over. The ship is gone." Well, we looked up and by thunder, so it was! Then the Doctor says to me, he says, "Silver, let's talk business!" And a strange business it were, Jim. Because the end of it was—*we* gets the stockade, *we* gets the food, *we* gets the guns, and they just up and disappears into the wood, God knows where.

MORGAN: And you was a fool to let 'em go, John Silver, just like you was a fool this whole voyage long!

(Silver looks at Morgan, raises his crutch and knocks him to the ground.)

SILVER: So anyways, Mister Hawkins. What's it to be? Are you with us or no?

JIM: *With* you, Mister Silver? I'll tell you how far I'm with you. You fooled me, yes, and I'm ashamed to say it. But if you find yourself in trouble now—and you do—I'm happy to say it's because of me! You say the ship is gone, Mister Silver? Not gone, sir—far from it. It was I who cut her cable, and it was I who killed the men you had aboard of her, and it was I who brought her where you'll never see her more, not one of you.

(The men curse and move toward Jim.)

MERRY: I'll wring his bloody neck!

SILVER: Hold your tongue, George Merry! I'll hear the lad out, I will!

JIM: Oh, you may kill me, if you please. Or you may spare me, and keep a witness to save you from hanging.

DANCER: Why, the boy is just beggin' for a cut throat, ain't he!

MERRY: *(Drawing his knife.)* Well I'd be pleased to oblige him in that!

MORGAN: I says, let's do for him now!

SILVER: Avast there! Who are you, Tom Morgan? Maybe you thought you were captain here perhaps. Cross me and you'll end up like Benn Gunn!

JIM: Benn Gunn…!

SILVER: He were a friend of ourn, Jim. Oh, but he made a mistake and he died, poor man, right here on this very island some three years ago. It were very sad, Jim.

MERRY: But the boy's to blame for everything, Silver!

DANCER: No, he ain't. You want to know where to put the blame, do you. You can put it square on one man. *Captain* Long John Silver.

SILVER: *(Roaring.)* Did any of you gentlemen want to have it out with *me?* Him that wants it shall have it. I've not lived this many years to have a son of a rum puncheon cock his hat athwart my hawser *now!*
(The men stand silent and grim.)

SILVER: That's your sort, is it? Then, by thunder, you'll obey! I like this boy, now. He's more a man than any two of you here, and what I say is this: Let me see the man that'll lay a hand on him!
(Dancer taps Morgan on the shoulder and whispers into his ear.)

MORGAN: Aye, John Dancer. *(To Silver.)* Askin' your pardon, Captain Silver. This crew has rights like any other crew, and we claims our rights to step inside for a council.

DANCER: Accordin' to the rules.

SILVER: Oh, by all means, Mister Dancer. Accordin' to the rules, by all means!
(Dancer gives Silver a sea-salute and goes into the stockade, followed by Morgan.)

REDCLIFF: *(Salutes Silver.)* Foc's'le council, Mister Silver. *(Goes into stockade.)*

MERRY: By the book, Cap'm.
(Goes into the stockade. Jim and Silver Left alone.)

SILVER: Now you look here, Jim Hawkins. You're within half a plank of death and John Silver's even closer. But mark you, I'll stand by you through thick and thin. I didn't mean to—no, not till you spoke up. But then I

says to myself, you stand by Hawkins, John, and Hawkins'll stand by
you.

JIM: You mean all's lost?

SILVER: Aye, by gum, I do! You're in a tight place, and I'm so near to the gallows my neck is stiff with thinking on it. But I'll save your life—if so be I can—and you save Long John from hanging.

JIM: What I can do, that I will do!

SILVER: It's a bargain! *(Takes a flask from his hip-pocket and drinks.)* Ahh, Jim, it's a strange business, first to last. Perhaps you can answer me one thing. Why did Doctor Livesey give me the map?

JIM: *(Shocked.)* The map!

SILVER: Hush, Jim! They don't know it—but it's true enough. Here it is— Flint's map. Livesey gave it me on the sly, he did.
(John Dancer pokes his head out of the stockade.)

SILVER: Ssst! *(Silver tucks the map away.)* Well, Mister Dancer?
(The four men file out of the stockade in silence.)

SILVER: Well, come on then! I won't eat you…hand it over!
(John Dancer steps up to Silver.)

DANCER: Put out your left hand, John Silver.

SILVER: I *know* the *rules*, Mister Dancer!
(Silver puts out his hand, Dancer puts his hand over it. Then Dancer turns and steps back.)

SILVER: Well, well, well. The black spot. Say now! Where might you have got the paper? You've gone and cut this out of a Bible, you have! Oh, that's not good, gents, that's not good at all. You'll all swing now, I reckon.

MORGAN: Belay the talk, John Silver. This crew has tipped you the black spot—now you just turn it over and see what's wrote there.

SILVER: Thanky, Tom. You always was brisk for business, wasn't you, Tom boy. Well, what is it anyway? Ah! *"Deposed and dead."* It's very pretty wrote, to be sure. Your handwritin', ain't it, Tom Morgan? Why, you're gettin' quite a leadin' man in this here crew. You'll be cap'm next, I shouldn't wonder.

DANCER: That's enough, Silver!

SILVER: *(Suddenly roaring, eloquent, all his powers in play.)* What's enough, Mister Dancer? Is it enough that you and fools like you have lost our ship for us? So I'm to blame for what's wrong here, am I? Well, now— you others know what I wanted—and you all know, if we had waited like I said, we'd been aboard the *Hispaniola* this night, every man of us alive and fit, and the treasure in the hold, by thunder! Well, who crossed me? Who tipped me the black spot the day we landed? Why, it were Israel Hands and you, Tom Morgan, and you, John Dancer. And you're the last alive of that same meddling crew; and you have the insolence to stand for captain over me, Tom Morgan? By the powers, it makes me sick to think!

JIM: And that's not the half of it, is it, Long John.

SILVER: Ha haaa! No and it ain't, Jim.

JIM: Perhaps you men forget why it was you came to this island, but we haven't.

SILVER: No, and we ain't, Jim.

REDCLIFF: What are they talkin' about, Tom?

DANCER: Shut up, Redcliff!

JIM: Mister Redcliff, sir. We're talking about a map, sir.

MERRY: Map?

REDCLIFF: The map?

MORGAN: You don't...you don't have the map!

SILVER: Oh, Mister Morgan—you ain't got the imagination of a cockroach. I'm sick, Jim. They make me sick. I'm done with it. I resign, by thunder. Elect whom you please to be your captain now. I'm done.

REDCLIFF: Silver! We want you, Mister Silver!

MERRY: Aye, that we do! Silver is Captain! Only tell us, Long John...have you got that map?

SILVER: Jim, lad—give it to them, I'm sick.

JIM: *(Taking it out of Silver's vest pocket.)* Aye, sir.
(Jim gives the map to Merry. The others "leaped upon it like cats upon a mouse. It went from hand to hand, one tearing it from another; and by the oaths and the cries and the childish laughter with which they accompanied their examination, you would have thought, not only they were fingering the very gold, but were at sea with it, besides... ")

MERRY: Yes, that's Flint, sure enough. "J.F. his mark," so he done ever!

REDCLIFF: Seven hundred thousands in gold!

DANCER: "Tall tree, Spy-glass Shoulder." We've got it!

MORGAN: Yes, but what good's it to us? How do we get away with it without no ship?

MERRY: You was the one lost the ship, Tom Morgan, so you can shut up quick!

REDCLIFF: You lost the ship, and Cap'm Silver found the treasure. Now who's the better man, Tom Morgan?

DANCER: Silver! Captain Silver!

SILVER: You change your tune with the wind, John Dancer. I'll remember that.

REDCLIFF: We're with you, Cap'm Silver.

MERRY: Aye, we are that. And we've got the map, so let's march!

SILVER: But what do I do with this here black spot, gents?

(The men fall silent, chagrined.)

SILVER: Do *you* want it, Tom Morgan? No? What about you, John Dancer. No again, eh? Well then, here, Jim. Here's a little token of Treasure Island. *(He gives Jim the black spot.)* Keep it till you die, Jim. Keep it till you die.

(Lights fade.)

ACT II
SCENE VI

Lights rise on a secluded part of the island—the treasure site. A skeleton hangs suspended upside down from a standing rock, Stage Right. Benn Gunn appears at the top of the Upstage rise, looking Left and hiding from the men who are approaching from that direction. He cackles madly.

BENN GUNN: Benn Gunn'll do what he can, says I. Fine with me, says you! Hahahaha! *(He runs Downstage Right to the skeleton, lifts the bone which was its arm and points toward the treasure hole—a mound of loose dirt above an empty hole in the earth. He cackles and drops the arm. He picks up a sturdy stick and props up the skeleton's arm with it. He points the arm directly at the treasure hole and leaves it there. He cackles.)* Cheese! Benn Gunn's gonna get some cheese, says he. Fine with me, says me. Hahahaha! *(Gunn runs to the treasure hole, looks in.)* Cheese, says me! *(Takes a gold doubloon from a pouch at his side, holds it up to the light, flips it in the air and catches it. Cackles.)* A little giftie! A little giftie for an old friend!

(He drops the doubloon into the treasure hole and runs off Left. After a moment, he runs back on carrying leafy branches. He covers the hole with them, and then runs off Right, just as the pirates come into sight.)

DANCER: *(Reading from the map.)* "Tall tree, Spy-glass shoulder, bearing a point to the N. of N. N. E." The tall tree! There it is!

SILVER: Oh, Mister Dancer. You think every tree's a tall tree when you're beneath it looking up!

JIM: *(A terrified cry.)* Ohhhh!

MERRY: What is it now!

(Merry looks where Jim is pointing: at the hanging skeleton.)

MERRY: Oh, my God!

(The others see the skeleton.)

DANCER: *(A nasty scream.)* Ahhhh!

MORGAN: It's a man!

REDCLIFF: Lord help us all!

SILVER: Look there! See how the bones are propped up like. Oh, if it don't make me cold inside to think of Flint. This is one of *his* jokes, and no mistake. There's your "spy-glass shoulder," mates... After he killed this one, he made a compass out of his bones!

MORGAN: Oh, he weren't natural, were Flint!

SILVER: Stow that now! You fools are no more than ten feet from seven hundred thousands in gold! You see where the bones is pointin', don't you? Well, pace off ten feet and you're standin' in a fortune.

DANCER: *(Pointing to the treasure hole.)* There it is!

(Runs to it, throws off the branches covering it. Redcliff, Morgan, and Merry follow.)

MERRY: *(Looking down into it.)* I don't see nothin'.

(Dancer jumps down into the hole, begins digging in the dirt frantically.)

DANCER: It's gone! It's gone! There's nothing left!

(Merry, Morgan, and Redcliff all leap down into the pit and begin digging themselves. Anguished cries from the increasingly desperate men. Silver backs away from the pit, draws Jim to him.)

SILVER: *(To Jim.)* Here, Jim, boy. Take this! *(Gives Jim one of his pistols.)* Stand by for trouble!

(Morgan appears out of the pit, holding up a single doubloon.)

MORGAN: Two guineas! Two guineas! So that's your seven hundred thousand pound, is it, Silver! You're the man for bargaining, ain't you? You're him that never bungled nothing, ain't you, you bloody-minded swab!

(The other men, with dirt-covered faces and wild eyes, stand in the pit and glare up at Silver.)

SILVER: *(Cool insolence.)* Dig away, boys. You'll find some pig-nuts soon, I shouldn't wonder.

DANCER: *(In a scream.)* Pig-nuts! Pig-nuts!

MORGAN: *(To the others.)* Do you hear that? I tell you, that man there knew it all along. Look in the face of him and you'll see it wrote there!

SILVER: Ahh, Mister Morgan. Standing for captain again? You're an ambitious lad, to be sure.

(The men scramble up out of the pit. Silver and Hawkins are at one side of the excavation, the others at the other side.)

MORGAN: Mates, there's two of them alone there—one's the old cripple that brought us all here and blundered us down to this. The other's that boy—that boy that I mean to have the heart out of! Are you ready, mates?

(Morgan draws his pistol. The others do the same.)

MORGAN: The boy is mine! Now!

(Crack! A musket shot flashes out of the thicket. Morgan falters and then tumbles down into the excavation. Livesey and Smollett appear from out of the thicket on one side; Hunter and Redruth from another. Merry fires at Livesey, misses; Ben Gunn appears behind Merry, knocks him over the head

with a bludgeon, and Merry sinks to the ground. John Dancer has darted around the pit behind Jim. He grabs Jim around the neck and holds a pistol at his throat. Dancer backs off, holding Jim as a shield.)

DANCER: Stop it right there or the boy's dead.

(The men hold their fire. Silver swings around to face Dancer.)

SILVER: Mister Dancer! I'd like a word with you!

(Dancer takes the pistol from Jim's head and points it at Silver. Just as he does so, Silver swings his crutch up and knocks the pistol, flying, from Dancer's hand. Dancer cries out in pain and shakes his hand. Redruth moves in on Dancer, pulling him aside and covering him with his gun.)

REDRUTH: That'll be enough out of you, Mister Dancer!

(Hunter moves behind Redcliff with his pistol.)

HUNTER: Mister Redcliff, sir. Let go your pistol, if you please.

(Redcliff drops his gun, puts his hands in the air. Livesey rushes to Jim and holds him.)

JIM: Oh, Doctor Livesey!

SILVER: Thank you kindly, Doctor Livesey. You came in in about the nick, I guess, for Hawkins and me.

(Smollett goes to Jim, puts his hand on Jim's shoulder.)

JIM: Captain Smollett, sir!

SMOLLETT: Hello, Jim.

LIVESEY: We've been watching you all day, Jim, following you and the others on their little treasure hunt.

JIM: What?

REDRUTH: It's true, Jim! And let me tell you, we had the devil of a time keeping Doctor Livesey from rushing out and snatching you away from those rogues!

JIM: Then, you've forgiven me? For running off against orders?

(Smollett laughs.)

SMOLLETT: Jim, my lad. Every step of the way it's been you who have saved our lives. Did you suppose by any chance that we were going to let you lose yours? That would be a poor return, my boy. You found out the plot, you found Benn Gunn—the best deed that ever you did, Jim—and Benn Gunn, who sees everything that happens on this island, tells us that you have even saved us our ship!

LIVESEY: It's been said before, I know, Captain Smollett, but this boy's a trump, he is. A genuine trump!

SILVER: *(To Benn Gunn, who has been shyly edging about.)* And so, Benn Gunn! It *was* you, then. Well, you're a nice one, to be sure!

GUNN: I am Benn Gunn, I am. And…and how do, Mister Silver! Pretty well, I thank you, says you. Long time no see, says I. Right you are, says you. Right you are.

SILVER: Ahh, Benn. You never was one for conversation, was you?

GUNN: The Squire, I gave him a little nudge and he said it'll be all right!

JIM: The Squire! Where is Squire Trelawney?

LIVESEY: He's guarding something that Benn Gunn dug up and hid some three years ago, Jim. The treasure of Treasure Island. Squire Trelawney, old fellow! You can come out now!

(The Squire appears at the top of the rise, lugging an enormous chest.)

SQUIRE: Someone help me with this blessed thing, will you?

(Redruth goes to him and helps him carry the chest Downstage Center.)

JIM: Squire Trelawney!

SQUIRE: Well, Jim! How de do, Jim! We've missed you, Hawkins, and that's a fact!

(Jim hugs the Squire. Then turns back to Livesey and Smollett.)

JIM: Doctor Livesey! Captain Smollett! Long John Silver is not what he should be and that's for certain. But he did save my life, and more than once.

SILVER: Thankee, Jim. Much obliged for that.

SMOLLETT: It will be taken into consideration, I assure you, Hawkins.

JIM: And Captain Smollett, sir?

SMOLLETT: Yes, Jim?

JIM: Can we go home now?

(The men burst out laughing.)

SMOLLETT: Very soon, Jim, very soon! And just think what your mother will say when she sees you, Jim Hawkins!

(The men laugh again, the music begins, and the lights begin to fade. The men all exit Upstage over the rise and off, with Jim in the rear. He turns back at last, and looks at his Treasure Island as the lights fade.)

VOICE OF JIM HAWKINS: *(During the exit of the men above.)* What my mother had to say took her three full days to say it in. As for Long John Silver—well, he was a pretty prisoner, to be sure. After only a few days of our homeward journey, he took a sack-full of gold doubloons in the dead of night, lowered one of the small boats, and slipped clean away. It was Squire Trelawney, Doctor Livesey, and the Captain who asked me to tell this whole story of Treasure Island. It was not a difficult task, for even now I can hear the sea crashing about its rugged coasts, and the sharp voice of Silver's parrot, crying, "Pieces of eight!" Besides, I still have that

tattered black spot that Long John gave me, and I shall keep it...I shall keep it till I die.
(Curtain down.)

END OF PLAY

Mark Twain's

The Adventures of Tom Sawyer

Directed by John Clark Donahue
Music Composed and Arranged by Roberta Carlson
Set Design by Dahl Delu

THE CHARACTERS

* Tom Sawyer, 11–14 years old
* Huckleberry Finn, 12–15 years old
* Mark Twain
* Aunt Polly
* Sid, 9–11 years old
  Jim, 9–12 years old
* Muff Potter
* Injun Joe
  Doc Robinson
  Mr. Dobbins
* Becky Thatcher, 11–14 years old
* Joe Harper, 11–14 years old
  Reverend Forbes
  Judge Thatcher
  Mrs. Harper
  Prosecutor
* Defender (Mark Twain)
  Other Children and Adults, Inhabitants of St. Petersburg, Missouri
  (Amy Lawrence, Ben Rogers, Susan Harper, Gracie Miller, Will Hanley,
  Jack Taylor, Hank, Sheriff Thompkins, Mother Hopkins, Riverboat
  Captain, Riverboat Crewman, etc.)

* *Denotes principal roles.*

This is a large-cast show, and I leave it to the ingenuity of the director to
double-and treble-cast actors to fill out the town of St. Petersburg.

THE SINGER

The Singer referred to throughout the script is the *musical narrative.* It may
be a single tenor voice, or a small instrumental and vocal ensemble,
depending on the form selected. In the original production, the Singer was
actually three costumed musicians, inhabitants of St. Petersburg; a fiddler, a
banjo player, and a guitar player; they also played harmonica and ham-bone
percussion; one was a tenor and another a bass. They moved in and out of
the action of the play, just as Mr. Twain both narrates and participates.

THE SETTING

The Mississippi River is the dominant unseen character in the play. A series of levels and platforms, all constructed of rough-hewn planks and all suggestive of a river wharf. Scattered hanging ropes and tackles. The set facilitates the almost continuous scene-to-scene flow of the script, with the assistance of area lighting and directorial focus.

General scenic locations are indicated in the script by the following labels:

The Slope (a series of broad steps which become the school room, courtroom, hillside, Aunt Polly's sitting room, etc.)

The Graveyard (at the top of the slope, also serves as preacher's pulpit, judge's bench, island lookout, etc.)

Center Pier (broad Down Center playing area, a portion of which lifts up from the floor to form the whitewash fence.)

The Cave (an opening just Left of Center, beneath the graveyard, used throughout the play for exits and entrances, a street, etc., before it becomes the dark gaping mouth of the cave.)

Upper Pier Left (which is also the singer's platform)

Lower Pier Left

Upper Pier Right (which is Tom's bedroom, the church choir loft, etc.)

Lower Pier Right

The Adventures of Tom Sawyer has a running time of one hour and forty-five minutes, including intermission.

For information concerning the original score by Roberta Carlson, contact The Children's Theatre Company of Minneapolis.

The Adventures
of Tom Sawyer

SCENE I

A single fiddle begins the hymn tune in the darkness. Then it is joined by the Singer.

SINGER: Shall we gather at the river
 Where bright angel feet have trod
 With the crystal tide forever
 Flowing by the throne of god
  Yes! We will gather by the river
 The beautiful, the beautiful river...
 (The distant barking of a dog. The Singer continues beneath the following speech, gradually fading.)

MR. TWAIN: St. Petersburg, Missouri. A shabby little village on the banks of the Mississippi. Eighteen forty-two, or thereabouts. I forget.
 (A distant indistinguishable shout of a mother calling her child home.)

MR. TWAIN: My name is Mark Twain, and I once wrote a story called *The Adventures of Tom Sawyer*. Some of you may have read that book. Others not. It is not a matter of great significance. Because I am going to tell it to you now. As best I can remember...Remember...St. Petersburg, and summer, and a boy, and the whole blessed town, early in June, eighteen forty-two. Or forty-three. I forget.

TOM SAWYER: *(In the graveyard area with Huck Finn.)* How does it go, Huck?

HUCK: Barley-corn, barley-corn, injun-meal shorts.
 Spunk-water, spunk-water, swaller these warts...
 (Lights on them fade.)

TWAIN: Remember a white-lace petticoat and a pair of pigtails, oh, Becky...
 (Becky Thatcher runs into a pool of light on the Center pier.)

BECKY: All right, Tom. I'll whisper it in your ear. But you must promise you'll never tell, will you, Tom? Ever? Ever and forever and forever...
 (She runs off and her light fades. It is replaced by a harsh midafternoon glare surrounding the cave entrance. Several men lean against posts and squat on the ground.)

TWAIN: Forever and ever…Remember…Muff Potter, forever drunk and in need of tobacco.

MUFF: Gimme a chaw'v tobacker, Hank.

HANK: Cain't. I hain't got but one chaw left, Muff. Ask Jack.

MUFF: I wisht you'd len' me a chaw, Jack, I jist this minute give Ben Thompson the last chaw I had…

JACK: You give him a chaw, did you? So did yer dead sister's cat's grandmother. You pay me back the chaws you've already borry'd off'n me, Muff Potter, and I'll loan you one or two ton of it.
(Lights on them fade.)

TWAIN: I remember a fella the townsfolk called Injun Joe. They called him Injun Joe cause they didn't like him. They didn't like him cause he was an Injun. That's what the God-fearing folk of St. Petersburg called logic. You figure it out, I can't.
(Lights rise on Injun Joe cornered by three men.)

JACK: The sun done set, half-breed. What you doin', still in town?

SHERIFF: You know the law, Injun Joe.

HANK: No Injuns or breeds 'lowed here 'bouts after sundown, now git!

INJUN JOE: I put in a day's work for you, Matthews, I come for my pay an' you know it.

SHERIFF: Too late, Joe. After sundown, don't owe you nothin'.

INJUN JOE: I come for my pay!
(Man One pulls a pistol.)

JACK: Git!

INJUN JOE: You'll pay. By an' by, I swear you'll pay.
(Joe turns and walks away with as much dignity as he can muster. Man Two picks up a clod of dirt and throws it at Joe's back—the three men laugh. Lights on the men fade.)

TWAIN: St. Petersburg, on the banks of the Mississippi. Summertime, eighteen forty-two, or maybe forty-three, I forget. I do remember…the Sabbath day.
(Lights up on the Preacher, standing at the top of the slope. The Choir sits in pews on the upper Right pier.)

PREACHER: *(A universal preacher's intonation.)* Remember the Sabbath-day, to keep it holy.
Which of you, by being anxious, can add one cubit to his span of life?
And why are ye troubled over what ye shall put on?
Consider the lilies of the field…
They neither toil nor do they spin…

Yet I say unto you, not even Solomon in aaallll his glory...

TWAIN: *(Suddenly appearing amid the choir on the upper Right pier.)* I remember Solomon in all his glory. Who wouldn't?

PREACHER: You there! In the choir! Please to hesh up!

TWAIN: *(Rising and walking down to the edge of the pier.)* The choir always tittered and whispered all through the services.

(A high female titter from the choir.)

TWAIN: There was once a church choir that was not bad-mannered, but I have forgotten where it was, now. It was a great many years ago, and I think it was in some foreign country.

THE CHOIR: Yes, we will gather by the river,

The beautiful, the beautiful river...

(Lights on Choir fade.)

TWAIN: The river! I remember the river!

(With whoops and cries and musical accompaniment on the banjo and fiddle, five boys run across the uppermost platform, leap Upstage in the air and plummet down into the river, with the sound of a great splash.)

TWAIN: The river and summer and summer nights thick with fog.

(All lights grow dim and murky and tinged with blue. The sound of a paddle-wheel steamboat on the river, a fog horn, and muffled shouts.)

RIVERBOAT CREWMAN: *(Standing with a measuring line on the lower Left pier.)* Half twain! Half twain! Half twain!

RIVERBOAT CAPTAIN: *(Standing on the upper Left pier, above the Crewman.)* Let her go about!

CREWMAN: Let her go about! East, starboard! Strong on the larboard! Starboard, give way!

CAPTAIN: Cramp her up to the bar! What are you standing up through the middle of the river for?

CREWMAN: Starboard, give way!

CAPTAIN: Whar'n the hell you goin' to? Cain't you see nothin', you egg-suckin', sheep-stealin', one-eyed son of a stuffed monkey!

(Lights on Captain and Crewman begin to fade, river sounds continue at lower level.)

TWAIN: *(In a pool of light on the lower Right pier.)* I wished I could talk like that.

CREWMAN: *(From the near-darkness.)* Mark twain!

TWAIN: *Bless* my soul, I wished I could talk like that.

(All river sounds fade.)

SINGER: Shall we gather at the river
That flows by the throne of god…

TWAIN: St. Petersburg. A little village in Missouri, so shabby that if I were given the choice of spending eternity in Heaven or there, I'd take St. Petersburg every time.

HUCK: *(Running on past Twain, with Tom following close behind.)* No, no, no! That ain' it!
Barley-corn, barley-corn, injun-meal shorts,
Spunk-water, spunk-water, swaller these warts…
and then you walk away quick, seven steps, with your eyes shut, and turn around three times, and all your warts is gone!

TOM: Well, it sounds right. Did you ever try it, Huck?

HUCK: No, but old Mother Hopkins told me.

TOM: Mother Hopkins! Well, I reckon it *is* right then. Becuz they say she's a witch.

HUCK: Say? Why, Tom, I *know* she's a witch…
(The boys part company with a ritualistic gesture that should be repeated at various times throughout the play: They both lick the tips of their thumbs and then press the thumbs together. Tom runs up the slope into darkness. Huck crosses Left slowly as Twain makes the following speech.)

TWAIN: Mother Hopkins wasn't quite what you'd call refined. Mother Hopkins wasn't quite what you'd call unrefined. Mother Hopkins was the kind of person that keeps a parrot.
(Mother Hopkins jumps out of the shadows beneath the upper Left pier, parrot on her shoulder squawks, Huck jumps and runs off. Light on her fades. Light on Tom in his bedroom rises.)

TOM: Lemme see.
Barley-corn, barley-corn, injun-meal shorts,
Spunk-water, spunk-water, swaller these warts!
(He examines his hands.) Must be it takes some time to work. *(He looks up and notices the Singer on the upper Left pier.)* Howdy.

SINGER: Howdy, Tom.

TOM: *(Addressing the audience directly.)* Anyway, my name is Tom Sawyer, and Mr. Twain, he put me in a book. And some of what he wrote is even true. As for the rest of it…well…Mr. Twain says that he was born honest. But it wore off later on. I don't know nothin' about that, but I'm glad he put my friend, Huck, in it. And Aunt Polly and my half-brother, Sid. Though I don't much care for him. I'm even glad he put Injun Joe in it, cuz what kind of a story would it be without him?

The Adventures of Tom Sawyer 181

(Lights on him fade.)

TWAIN: Summertime. St. Petersburg. The Mississippi, and a boy named Sawyer. Tom Sawyer.

(During the preceding speech, Twain walks up the slope. As he passes, Aunt Polly appears, wiping her hands on her apron.)

AUNT POLLY: Tom? Tom! *(She bustles past him down the slope.)*

TWAIN: He was not the Model Boy of the village.

AUNT POLLY: You—Tom! I never did see the beat of that boy! You-u-u-u *Tom!*

TWAIN: Oh, the village *had* its Model Boy. And he had our undivided contempt.

SID: *(Coming down from his bedroom to Aunt Polly.)* Tom's hiding in the fruit cellar, Mother. He's been into the jam.

AUNT POLLY: *(With barely disguised distaste.)* Thank you, Sid. *(Shouting into the fruit cellar.)* You—Tom! *(She pulls Tom out by an ear.)*

TOM: I'll *get you* for *that*, Sid. *See* if I don't.

AUNT POLLY: *Tom!* Look *at* your hands! And look at your mouth! What *is* that truck?

TOM: I don't know, Aunt Polly.

AUNT POLLY: Well I do. It's jam—that's what it is. Forty times I've said if you didn't let that jam alone I'd skin you. Hand me that switch. *(The mimed switch is produced, Aunt Polly brandishes it above Tom, the peril is desperate.)*

TOM: *(Pointing Offstage.)* My gracious! Look a' there, Aunt Polly!

AUNT POLLY: *(Whirling around and shrieking.)* What is it!

(Tom gives one jab to Sid's belly, two to his ear, jumps up, runs Right past Sid, catches hold of upper pier Right, spins and drops to the floor.)

SID: Owww!

AUNT POLLY: Tom!

TOM: *(Whooping like an Indian.)* Woo-woo-woo-woo-woo-woo-woo!

(He turns and runs off. Aunt Polly stands surprised for a moment, then begins to laugh. Sid is whimpering.)

AUNT POLLY: Hang that boy, can't I never learn anything? Ah, but old fools is the biggest fools there is. *(To Sid.)* What are you carrying on for, boy? You ain't gonna die from it, I suppose. Now get off with you and get to school.

SID: *(Sulking.)* Yes, ma'am. *(Sid turns and mopes slowly off.)*

AUNT POLLY: And make sure Tom gets there, too!

SID: *(Instantly jubilant.)* Oh, yes, ma'am, I shore will, ma'am! *(He runs out.)*

AUNT POLLY: *(Sweeping the down Right pier with a real broom.)* I ain't doin' my duty by Tom Sawyer, and that's the Lord's truth. But laws-a-me, he's my own dead sister's boy, poor thing, and I ain't got the heart to thrash him, somehow. Though I oughter. And if it's the Lord's will I thrash that boy, then I just will…the next time. Only I pray the Lord Tom don't make me laugh again—it's so dang hard to hit him when I'm a-laughin'.

SCENE II

Continuous with the preceding. A rush of children from Left to Right, laughing and shouting, schoolbooks in their arms. Cries of "Morning, Miss Polly!" They exit off Right, Aunt Polly climbs the slope and exits. Doc Robinson appears beneath the upper Right pier. He looks about him furtively and then motions to the dark shapes behind him in the shadows. They come down and join him on the lower Right pier: Muff Potter and Injun Joe.

DOC ROBINSON: What the devil are you two hounding me in the streets for? And in broad daylight! You have your instructions!

MUFF POTTER: Oh, we got yer instrukshuns awright, Doc. We jist ain't got yer money yet.

DOC ROBINSON: I told you I'd make payment when you'd finished your work, Muff Potter.

MUFF: Well, what you tol' us and what we wants is two diff'rent things, seemin'ly.

INJUN JOE: You give us that money now, Robinson.

ROBINSON: You listen to me, Joseph…

INJUN JOE: *Injun* Joe is good enough for me, *Doc.*

ROBINSON: *(After a brief hesitation.)* Oh, curse you both! *(He takes bills from his pocket.)* There! Five dollars. And see you don't spend it on whiskey, Muff Potter. You're no good to me drunk.

INJUN JOE: Oh, we're plenty good to you, *Doctor* Robinson. You couldn't do without us, I reckon.

ROBINSON: Now leave me alone…

INJUN JOE: Till tomorrow night, Doc. In the graveyard, with two shovels and a pine box.

ROBINSON: …And don't ever talk to me in the street again!

(Robinson strides off Upstage Center to the mouth of the cave, where Tom and Huck have just appeared. Injun Joe and Muff Potter fall back into the shadows beneath the pier and vanish.)

TOM: Mornin', Doc.

ROBINSON: *(Startled.)* What? Oh. Good morning, Thomas. Huckleberry.

(Robinson exits Upstage through the cave.)

HUCK: *(With a gratified chuckle.)* That Doc Robinson—he allas treats me like I was folks. I like that in a man, makes me feel good.

SID: *(Running down out of cave to the boys, but keeping his distance.)* Tom—you git on to school!

TOM: I don't gotta mind you, Sid!

SID: I'm tellin' Aunt Polly you talkin' with the riffraff!

HUCK: *(Picking Sid up by the back of his trousers.)* Riffraff!

(Sid "runs" without getting anywhere.)

HUCK: You best keep on runnin, boy!

(Huck releases Sid, who edges past and then breaks into a run, Right. Tom mimes picking up clods of dirt and hurtling them after Sid.)

TOM: I'll lick you, Sid! I swear I will!

(Exit Sid Right. Enter Mark Twain, Right, dusting off his white jacket which has received the benefit of Tom's anger—real dirt on his jacket.)

TWAIN: *(To the Audience.)* It's a bombardment. It's an outrage. It's dirt.

(A light on Huck alone, amusing himself. Perhaps he flaps his wings like a bird, turns his back to the audience and pees, lights his pipe and checks the contents of the sack he carries. All this slowly, in a contemplative fashion, while Twain speaks.)

TWAIN: That creature there is Huckleberry Finn, son of the town drunkard. Huckleberry comes and goes as he pleases—he does not have to go to school, or to church, and there is no one to tell him to wash or to put on a clean shirt. He knows how to smoke a pipe and he can swear wonderfully. In short, everything that goes to make life precious, that boy has. Huckleberry is cordially hated by all the mothers in St. Petersburg, because he is idle and lawless and vulgar and bad—and because all their children love him. Tom, of course, is under strict orders not to play with him.

(We see Tom poke his head out from behind a post.)

TWAIN: So he plays with him every chance he gets.

(Tom runs up to the graveyard platform to join Huck. Twain walks slowly off Left.)

TOM: What's that you got in the bag, Huck?

HUCK: Dead cat.

TOM: Lemme see him. *(Tom digs in the sack and comes out with a rigid cat.)* My, he's pretty stiff. Where'd you get him?

HUCK: Bought him off'n a boy.

TOM: Say—what is dead cats good for, Huck?

HUCK: Cure warts with.

TOM: Bob Tanner tried it with a dead cat, and it didn't work.

HUCK: Bob Tanner is the wartiest boy in this town. Bob Tanner wouldn't have a wart on him if'n he know how to *work* dead cats.

TOM: How *do* you do it, Huck?

HUCK: Well, you jist take yer cat and go to the graveyard 'long about midnight when somebody that was wicked has been buried. And when it's midnight, a devil will come, or mebby two or three, and when they're takin' that wicked feller away, you throw yer cat after 'em and say "Devil follow corpse, cat follow devil, warts follow cat, *I'm* done with you." Shoot. Fetch any wart.

TOM: Say, Huck. When you going to try that cat?

HUCK: Tomorrer night. They're a-buryin' old Hoss Williams, and *he* was wicked enough, I reckon.

TOM: Kin I go with?

HUCK: O'course—if you ain't afeard.

TOM: That ain't likely. Will you meow beneath my winda?

HUCK: I suppose—but you meow back this time. Last time, you kep' me a meowin' around till the neighbors went to throwin' rocks at me.

TOM: I will, Huck, for sure this time. Tomorrer night.

HUCK: Tomorrer night.

TOM: *(Running Offstage.)* Meee-oow!

SCENE III

In an instant, the school children spill over the top of the uppermost platform and down the slope into the schoolroom, noisily taking their seats. Mr. Dobbins appears, Right, standing at his desk. He brings his stick down on the desk with a crack and all is silent.

MR. DOBBINS: Children?

CHILDREN: *(Singsong unison.)* Good morning, Mr. Dobbins.

DOBBINS: *Decent* children sit up straight in their seats, like little soldiers.

CHILDREN: *(Readjusting themselves to imitate little soldiers.)* Yes, sir, Mr. Dobbins.

DOBBINS: *Decent* children don't slouch in their seats like Joe Harper there. Stand up, Harper.

JOE: *(Standing.)* Yes, sir.

DOBBINS: *(Standing above him.)* Now, class. Is this boy a good little soldier?

CHILDREN: *(Drearily.)* No, sir.

DOBBINS: No, indeed. Sit down, Harper.

(Joe Harper sits. Mr. Dobbins continues his rounds.)

DOBBINS: Oh, oh, oh. I see one little girl who is looking out the window. I am afraid she thinks that I am out there somewhere—perhaps up in one of the trees, making a speech to the little birds...

(Mr. Dobbins enjoys his own devastating wit for a moment. Polite titter from the class. Dobbins suddenly interrupts it with a crash of his stick on the desk.)

DOBBINS: Silence!

(There is silence.)

DOBBINS: Amy Lawrence.

(She pops up out of her seat.)

DOBBINS: Spell the word, "latitude."

AMY: "Latitude." L-A-T-I-T-U-D.

(Mr. Dobbins harpoons a glance at her.)

AMY: E. "Latitude." *(She sits down.)*

DOBBINS: Joe Harper?

(Joe Harper stands. As he does so, Dobbins turns his back and two boys on either side of Harper tickle him.)

DOBBINS: What is the meaning of the word..."latitude."

JOE: *(Trying to recover.)* Oh, uh..."latitude. "L-A-T-I-T—"

DOBBINS: Joe Harper!

JOE: Uh, yes sir, Mr. Dobbins? What was it you wanted to know again?

DOBBINS: Sit down, Harper!

(He attempts to do so, but the boy to his Right has placed a ruler on end for Joe to sit on. Joe springs up again.)

DOBBINS: Harper!

JOE: Yes, sir.

DOBBINS: Sit down!

JOE: *(Doing so.)* Yes, sir.

DOBBINS: You will write forty lines. "I will not be such a fool in the future."

JOE: Yes, sir.

DOBBINS: The rest of you. Open your readers to page twenty-one.

(The children open their books and bend over them studiously. In the subsequent hush, Tom Sawyer appears at the top of the uppermost platform.)

DOBBINS: Sawyer! Come here!

(Tom hesitates, begins to do an about-face.)

DOBBINS: Thomas Sawyer! Come back here at once!

(Tom turns back and descends the slope until he is face to face with Dobbins at his desk.)

DOBBINS: Well. What was it this time, to make you so late? Hmm? Is your Aunt Polly on her deathbed again? Like she was on Tuesday? Or did you stop to give a basket of eggs and ham to a poor family, as you so kindly did on Monday?

TOM: *(After a slight hesitation and a backward glance at Becky Thatcher.)* No. sir. No…I stopped…I stopped to talk to Huckleberry Finn!

(A gasp from students and teacher alike, and then a dreadful pause.)

DOBBINS: *(Quietly, with relish.)* This is the most astonishing confession I have ever heard! You will be whipped, boy! You will remain after school to be whipped!

TOM: Yes, sir.

DOBBINS: And in the meantime, you can go sit with the *girls*.

(Titter from the class, catcalls as Tom makes his way into the girls' section. He sits down next to Becky Thatcher and the lights on the schoolroom fade. A thin, lyrical melody from the fiddle.)

TWAIN: Which, of course, was exactly what Tom wanted. A seat next to a lovely blue-eyed creature named Becky Thatcher. Until a week ago, Tom had loved a certain Amy Lawrence. To distraction. He would have gladly died for her. But of course, that was last week.

(Lights on Tom and Becky intensify, remain dim on the rest of the class.)

TOM: Do you like rats?

BECKY: Rats? Of course not! I hate them!

TOM: *(Switching tactics.)* Oh! Well, o'course, I hate 'em too. *Live* ones. But I mean, dead ones, to swing around yer head with a string.

BECKY: No, I mostly don't care for rats either way. What *I* like is chewing gun.

TOM: Oh, I should say so! I wisht I had some right now.

BECKY: Do you? I've got some. I'll let you chew it awhile, but you have to give it back.

(The wad of chewing gum changes hands furtively.)

TOM: It's all right. Nobody's lookin'. Say, Becky, was you ever engaged?

BECKY: What?

TOM: Engaged to be married.

BECKY: Why, no.

TOM: Would you like to?

BECKY: I suppose so. I don't know. What's it like?

TOM: Like? Why it ain't like anything. You only just tell a boy that you love him forever and ever, and then you kiss and that's all there is to it. Shoot. It's easy.

BECKY: What do you have to kiss for?

TOM: Why, that's, *you* know—well, they *always* do it.

BECKY: Everybody?

TOM: Why, sure! Come on, say you love me.

BECKY: No!

TOM: Please?

BECKY: ...Tomorrow.

TOM: No, *now*. Just whisper it, that's all.

BECKY: Well, you turn your face away so you can't see. And you mustn't ever tell anybody—will you, Tom? Ever?

(Tom shakes his head. Becky leans close to his ear and whispers.)

TOM: Hooo-ee! Now it's all over but the kiss, and that ain't nothin' at all.

(Tom raises Becky's slate in front of their faces and they kiss behind it.)

TOM: See? Ain't it nice to be engaged?

BECKY: Oh, Tom it's ever so nice! I never even heard of it before.

TOM: Oh, shoot. It's lots of fun. Why, when me and Amy Lawrence was engag... *(Tom suddenly realizes his blunder.)*

BECKY: Oh, Tom! You mean I ain't the first girl you've ever been engaged to? *(She bursts into tears.)*

TOM: Don't cry, Becky! Me and Amy. we wasn't *really* engaged, not like you and me...

(Mr. Dobbins appears directly behind Tom like one of the avenging angels. He takes Tom by the ears and slowly lifts him out of his seat.)

DOBBINS: Becky Thatcher?

BECKY: *(Cowering with fright.)* Yes, sir.

DOBBINS: This boy bothering you?

BECKY: *(Relieved.)* Oh. Oh, yes! That's for certain, Mr. Dobbins, he certainly *was* botherin' me...

(The action shifts to slow motion and although people's mouths move, no sound comes out. Mr. Dobbins, in slow motion, shaking Tom back and forth, Becky looking on, a low light on the other school children reveals them laughing, pointing, jeering with grotesque exaggeration.)

SINGER: Blest be the tie that binds

Our hearts in Christian love.

The fellowship of kindred minds

Is like to that above.

TWAIN: Let us draw the curtain of charity over the remainder of this scene.

(The lights on the schoolroom fade.)

(Twain joins in singing the next verse.)

SINGER & TWAIN: We share our mutual woes,

Our mutual burdens bear,

And often for each other flows

The sympathizing tear.

(All lights fade except on Twain.)

TWAIN: Tom was miserable. It seemed to him that his life was nothing but trouble. In fact, he would almost be willing to pass on into a better world, right there and then, if only his Sunday-school record were clean. Which it wasn't. Oh, she would be sorry some day—they'd all be sorry—when it was too late. Tom went to bed that night devoutly wishing that he could die—but temporarily, temporarily…

SCENE IV

Tom in his bed. His vision.

DOC ROBINSON: *(Closing up his black bag and departing.)* I'm sorry, Aunt Polly. I'm afraid there's nothing more we can do. That sore toe has mortified beyond recall. He was a splendid lad.

(Robinson leaves. Aunt Polly kneels beside Tom's bed.)

AUNT POLLY: Oh, Tom, Tom—don't leave us now! I'm sorry for all those thrashings and scoldings I gave you, Tom—please, please…

TOM: *(In a faint and holy voice.)* That don't matter none, Aunt Polly. I know you liked Sid best, and I don't blame you.

AUNT POLLY: No, Tom, no!

TOM: I forgive you. I forgive you all.

MR. DOBBINS: Thomas Sawyer was the finest student I ever had. Oh, if only I hadn't treated him so badly. Thomas, if you'll only come back, you may sit at the head of the class…at the head of the class…Sid! Sidney! Stop scratching your nose! Can't you be a good little soldier, like Tom here?

AUNT POLLY: Sid! Go sit in the cellar!

TOM: No, Aunt Polly. Don't send him away. He can't help the way he is.

AUNT POLLY: *(With a melodramatic gasp.)* Ahhh! Here *she* comes!

(Becky Thatcher, with a wrapped present.)

BECKY: Oh, Tom, I didn't mean to be so cruel! I love you, Tom, forever and ever! I brought you a present, Tom. Please take it, and say you forgive me. I wrapped it up special for you, Tom. It's a package of chewing gum and a dead rat. Please, Tom...

(Tom puts a hand to his brow and turns away.)

AUNT POLLY: *(Shaking him gently by his nightgown, and sobbing piteously.)* Oh, Tom! Tom! Tom!

SCENE V

All the others vanish. Aunt Polly's voice changes to an angry tone. She is still shaking Tom.

AUNT POLLY: Tom! Tom! You—Tom! Wake up, you idle thing! Did you expect to sleep clear through Saturday?

TOM: *(Dreamily.)* I forgive you, Aunt Polly.

AUNT POLLY: You forgive *me?* What a notion! I'll forgive you when you've whitewashed that fence like I told you to.

TOM: But what about my mortified toe?

AUNT POLLY: Your *what?*

TOM: You mean...I'm gonna live?

AUNT POLLY: I am distinctly afraid that that is the case, Tom Sawyer. Now git up outta that bed, you ridiculous creature! And take your mortified toe with you! Forgive *me,* indeed!

(She leaves the bedroom, Tom pulling on his trousers beneath his nightgown, then pulling the nightgown over his head.)

AUNT POLLY: *Two* coats a' whitewash, Tom! You hear me?

(Aunt Polly collides with Twain on her way out.)

AUNT POLLY: Oh! My gracious, I nearly run you down!

TWAIN: That you did, Miss Polly, that you did. You're a tropical storm this morning, Miss Polly—and I pity the man or boy who gets in your way.

AUNT POLLY: *(Delighted.)* Oh, the way you talk, sir. I declare, it's almost a pleasure to listen to your foolishness...

(Jim runs between them.)

AUNT POLLY: Jim! *(To Twain.)* I beg your pardon.

(To Jim, who has halted in his tracks.)

AUNT POLLY: Jim, get a bucket and fetch the water from town.

JIM: Yes'm.

AUNT POLLY: And Jim…

(Jim goes to her. She excuses herself to Twain.)

AUNT POLLY: Pardon me. *(She whispers something in Jim's ear.)*

JIM: Yes'm, Miss Polly. Doan you worry 'bout that. *(Jim runs Offstage.)*

TWAIN: Good day to you, Miss Polly.

AUNT POLLY: Good day to you, sir.

(Aunt Polly exits off the slope, Upstage Center. A little girl jumps rope Downstage from Left to Right and Off. Twain walks down Center. He stoops and lifts up a portion of the plank floor, which is counterweighted, to form the white-wash fence. He gives the audience a meaningful look and then exits Upstage Center, puffing on his cigar. Tom Sawyer enters from Downstage Left, carrying a bucket and brush. He stops in front of the fence and surveys it with dismay. "Buffalo Gals" starts up on the banjo.)

TOM: *(Grieving.)* Jiminy. *(To the Audience.)* A body could grow old and die before he was finished with this here fence.

(Tom dips his brush in the bucket—there is no whitewash in it, by the way—and makes a pass at the fence. Then another, and then a third swipe. He steps back to look at his work—compares the insignificant "whitewash streak" with the far-reaching continent of the un-whitewashed fence, and sits down on a lower step of the slope, utterly discouraged. Jim enters from Left with a tin pail, singing "Buffalo Gals" on his way to the town pump.)

JIM: Buffalo gal, won't you come out tonight,

Come out tonight,

Come out tonight?

Buffalo gal, won't you come out tonight,

And dance by the light of the moon…

TOM: Hey, Jim.

JIM: Howdy, Tom.

TOM: Say, Jim, I'll fetch the water for you, if you'll whitewash some.

JIM: Cain't Tom. Miss Polly, she tole me I got to go an' git dis water an' not to stop foolin' round wid nobody. She say she spec' you going to ax me to whitewash, an' she tole me to get along and not let you do it.

TOM: Oh, never mind what she said, Jim. That's the way she always talks. Gimme that bucket—I won't be gone only a minute. *She* won't ever know.

JIM: Uh-uh. Miss Polly, she'd take an' tar de head off'n me, she would.

TOM: Oh, shoot! She never licks anybody. Only whack's 'em over the head with her thimble, and who cares for that, I'd like to know. Jim—I'll give you a marble. I'll give you this white alley!

JIM: That's a mighty nice marble.

TOM: A white alley, Jim!

JIM: But I'm powerful 'fraid a' Miss Polly...

TOM: And besides, if you whitewash some, I'll show you my sore toe!

JIM: *(Genuinely excited now.)* Your sore toe! You mean it?

(Tom squats to unwind the bandage around his toe. Jim bends over it with consuming interest. Aunt Polly appears unseen by the boys. She elaborately creeps up behind them, fitting a thimble over her middle finger as she goes. Crack! It comes down on Jim's head, followed by a mild slap to his rear. Jim picks up his bucket and runs off while Polly gives a perfunctory twist to one of Tom's ears. Tom begins whitewashing furiously, even while she has hold of his ear.)

AUNT POLLY: That's a mighty fine start you got there, Tom. Remember now, *two* coats.

(Aunt Polly retires, triumphant. Enter Joe Harper, eating an apple and imitating a riverboat.)

JOE: Ding, ding, ding, ding! Let her go about! Ding, ding, ding! (Breaking *off.*) Hey, Tom.

(No answer from Tom.)

JOE: You're up a stump, ain't you!

(No response from Tom, who is suddenly very fastidious about his labors.)

JOE: Hey, Tom! You got to *work*, huh?

TOM: *(Wheeling around suddenly.)* What? Oh! It's *you*, Joe. I weren't noticing.

JOE: Sure you weren't. Say, Tom, I'm goin' in a-swimmin'. Wanna come?— Oh, no! I suppose you'd druther work, wouldn't you...

TOM: *(He resumes whitewashing.)* Whatta you call work?

JOE: *(A little hesitation.)* Why...ain't *that* work?

TOM: *(Punctuating the following with strokes of his brush.)* Mebbe...mebbe not. All I know is, it suits Tom Sawyer.

JOE: Oh, come on...you don't mean to let on that you *like* it?

TOM: Like it? Don't see why I oughtn't to like it. Does a boy get a chance to whitewash a fence every day?

JOE: *(After a considerable pause, watching Tom.)* Say, Tom...let *me* whitewash a little.

TOM: Mmmm...no. No, I reckon it wouldn't hardly do, Joe. You see, Aunt Polly's awful particular about this fence—right here on the street and all...If it was the back fence, I wouldn't, and *she* wouldn't mind...buuuut...

JOE: Oh, come on…lemme just try. I'd let you, if you was me, Tom.

TOM: *(So sincere.)* Joe, I'd like to, honest injun. But Aunt Polly—well, Jim wanted to do it, but she wouldn't let him. Sid wanted to do it, and she wouldn't let Sid. Now, if you was to tackle this fence and anything was to happen to it…

JOE: Oh, shucks. I'll be careful. I'll give you half my apple if you let me.

TOM: No. *Joe,* now don't. I'm afreard…

JOE: I'll give you *all* my apple!

TOM: Welllll…

(Tom hands over the brush, takes the apple. As Joe begins to work, Tom settles himself comfortably on the slope, apple in mouth, legs dangling. Then he sings.)

TOM: Buffalo gal, won't you come out tonight,

Come out tonight,

Come out tonight?

("Buffalo Gal" is taken up on the banjo, and from this point until the "freeze" at the end of the scene, it gradually accelerates in tempo. Enter Ben Rogers, carrying a kite. He stops before Joe Harper, who hardly looks up from his labors.)

BEN: Hey, Joe. Whatcha doin'?

JOE: Hmm? Oh. Tom is lettin' me whitewash his fence for'm.

BEN: Whatta you mean, he's *lettin'* ya?

JOE: I give him an apple for a chance at it. Now don't bother me, Ben. You gotta be careful with these fences.

(Ben stands and watches Joe work.)

TOM: *(To himself.)* Buffalo gal, won't you come out tonight,

And dance by the light of the moon…

(Ben looks at the fence, at Joe, at Tom, at the fence, at his kite. He squats down by Tom.)

BEN: Hey, Tom. I'll give you my kite if I kin whitewash some.

TOM: *(Examining the kite.)* Welll, I don't know…

(Tom capitulates and produces a brush for Ben to work with. The scene at this point assumes a certain stylization, performed in mime from now on to the quickening pace of the banjo. Boy after boy enters, observes, barters with Tom and receives a brush—the "miraculous" store of brushes is concealed just up of the fence, Tom unobtrusively reaches behind it for them. By about the fifth time through "Buffalo Gals" the tempo is frantic and the actions of the boys painting the fence reflect it: a whole line of them from one end of the fence to the other, jerking madly like an old-time movie. Finally, the Singer

strums the final chord of the final chorus to "Buffalo Gals." The boys freeze. Mark Twain enters.)

TWAIN: By the end of the afternoon, Tom was literally rolling in wealth.

(The boys come to life in slow motion, still painting, but slowly moving off Left as they do.)

TWAIN: He had twelve marbles, part of a jew's harp, a piece of blue bottle glass to look through, a key that wouldn't unlock anything, a couple of tad-poles, six firecrackers, a brass doorknob, a dog collar—alas, no dog—and four pieces of orange peel.

(By this time, the last of the boys has exited in slow motion. Tom gathers up his treasures—also in slow motion and moves up to his bedroom. The lights are dimming.)

TWAIN: As for Aunt Polly's fence—well, *it* had *three coats* of whitewash. Tom decided the world wasn't such a bad place after all. *(Twain gently lowers the fence back down to its boardwalk position.)*

SCENE VI

Continuous with the preceding scene.

TWAIN: Away off above St. Petersburg, in the dying sunshine, Cardiff Hill lifted its soft green sides through a shimmering veil of heat. The cows dozing on the hillside looked like statues in the dusk. The hum of bees gave way to the gibber of crickets, and the only birds aloft now were the lonely circling nighthawks. St. Petersburg was falling asleep.

(Tom strikes a match in his bedroom and lights a candle. The sounds of crickets and other vague nighttime noises. Tom takes candlestick to Sid's bed and leans over the sleeping form.)

TOM: Hssst. Sid. You asleep? *(Pause.)* Sid?

(A snore from Sid. Tom is pleased. He tucks his nightshirt into his trousers. From beneath the bedroom comes a sudden scraping and then a "meow.")

HUCK: *(Standing beneath the upper Right pier.)* Meee-ow!

TOM: *(Goes to the Downstage edge of the upper Right pier, leans out.)* Mee-ow!

(Tom and Huck "talk" to each other in cat language for a moment. Then, the sound of a neighboring window being thrown up: single light on a woman's face.)

TOM: Damn cats! Hssst! Scat!

(The crash of something hurtled from the neighbor's window to the ground.

The sound of the window slammed shut: The women disappears. Tom climbs out the window ledge, turns back to blow out the candle, and then drops to the ground. Tom and Huck exit into the shadows.)

(In the moonlight, we see Sid jump out of his bed and creep to the Downstage edge of the upper Right pier. He looks out the window, and then looks at the audience, reflectively.)

SID: Should I tell on him now? Er should I wait until mornin'... *(He picks his nose thoughtfully as the light on him fades.)*

SCENE VII

Moonlight on the tombstones of the graveyard, and fog swirling among them. Tom and Huck cautiously climbing the slope to the graveyard.

TOM: Huck?

HUCK: What?

TOM: I was wonderin'. Do you believe the dead people like it for us to be here?

HUCK: I wisht I knowed. It's awful solemn-like, ain't it?

TOM: It shore is. *(Pause.)* Got yer cat?

HUCK: Right here in the bag...Sh!

TOM: What is it!

(Pause.)

HUCK: Nothin'.

TOM: Hucky? When the devils come, will they know *we're* here?

HUCK: Sh! What was that?

(The faint sound of muffled voices.)

TOM: Huck! It's them!

HUCK: Sh!

(The voices somewhat louder.)

HUCK: Oh, lordy, Tom, they're coming, sure! I wisht I was somewheres else.

TOM: What'll we do?

HUCK: Just keep still an' hope they don't pay us no mind. Oh, look, Tom—*(Pointing offstage.)* ...there they are! Three of 'em.

TOM: Lordy.

HUCK: We're goners, Tom. Kin you pray?

TOM: *(Instantly kneeling.)* "Now I lay me down to sleep, I pray the Lord my soul to keep, if I should die..."

HUCK: Shhh! Tom! They're *humans!* Leastwise, one of 'ems Muff Potter—
that's his voice!

(They listen, the voices growing louder.)

TOM: Huck—I know another of them voices. It's Injun Joe.

HUCK: Oh, Lordy, Tom. I'd druther have a devil than Injun Joe.

TOM: Hush!

*(The three figures come into view: Doc Robinson, Muff Potter, and Injun
Joe. Tom and Huck crouch beneath them, just below the top graveyard level.)*

ROBINSON: Here's the grave. Now get to work.

HUCK: *(Whisper.)* That's Doc Robinson!

TOM: Shhh!

ROBINSON: What are you waiting for? Dig him up!

INJUN JOE: You just hold on, Doc. Me and Muff—we decided we're worth
more money than you done paid us. Now you just out with another five,
or you don't get no corpse tonight.

MUFF: That's the talk!

ROBINSON: Thieves! You required your pay in advance and I've paid you!

INJUN JOE: Yes, and you done more than that. All this time I been diggin' up
bodies for you and your experiments, you been forgettin' something,
ain't you Doc? One night, five years ago, I came to your father's door. I
was asking for food. You said I weren't there for no good and drove me
away. And when I swore I'd get even with you, your father put me in jail
for a vagrant. Did you think I'd forget that? Not likely. You're just like
all the rest, all of you against me. And now, I've got you, and you're
going to settle...

(Injun Joe stalks the Doctor, the two of them moving in a circle.)

MUFF: Wait a minute, Joe...What're you doin'? I dint know you meant
nothin' like this...

(The Doctor strikes out at Injun Joe, knocks him down.)

MUFF: Don't you hit my pardner, Doc!

*(Muff hits Robinson, and the two of them struggle. Joe gets up and draws a
knife. He circles around the fighting men. Robinson knocks Muff unconscious. Injun Joe rises up behind Robinson with his knife high.)*

INJUN JOE: Now!

*(Injun Joe plunges the knife into Robinson's back. Robinson screams and falls
to the ground.)*

INJUN JOE: There, damn you...the score is settled.

(Potter is unconscious. Injun Joe pulls the knife out and goes to Muff. He

picks up one of Potter's hands and puts the knife into it. Then he sits down and waits.)

MUFF: *(After a moment, sitting up with a moan and looking about him.)* Ahhhhh… *(Sees Robinson's body at his feet.)* Ah! God a'mighty! What's that!

INJUN JOE: It's a dirty business, Muff. What did you go and kill him for?

MUFF: Me! I never done it!

INJUN JOE: Look, Muff. That kinda talk won't wash. What's that you got in your hand, if you didn't do it?

(Muff realizes that he is holding a bloody knife.)

MUFF: Ahhh! *(He drops the knife.)* Oh, God! Why did I drink tonight? I'm all in a muddle…I cain't recollect nothin' hardly. Tell me, *Joe*—honest now—did I do it? *(Silence.)* Oh, Joe, I never meant to…God help me, I never meant to do it. Oh, it's awful Joe…and him so young and promising. How did it happen?

INJUN JOE: You was scuffling and he knocked you down. You come up, all reeling and staggering, like, and snatched the knife and jammed it into him, just as he fetched you another clip. And here you laid, as dead as a wedge till now.

MUFF: Oh, God have mercy on my soul! I didn't know what I was a-doin', I swear I dint. Joe, Joe, don't tell! Say you won't tell, Joe. I always liked you, Joe, and stood up for you, dint I, Joe? Don't you remember? Joe?

INJUN JOE: That's enough of that. This ain't any time for your blubbering. You be off yonder way and I'll go this. Move, now!

MUFF: *(Hesitantly beginning to leave.)* Joe. Please, Joe. I never meant it. Joe? *(Muff turns and runs into the darkness. Injun Joe stands still for a moment above the body. Then he too turns and stalks into the darkness. Tom and Huck crawl out from their hiding place and approach the body.)*

TOM: *(After a pause.)* Hucky? There's goin' to be a hanging, ain't there.

HUCK: Shore there's gonna be a hangin', and you know who's gonna hang for it, don't you.

TOM: Not Injun Joe.

HUCK: Muff Potter'll hang.

TOM: An' he didn't do it.

HUCK: Nope.

TOM: If we was to tell what we saw, Muff Potter wouldn't hang.

HUCK: Nope. But s'pose something happened and Injun Joe didn't hang. He'd kill us, too. Dead as dead.

TOM: That's jist what I was thinkin'.

HUCK: We cain't ever tell what we saw, Tom.

TOM: I know it, Huck.

HUCK: We gotta swear on that, Tom. Swear good and proper.

(The boys join hands.)

TOM: Huck Finn, and Tom Sawyer...swears they will keep mum about what they seen here tonight...forever. And they wish they may drop dead in their tracks if they ever tell and rot. Swear.

HUCK: I swear. Swear.

TOM: I swear.

(The sound of the wind. The two boys remain for a moment, locked in their ritual handclasp.)

HUCK: Pore Doc Robinson.

TOM: Pore old Muff.

(They break apart, and Tom and Huck run off their separate ways.)

SCENE VIII

Tom climbs up and into his bedroom window—the upper Right pier—taking great care not to make noise. The room is dim and Tom does not see Aunt Polly waiting for him—and neither do we.

TOM: *(Testing.)* Sid? You still asleep?

(No response. Relieved, Tom flops down onto his bed. Instantly, Sid pops up.)

SID: *(Mimicking.)* "Sid? You still asleep?"

TOM: *(Starting up.)* Sid, so help me, if you ever tell Aunt Polly 'bout this...

(Sid folds his arms triumphantly and turns expectantly to Aunt Polly who emerges from a shadow. Tom gasps.)

TOM: Aunt Polly! I...I heard a noise down below and I jist went out to see if mebby it was...

AUNT POLLY: Please, Tom. Please don't lie. I just can't bear it. *(She begins to weep.)*

TOM: Oh, Aunt Polly. Don't cry, *please* don't cry. I wish you'd thrash me instead, it's a hundred times better'n when you cry.

AUNT POLLY: I ain't got no more thrashing left in me, Tom. I love you so, Tom, and then you go and break my old heart...I don't know how you kin do it to me, Tom.

TOM: I don't mean to trouble you so, Aunt Polly...I truly don't.

AUNT POLLY: Where was you all night, Tom? I was sick to death with worryin'
for you.

(*Tom hangs his head and doesn't answer.*)

AUNT POLLY: Tom? (*Still no answer.*) All right, then, Tom Sawyer, go ahead
and ruin yourself. And send me to my grave with sorrow and heaviness
of heart... (*She turns and leaves the room.*)

SID: (*To Tom.*) Nnya, nnya, nnya, nyya nnyaaa!

(*Tom is too downcast to take up the bait. He lies face down on his bed and
covers his head with his arms. The lights on them fade.*)

SCENE IX

*Lights rise almost immediately to a gray morning drizzle. A villager runs out
onto the down Center pier and shouts.*

JACK TAYLOR: Murder! Murder! Doc Robinson's bin murdered!

(*A passerby takes up the cry.*)

PASSERBY: Murder? Oh, my Lord! Murder! Murder!

(*It takes no time at all for the street to fill with people, all dressed for the
rain, some carrying umbrellas. Crowd ad-libs: Murder? Doc Robinson! Who
done it? Where is he? What happened? Murder! Where's the Sheriff? Doc
Robinson's been murdered! etc.*)

JACK TAYLOR: It's Doc Robinson! He's bin stabbed! Up in the cemetery! I jist
heard it from the Sheriff! He's got hold of Muff Potter!

CROWD: Muff Potter!

JACK TAYLOR: Muff Potter was covered with blood when the Sheriff found
'im!

CROWD: Muff Potter! Murder! And Doc Robinson, such a fine young man! If
he was such a fine young man, what was he doin' in the cemetery?
Robbin' graves, that's what! Grave-robbing! It's the hand of the Lord!
Muff Potter! Where is he! Lynch 'im, I say!

(*Tom has crept out of his room and stands apart from the crowd, listening.
Huck Finn slips up beside him, and together they watch the proceedings in
mute terror. Joe Harper is prominent in the crowd, maneuvering for a good
position, but continually yanked back by Mrs. Harper. The Sheriff enters
with Muff Potter in tow, assisted by a couple of townsmen.*)

CROWD: There he is! Look at 'im! Murderer! Murderer!

SHERIFF: (*To the crowd.*) Hesh up!

(Most of the crowd fall silent.)

JACK TAYLOR: Murderer!

SHERIFF: You, there! Jack Taylor! You heard me, boy, you hesh up that bellerin'!

(Silence.)

SHERIFF: Now, then. There's been murder done. Now I have this yer suspek in custidy but I want to know if there's any of yew knows anything about this yer.

(Small murmur, then silence. Then, from the tick of the crowd, Injun Joe steps forward.)

MUFF: *(Seeing him.)* No! No! *Please,* Joe!

INJUN JOE: You might as well tell 'em, Muff. And get it over with.

(Angry murmur from the crowd.)

SHERIFF: *Hesh up!*

(Silence.)

SHERIFF: Injun Joe. You know somethin' 'bout this yer?

INJUN JOE: I ain't the sort of man to rot on his friend. But I expect there ain't much point in holding out any longer, Muff. They got you, sure as sure.

MUFF: Joe! Oh, God a'mighty. I never meant to do it.

SHERIFF: Yawl come with me.

(The Sheriff leads Muff out, followed by Injun Joe, and then the crowd, ad-libbing shouts of anger and revenge. Joe Harper attempts to follow, but is held back by his mother. Mrs. Harper and Aunt Polly have gravitated toward each other during the preceding. Now they stand together, looking off after the exiting crowd. Huck Finn—not a popular one with mothers, hangs back while Tom slouches dismally against a post.)

AUNT POLLY: Well, Sereny Harper. Did you ever think you'd see the day when *this* sorta thing come to St. Petersburg?

MRS. HARPER: As I stand here talkin' to you, Polly, I swear I did not. I never did. I feel downright faint. Why, I seen Doc Robinson just day before yesterday, lookin' a-fine and fit and up-comin' a young man as you'd ever...

AUNT POLLY: Day *before* yesterday? Why, I just seen him myself *yesterday.* Yesterday ev'nin'. Gettin' on towards *eight, I* seen him. He was...

MRS. HARPER: It's a tragidy, that's all there is to it. Joe Harper, you git back here! It's a downright tragidy. It's all I can do to keep m' tears back. Joe Harper, you take one more step in that direction and I'll blister yer bottom, boy! *(To Aunt Polly.)* He got inta my rasberry preserves this morning, Polly. What's a woman to do?

AUNT POLLY: Tom's a-tormentin' me, as usual. I wouldn't bet a plug nickel but what he's up to mischief with that Huckleberry Finn. Will you take a nice cup of tea, Sereny Harper, and get in outta this drizzle?

MRS. HARPER: Why, *yes,* thank you, Polly, I'd be much obliged to you for a little refreshment. Huckleberry Finn! Why, I'd never let my Joe go around with the likes of Huckleberry Finn. Joe! I'm a-warnin' you!

(The two ladies proceed up the slope and exit into the house.)

AUNT POLLY: *(Thrown away, as they exit.)* Oh, I'm not suggestin' that I *allow* Tom to 'sociate with Huck Finn. That don't even enter in. No, I'm always sayin' to him...

(The ladies are gone. Tom and Joe remain. Huck emerges from his hiding place to complete the unhappy trio. They sit on their haunches at the bottom of the slope. Twain stands above them.)

TWAIN: Has the world ever beheld three such miserable boys? It's not likely. Joe Harper hadn't even touched those raspberry preserves. Least, he didn't *recollect* having done so. No, no, it was plain to Joe Harper that his mother simply had no further use for him, and wished he would go away. Tom Sawyer felt the same about his Aunt Polly. If her life would be better off without him, so be it. Huck Finn didn't have a loving mother or a kindly aunt to make *him* feel miserable, but he was in mortal terror of Injun Joe. So the three of them decided there was only one honorable choice open to them. They'd run away.

(We see the three boys discussing their possibilities, but they make no sound.)

TWAIN: Joe Harper was all for becoming a hermit, and living in a cave, and dying of starvation. Well, that sounded pretty tempting to the boys, but Tom Sawyer finally convinced them that there were more advantages to a life of crime. And so they all became pirates. Then and there.

(The boys leap to their feet, lick their thumbs, and press thumbs together all around. Then all three run off in separate directions. The Singer begins as the boys jump up.)

SINGER: Get on board, little children,

Get on board,

While the moon is shinin' bright. (Shinin' bright)

Get on board, down the river float,

Gonna raise a ruckus tonight.

(We see the boys sneaking stolen provisions onto a raft.—N.B. In the original production, it was located down of the apron, in the orchestra pit. It was a plank raft mounted on automobile springs that in turn were mounted on a wagon. Once the boys cast loose from their moorings, a crew member in the

orchestra pit moved the wagon slowly from Right to Left across the pit.
Subdued lighting and the motion of the spring-mounted planks created the
illusion.)

(Midway through the following stanza, the lights on the boys fade.)

SINGER: Get on board, little doggies,

Get on board,

While the moon is shinin' bright

Get on board and down the river float,

We gonna raise a ruckus tonight.

TWAIN: About a mile below St. Petersburg, where the Mississippi was particularly wide, there was an island. Jackson's Island. There they beached
their raft, staked out their camp, and began their lives as cutthroats. Or
maybe they'd be Indian warriors. It was hard to say.

SCENE X

A screaming Banshee, half-naked and painted with stripes of charcoal, runs
shrieking down from the topmost platform, leaps off the over-hanging edge,
and falls with deadly intent upon another Indian brave directly below. It is
Tom Sawyer, doing in Joe Harper. Tom raises his tomahawk and strikes Joe
a mortal blow. Joe crumples and falls dead. From nowhere, a third painted
devil comes roaring out at Tom and fells him after a brief struggle. Huck
stands triumphant over the corpses, one of which is still twitching piteously.
However, the twitching corpse—Tom Sawyer—suddenly leaps up and tom-
ahawks Huck on the back of the neck. Huck merely turns and looks at Tom
with disgust.

TOM: Fall, Huck! Yer supposed to *fall!*

HUCK: Whadda you mean, fall? I kilt you *dead,* Tom Sawyer! Once yer dead,
you stay dead!

JOE HARPER: *(Still supine.)* You lie back down, Tom!

TOM: I weren't dead. I were only wounded!

JOE: *(Jumping up.)* That ain't playin' fair, Tom an' you know it!

HUCK: *(To Joe.)* What're you doin', Joe Harper? I spose you was only
wounded, too!

(A general melee breaks out among the three of them, ending only when all
three Indians have fallen. They lie there, luxuriating in the prospect of a life

without care, their heads cupped in their hands, staring at the sky, or propped up on an elbow.)

TOM: Ain't it bully out here on this here island?

JOE: It shore is, Tom. Gosh, if the other boys could see us now.

TOM: You know, there's spose to be treasure buried on this island.

HUCK: That's what Mother Hopkins says. She tole me that this yer island was a camp once, fer river-bandits. An' they buried heaps a' treasure right here somewheres. Unless somebody already done found it.

(A low and distant booming sound.)

JOE: What's that?

HUCK: What's what?

JOE: That noise.

(It grows louder.)

TOM: I hear it too.

HUCK: It ain't thunder.

TOM: It's comin' from the other side of the island.

(They get to their feet and scramble up the slope until they stand looking Upstage off the other side of the island over the river.)

JOE: What's that ferryboat doin'? Goin' back an' forth across the river like that?

HUCK: An' all those skiffs, jist a-floatin' with the stream?

TOM: *(Excited.)* I know what it is! Somebody's drownded!

HUCK: That's it, Tom! They done that last summer, when Bill Turner got drownded! They fire a cannon over the water, and that makes the body come up. I wonder who it is…

JOE: I'd give heaps to know who drowned. By jings, I wisht I was over there now…

TOM: Wait a minute…wait a minute…Huck! Joe! I know who got drownded! It's *us!* They all think we got drownded when we never came back, and they're a-lookin' for us now—at the bottom of the river!

HUCK: Whooopeee!

JOE: *(Jubilant.)* We's drownded!

TOM: An' they're all a-cryin' and a-moanin' for us…Oh, jiminy! It's bully, that's what it is!

(The boys scramble halfway down the Upstage side of the set. We can still see their backs, when a man stalks furtively out from the planks beneath them. He wears a long cape and a hood. He stops beneath the overhanging ledge and looks about him. He unfolds a map and takes his bearings. He paces off a short distance, gets down on all fours and crawls beneath the slope. He

immediately finds what he's looking for, and begins to drag it out. It's a small chest, but obviously very heavy. Huck and Joe are still engrossed in the activities on the river, but Tom hears the noise and slowly walks down to the overhanging ledge. By this time the man has got the chest all the way out of its hiding place. He straightens up and catches his breath just as Tom leans over the edge for a look. Tom drops flat. The man throws off his hood—it's Injun Joe.)

TOM: *(Terrified, he hisses back to the other boys.)* Hsssst!

(The boys turn and look at Tom who motions to them. Silently, Huck and Joe climb down behind the Upstage side of the set. But Injun Joe has heard the "hiss" too, and draws his knife. Tom slithers in beneath one of the plank steps as Injun Joe goes to the foot of the slope and then starts up it. Tom is hanging now like a monkey to the underside of the over-hanging ledge. Injun Joe walks Right over him to the top of the riverbank. He sees no one and starts back down the slope. He sees the raft moored at the edge of the apron. He stops. Then he goes to it.)

TOM: A raft.

(He wheels around and looks over the area. He turns back to the raft.)

INJUN JOE: Mighta been left here some time ago. *(Pause.)* Might not. *(He wheels around again and stands motionless. Then he walks to where the chest lies, picks it up, and walks back to the raft. He sets the chest down.)* We'll just let this here raft travel some…on its own. *(The raft is moored to the island by a rope tied to a post. Injun Joe unties it and tosses the rope onto the raft. He gives the raft a shove and watches it move off from the island. Then he picks up the chest and exits off Right.)*

(Tom drops from his perch to the ground. Huck and Joe slowly emerge from their hiding places. They walk to the edge of the apron and look out disconsolately over the river at their disappearing raft. Their faces are frightened.)

SINGER: I am a poor wayfaring stranger,
Traveling through this world of woe,
And there's no sickness, toil or danger
In that bright land to which I go.
(The lights begin a very slow fade on the boys.)
I'm goin' there to meet my brother,
I'm goin' there no more to roam,
I'm just a-goin' over Jordan,
I'm just a-goin' over home.
(Lights out.)

Intermission

SCENE XI

The mourners assembling in the church, "Shall We Gather at the River" on the organ. At the conclusion of the hymn, when the congregation is seated, the Preacher takes the pulpit.

PREACHER: *(Nodding to each in turn.)* Miss Polly...Mrs. Harper...Friends and family of the departed...I take my text from the one hundred and twenty eighth chapter of the Book of Psalms, beginning at the third verse: "Your children will be like olive shoots around your table." *(Pause.)* "Your *children* will be like olive *shoots* around...your table."

CONGREGATION MEMBER: Amen.

PREACHER: Dearly beloved, we are here today to mourn the passing of three tender...olive...shoots. Tom Sawyer...

(A moan from Aunt Polly.)

PREACHER: ...Joe Harper...

(A sob from Mrs. Harper.)

PREACHER: ...and Huckleberry... *(Consulting his notes.)*...and Huckleberry Flinn.

AMY LAWRENCE: *(Stage whisper to her mother.)* No—*Finn*. It were Huckleberry *Finn*.

PREACHER: That's right, Amy—we know how much you miss your little play-mate.

AMY: Oh, no, Preacher. Mama *never* let me play with Huckleberry Finn—he cussed too much!

MRS. LAWRENCE: Amy! *(She jabs her daughter in the ribs.)*

PREACHER: Three young lives...swallowed up...by the cruel...Mississippi. The Lord giveth and the Lord taketh away, blessed be the name of the Lord. Oh, these were not angels—these boys—but we all know that their piping voices can be heard today in the angelic...choir. Many's the time I remember, personally, giving Tom Sawyer's curly little head a good rap—with a hymnal—right here in this very church.

SEVERAL CONGREGATIONS MEMBERS: Amen. Amen. Amen.

PREACHER: But I'd always say to Tom Sawyer, while I was twisting his ears or rapping those little knuckles...Tom, I'd say, when you are the President of these United States, you'll remember your old Preacher back in St. Petersburg and you'll thank him. And Tom would always looks up at me and he'd say, Oh, I'll remember, all right, Preacher, I'll remember...

(Sobs from the congregation.)

PREACHER: And Joe Harper...what a dear lad. I always thought of Joe as one of God's little jokes that he plays with mankind—to make us smile, to make us remember to suffer the little children. And now...if we could hear from family? Testimonials from the families of the deceased. Miss Polly?

AUNT POLLY: *(Standing up timidly.)* Tom...Tom...he warn't *bad,* so to say. Only mischeevous. Only just giddy, and harum-scarum, you know. He never meant any harm, and he was the best-hearted boy that ever was... *(She breaks down crying.)*

PREACHER: Mrs. Harper?

MRS. HARPER: *(Standing up.)* Oh, it were the same with my Joe. Only last Saturday, he set off a firecracker right under my nose and I knocked him down. Little did I know then...oh, if I had it to do over again, I'd hug him and bless him for it... *(She bursts into tears.)*

PREACHER: Thank you, Mrs. Harper. Thank you, Aunt Polly.

TOM SAWYER: *(Standing up in the back row of the choir, throwing off the woman's shawl which had disguised him.)* It ain't fair!
(The Preacher and congregation do a unison double take.)

TOM: Aunt Polly, it jist ain't fair! Somebody's got to say something good about Huck!

AUNT POLLY: Tom!
(Joe Harper and Huck throw off their shawls.)

MRS. HARPER: Joe!
(The Congregation is in an uproar. Tom and Joe run down to embrace Aunt Polly and Mrs. Harper, respectively. Huck lingers uncomfortably in the choir.)

TOM: We was marooned, Aunt Polly! Marooned on an island!

AUNT POLLY: Oh, Tom! Huckleberry! Huckleberry Finn, you come right down here! I've got something to say to you, Huckleberry!
(In anguish, Huck approaches Aunt Polly. She looks him up and down, and then smothers him with a big hug and kiss.)

AUNT POLLY: I'm glad to see you, Huckleberry—you poor motherless thing!
(Huck retreats as best he can in utter agony.)

TOM: We had to swim near a mile to git back home, Aunt Polly!

AUNT POLLY: Tom, I don't know whether to kiss you or to thrash you. Matter of fact, I've a mind to do *both! (She gives him a big kiss.)* We'll save the thrashin' for later.

PREACHER: *(Shouting.)* Praise God From Whom All Blessings Flow! Everybody, now! Sing!
(The congregation breaks jubilantly into the Old Hundreth. As they sing,

they stand and file out of the church. When the crowd has cleared, we see Mark Twain sitting alone in a pew, reading a newspaper. When he realizes he has been discovered, he quickly folds up the paper.)

TWAIN: *(Standing and approaching the audience.)* Tom Sawyer received more kisses and more thrashings during the week that followed than he had earned before in a year. He finally realized that being a hero can be fatal—or nearly. And, despite all the glory that the town heaped upon him, he did not *feel* like a hero. Tom and Huckleberry Finn were both suffering from the most uncomfortable of all diseases. A guilty conscience. Their thoughts were occupied by a single, lonely prisoner in the St. Petersburg jail.

(We see Muff Potter lying on the upper Left pier, which becomes the jail cell.)

TWAIN: Muff Potter was destined to hang for a crime he did not commit. And, as the date set for his trial approached, he began to have visitors— two of them, every day, bearing gifts.

SCENE XII

Tom and Huck enter from Left, beneath the upper Left pier. Huck knocks on the wooden post by Muff's head to rouse him.

MUFF: What! Oh—boys, boys. God bless you both. Tom. Huck.

HUCK: We brung ya some chaw, Muff.

TOM: *And* some smokin' tobacker…

HUCK: And I don't need this yer pipe, Muff. What do I want with two of 'em?
(They hand their gifts up to Muff.)

MUFF: You've been mighty good to me, boys…better'n anybody else in this town. And I don't forgit it, I don't. Time was, I used to mend all the boys' kites and such, and show 'em where the good fishin' places was, and now they've all forgot old Muff, now that he's in trouble. But Tom don't, and Huck don't—*they* don't forgit him, and I don't forgit them. I done an awful thing, boys—drunk and crazy at the time—that's the only way I kin account for it. Well, we won't talk about that. It's a prime comfort to see friendly faces when a body's in such a muck of trouble. Here—git up on Huck's back, Tom…go on, jist climb on up here…
(Tom gets a boost from Huck to the jail cell window. Muff puts his hand on Tom's head in blessing.)

MUFF: Bless you, boy.

(Tom drops down.)

MUFF: Huck?

(Huck reaches his hand up to touch Muff's.)

MUFF: Bless you, Huck. You boys have helped Muff Potter in his time of trouble. And I know you'd help him even more, if you could. Git along now, boys. And, I thankee…

(We hear a rattle of keys and the voice of the Sheriff.)

SHERIFF: *(From offstage.)* What you doin' in there, Muff? You settle down, boy, an' git some rest.

(As the boys move away and the light on Muff fades.)

MUFF: Thankee, boys…

(Light on Muff out. The two boys sit on the edge of the down Center pier.)

TOM: Huck, nobody could git you to tell the truth about…that night, could they?

HUCK: Git me to tell? Why, shore they could. If I wanted Injun Joe to put me in a sack and drownd me.

TOM: I wisht we could git him outta there, Huck.

HUCK: Well, I do too, Tom. But we wouldn't be alive more'n two days if Injun Joe was to git at us.

TOM: I wisht Muff wouldn't a' blessed us quite so much.

HUCK: I know. Puts a body in a sweat, all them "bless yous."

(Sid and Becky Thatcher appear from Left, walking together carrying schoolbooks.)

SID: *(Seeing Tom.)* Tom Sawyer. Where you been this lunch hour? Third time this week you ain't come home fer lunch, an' Aunt Polly's fixin' to skin you.

TOM: It ain't none a'yer business where I been, Sid. Howdee, Becky.

BECKY: *(Ignoring him.)* Tell me, Sid—don't you think that sartin folks has got mighty uppity…ever since their funeral?

SID: I shore do, Becky.

TOM: Becky, I'm sorry if I acted that way…I won't ever do it agin, I promise!

BECKY: I'll thank you to keep yourself *to* yourself, Thomas Sawyer. *(All honey.)* Oh, Sidney…my ma's lettin' me have a picnic!

SID: Do you think she'll let *me* come?

BECKY: O' course she will! She'll let anybody come that I want, and I want you!

SID: Oh, Becky…that's ever so nice!

TOM: *(Mimicking Sid.)* Oh, Becky…that's ever so nice!

BECKY: I don't ever want to talk to you agin, Tom Sawyer!

TOM: So who cares, Miss Smarty-pants! *(He yanks her hair.)* Come on, Huck! *(Tom and Huck run offstage.)*

SID: *(Indignation.)* Well! *(Coy.)* Say, Becky…I'll walk you the rest a' the way to school…

BECKY: *(Suddenly turning on Sid, in rage.)* Oh, will you stop pesterin' me! I hate you! Git away from me!

(She hits Sid on the head with a schoolbook, bursts into tears and runs off, leaving a bewildered Sid. Twain approaches Sid. Sid, after thinking about it for a moment, bursts into tears himself.)

TWAIN: *(To Sid.)* Don't try to figure it out, son. It would be a waste of time. Now, here's a piece of rock candy for you…no, no that's a cigar. *Here's* a piece of rock candy. Now get along to school.

(Sid takes the candy and runs off.)

TWAIN: *(Who watches Sid run off and then turns to us.)* I don't suppose it would be charitable to hope he breaks a tooth on it…

SCENE XIII

Continuous with preceding.

TWAIN: Well, Miss Thatcher arrived in the schoolroom before any of the others—lonely, unhappy, and angry, all at once.

(We see Becky appear at the top of the slope, sulking.)

TWAIN: Just the sort of mood to get a body into trouble.

(Mr. Dobbins enters from Right and, without noticing Becky, goes to the podium down Right. As Twain speaks the following, Dobbins mimes the corresponding action.)

TWAIN: Now, Mr. Dobbins had not *wanted* to become a village schoolmaster. Who would?

(Mr. Dobbins takes from the lift-top podium an apple and a knife.)

TWAIN: No, his lifelong ambition was to be a doctor…

(Dobbins sets the apple on the podium and gripping it with one hand, he carefully saws through it with the knife, in the manner of a surgeon.)

TWAIN: …but his own talents had decreed otherwise.

(Mr. Dobbins "saws" into his own hand, drops the knife, and sucks at the wound.)

TWAIN: He did have one comfort, however. Every day, he took a mysterious book out of his desk and read it devoutly.

(Mr. Dobbins rather furtively takes a large book from out of the desk and opens it.)

TWAIN: It contained medical diagrams of the human body…but no one except Mr. Dobbins knew that. And there was not an urchin in school that was not perishing for a glimpse inside that book.

(A muffled burst of boys' voices from offstage, and then a lump of clay flies in through the schoolroom "window" and lands at Mr. Dobbins's feet. Dobbins stoops, picks it up, and marches offstage to locate the offenders.)

TWAIN: Well, Miss Thatcher saw her chance and she took it.

(Becky dashes furtively down to Mr. Dobbins' podium. She opens the book and starts paging through it. After a moment, Tom Sawyer appears at the top of the slope.)

TOM: Becky…

(Becky gives out a terrific start, and in doing so, tears a page of the book so that it comes out in her hand.)

BECKY: Oh! I ripped a page…! *(Becky fumbles with the book, sticking the torn page back in and closing it. Then she turns on Tom in a panic.)* Tom Sawyer, how could you be so mean! To sneak up on a person and look at what they're lookin' at!

TOM: How could *I* know you was lookin' at anything?

BECKY: And now you're goin' to tell on me, and I'll be whipped! I'll be whipped, and I was never whipped in school before!

TOM: No, Becky, I…

BECKY: Just *be so* mean, if you want to, Tom Sawyer! Hateful!

TOM: Listen, Becky! I swear I…

MR. DOBBINS: *(Who has just re-entered.)* That will be enough of that, Sawyer! *(Other school children begin to come into the schoolroom.)*

MR. DOBBINS: Take your seats all of you.

(The children take their seats, Tom and Becky watching Mr. Dobbins intently.)

MR. DOBBINS: Open your readers to page thirty-six and commence. In silence! *(A yawn from Mr. Dobbins. He pulls on his reading spectacles and leisurely opens the book on his podium. He turns a page, contentedly. He turns another. He turns a third page and it comes out in his hand. Dobbins looks up and down in disbelief and rage. Then, with relish, he closes the book and removes his spectacles. After a considerable pause during which he gathers his wrath.)*

MR. DOBBINS: Who…tore…this…book?

(A quiver of fear passing through each young body. Then all is utterly still.)

MR. DOBBINS: Benjamin Rogers. Did you tear this book?

BEN: *(A tiny voice.)* No, sir.

MR. DOBBINS: Joe Harper. Did you tear this book?

JOE: No, sir, Mr. Dobbins.

DOBBINS: Amy Lawrence?

AMY: No, sir.

DOBBINS: Gracie Miller?

(Gracie shakes her head "no.")

DOBBINS: Susan Harper, did you do this?

SUSAN: No, sir.

DOBBINS: Rebecca Thatcher, did you tear...no, look me in the face! Did you tear this book?

(Becky teeters for a moment on the brink of disaster.)

BECKY: I...I didn't...

TOM: *(Springing up out of his seat.)* I done it!

(A collective gasp and then deadly silence from the schoolroom.)

DOBBINS: *(Quietly.)* The rest of you are dismissed for the day.

(Mr. Dobbins turns and faces us, removes his jacket and rolls up his sleeves. The children stand and file silently out of the schoolroom, occasionally casting glances of wonder and pity back at Tom. Sid pauses by Tom and makes a significant gesture. Tom regards him for a moment, then gives him a slug that sends Sid running out with a yelp. Meanwhile, Becky has gone to stand by Tom. The following moment is suspended in eternity, and if the fiddler has a love-theme for Becky, he should play a bar of it now.)

BECKY: Oh, Tom! How *could* you be so noble!

(She plants a kiss on Tom's cheek. Mr. Dobbins turns back to face them, breaking the spell.)

DOBBINS: Rebecca Thatcher, class is *dismissed!*

(Becky runs out, with one more backward glance at Tom. Dobbins opens his desk and take out a large switch. He approaches Tom slowly.)

DOBBINS: Remove your shirt.

(Tom does so, Mr. Dobbins raises the switch above Tom's back and the lights black out on them with a huge crash of thunder.)

SCENE XIV

Night, a thunderstorm, Tom's bedroom and various locations. A "double" of Tom lies in Tom's bed, thrashing under the covers. A particularly bright flash of lightning is followed by a deafening thunderclap. Suddenly, we see Becky Thatcher in a shaft of light.

(This entire section will be most effective if the actor's voices are recorded and played with an amplified reverberation.)

VOICE OF BECKY THATCHER: Oh, Tom! How *could* you be so noble!

BECKY THATCHER AND OTHER VOICES: How could you be so noble…could you be so noble…so noble…so noble…so noble.

(Becky fades away. Single light on Muff Potter in his cell.)

VOICE OF MUFF POTTER: God bless you, Tom. God bless you, Huck. You boys have helped Muff Potter in his time of trouble, and I know you'd help him even more, if you could…even more, if you could…if you could…if you could…

(Light on him fades. Light up on Injun Joe and Doc Robinson in the grave-yard.)

VOICE OF INJUN JOE: Aaaaah!

(He stabs Robinson in the back, Robinson screams and falls. The screams echo. Light out. Light up on Aunt Polly, standing in church.)

VOICE OF AUNT POLLY: Tom…Tom—he warn't *bad*. He never meant any harm, and he was the best-hearted boy that ever was…the best-hearted boy…best-hearted boy…

(Lights up on the "real" Tom and Huck in the graveyard.)

VOICE OF TOM SAWYER: Huck Finn and Tom Sawyer swears they will keep mum about what they seen here tonight…forever. And they hopes they may drop dead in their tracks if they ever tell and rot. Swear.

VOICE OF HUCK FINN: Swear…swear…swear…

(Light on Becky Thatcher.)

VOICE OF BECKY THATCHER: Oh, Tom! How could you be so noble!

VOICE OF HUCK FINN: Swear, Tom…swear!

VOICE OF MUFF POTTER: And you'd help Muff Potter even more, if you could…if you could…if you could…

VOICE OF BECKY THATCHER: How *could* you…how *could* you…Tom? How could you be so…

VOICE OF HUCK FINN: Swear, Tom! Swear! Swear! Swear!

VOICE OF TOM SAWYER: I swear! I swear! I swear!…

(Blackout.)

SCENE XV

No break between this and the preceding, the participants having gathered quietly in the courtroom during the undulating light and darkness of scene

XIV. Lights up full on the courtroom. The entire village has assembled for Muff Potter's trial. Prominent among them: Judge Thatcher, the Prosecutor, the Counsel for the Defense—who is Mark Twain, Muff Potter. At this moment, the Sheriff is on the witness stand, being sworn in by the Judge.

JUDGE: *(To the Sheriff.)* Do you solemnly swear to tell the truth, the whole truth, and nothing but the truth, so help you God?

SHERIFF: Ah do.

JUDGE: Your witness, Mr. Prosecutor.

PROSECUTOR: Thank you, Judge Thatcher. Sheriff Thompkins, would you please tell this court whether you had occasion to see the accused, Muff Potter, during the early morning hours of June the eighth?

SHERIFF: Yessir, Ah did. Ah seen him sometime 'round four in the mornin'.

PROSECUTOR: And where did you see the defendant?

SHERIFF: Ole Muff, he were kneelin' at the edge of the brook jist beneath the cemetery.

PROSECUTOR: Were you able to tell what the defendant was doing there at the edge of the stream?

SHERIFF: Why, shore. He were a-washin' hisself. In the brook.

PROSECUTOR: And could you determine if there was any particular reason for him to be washing himself in the brook at that hour of the morning?

SHERIFF: Well, I reckon so. He were covered with blood.

(Huge response from the courtroom.)

JUDGE: *(Banging his gavel.)* Silence! The gallery will come to order! *(He gavels again.)* You may proceed, Counsellor.

PROSECUTOR: Now then, Sheriff. I want you to examine this knife and tell the court if you've ever seen it before.

SHERIFF: Yessir, Ah seen this yer knife before.

PROSECUTOR: When you last saw this knife, where was it?

SHERIFF: Why, it were lyin' aside the body a' Doc Robinson.

PROSECUTOR: Do you recall having seen it *before* that time?

SHERIFF: O' course Ah do. That's why Ah went lookin' fer Muff Potter till Ah found 'im by the brook.

PROSECUTOR: I'm sorry, Sheriff. I don't quite follow you. *Why* did you go looking for Muff Potter when you had found this knife?

SHERIFF: Why? Because it was *his knife,* dang it!

(Uproar from the gallery.)

JUDGE: Sheriff Thompkins—please keep yourself in order.

PROSECUTOR: I have no further questions your honor.

JUDGE: Counsel for the Defense—your witness.

TWAIN: I have no questions for this witness, your honor.

(Buzz from the courtroom, the Judge gavels.)

JUDGE: Counsellor—this man has just given very damaging testimony... damaging your client. And you do not wish to cross-examine him?

TWAIN: No, sir, your honor.

JUDGE: Just as you did not wish to cross-examine any of the prosecution witnesses that have testified today?

TWAIN: Your honor. In our remarks at the opening of this trial, we stated our intent to prove that the defendant committed this fearful crime while under the delirious influence of alcoholic drink. Early this morning, however, I received a visitor who claimed to have a new light to shed upon this matter. As a result of that visit, I now wish to do two things: change the defendant's plea to not guilty, and...call to the witness stand... Thomas Sawyer.

(Tumult in the gallery.)

JUDGE: *(After gavelling for quiet.)* Thomas Sawyer, approach the stand!

(Tom does so.)

JUDGE: Do you swear to tell the truth, the whole truth, and nothing but the truth, so help you God?

TOM: I swear.

JUDGE: Proceed.

TWAIN: Thomas Sawyer, where were you between a quarter to twelve, June the seventh, and the early morning hours of June the eighth?

TOM: *(Quietly.)* In the graveyard.

TWAIN: Louder, boy...don't be afraid.

TOM: *(Too loud.)* In the graveyard!

TWAIN: Were you anywhere near Horse Williams's grave?

TOM: Yes, sir.

TWAIN: How near?

TOM: Near as I am to you.

(Murmur from the crowd, Injun Joe half-rises in his seat, and then sits back down.)

TWAIN: Was there anyone with you?

(Tom hangs his head in silence.)

TWAIN: Thomas, was there anyone with you in the graveyard?

HUCK FINN: *(Jumping up from his place in the gallery.)* Go ahead, Tom! You already done broke yer oath. I was there with 'im!

(Buzz from the crowd, Judge gavels.)

TWAIN: Is that true? Was Huckleberry Finn with you?

TOM: Yessir.

TWAIN: Now, Tom. Will you tell us what you saw there?

TOM: Well…*(Tom glances at Injun Joe throughout this.)* Muff Potter and Doc Robinson were standin' around the grave with…with Injun Joe.
(Low murmur from crowd.)

TOM: And Injun Joe, he said something to Doc Robinson about settlin' a score. And then, them two was fightin' and Doc knocked Injun Joe down. Muff started in on the Doc, but Doc Robinson—he put Muff Potter out cold. That was when…that was when Injun Joe come up from behind…with the knife…
(Injun Joe leaps out of his seat. Women in the courtroom scream. Injun Joe knocks people out of his way as he scrambles up over them and dives off the slope. The Sheriff and other men leap after him but fall in a tangle. Injun Joe runs Upstage and out through the "cave" opening. A chaos of shouts as the lights fade.)

SCENE XVI

There is one figure Left in the courtroom, sitting in the gallery, his back to us. After a moment, he turns about suddenly: Mark Twain.

TWAIN: *(As he speaks, a court clerk enters and slowly sweeps out the courtroom. The Singer hums a ballad beneath Twain's speech. Its tune foreshadows the hoedown melody which will be heard in the following scene.)* Rewards were offered, of course…and the countryside was scoured, but no Injun Joe was found. The local officials even went so far as to hire a "de-tec-tive," who came all the way from St. Louis. Well, this fellow moused around, and shook his head mournfully, and looked altogether wise. And eventually, he even found a *clue.* Injun Joe's pocket-handkerchief. But, since you can't hang a pocket-handkerchief for murder, they sent the detective back to St. Louis. As the days went by, however, even the whereabouts of Injun Joe sank into secondary importance. *(Twain rises and walks down the slope during the following speech.)* For there was going to be a picnic—Miss Becky Thatcher's long awaited picnic on the banks of the Mississippi. There would be singing and dancing and lemonade, and explorations into the massive cave that spread like tentacles for miles beneath St. Petersburg. *(During this last line, Twain produces a candle, strikes a match and lights it, and passes into the cave opening.)*

SCENE XVII

The area before the mouth of the cave is suddenly filled with children and young men and women, dressed in summer finery and arranged for dancing. The Singer, the fiddler and the banjo player are prominent.

SINGER: Ladies and gents! Boys and girls! Up on yer toes and ready to whirl! Oh...I...
(The hoedown dance.)
SINGER: Love my wife, I love my baby,
Love my biscuits sopped in gravy.
Shoo, pretty little black-eyed Susie,
Shoo, pretty little black-eyed Susie, shoo.
Oh, you be the horse and I'll be the rider,
We'll go home and get some cider.
Shoo, pretty little black-eyed Susie,
Shoo, pretty little black-eyed Susie, shoo.
I asked her to be my wife.
She rushed at me with a barlow knife.
Shoo, pretty little black-eyed Susie,
Shoo, pretty little black-eyed Susie, shoo.
Jump up, kitty puss, jump up higher,
Jump up, kitty puss, your tail's on fire.
Shoo, pretty little black-eyed Susie,
Shoo, pretty little black-eyed Susie, shoo.
All I want to make me happy,
Two little girls to call me pappy.
Shoo, pretty little black-eyed Susie,
Shoo, pretty little black-eyed Susie, shoo.
(The musicians finish and the dancers fall apart with much laughter and panting and the waving of fans in front of young ladies' faces. Many of them collapse happily on the grass, talking, giggling, flirting, and feigning exhaustion. We see Huck hanging about the fringes of the group, Right at the river's edge. We see Tom and Becky Thatcher happily together. We see other familiar faces, among them—Muff Potter. He is totally out of place with these

people, but since his "redemption" he has received many such invitations. After a few moments of indistinguishable ad-libbing, a boisterous young man stands up and shouts.)

WILL HANLEY: Whooo-ee! May I have yer atten-*tion!*

(The chatter gradually subsides.)

WILL HANLEY: Thank yew. May I *pro-pose*...an at*tack*...on McDougal's *cave!*

(Cheers from the crowd, scattered with groans and "no's!")

WILL HANLEY: Ah'd propose more, only mah girl, Sally Jones, she won't *have* me!

(Laughter.)

ANDY TANNER: *(Who is perhaps the Singer.)* Let's have a cheer for Sally Jones's good sense!

(A cheer.)

WILL HANLEY: Don't you speak too soon, Andy Tanner! Me and Sally, we're goin' to get lost in that there cave, and never come out—and that were *Sally's* ideer!

(Laughter; people getting up off the ground, brushing off their clothes.)

ANDY TANNER: Has everybody got a candle.

(A chorus of "yesses.")

WILL HANLEY: Then let's go!

(The young couples and the boys and girls light their candles, while excitedly talking about the mysteries of the cave. Sample ad-libs: "I'm gonna carve my name onna wall!" "I'm gonna carve Mr. Dobbins's name onna wall, an' write words beneath it!" "You hold onto me, Andy. I'm afraid o' the dark!" "You hold onta him, and that ain't all you got to be afeard of!" "Hesh yer mouth, Will Hanley!")

(With lit candles, the group passes in through the mouth of the cave. Becky waits just outside, while Tom goes down to Huck.)

TOM: Ain't you a-comin', Huck?

HUCK: I don't reckon.

TOM: Why ain't ya?

HUCK: *(Too distinctly.)* Cause of I don't *care* to. Sides. Me an' Muff. We're gonna do some fishin' off the bank.

BECKY: *(Shouting.)* Come one, Tom! We'll be the last ones!

(Tom turns and runs Upstage to Becky, who holds two lighted candles. She gives one to Tom and they enter the cave. The stage is plunged into darkness.)

SCENE XVIII

The cave. Only the flickering candles light isolated faces and the faces of couples. The sound of voices is suddenly hollow and echoing.

AMY LAWRENCE: It's so cold in here!

WILL HANLEY: *(Shouting for an echo.)* Hello!—ello—ello—ello...

BETH PARSONS: Touch the wall just here...go ahead, touch it!

SALLY JONES: Oooo! It's all slimy and drippin'!

BEN ROGERS: Look out for bats, Gracie Miller!

GRACIE MILLER: Don't you talk to me about bats, Ben Rogers!

SALLY JONES: Watch out! Lord a'mighty, Susan Harper! If you'd a-stepped off that there ledge, you'd still been fallin' next Tuesday!

JOE HARPER: Listen! I'll drop a rock off'n it.
    (Pause.)

SUSAN HARPER: It never hit bottom!

WILL HANLEY: They ain't no bottom, Susan Harper. It jist goes down and down.

AMY LAWRENCE: Oh, let's go through here!

ANDY TANNER: All right! Everybody follow me!
    (The voices begin to fade in volume as the party follows twistings and turnings out of sight. Gradually, the candles begin to disappear.)

AMY LAWRENCE: Over here, Gracie!

GRACIE MILLER: I'm comin', Amy!

ANDY TANNER: Watch your step here...

SALLY JONES: My, it's narrow...
    (The last candle disappears.)

SCENE XIX

The sound of dripping water echoes and intensifies. A flutter of bat wings passes by. Finally, a match is struck in the darkness, and a candle is lit. An isolated pool of light grows around Tom and Becky Thatcher.

BECKY: Please don't let it go out like that again, Tom. I do wish we hadn't let the others get so far ahead of us.

TOM: It don't matter, Becky. I know my way.

BECKY: I cain't hear 'em anymore, Tom. Can you?

(Pause while they listen. Then there is a faint, echoing laugh.)

TOM: There! You hear that? Now we just follow that voice…down this way, I reckon…

(They begin to descend. Suddenly, a distant echoing curse from a different direction. Tom and Becky stop.)

BECKY: Oh, Tom! Everything's mixed up in here.

TOM: Now that voice were above us…and to the right, I think. Just take my hand, Becky. *(Tom leads her up again in the direction they just came from.)* Hello!—ello—ello—ello—ello…

BECKY: Don't shout so, Tom! It makes such a horrid noise.

(They come into view again at another location.)

TOM: I know, Becky, but it just might be they'll be able to hear us.

BECKY: *Might* be? Oh, Tom…Tom, I'm scared…

TOM: It's all right, Becky. The others'll be sure to miss us…

BECKY: Yes. Yes, they'll miss us and they'll start huntin' for us…

TOM: Why, shore they will.

BECKY: Maybe they're huntin' for us right now, Tom!

TOM: I…I reckon, maybe they are.

BECKY: *(A hint of growing hysteria.)* They're probably lookin'…they're lookin' all over, right now…for us…and they're a-shoutin' for us and…*(Mood shift.)* Tom, I don't hear no shouting…they ain't lookin' for us at all, Tom…They don't even know we're *lost*, Tom, they don't even *know*…

TOM: Shhht! What was that?

(Silence. Then, echoing footsteps. The footsteps suddenly stop.)

BECKY: Tom! Tom, it's them! *(Becky breaks away from Tom and runs blindly in the direction of the sound.)* Hello? Help! Help!

TOM: Becky, come back! *(He runs after her, trips and falls in the dark.)*

BECKY: I see a light, Tom! We're saved! Hello! Over here! We're over here! Becky Thatcher and Tom Sawyer!

(Becky is groping her way frantically in the darkness. Tom gets to his feet and tries to follow her.)

TOM: Becky, stop! You'll fall off a ledge up there! Wait for me!

BECKY: Oh, Tom! I cain't see it no more! The candle! It was coming toward us, and now it's gone!

TOM: *(Catching up to her.)* Wait, Becky!

(Injun Joe leaps out from behind a rock barrier.)

BECKY: *(A scream.)*

(Injun Joe towers over Becky, not five feet from her, his lantern lighting his face from below. Tom and Becky are frozen for a moment in terror.)

INJUN JOE: Well, if it ain't Miss Thatcher. Judge Thatcher's daughter. You know, your pappy put a price on my head, little girl. Five hundred dollars, dead or alive. That's a heap of money.

(Injun Joe slowly draws his knife. In an instant, Tom makes a dash for Becky, placing himself in front of her, just as Injun Joe slashes out with his knife. Tom stands facing Injun Joe, holding Becky behind him.)

INJUN JOE: And little Thomas Sawyer. Star witness for the defense. Big hero. Little Thomas Sawyer who wants to put Injun Joe's neck in a noose.

(Injun Joe starts to edge toward them. Tom backing up and pushing Becky behind him.)

INJUN JOE: But Joe ain't gonna hang. Joe's a rich man. I've got thousands... *thousands*...in a little chest I keep back there a ways.

TOM: *(Scared, defiant.)* I know all about yer little chest. I seen you fetch it off Jacksons' Island.

INJUN JOE: My, my, my. Always eavesdropping and snooping...in graveyards and on islands...You put your nose into my affairs once too often, Tom Sawyer. I just might have to cut if off for you.

(Injun Joe makes a feigning stab through the air, Tom retreats another step, Becky screams.)

TOM: Don't you take another step. The others are lookin' for us right now. They'll find you.

INJUN JOE: Oh, no—they won't find me. But they'll find you all right. They'll find you and little Miss Thatcher. They'll find you right where I leave your bodies...

(He lunges at Tom with the knife straight out. Tom dodges, pulling Becky with him. Injun Joe lurches past them and steps into air: a crevasse. We hear his scream as he falls.—N. B. The actor steps off the edge of the uppermost platform and falls into the darkness onto a gymnastics mat; the scream is a recorded voice-over, and its length, fading into the depths, creates the illusion.—Tom rushes to the edge of the crevasse and looks down. Silence. Then, Becky bursts into hysterical sobbing. Tom turns back to hold her. Lights on them fade.)

SCENE XX

In the darkness, the sound of men's voices approaching. We see a lantern, and then three lanterns lighting up isolated faces. They are carried by the Sheriff, Muff Potter, and Will Hanley. There are others surrounding them, including Huck Finn.

SHERIFF: Well, boys. Her's a passage we ain't bin down yet. Huck—Muff. You try up that way.

HUCK: Yessir, Sheriff.

SHERIFF: Will—you come with me.

(The Sheriff and his men exit Left. Huck and Muff climb the slope, Huck in the lead.)

HUCK: Come on, Muff.

MUFF: Hold on, Huck. I cain't keep up!

HUCK: *(At the top of the slope, looking off Right.)* A light! I see a light, Muff!

MUFF: Where?

HUCK: Tom! Becky!

TOM: *(From offstage.)* Huck!

HUCK: It's them! It's them! We found 'em! It's them!

(His voice fades as Huck and Muff exit into the gloom. Blackout.)

SCENE XXI

Lights rise on a dismal group gathered outside the mouth of the cave. The fiddler and banjo player among them.

WILL HANLEY: *(From within the cave, hollow-sounding.) It's them!* It's them! We found 'em! It's them!

(The people outside the cave give up a cheer. The Fiddler and banjo player strike up a jubilant variation of the hoedown melody on their instruments. From out of the mouth of the cave come Muff, carrying Becky Thatcher in his arms, followed by Tom, and then Huck, who carries Injun Joe's treasure chest. The Sheriff and the others follow them out. The music rides over the laughter, expressions of relief, and explanations that pass among the party. They all exit except for the fiddler and one elderly white-haired gentleman who has been picking over the remains of a picnic lunch.)

TWAIN: *(Turning with a chicken leg in one hand, a picnic basket in the other, to address us and the fiddler.)* Fried chicken. Oh—the meals I enjoyed as a boy on the Mississippi. Well, it makes me cry to think of them: corn bread and hot biscuits and fried chicken. These things have never been properly cooked in the North—the art cannot be *learned* north of the line of Mason and Dixon, nor anywhere in Europe. This is not hearsay; it is experience that is speaking. Well…never mind.

(Throughout the above, the fiddler has played a wistful country melody. Now Twain turns to him, gives him the chicken leg, and the fiddler exits.)

SCENE XXII

Continuous with the previous, Twain still holding the picnic basket.

TWAIN: Tom Sawyer and Huckleberry Finn were now the wealthiest citizens of St. Petersburg. The contents of the treasure chest which they found in the cave come to twelve thousand dollars—almost enough to buy the town of St. Petersburg. For Tom and Huck, the pleasure of being wealthy lasted a good day and a half. Then they found out that having money means people fussin' over you, and wearing neckties and fancy clothes that don't let the air in anywhere, and even wearing *shoes*—on a Saturday!

(As Twain speaks, a party gathers in Aunt Polly's sitting room: Aunt Polly, Becky Thatcher, Judge Thatcher, Mr. Dobbins, the Preacher, Sid, young men and women. Tom and Huck are dressed fit to suffocate. One of the young women mimes playing a pump organ while a recorded sound track plays: a "pretty" tune for sitting room celebrations.)

TWAIN: That was bad enough. But when Aunt Polly took to giving *socials*, and inviting people over just to *look* at Tom and Huck, it was too much.

(One of the young ladies begins to sing "Shall We Gather at the River" in a dreadful vibrato voice. Mark Twain looks up at her with distaste, and then back at us.)

TWAIN: Well, I can't take it. I am going to escape.

(He looks up at Tom and Huck, who have begun to edge uncomfortably away from the group. He addresses them directly.)

TWAIN: And I would advise you boys to do the same!

(The party continues, unaware that its featured attractions are escaping. The sound of the lady singer fades, along with the light on the party. The Singer now takes over "Shall We Gather at the River" in a lovely, clear voice. Tom

and Huck are stripping off their fine clothing, and we begin to be able to hear what they are saying.)

HUCK: Well, that sounds bully, Tom! Bein' a robber sounds even better'n bein' a pirate!

(As they both shed their clothes.)

TOM: Oh, it is, Huck, it is! Of course, we'll have to let Joe Harper in on it...and Ben Rogers, because there's got to be a Gang, or else there wouldn't be any style about it. Tom Sawyer's Gang—that sounds pretty good, don't it, Huck?

HUCK: Well, it just does, Tom. And who'll we rob?

(Their jackets, shirts, and trousers have been discarded, and their shoes and stockings. They roll their underwear up from the feet and down from the chest. They're nearly to the edge of the upper pier.)

TOM: Oh, most anybody. Come on, Huck!

(Tom and Huck each grab one of the ropes that are strung across the proscenium. They detach them from their moorings and swing out over the Mississippi and back again. On the second swing out, they drop down into the river and two tall jets of water shoot into the air.)

END OF PLAY

Aladdin and the Wonderful Lamp

Directed by Gene Davis Buck
Produced by John Clark Donahue
Music Composed by Steven M. Rydberg
Scenic Design by Dahl Delu
Costume Design by Gene Davis Buck
Lighting Design by Jon Baker
Choreography by Myron Johnson

CHARACTERS

* Sorcerer, The Maghrabi
  Voice of the Sand
  Dabba,(Dahb-ba) slave of the Sorcerer
* Fatmaa, (Faht-má) widow of Mustafa Ali, mother of Aladdin
* Aladdin, (Allah-ah-deen) son of Fatmaa and Mustafa Ali, 13–16 years old
  Hassan, (Hah-sahn) friend of Aladdin, about 14 years old
  Careem, (Kah-reem) friend of Aladdin, about 14 years old
  Ali, (Ah-leé) friend of Aladdin, about 14 years old
  Abdo, (Ahb-doó) friend of Aladdin, about 14 years old
  Abdul, (Ahb-dool) Fruit Vendor,
  Eunuch, servant of the Sultan
* Abdel-A-Teef, (Ahb-dell-ah-teef) Cloth Merchant
  Jinn of the Ring, Daughter of Rokh
* Jinn of the Lamp, Son of Rokh
* Princess Badr-Al-Badur, (Bah-drool-boo-dooer) daughter of the Sultan, 14 or
      15 years old
* Sultan Harun-Ar-Rashid, (Hah-roon-ar-rah-sheed) ruler of Al-Kalas
  Grand Wezir Achmed, (Veh-zeer Ahk-med) servant of the Sultan
  Lampseller
  Attendants to the Sultan and the Princess, Ambassadors, Petitioners,
  People of Al-Kalas

Denotes principal roles.

Aladdin has a running time of one hour, forty-five minutes, including intermission.

For information concerning the original score by Steven Rydberg, contact
The Children's Theatre Company of Minneapolis.

Aladdin and the Wonderful Lamp

PROLOGUE

As house lights dim, the cry of Mohammed the Lampseller. He enters Stage Right, carrying a wooden "tree" upon which hang many oil lamps.

LAMPSELLER: Lamps for Sale! Brass and copper lamps! Two dinars for a lamp! Lamps for sale!
(A little street urchin runs by from Downstage Left toward Stage Right.)
LAMPSELLER: Abdo! Where are you going in such haste?
ABDO: *(Stopping.)* Nowhere.
LAMPSELLER: Nowhere? A fine answer! Why, you are nearly as foolish a boy as Aladdin.
ABDO: "Foolish?!" Why, Aladdin was a great prince!
LAMPSELLER: A very great prince, and wise beyond his years—but he was not always so. As a boy he was always in trouble; a ne'er-do-well. He was rude, he was boisterous, and, for the most part, unwashed. Much like you, Abdo, much like you.
ABDO: But Mohammed, I am not unwashed…
(He lifts his arms to show Lampseller, but the man continues on about Aladdin.)
LAMPSELLER: Still we remember Aladdin and value his memory and tell each other his story as often as we can. Do you know where it begins?
ABDO: No.
LAMPSELLER: It begins in the sands of Morocco, far from Al-Kalas. It begins with a Sorcerer: an evil man, with darkness in his heart. This man was looking for a treasure—the treasure of treasures—which would give him power and riches and glory. And to do this he asked questions of the sand.
ABDO: He asked the *sand* questions?
LAMPSELLER: This sand had the power of prophecy…it spoke in voices…
ABDO: What did the sand say?
LAMPSELLER: It told him to look for a lamp. Now imagine that! I have carried

lamps upon my back all these years and I have never found a magic one. Abdo, where did you say you were going?

ABDO: Nowhere.

LAMPSELLER: Good. Then I shall accompany you.

(*They slowly start to walk.*)

LAMPSELLER: You know, Abdo—in Aladdin's time there was a saying in Al-Kalas: A child is the lamp of a dark house. Do you know what that means, Abdo?

ABDO: No. I don't.

LAMPSELLER: Good. Neither did Aladdin. But perhaps you'll learn…

(*Lampseller and Abdo are Offstage Left.*)

ACT I
SCENE I

The Act Curtain—a scrim—is an illuminated Persian miniature. Interlocking gardens connect three main areas: Aladdin holding the Lamp with his Princess beneath a little pavilion; the Sultan on his throne beneath a canopy; the Sorcerer on his tower with necromantic figures above his head. Music. The music gives way to the sound of a dry and rasping wind over sand. The wind rises and peaks and falls and rises. The image of the Sorcerer on the scrim begins to glow with a harsh, reddish light, while the rest of the miniature fades. The wind rises to a new fury and then subsides to a whisper as the glowing illustration burns through to reveal the actual Sorcerer in his tower. The Sorcerer is calling upon the oracular Voice of the Sand to speak: He sits with a tray before him; he picks up handfuls of sand and allows it to run through his fingers.

SORCERER: Sabba raml, zaraba raml, Sabba raml, zaraba raml, Zaraba raml, saba raml…

VOICE OF THE SAND: Strike the sand. He strikes the sand. The sand is cast. He strikes the sand. The sand is cast.

SORCERER: Speak!

VOICE OF THE SAND: Speak! The sand will speak.

SORCERER: Tell me!

VOICE OF THE SAND: Tell me what you wish to know, tell me what it is you wish.

SORCERER: Tell me whither is the treasure...the treasure of all treasures...What is it?

VOICE OF THE SAND: Is it? Is it? A lamp. It is a lamp. A lamp is what you seek.

SORCERER: A lamp?

VOICE OF THE SAND: Wonderful Lamp...the Wonderful Lamp.

SORCERER: Where is it?

VOICE OF THE SAND: Is it? In a city of the cities of the east. A city named Al-Kalas. The Lamp you seek is beneath the earth.

SORCERER: Beneath the earth? How can I fetch it?

VOICE OF THE SAND: You cannot. You cannot.

SORCERER: I must have it!

VOICE OF THE SAND: Have it, then—have it.

SORCERER: How?

VOICE OF THE SAND: There is one who can fetch it. The Lamp is kept in his name.

SORCERER: His name! What is his name?!

VOICE OF THE SAND: Aladdin.

SORCERER: Aladdin...

VOICE OF THE SAND: His name is Aladdin.

SORCERER: What is this Aladdin? A king?

VOICE OF THE SAND: Not a king. A boy. Aladdin is a boy.

SORCERER: How will I find him?

VOICE OF THE SAND: Look for him in the sand.

SORCERER: Where?

VOICE OF THE SAND: His name will be written in the sand.

SORCERER: Tell me more!

VOICE OF THE SAND: *(Fading as the wind rises.)* No more. There is no more. The sand is still. Still. The sand is still.

(Silence, but for the wind.)

SORCERER: *(He claps his hands.)* Dabba!

(A chattering little misshapen creature appears.)

DABBA: Maghrabi!

SORCERER: *(Giving the tray of sand to the Dabba.)* Prepare the carpet.

DABBA: The Maghrabi is going on a journey?

SORCERER: Silence, slave! *(Sorcerer strikes Dabba.)* Prepare the carpet! Hurry!

(Dabba chatters in fright and lurches off.)

SORCERER: The Maghrabi is going on a journey...

(Ominous music as lights fade on Sorcerer and Act Scrim warms again.)

SCENE II

Music crossfades to voice of the muzzein and distant sounds of the city as Act Scrim rises. Sultan's Servants, Aladdin, and Fatmaa enter, bow to audience. Aladdin and Fatmaa assume pose and freeze as Servants shift screens to city setting, and stand in waiting. Aladdin is bent over while his mother attempts to sew a rip in the seat of his trousers; the boy is restless.

FATMAA: Aladdin! Aladdin Mustafa, son of Mustafa Ali! I pray you by Allah, *(Both gesture.)*

FATMAA: Move not thy bottom so!

(Aladdin continues to fidget.)

FATMAA: Aladdin! *(Indicating her needle.)* There is great danger behind thee!

ALADDIN: I am hungry, my mother.

FATMAA: Hungry!? How is it possible? Did I not just feed thee and thy brown belly breakfast?

ALADDIN: Yes. I am hungry still, my mother.

FATMAA: I am hungry still, I am hungry still…Keep thy body still, or it will come to harm! *(She continues sewing.)* A son should be the lamp of a dark house, Aladdin. Thou art in the fifteenth year of thy age—nearly a man, Aladdin Mustafa—and yet you do no job of work. You eat, and little else.

ALADDIN: *(Pivots and sits on Fatmaa's lap.)* But my mother, work does not suit me.

(Fatmaa gives a start of anger; in doing so she pricks her finger.)

FATMAA: Ahh! *(She sucks her finger, then lifts Aladdin from her lap and moves to clay cooking pot.)* Work does not suit thee, but food suits thee well! Oh, Aladdin Mustafa,

(Aladdin has moved to pot and reaches his fingers in for food. Fatmaa threatens him with the needle again.)

FATMAA: You tempt me to commit a great wrong upon the end part of the son of my husband!

(Aladdin, recognizing the danger, spins around and wards off the needle with the pot lid.)

ALADDIN: I would not have you sin on my account.

FATMAA: *(Grabbing for the thread that is still connected to Aladdin's seat and the spool rattling on its spindle.)* Aladdin!

ALADDIN: Farewell, my mother!

FATMAA: *(As Aladdin starts Offstage Left.)* Come back! Oh, if thy father were still alive!

ALADDIN: *(Returning to Fatmaa.)* Oh, my mother! I had forgot—What are you preparing for the noon meal?

FATMAA: What am I preparing? Oh! Out! No! Come back! My thread! Aladdin!

(Music as Aladdin rushes out, thread racing from spool. Lights fade on Fatmaa entangled in thread, pose. Screens shift to city.)

SCENE III

Full market activity. A seller of lamps, a fruit merchant, veiled women buy-ing, children playing. Abdel-A-Teef, the cloth merchant, has a shop Stage Left. Aladdin rushes in and tugs at the robes of the fruitseller, Abdul.

ALADDIN: *(Pointing up Stage Right stairway, anxiously.)* Look there, Abdul! Thieves, bandits in the street! Coming this way, I think…and hungry for pomegranates!

ABDUL: *(Setting down his basket and looking off where Aladdin indicated.)* Where?

ALADDIN: *(Taking one, two, three pomegranates.)* Closer than you think, Abdul, and very hungry!

ABDUL: By my beard, they'll have none of mine!

(Aladdin hides the fruit in his shirt.)

ALADDIN: Very good, Abdul! Stand guard now and watch!

ABDUL: *(Returning to his basket.)* Many thanks, Aladdin! Please take a pome-granate for your pains!

ALADDIN: *(Taking another and ascending stairs.)* Many thanks to *you*, Abdul. Farewell!

(Aladdin sees his friends Careem and Hassan pass; he waves to them.)

HASSAN: Aladdin! We'll meet you at the river!

(Aladdin nods in acknowledgment. He has reached the entrance to the Hammam, which is guarded by a Eunuch. From within, the sounds of splashing water and women's laughter.)

ALADDIN: *(To Eunuch.)* Hail to thee, Keeper of the Hammam!

(Aladdin offers a deep salaam. Eunuch condescends to return the salutation with a deep bow as well; as he does so, Aladdin attempts to pass by into Hammam entrance. Eunuch grabs Aladdin by the seat of his trousers.)

EUNUCH: Stop there, street boy! The baths are forbidden to such as you. Besides, it is the hour of the day when the women are bathing. You cannot go in!

ALADDIN: A thousand pardons, gentle sir. Indeed, I can hear the women laughing now, I had forgot. My message from the Sultan must wait.

EUNUCH: Message from the Sultan! What?

ALADDIN: Princess Badr al-Badur wishes to bathe later in the day. You must prepare the Hammam for her arrival.

EUNUCH: The Sultan's daughter! Leave me, urchin! I must prepare the bath! *(Eunuch turns, opens the door to the Hammam and passes in. As he does so, Aladdin sneaks a peek inside, takes one of his pomegranates and tosses it into the Hammam. Women shriek from within. Aladdin laughs as Eunuch runs out again after Aladdin.)*

EUNUCH: You are not the Sultan's messenger! Stop! *(Eunuch rushes at Aladdin, who stops, puts his foot out, and trips the large, round man. Aladdin runs off, laughing, but Abdel-A-Teef, who has been observing Aladdin's pranks, stands outside his shop Stage Left and trips Aladdin. Sorcerer appears as Abdel-A-Teef and Aladdin converse.)*

ABDEL-A-TEEF: Good morning, Aladdin. Did you fall? *(He picks Aladdin up by an ear.)* Yet so early and already into mischief? A son is the lamp of a dark house, Aladdin, but you do not light your mother's heart. I knew your father, Mustafa Ali, and while he lived he was an honest man and good. Would he not now be ashamed to see the rough and idle life you lead, my boy? *(Aladdin hangs his head in shame.)*

ALADDIN: It was only sport, Abdel-A-Teef.

ABDEL-A-TEEF: Sport! *(Aladdin's friends: Careem, Hassan, Ali, and Abdo appear and play at edge of orchestra pit, which represents the river. They wave to Aladdin and freeze. Sorcerer disappears.)*

ABDEL-A-TEEF: Go play your idle games in the sands! Find your friends, who are no friends at all! Go! *(Aladdin runs off, down the staircase Stage Left as lights fade to focus on Abdel-A-Teef's shop. Sorcerer steps from the shadows Stage Right)*

SORCERER: *(Crossing to Abdel-A-Teef.)* That boy with whom you spoke. Do you know him?

ABDEL-A-TEEF: *(Arranging his merchandise, uninterested.)* I know the boy better than I know you, sir. What do you do here, and what do you want with him?

SORCERER: Forgive me. I am a stranger in Al-Kalas. My home was in the Sunset-lands.

ABDEL-A-TEEF: Africa!

SORCERER: Yes. I have traveled far to Al-Kalas, and seek a likely lad to work with me.

ABDEL-A-TEEF: What is thy business, if I may ask?

SORCERER: Lamps.

ABDEL-A-TEEF: Then do not seek the boy with whom I spoke. He is a lazy lad and will not work.

SORCERER: Where can I find the boy?

ABDEL-A-TEEF: I am fond of him, but I fear that he will come to no good...

SORCERER: *(Losing his patience.)* That may be. Where can I find the boy? *(Sorcerer takes Abdel-A-Teef by the arm.)*

ABDEL-A-TEEF: Since you insist, *(Pulling his arm away.)* you will find him in the sands.
(Abdel-A-Teef bows curtly to Sorcerer and steps into his shop, but is pulled back by the Sorcerer. Lights begin to slowly rise on boys, playing in the sand with sticks.)

SORCERER: *(Very excited.)* In the sands, you say! What do you mean?

ABDEL-A-TEEF: Well, by the river, of course. The sands by the river.

SORCERER: *(To himself.)* In the sands by the riverbank! As simple as that! *(Sorcerer quickly rushes Offstage Right.)*

ABDEL-A-TEEF: *(Shouting after Sorcerer.)* The boy will do no work! *(Disgusted.)* Hmmph! Foreigners!
(Lights fade on Abdel-A-Teef as he steps into his shop and closes the shutters.)

SCENE IV

Aladdin and his young friends each have sticks that serve for them as scimitars. They prepare for "battle."

ABDO: Draw the line, Aladdin! Draw the line!
(Aladdin draws a line in the sand with his stick.)

HASSAN: What's your hurry, Abdo? You are bound to lose!

ALADDIN: For that, Hassan, you will lose your toes!

CAREEM: Aladdin! How would you look without a nose?!

HASSAN: Much better, Careem—much better, I'm sure.

ALI: Stop talking, now, and take your sides!

(Aladdin and Careem take positions facing each other across the line, their "scimitars" at the ready. Abdo moves directly behind Aladdin, Hassan stands behind Careem. All behave rather solemnly. Ali stands as judge.)

ALI: Now!

(Aladdin and Careem immediately crouch, Abdo and Hassan jump onto the shoulders of their respective partners who stand upright again. The sword-play commences with grunts and shouts, both levels dueling.)

ALI: You're over the line, Careem!

(Hassan pushes Abdo, who falls backward, but still clings to Aladdin with his legs around Aladdin's neck.)

ALI: None of that! Play fair! Look out, Abdo! Look out!

(Hassan jumps down from Careem's shoulders to take advantage of the situation. Aladdin turns around, so that the upside-down Abdo may duel with Hassan. Careem moves Upstage to fight Aladdin. Aladdin duels and walks backward, Abdo valiantly battling Hassan. Hassan is being forced to walk backwards, Downstage, as Aladdin walks backwards. Hassan takes one step too many and falls into the river with a splash. The fighting ceases; great laughter at Hassan.)

ALI: Aladdin's side is victorious! Let his name be written in the sands!

(Hassan pulls himself out of the pit, refusing the offer of aid by Aladdin.)

HASSAN: I'll get you, Aladdin!

(Hassan shakes his fist and runs off. Careem puts his arm around Aladdin's shoulder and they laugh at Hassan's ill humor. Abdo capers with delight. Ali takes his stick and writes in the sand.)

ALI: Al...a...ddin! Victorious!

(The muzzein is heard in the distance, singing the call to noon prayers.)

ALADDIN: Listen! It is time for prayers, and then—time to eat! *(Aladdin runs off via steps Stage Right.)*

CAREEM: Come, Ali. Abdo.

(Ali and Careem start to exit Stage Left.)

CAREEM: Abdo! Are you coming?

(They exit, as Abdo lingers to write his own name in the sand next to Aladdin's. Sorcerer appears from under steps Stage Right and observes.)

ABDO: Ab...do! Aladdin. There!

(Sorcerer runs up to Abdo, lifting him high into the air with one hand. Abdo shrieks and kicks at the air.)

SORCERER: What have you written there in the sand?!

ABDO: *(Terrified, piping voice.)* My name...Abdo...

SORCERER: Not that! The other one!

ABDO: Aladdin, sir. Aladdin. Our side won.

SORCERER: *(As he carries Abdo into the shadows Stage Right.)* Tell me about this Aladdin! Where he lives, his parents' names, everything!

(Lights fade.)

SCENE V

(Screens immediately open and reveal Aladdin and Fatmaa in their home. Fatmaa sits on the bench as Aladdin kneels; he eats with his customary passion.)

FATMAA: Slower, Aladdin! How can you eat so? A wise man, knowing that there was no more, would make what little he had linger in his bowl! *(Aladdin pays no heed.)*

FATMAA: I can't believe it. The boy will surely choke.

ALADDIN: *(Setting his bowl down and licking his fingers.)* Ahh. That was very nice, my mother. May I have some more? *(Aladdin crosses to the brazier.)*

FATMAA: Aladdin! Is it true your ears are stuffed with beans? I tell you, son— there is no more.

ALADDIN: *(Looking in pot; grieved.)* None?

FATMAA: Not a morsel. And unless I sell some cloth today, there will be none tomorrow. But come. I have not finished mine, and today I do not feel so hungry. Take it, Aladdin. *(She offers him her bowl.)*

ALADDIN: *(Accepting.)* Blessed be my mother. Do not fear—Allah will provide. We shall not starve.

(Sorcerer slowly enters; he eavesdrops at base of stairs.)

FATMAA: Allah—may his name be praised—would be pleased if *Aladdin* did some of the providing!

(Sorcerer knocks against proscenium.)

FATMAA: Now who is that? Aladdin—go and see who it is that knocks.

(Aladdin starts down stairway.)

FATMAA: And be polite!

ALADDIN: *(Garbled, his mouth still full.)* Yesh, by bother.

(As Aladdin descends, Fatmaa clears away dinner bowls. Aladdin stops on landing and sees Sorcerer at base of steps.)

ALADDIN: Mother! It is a man!

(Sorcerer starts to ascend.)

FATMAA: I gave birth to a ninny. Invite the man *up!*

(Fatmaa quickly arranges her clothing and veils herself. Sorcerer stands

beside Aladdin for a moment and looks deeply into the boy's eyes. Aladdin steps back, frightened, and the Sorcerer continues up into the room, followed by Aladdin.)

FATMAA: *(Quavering voice, nervous.)* How do you do? *(Silence.)* Allah be praised. *(Silence.)* Would you like anything? Water, perhaps? *(Silence.)* You're very tall, aren't you? This is my son, Aladdin.
(Aladdin moves to his mother's side.)

SORCERER: I know. Aladdin—son of my brother.
(Pause.)

FATMAA: I beg your pardon?

SORCERER: Aladdin Mustafa, son of Mustafa Ali, my brother. And you— Fatmaa—wife of my brother, who has gone to mercy in the arms of Allah. I am your husband's brother, uncle to Aladdin.

FATMAA: I am sorry, sir. There must be some mistake. My husband, Mustafa Ali—who has found mercy—had but one brother and he is long since dead.

SORCERER: Not dead. But lost—wandering these forty years among the wild places of the world. Through the lands of Al-Hind I traveled, and Al-Sind, deep into Egypt and beyond, until at last I journeyed to the regions of the Setting Sun.

FATMAA: *(Not really taking it in.)* Fancy that…the Setting Sun, you say?

SORCERER: There I dwelt for the space of thirty years. But one day of days, O wife of my brother, a messenger came with a message long delayed. My brother was dead. Then said I to myself: Go! Search out the one thing that is precious to thee, the treasure of treasures—thy brother's only son.
(Sorcerer reaches out to Aladdin, who sits next to Sorcerer on bench.)

ALADDIN: Me? *(A whisper to Fatmaa.)* Mother—does the man mean me?

FATMAA: Shhh!

SORCERER: *(Putting his hand on Aladdin's shoulder.)* I shall make a man of my nephew, Aladdin! I shall help you, good Fatmaa, to raise him up, and shall teach him wisdom and courage, and the knowledge of my years.

FATMAA: *(Gently taking her son from Sorcerer and standing between them.)* Well, sir—brother-in-law, if that's what you are—I'm afraid you have your work cut out for you. The boy does not know the meaning of labor. I love him, for all that, but his head is stuffed with beans, and all he ever cares to do is eat.

ALADDIN: *(His pride a bit wounded, moving back to Sorcerer.)* Please, my mother—what you say is true. But I promise you by Allah the Merciful,

I shall mend my ways, and with my uncle's help, I shall become the lamp of this dark house.

SORCERER: Lamp! You speak of lamps, Aladdin Mustafa?

ALADDIN: It is a saying we have in Al-Kalas.

SORCERER: Of course. *(Pause.)* Now, the first thing this family needs…

ALADDIN: …is food!

FATMAA: Aladdin! Hush! *(To Sorcerer.)* You see what I mean?

SORCERER: *(Standing.)* But the boy is right—first we buy food, and then a new suit of clothes for Aladdin!

(From the street, we hear a Crier of the imperial procession.)

CRIER: Hide your eyes! Hide your eyes! The Princess passes! Hide your eyes!

FATMAA: The Sultan's daughter! Quickly—close the blind! *(To the Sorcerer.)* It is forbidden to look on the Sultan's daughter, Princess Badr-al-budur.

(Aladdin closes the screens as lights fade on home. Townspeople scatter as music approaches. Procession enters from Stage Left: the Princess sits within a gilt box carried on a litter by two Servants. Three Ladies in Waiting and the Eunuch accompany her.)

EUNUCH: Hide your eyes! Hide your eyes! Khabbi-eeneki! Khabbi-eeneki! By command of our magnificent master, let all the folk lock their shops and stores and retire within their homes! The Princess passes! The Princess passes!

(The procession moves Offstage Right.)

EUNUCH: Khabbi-eeneki! Khabbi-eeneki! Hide your eyes! Hide your eyes!

(The voice fades with the music.)

SCENE VI

Vendors and townsfolk resume their business, re-opening their stalls for trade. From out of Abdel-A-Teef's shop, Stage Left, come Aladdin dressed in a new suit of clothing, Sorcerer, and Abdel-A-Teef.

ABDEL-A-TEEF: There's a fine suit of clothes for you, Aladdin. Wear it in good health and be sure to wash your elbows.

SORCERER: How much do I owe you?

ABDEL-A-TEEF: Five dinars, if you please.

(Sorcerer gives him the money.)

ABDEL-A-TEEF: If I had known that you were the boy's uncle, I would have treated you with greater courtesy…

SORCERER: *(Cutting him off.)* We are in a hurry.

ALADDIN: *(To Hassan and Ali who pass below.)* We are going on a journey!

SORCERER: *(Taking Aladdin by the arm.)* That is enough, Aladdin. *(Over his shoulder to Abdel-A-Teef.)* Thank you. Good-bye.

(Sorcerer and Aladdin exit Stage Right. Abdel-A-Teef looks after them, shrugs, looks at the coins he was given, bites one. He shrugs again and exits into his shop. Blackout.)

SCENE VII

The sounds of the market crossfade to wind. Almost immediately, lights rise to reveal Aladdin and Sorcerer climbing staircase. Aladdin stops midway.

SORCERER: Do not be afraid. Climb on. Climb on!

(A painted mountain landscape appears behind them.)

ALADDIN: Listen to the wind—how it blows at the top of the mountain.

SORCERER: Sit thee down and take thy rest, Aladdin, for this is the very spot that we have been seeking.

(Aladdin sits at the Sorcerer's feet. The ladder they ascended rises and disappears.)

SORCERER: Beneath this earth lies a treasure kept in your name. *Your name,* Aladdin! The treasure of treasures, wealth beyond the wealth of many kings!

ALADDIN: I do not understand what you say, Uncle.

SORCERER: *(Revealing his true nature; a growl.)* Then be still and listen!...
(Suddenly gentle.) ...beloved...nephew. *(He kneels down beside Aladdin.)*
There is magic beneath the Mountain Barakat: a Wonderful Lamp, and powerful—and you have been chosen. No one may pass into the earth to fetch it but you.

ALADDIN: Beneath the mountain? I cannot travel in the earth!

SORCERER: Your *name,* Aladdin, will open the earth—and close it.

(Slight pause as Aladdin tries to comprehend.)

SORCERER: Find the Lamp and bring it straight to me. Do you hear? Do you understand?

ALADDIN: Yes, my uncle. I bring the Lamp to you.

SORCERER: If you find yourself in any danger, say your name. It will protect you.

ALADDIN: Protect me? From what?

SORCERER: The Guardian of the Lamp.

ALADDIN: What is that?

SORCERER: Not…to be spoken of.

(Aladdin gulps.)

SORCERER: Remember, your greatest protection, Aladdin, lies in your very name, and in your father's.

ALADDIN: Our names?

SORCERER: (Removing a ring from his hand.) To this I add my protection. Take this ring.

(Aladdin puts the ring on his finger.)

SORCERER: Now stand, Aladdin! Take courage and observe! (Sorcerer takes a pinch of powder from a small box and throws it to the earth. He shouts.) Aladdin Mustafa! Son of Mustafa Ali!

(A crash of thunder. Flame and smoke leap up into the sky behind them.)

ALADDIN: Stop! I am afraid!

(Aladdin turns to run, but Sorcerer grabs him back and strikes him. Aladdin falls to the ground from the force of the blow.)

SORCERER: Coward, obey!

ALADDIN: Uncle!

SORCERER: Obey me as you would your father. For your own good.

ALADDIN: (Trembling with fear.) Yes, sir.

(The rumbling of thunder has become the creaking and moaning of the earth itself. Slowly, a staircase appears on the Stage Right area of the platform, leading into darkness.)

ALADDIN: Uncle! There is a door now in the earth!

SORCERER: Yes! Descend—and find the Lamp!

(Hesitantly, Aladdin stands and begins down the staircase.)

SORCERER: Find the Lamp…find the Lamp…

(Lights dim as Sorcerer sits in meditating posture Center. Aladdin reaches the bottom of the staircase and slowly gropes in the darkness. Echoing drops of water. As Aladdin makes his way Stage Left, suddenly we see a pair of eyes, glowing in the darkness—mammoth, and following Aladdin's every step. Aladdin trips and falls. Immediately the eyes move toward him, seizing the opportunity to attack. Aladdin rolls over onto his back, sees the eyes, and screams. He edges away in terror, as the eyes draw nearer with immense, groaning breath.)

ALADDIN: (Faintly.) Aladdin!

(His voice echoes: "Aladdin, Aladdin, Aladdin, Aladdin…")

ALADDIN: Aladdin Mustafa! Son of Mustafa Ali!

("Ali, Ali, Ali, Ali..." The eyes halt their forward progress, blink. Aladdin rises, emboldened.)

ALADDIN: I am Aladdin! Son of Mustafa!

(Eyes blink again and retreat a bit.)

ALADDIN: Aladdin Mustafa, son of Mustafa Ali!

(An almost indistinguishable chorus of tiny, high voices echo Aladdin's words until the cavern is filled with the sound. Then, a deep, bestial bellow emerges from the Guardian of the Lamp, and the eyes retreat up into the darkness, blink twice, and close again. Aladdin sighs in relief and congratulates himself.)

ALADDIN: Well *done*, Aladdin.

(A faint glimmer of a treetop appears. Aladdin notices the tree—bedecked with fruit of precious gems—and he goes to it. The light of the jewels grows in intensity until the entire tree is spectacularly visible. Aladdin begins to climb down the tree. He pauses and plucks a jewel, bites it to see if it is edible fruit, holds his jaw in discomfort at biting the hard surface. He holds it before him, admiring its beauty, and tucks it and several other gems in his shirt. He steps down into the Chamber of the Lamp. The light of the tree fades a little, and the music of the Lamp can be heard. With it, the light rises on the Lamp itself which rests upon a lilypad at the Downstage edge of the orchestra pit. Aladdin approaches, and finds that he must step on a series of large, ornate "lilypads" to reach the Lamp. He does so, stepping from one to the other, precariously, until he reaches the Lamp. Aladdin gently, reverently lifts the Lamp from its resting place, holds it for a moment, then puts it in his shirt and quickly leaves the Chamber, climbs the tree, and goes to the base of the stairway.)

SORCERER: *(Slowly rising, his voice first distant, then louder.)* Aladdin! Bring it to me! Bring the Lamp! *(Seeing the boy at the base of the stairs.)* Aladdin! Do you have it? The Lamp?

ALADDIN: I have it, Uncle.

SORCERER: *(Urgently)* Then give it to me! Give the Lamp to me!

ALADDIN: *(Starting up the stairs.)* *Have* the Lamp! And all things else! Just help me out of this hole.

SORCERER: *(A mad roar.)* No! Not until I have the Lamp!

ALADDIN: *(Halting midway.)* What?!

SORCERER: *(Wild.)* Son of a dog! I know your evil plans! You mean to keep the magic Lamp for yourself!

ALADDIN: *(With horrible understanding.)* You are not my father's brother...

SORCERER: Your father might have been a dog for all that I know! Wretched boy, give the Lamp to me!

ALADDIN: *(Shouting back, defiant.)* You are an evil man! My father's name was Mustafa Ali, and he gave his name to me: Aladdin Mustafa, son of Mustafa Ali!

(At the mention of the names, rumbling of the earth.)

SORCERER: Stop! Do not say those names!

(The staircase begins to rise, jolting Aladdin, who falls backward.)

SORCERER: *(A scream.)* The Lamp! Wretched Aladdin!

(A huge clap of thunder as the staircase disappears.)

ALADDIN: *(Jumping to catch the staircase.)* Help! Don't leave me here! Allah, help me!

(The trap is sealed with a tremendous hollow crash. All is dark. The crash reverberates in the hollow blackness. Gradually a dull, almost phosphorescent light illumines Aladdin, slumped on the floor, weeping. He kneels, his hands resting on his stomach, one on top of the other, in the attitude of prayer.)

ALADDIN: Allah, there is no God save Thou alone. Most Great, Omnipotent, All-Conquering, Quickener of the Dead, by Thy mercy, free me from this my doom... *(He rubs his hands in anguish and cries out.)* O! To be buried alive! Will no one save me?!

(As he rubs his hands together, there is a circular flash of fire Stage Left. The Jinn of the Ring appears within the circle—a woman with eight arms in the lotus position.)

ALADDIN: *(An exclamation of astonishment.)* Ahh!

JINN OF THE RING: I hear and I obey.

(Silence for a moment while Aladdin beholds the Jinn in amazement.)

ALADDIN: What...Who are you?

JINN OF THE RING: I am the Jinn of the Ring, and the servant of him who wears the Ring.

ALADDIN: A Jinn!

JINN OF THE RING: You rubbed the ring. I am the servant of the ring you wear on your hand.

ALADDIN: *(Suddenly looking at the ring on his hand.)* I had forgotten!

JINN OF THE RING: As long as you wear this ring, whatsoever you wish for, that will I give you.

ALADDIN: Anything?

(Jinn responds with a warm and comforting laugh.)

ALADDIN: Oh, take me home! Please—take me to my home!

JINN OF THE RING: I hear and I obey!

(Suddenly Aladdin is encircled by a ring of fire, as is the Jinn of the Ring. Blackout.)

SCENE VIII

Lights up immediately on Aladdin's home. Aladdin is seated slightly Right of Center, exactly as in previous scene. Fatmaa sits on the bench Left, unaware of Aladdin's presence. She frets and weeps.

FATMAA: Why did I let him go off with such a man? Brother-in-law! Sunset Lands, indeed! If the man is who he says he is, he'll answer to me!

ALADDIN: Hello, Mother.

FATMAA: *(Paying no attention.)* We'll be home in time for dinner, says he! With riches—wealth for Aladdin and his mother. Why did I believe him? *(Sobbing into her apron.)* O, Aladdin...

ALADDIN: *(Crawling to Fatmaa, resting his head on her lap.)* I am hungry, Mother.

FATMAA: *(Sobbing, still unaware that he is really there.)* Of course you're hungry—when aren't you hungry, Aladdin. *(Pause.)* Aladdin! (Fatmaa jumps up and hugs her son.) Aladdin! How...? Whaa...? Whe...? O! I cannot bear it, I must sit down.

ALADDIN: Mother?

FATMAA: Yes.

ALADDIN: You know that man?

FATMAA: Yes...?

ALADDIN: That was not my uncle.

FATMAA: I knew it all along! Your father would never have such a man for a brother! Where have you been? *(Seeing Lamp on the floor, she picks it up.)* And what is this?

ALADDIN: A lamp.

FATMAA: And what are all those *things* in your shirt?

ALADDIN: Some pieces of glass that I picked from a tree. *(Aladdin trades jewels for Lamp; he sets lamp on table, then sits back down on bench, exhausted.)*

FATMAA: Glass from a tree? I don't understand a word.

ALADDIN: Mother, I am truly hungry and very tired. May I have some food?

FATMAA: There is no food. That wicked man promised to provide for us, but that was just another of his lies. Well, make the best of it, as your father would say. *(She puts the jewels in a handkerchief and sets them down at Left*

edge of bench. She comforts Aladdin for a moment, then the Lamp catches her eye.) The lamp! We'll sell that lamp and buy a little food! *(She crosses to Lamp and examines it.)* A *very* little food, indeed. It's filthy! Why you brought *this* back, of all things…You certainly don't have an eye for value, Aladdin. *(Taking the corner of her apron.)* I'll clean it up. Pieces of glass…from a *tree!*
(She sets the Lamp back on the table and begins to rub it with her apron. A stream of smoke shoots from the spout. The Center panel of the city painting behind them drops like a shutter, revealing the Jinn of the Lamp—from waist up—hovering "above" the Lamp. Fatmaa sees him, slowly turns back and faints. Aladdin looks up and sees his mother on the floor.)

JINN OF THE LAMP: Aladdin. I am the Jinn of the Lamp, and thy servant. Whatsoever you wish for, that will I give you.

ALADDIN: *(Backing away in fear.)* Jinn? Jinn of the Lamp? I do not understand.

JINN OF THE LAMP: I am the Spirit—the Jinn of this Lamp which is my home. There I live and have lived for time beyond count. I am Servant to all who hold the Lamp.

ALADDIN: Even me?

JINN OF THE LAMP: Of course, my Master—Master Aladdin. Whatsoever you wish for, that will I give you.

ALADDIN: Then give me food! Please, sir, for I am hungry. And for my mother, who gives me always her share. Some beans, perhaps—a large bowl—and figs…?

JINN OF THE LAMP: I hear and I obey. *(Jinn bows and begins to turn away.)*

ALADDIN: One moment—O Jinn. Whatever you fetch to eat, let it be toothsome beyond our fondest dreams.

JINN OF THE LAMP: *(A smile.)* It shall be toothsome, Master Aladdin.
(Jinn turns, just one smooth revolution. From the void he has obtained a silver tray laden with marvelous foods. Aladdin, awestruck, takes the tray from the Jinn and sets it down on the bench.)

ALADDIN: O my! I wish my mother could see this sight.

JINN OF THE LAMP: I hear and I obey.
(He bows and gestures to Fatmaa. Fatmaa revives, she rises exactly as she fainted, as if a film was run backward. She sees the food, sees the Jinn, and faints back down again.)

JINN OF THE LAMP: Your wish is my command.

ALADDIN: *(A laugh.)* I shall have to be careful what I wish for! *(Aladdin laughs again in wonder.)* This is splendid! My head turns 'round! And the food! *(He takes a morsel and eats.)*

JINN OF THE LAMP: Does my master desire anything more?

ALADDIN: O, yes—please—Who was the man who brought me to the Mountain?

JINN OF THE LAMP: That man was the Maghrabi: the Sunset Dweller, the African Magician, Learned in Evil...the Sorcerer.

ALADDIN: *(A shudder.)* And had *he* now this Lamp, would you serve *him?*

JINN OF THE LAMP: I am the Servant of the Lamp, and him who holds it.

ALADDIN: Are...you...evil?

JINN OF THE LAMP: I am the Servant of the Lamp, and him who holds the Lamp. That is all.

(Aladdin takes another morsel of food and eats, thoughtfully.)

ALADDIN: *(Almost to himself.)* I see that I must be very careful, indeed. *(To Jinn.)* If I should ask you to bring me the Mountain Barakat, would you do that?

JINN OF THE LAMP: I shall only be gone a moment...

ALADDIN: No! Wait! I do not require a mountain. Only food enough for us, and clothes. And some wisdom, if you have that. I know so little... *(Small pause. Aladdin is lost in thought.)*

JINN OF THE LAMP: Master? My Master?

ALADDIN: *(Coming out of a daydream.)* Yes?

JINN OF THE LAMP: Do I have your leave to go?

ALADDIN: Yes. You may go.

JINN OF THE LAMP: I hear and I obey.

(Jinn bows. Burst of smoke from Lamp and shutter closes. Aladdin moves to Fatmaa and cradles her head in his arms.)

ALADDIN: My mother! Please wake up! It's time to eat!

FATMAA: *(Rising to her feet, groggy.)* Aaa...my head... *(She stands, remembers, looks around suspiciously with her eyes.)* Aladdin...is your "friend" still here?

ALADDIN: *(A chuckle.)* Look, mother! Food—such as we have never eaten in our lives!

FATMAA: *(Nervous.)* That's wonderful, Aladdin. *(Furtive whisper.)* What was that I saw?

ALADDIN: A Jinn, Mother. The Jinn of the Wonderful Lamp! *(He takes the Lamp from the table and crosses to his mother.)*

FATMAA: *(Stepping away.)* A Jinn? I thought they were only for stories.

Aladdin—take that lamp and keep it hidden. I don't much care to see it. Do you mind?

ALADDIN: Of course not, Mother. I shall keep it hidden.

FATMAA: Well, then. I'm hungry.

(Fatmaa samples some food. Blackout.)

SCENE IX

The marketplace. Abdel-A-Teef stands outside his stall speaking to another Merchant. Hassan, Ali, Abdo, and Careem stand at edge of orchestra pit and throw "rocks" into the audience. Aladdin enters. Time has obviously passed, for Aladdin has grown a mustache, is clean and well-kept. He carries a small burden in a cloth bag. As Aladdin starts to mount staircase Left, Abdo spots him.

ABDO: Aladdin! Come and play with us!

(Aladdin stops and turns to them.)

ALADDIN: Thank you, Abdo, but I have much to do.

HASSAN: *(Mimicking.)* "Thank you, Abdo, but *I* have much to *do!*"

CAREEM: Aladdin, you always have much to do!

ALI: You are always too busy to play with us!

ABDO: We are throwing stones into the river; you'd *like* it!

ALADDIN: *(With a gentle smile.)* I'm sure I would, Abdo. Perhaps another time.

(Aladdin turns and climbs the staircase. Hassan rushes after him, grabs his arm and pulls him around.)

HASSAN: *(Fiercely.)* You'll come to wish you weren't so high and mighty, Aladdin!

(The two stand tensely looking at each other. Then Hassan releases Aladdin's arm and spits on the ground. Aladdin turns as Hassan runs back and calls the others into a silent, excited huddle. Aladdin crosses to Abdel-A-Teef; Merchant gestures "farewell" and exits.)

ABDEL-A-TEEF: Good morrow, Aladdin.

ALADDIN: Good day, Abdel-A-Teef. I have come to you for some advice.

ABDEL-A-TEEF: Advice from me? Such flattery for an old man. But for over a year, now, Aladdin, you come to my shop to learn what little I have to teach; you care for your mother and provide for her. You have become a lamp for a dark house, and your father would now be proud to be your father.

ALADDIN: Your words are kind, Abdel-A-Teef. I thank you. But I could still steal a pomegranate if I wanted to…

ABDEL-A-TEEF: I'll wager you could. Just try it and I'll give your ears such a smack! But come, you wanted more than idle talk.

ALADDIN: *(Holding forth his cloth bag.)* Look at these and tell me what they're worth.

(Abdel-A-Teef reaches in and takes out some of the jeweled fruit from the Chamber of the Lamp. The old man stands astonished, open-mouthed, looking at Aladdin.)

ALADDIN: At first I took them for pieces of glass, but now I think that is not so.

ABDEL-A-TEEF: Pieces of glass! These are jewels of such size and value as would make a sultan weep. Priceless! Where did you get them?

ALADDIN: Alas, I cannot tell you.

ABDEL-A-TEEF: There is some mystery behind this, I can see. But one thing is clear—Allah has smiled on you. Guard them well—you hold a fortune in your hands.

(From Offstage, the voices of Criers.)

CRIERS: Hide your eyes! Hide your eyes! The Princess passes! Khabbi-eeneki!

ABDEL-A-TEEF: *(Closing up his shop.)* Hurry, Aladdin! You must be off the streets before the Sultan's daughter makes her passage!

ALADDIN: Good-bye, Abdel-A-Teef. Allah be praised!

(Abdel-A-Teef exits. Aladdin turns and rushes off, but has not gone more than a few strides toward Stage Right when Abdo runs past, knocks into him, and causes Aladdin to lose his balance and fall into the arms of Careem and Hassan. Ali has carried on a huge earthenware jar and opens the lid. Careem and Hassan shove Aladdin into the jar. They have bound his hands with a cloth belt.)

HASSAN: You wish to see the Princess, don't you, Aladdin?

(He shoves Aladdin's head down and fits the lid over the top. They carry the jar Upstage as Abdo furtively opens the gate of the Hammam; they place the jar within and the four boys quickly exit. Immediately, the Princess and her three Attendants enter the Hammam from Upstage. They perform a ritual dance, unveiling the Princess, layer by layer. Finally, the Princess herself lifts the final covering from her face. One Attendant goes to the jar and lifts the lid. She sees Aladdin and gasps in horror. Aladdin stands and is revealed. For a moment, the four women are frozen in confusion; Aladdin looks at the Princess, transfixed. The Princess returns his gaze. Two Attendants turn to

run Upstage and fetch the Eunuch. The Princess holds up a hand to stop them.)

PRINCESS: Stop! Oza! Nihal! Make no sound!

(Attendants freeze, kneel. The Princess turns back to Aladdin, hiding her face with her Left hand over her Right cheek.)

PRINCESS: Thou hast looked on me when I was unveiled. The penalty for such a crime is very great.

ALADDIN: While I was yet ignorant of the prize, I feared the crime. Now I give thanks to Allah that I have seen thee.

(Eunuch enters, carrying a tray of scents and oils. He sees Aladdin, stops in his tracks, then puts the tray down and goes for his scimitar.)

PRINCESS: Eunuch! Thou wilt not need they scimitar. This man—however he came to be here—is pardoned.

EUNUCH: But my liege…

PRINCESS: Release him, I say, and let him go to his home.

EUNUCH: *(Kneeling.)* Hearing and obeying.

(Princess gestures for Attendants to replace the veils.)

ALADDIN: Glory be to Him who created thee, and who adorned thee with this loveliness and grace.

(Princess lowers her head, overcome, and turns to leave. She stops.)

PRINCESS: Thou art a boy of the streets, but thou speakest like a prince.

(Aladdin bows to the Princess, and she exits, followed by Attendants and the displeased Eunuch. Aladdin slowly climbs out from the jar and steps Downstage as lights dim to a single pool on the lovestruck young man.)

ALADDIN: *(With reverence and joy.)* Alhamdolillah!

(He claps his hands, spins, and runs off happily. Blackout.)

SCENE X

Lights rise on Aladdin's home. Fatmaa stands at brazier, preparing dinner. Aladdin enters without a word and goes Upstage to gaze out window.

FATMAA: Aladdin Mustafa! You took your time—I almost thought you would be late for supper. *(She laughs at the absurdity of such a notion.)* Imagine that! You! Late for supper! *(Another laugh.)*

ALADDIN: That's all right, my mother. I am not hungry.

FATMAA: *(Instantly sober.)* Lie down. You're sick. Get into bed and lie down.

ALADDIN: I am not ill. I simply do not care for food.

FATMAA: *(Panic.)* He's dying! Allah the Merciful, have compassion on him!

ALADDIN: *(Turning to her.)* My mother, please! Try to calm yourself. I...have looked on a lady.

FATMAA: *(A gentle laugh. She crosses to him and holds him in her arms.)* My son has grown, indeed! In love, Aladdin? Your father was younger than you, when he chose me. It is cause for celebration! Who is the girl?

ALADDIN: Princess Badr-al-Budur, the Sultan's daughter.

FATMAA: Lie down. You're sick. Get into your bed and sleep!

ALADDIN: No, Mother. You may think me mad, but I am resolved. I shall marry the Princess Badr-al-Budur.

FATMAA: *I've* got to lie down. *I'm* sick. Help me to my bed.

ALADDIN: Please, my mother, you must be very strong I must ask you to go to the Sultan yourself. Since my father has found mercy in the arms of Allah, you must go in his stead, and ask the Sultan for his incomparable daughter's hand in marriage.

FATMAA: Aladdin! You are the son of a tailor! The poorest of the poor! It's not possible!

ALADDIN: Remember the pieces of glass I picked from a tree? *(He holds out the cloth bag.)* They were not glass, but gems of surpassing value. None of the Kings of Kings has jewels like these. Take them, Mother—take them to the Sultan and ask his daughter's hand in marriage for thy son. *(He places the bag in his mother's hand.)*

FATMAA: He'll sever my head from my body—I know he will...

ALADDIN: *(Joyfully.)* O, my Mother—you are the kindest of women...

(Aladdin exits. Fatmaa stands, petrified.)

FATMAA: He'll sever my head! "Chop it off!" he'll say...

(She takes her finger and "slices" her neck in illustration. Freeze. Blackout.)

SCENE XI

Music: a royal fanfare, Sultan's Servants enter and part panels to reveal Sultan's throne room. Seated on his throne is the Sultan: Harun-ar-Rashid. Princess sits on pillow to his Left. A grand staircase appears; Grand Wezir Achmed stands upon it. Ambassadors and Petitioners gather and kneel with heads bent. Servants position themselves: one holding canopy above Sultan's throne; one stands Upstage of throne; two sit at Right and Left and hold large feathered fans; two stand at base of stairs with scimitars. Grand Wezir claps his hands and addresses the gathering; while he speaks, Sultan and

Princess play some type of eighth century Arabic card game; they whisper to each other and laugh occasionally.

GRAND WEZIR: By the command of our Magnificent Lord and Master, the glorious Sultan, Harun-ar-Rashid, I call this his sovereign court to order. By the magnanimous grace and compassion of our Master, all who grieve or harbor some grievance may come, and make their complaint before the King of the Age... *(Breaking off his speech, annoyed.)* Silence! Someone dares to speak while I am speaking? Who is that? I heard speech and laughter!

SULTAN: It was I who spoke, O Grand Wezir, and it was my daughter, the Princess, who laughed. Do you wish to scold us for interrupting your speech?

GRAND WEZIR: *(Horrified.)* No, my Lord! Rather I should find toads in my bed!

SULTAN: You desire toads in your bed? You shall have them. Next request! *(Princess giggles.)*

GRAND WEZIR: *(Lamely.)* Thank you, indeed, my Lord.
(Fatmaa enters, carrying the cloth bag of jewels. She is obviously petrified in this grand context, and ignorant of protocol. She rather desperately attempts to make herself inconspicuous, with the effect of eventually becoming very conspicuous indeed. Grand Wezir consults his list of petitioners.)

GRAND WEZIR: The Ambassador from the Western Isles salutes thee, Harun-ar-Rashid, and brings greetings from his people.
(Ambassador steps forward one step and does obeisance to the Sultan: bowing, kneeling, and touching his forehead to the floor.)

SULTAN: The Sultan returns the greetings to the Ambassador of... *(To Grand Wezir.)* Where did you say the fellow was from?

GRAND WEZIR: *(A whisper.)* The Western Isles, my liege...

SULTAN: That's the one. Greetings to thee and thine. Get off the floor now.
(Ambassador rises and steps back to his place, which Fatmaa has since taken. Ambassador accidentally steps on Fatmaa's foot.)

FATMAA: Ow!
(She hops. Heads turn in her direction.)

GRAND WEZIR: Silence!

FATMAA: *(Deprecating; limping, explaining to the crowd.)* It's nothing. Don't worry about me. Man stepped on my foot.
(She turns to a petitioner who has been watching her in silence, and puts her finger to her lips.)

Aladdin and the Wonderful Lamp 249

FATMAA: Shhh!

GRAND WEZIR: Silence!

(Fatmaa dips and bows and edges her way to another location.)

GRAND WEZIR: Next—the courier of the Caliph Abdel-Salam brings a tribute of forty span of oxen...

(Courier steps forward and prostrates himself.)

GRAND WEZIR: ...twelve caskets of herbs, oils and fragrance, one golden ring, sixteen doves...

(Sultan is becoming more and more interested in the nervous antics of Fatmaa. He leans out further and further to catch glimpses of her as she jockeys for an inconspicuous position. She is constantly apologizing to people for her being in the way.)

GRAND WEZIR: ...the tusks of two elephant and twelve boar, a dancing girl and her brother who is an acrobat...

FATMAA: *(Throughout Grand Wezir's previous speech.)* Psst! How do you get your name on the list?

(Petitioner looks at Fatmaa in amazement.)

FATMAA: Do you speak the language?

(Over-enunciating as Petitioner tries to ignore her.)

FATMAA: I...get...my name...How...do...

GRAND WEZIR: Silence!

(Fatmaa bows and moves to Eunuch, and tugs at his pants to get his attention.)

GRAND WEZIR: ...one dancing girl and an acrobat, six jars of costly ambergris...

FATMAA: *(Tugging harder as Eunuch tries to ignore her.)* Psst! Psst! You! How do I get my name on the li...

(Fatmaa has tugged too hard and Eunuch's pants rip down the seat. Everyone in the court except the Grand Wezir has been watching; Eunuch runs off in horror as all laugh, except Grand Wezir. Fatmaa calls after Eunuch.)

FATMAA: O! I am terribly sorry! Forgive me! I just wanted to ask a question of you...

GRAND WEZIR: *Silence!*

(Fatmaa stops in terror.)

SULTAN: *(Chuckling.)* O, be still, Achmed. I must see this woman. Never has my court been so richly entertained.

FATMAA: *(Mortified.)* I'm so sorry, I...

SULTAN: Woman—approach the throne. The rest are dismissed.

(With much bowing, Ambassadors and Petitioners exit, leaving Sultan, Princess. Grand Wezir, Servants, and Fatmaa.)

SULTAN: Approach, I say, and tell me why thou hast come.

FATMAA: *(Kneeling.)* I pray to Allah for the continuance of the Sultan's glory, and for the everlasting permanence of thy prosperity. *(She kisses her fingertips, touches them to her forehead, and bends her forehead to the ground: hitting it on the floor with a loud bump.)* Ow!

(Sultan laughs; Princess stifles a giggle.)

SULTAN: O woman, I must tell thee—thou art a wonder! Speak to me of thy desire, and I shall grant it.

FATMAA: First, good Lord and Master, promise me one thing...

SULTAN: What shall I promise?

FATMAA: Not to sever my head.

SULTAN: *(Another laugh.)* Consider it done. I shall not sever thy head.

FATMAA: *(A deep breath.)* O Lord, our Sultan—I have a son. Aladdin. And he hath required of me that I should ask the Sultan... *(She is afraid to go on.)*

SULTAN: Continue.

FATMAA: *(Another breath; quickly getting it over.)* ...for thy daughter's hand in marriage. *(She bows again.)*

(Beat.)

SULTAN: Sever her head from her body!

(Servants advance on Fatmaa, who yelps in fear.)

SULTAN: No! Wait! I gave my word and I shall not break it now.

(Servants return to their places.)

SULTAN: But is thy son mad, this "Aladdin?"

FATMAA: *(After a sigh of relief.)* Quite...possibly. *(Ascending the steps toward the Sultan, forgetting propriety.)* But he's not bad looking and he *is* a dear boy and would make a fine husband...

(Grand Wezir quickly blocks Fatmaa from getting too near Sultan.)

GRAND WEZIR: The woman is clearly possessed. Shall I remove her?

SULTAN: No—not yet, Achmed. I am fascinated. *(To Fatmaa.)* What makes this son of yours think he is worthy to marry with the Princess Badr-al-Budur?

FATMAA: Well, his heart is honest and good...and he loves the lady. He did send a little token of his love...

SULTAN: Let us see a love-token worthy of our daughter.

(Fatmaa sets the cloth bag down on the steps and opens the top of the bag. The jewels rest in a small pile and the hall is filled with flickering, colored light. Stunned silence. Sultan rises and slowly descends the steps and sits next to the jewels—holding a couple in his trembling hand.)

SULTAN: I see it, and yet I have to struggle to believe it. Astonishing! In all my

Treasury, which is unthinkably vast, there is not one jewel to match the least of these! Truly, king has gone to war with king for treasures not one-half as precious as this. Good woman, your son has made a marriage offering most worthy of the Princess Badr-al-Budur.

PRINCESS: *(Rising from her pillow.)* But Father! I do not wish to marry this man. "Aladdin," she says, but I know him not...

(Sultan picks up the bag and ascends the stairs to Princess.)

SULTAN: You speak as one who has *another* in her mind.

PRINCESS: Truly, I did look upon a young man with favor, but he was far beneath my station.

SULTAN: Then put him from your thoughts and look on these gems!

GRAND WEZIR: O Sultan, I too would speak against this Aladdin. The jewels are marvelous, indeed, but the man himself—he must be a common fellow...look at his mother!

(Fatmaa gasps and steps up to Grand Wezir, her nose to his.)

FATMAA: Begging your pardon, sir, but what do you mean?!!

SULTAN: Stay your anger, good woman.

(Fatmaa sits.)

SULTAN: We must confer.

(Sultan gestures for Grand Wezir to approach throne. Sultan sits; Grand Wezir and Princess lean in from either side. They freeze. Aladdin with Lamp and Jinn of the Lamp appear.)

JINN OF THE LAMP: My Master. Speak your request and it shall be done.

ALADDIN: Provide for me whatever the Sultan may require.

JINN OF THE LAMP: I hear and I obey.

(Sultan, Grand Wezir, and Princess finish their consultation. Sultan stands and addresses Fatmaa.)

SULTAN: It is settled, then. Your son, Aladdin, has made a suitable offering for my daughter.

(Cry of joy from Fatmaa; Princess, dismayed, steps Stage Left and turns away.)

SULTAN: *However...*it is not enough, not for my Princess. Aladdin may marry with the Princess Badr-al-Budur if he brings to me ten times this number of jewels.

FATMAA: *(Crushed hopes.)* How is it possible...

SULTAN: Furthermore, this Aladdin must provide a fitting home for the Princess. A palace, good woman—your son must build a palace worthy of the beauty of Badr-al-Budur.

(Jinn of the Lamp gestures over the throne room and exits with Aladdin. A distant music is heard.)

FATMAA: *(Despair.)* It was hopeless from the beginning. Now all is lost. I know my son—this news of yours will kill him.

PRINCESS: Do not weep, good lady—I am sorry for your son.

(The music grows.)

GRAND WEZIR: Now what is this I hear? Some commotion in the streets…Shall I dispatch the Sultan's guards, my Lord?

SULTAN: It does not sound like a disturbance…

PRINCESS: It is music, Father—lovely, lovely music—and coming closer…

(A procession of people dressed in radiant garments enters the court. Acrobats, dancing girls, and two men carrying a litter upon which rests a huge bowl filled with gems—identical to the jewels Fatmaa presented to the Sultan. The room is again filled with dancing, colored light. Sultan runs down and tosses the jewels into the air with joy and wonder. Aladdin, splendidly dressed, rides in on horseback and catches one of the gems. Stunned silence in the court.)

FATMAA: *(After a beat, breaking the silence.)* Aladdin! What a pretty shirt you've got on!

PRINCESS: *(Descending the steps.)* This is Aladdin? This is the very man whose image I have kept in the secret places of my heart!

ALADDIN: Your words give me joy, my Princess.

(Aladdin and his horse bow. Aladdin addresses the Sultan.)

ALADDIN: Harun-ar-Rashid, Glorious Sultan, I ask for thy daughter in marriage.

SULTAN: *(Crossing to Princess.)* And I give thee my consent—with all my heart!

GRAND WEZIR: *(Running down steps to Sultan.)* No! Forgive me, Majesty, but this must not be! Surely these wonders are the works of trickery, and sorcery!

SULTAN: Silence! I do not look at the jewels alone! I look deep into men's eyes, and try their souls and this man's soul is pure and free from evil.

GRAND WEZIR: But my Sultan! He has not fulfilled thy request. You said yourself, he cannot marry the Princess until he builds for her a fitting palace!

SULTAN: So I did. Can you do this for her, Aladdin?

ALADDIN: Sire—order the eastern windows of this room cast open. There, beyond a deep reflecting pool, the Palace which I have builded for Badr-al-Budur.

GRAND WEZIR: You see? As I told thee, the man is as mad as his mother!

SULTAN: *(Ascending the steps to his throne.)* Open the windows, Achmed. Open them now!

(Sultan sits. Grumbling, Grand Wezir descends the stairs and walks to edge of orchestra pit Downstage Center. He mimes the slow opening of massive shutters. Music. A blinding line of white light grows in breadth as the shutters are opened, until all onstage are bathed in it. They surge forward, looking out over the audience, at the miraculous palace. The music builds and the crowd moves backward as a group, Upstage of proscenium line. The stairway withdraws. Aladdin gallops on his horse with joy. Rose petals shower the stage and Act Curtain falls as Music crescendos and fades.)

Intermission

ACT II
SCENE I

The Act Scrim is burned through, revealing Sorcerer seated on his magic carpet, casting in the sand.

SORCERER: Sabba raml, zaraba raml, Sabba raml, zaraba raml, Zaraba raml...

VOICE OF THE SAND: Sand. Strike the sand. He strikes the sand. The sand is cast...

SORCERER: I call on the sands to speak!

VOICE OF THE SAND: The sand will speak, will speak...

SORCERER: I am troubled in my spirit...

VOICE OF THE SAND: In thy spirit...?

SORCERER: I want to know about the death of Aladdin...

VOICE OF THE SAND: Ah—Aladdin, Aladdin...

SORCERER: It would comfort me to know he suffered. Tell me what agonies he suffered in the earth...

VOICE OF THE SAND: In the earth...?

SORCERER: Tell me now! How did Aladdin die?

VOICE OF THE SAND: Aladdin die? Did not die...Aladdin did not die...

SORCERER: What?!

VOICE OF THE SAND: Aladdin did not die, not die, not die...

SORCERER: No!

VOICE OF THE SAND: No, no, no...Aladdin lives...he lives in splendor...

SORCERER: This cannot be true!

VOICE OF THE SAND: ...be true, be true. He has the Lamp, the Lamp, the Lamp...

SORCERER: The Lamp!

VOICE OF THE SAND: The Lamp, the Lamp, the Lamp, the Lamp...

(Beside himself with rage, Sorcerer takes the tray and lifts it high above him, letting the sand cascade off.)

SORCERER: *No!*

VOICE OF THE SAND: *(A dying wail.)* No, no, no, no, nooooo...

SORCERER: *I shall destroy him! I shall destroy him!*

(The carpet rises off the floor, hovers for a moment, then carries Sorcerer through the air as lights fade.)

SCENE II

Act Scrim out. Lights reveal a room in Aladdin's palace. The Lamp rests on a pedestal Center. Aladdin rubs the Lamp. A jet of smoke heralds the appearance of the Jinn of the Lamp.

JINN OF THE LAMP: Good morrow, Prince Aladdin. Your wish is my command.

ALADDIN: O faithful Jinn, in the space of two days time I shall have been married to the Princess for one year. I desire from you a suitable gift to give her.

JINN OF THE LAMP: Of course, my Master. Shall I fetch a herd of snow-white deer from the frozen northern wastes?

ALADDIN: *(Chuckles.)* Something simpler, I think, and less difficult to admire. Perhaps a dove or two, in a pretty cage.

JINN OF THE LAMP: I hear and I obey.

(Jinn bows, turns, and faces front again, holding a large golden cage with two white doves within. Aladdin takes it from him.)

ALADDIN: Very nice, O Jinn. *(He sets the cage down beside him.)* You have been my servant and have served me now for more than two years. In all that time you have never denied my wishes. Is there nothing I could ask of you that you would refuse?

JINN OF THE LAMP: Indeed, Prince Aladdin, there is one request, that should you make it, not only would I refuse you, I would have to destroy you.

ALADDIN: Destroy me! What is this thing?

JINN OF THE LAMP: You must know, Aladdin, that I am very old—older than old by the reckoning of the years of humankind. Yet I, too, had a time of birth, and parents. Far away, high in the heights of the Caucasus Mountains, there lives a bird—huge and ancient and all-powerful the Great Bird Rokh, oldest of all beneath the sun. She is my mother, and all her offspring my brothers. If any man were so foolish as to ask for the Rokh, or any of her eggs, I would destroy him utterly.

ALADDIN: *(After a pause.)* I see.

JINN OF THE LAMP: My master Aladdin, the Princess is approaching this room. Perhaps you would not wish her to find me here?

ALADDIN: Yes, my servant. Thank you. You may go.

(Jinn disappears into the Lamp. Princess enters from Stage Left. Aladdin rises and takes her hands.)

ALADDIN: The stars of her sky, moon of the moons, the night of her eyes...
(*Aladdin kisses Princess's hand.*)

PRINCESS: (*Seeing the cage.*) O, what lovely birds! For me, Aladdin?

ALADDIN: No, I am giving them away.

PRINCESS: Ohhhh...

ALADDIN: (*Laughing.*) Of course the doves are for you, My Princess. Who else?

PRINCESS: (*Kneeling down to admire her gift.*) You are a good husband, even if you are lacking in wit.
(*She touches Aladdin playfully on his nose. They laugh together.*)

PRINCESS: My father is coming, and your mother, and others of the court.

ALADDIN: Good. I have some news for all of them.

PRINCESS: (*Seeing the Lamp.*) Aladdin. Look at that lamp. All battered and old...Why do you keep such a thing? You have such wealth, you could have a thousand and one new lamps.

ALADDIN: Sometimes there is value to be found in that which is old.

PRINCESS: Pray, keep it out of sight, at least—it is ugly.
(*Fanfare. Sultan enters, together with Grand Wezir and Fatmaa. Aladdin stands and bows to Sultan. Princess picks up birdcage.*)

PRINCESS: Look, my father, what Aladdin has given me.

SULTAN: It is a fine gift, my Princess. Greetings, Aladdin!

ALADDIN: Hail to thee, my Sultan! Good morrow, Mother...Achmed. Please be seated, all of you. I have some news.
(*They sit upon the satin pillows.*)

FATMAA: Nothing too dreadful, I hope. I always tremble when people say they have "news." (*Confidentially to Grand Wezir.*) It's usually bad.

GRAND WEZIR: (*Still not comfortable with Fatmaa as a member of court.*) Please, my lady. Always hope for the best.

FATMAA: Well, that's just what my husband Mustafa used to say!

ALADDIN: I am going on a journey!

PRINCESS: (*Dismayed.*) Ohhh.

ALADDIN: But only for a day! I am going on a hunt—to capture a wild boar for the court of the Sultan Harun-ar-Rashid!

SULTAN: (*Rising and taking Aladdin's hand.*) Thou art a fine adopted son, Aladdin—indeed, thou art the lamp of this my house. I shall send for the royal hunters to assist you.

ALADDIN: No, my father—I have other plans. Achmed—did you fetch the Man of Wisdom as I asked?

GRAND WEZIR: *(Standing.)* Yes, my lord. *(Moving Stage Right and clapping his hands.)*

GRAND WEZIR: Abdel-A-Teef! Enter!

(Abdel-A-Teef enters from Stage Right, followed by Hassan, Ali, Abdo, and Careem under guard.)

ABDEL-A-TEEF: Greetings, Aladdin. Here are the boys you called for.

(The boys throw themselves to the floor.)

ABDO: We are sorry, Aladdin, for what we did.

ALI: We wish we hadn't.

CAREEM: It was a shameful thing!

HASSAN: And all my fault. I made the others do it!

ALADDIN: *(With authority.)* Stop!

(A moment of silence; the boys tremble in suspense.)

ALADDIN: You are expecting me to punish you? You four captured me and placed me in a jar. For that, my friends—you shall be rewarded!

(Aladdin crosses and takes his bride's hand as the boys look up with joy and relief.)

ALADDIN: Never, otherwise, would I have found my Princess. I proclaim you to be Royal Hunters to the Court! Achmed—fetch for them the livery of the Guard.

(Grand Wezir exits Stage Left.)

ALADDIN: We shall capture a wild beast as you once captured me!

(Boys bow again in gratitude as lights fade and panels close.)

SCENE III

Lights rise. Lampseller enters from Stage Right. A cloaked figure—the Sorcerer stands in the shadows Stage Left.

LAMPSELLER: Lamps for sale! Brass and copper lamps! Lamps for sale! Two dinars for a lamp! Bright, shining lamps! Lamps for sale!

SORCERER: *(Stepping from the shadows.)* Lampseller! Lampseller!

(Lampseller approaches Sorcerer.)

SORCERER: Have you heard of a man called Aladdin?

LAMPSELLER: *Heard* of him? Are you mad? Or do you live in a hole?

SORCERER: *(Growling.)* You settle your tongue or I'll cut it out and roast it!

LAMPSELLER: O, I can see you *are* mad. There is not a man in Al-Kalas who does not know the wonderful Aladdin. He is the Prince of this realm, the

Sultan's son-in-law. For one so young, he is full of wisdom and kindness, and always doing what he can for the poor.

SORCERER: Where can I find him?

LAMPSELLER: You stand before his palace now. But if you seek an audience with Aladdin, you must wait. He was off this morning, him and his hunters. There is only his bride here now, Badr-al-Budur. *(Lampseller begins to move off Stage Left.)* Lamps for sale! Brass and copper lamps!

SORCERER: *(After a moment's thought.)* Stop there, Lampseller. Give me all of your lamps.

LAMPSELLER: I'll give you nothing! These lamps are two dinars each!

SORCERER: *(Taking a small money pouch from his cloak.)* Here are one hundred dinars. Now give me the lamps!

LAMPSELLER: One hundred dinars! You are mad, indeed. But I will gladly take your money from you. Here! Take the lamps. They are yours.
(Lampseller exchanges the lamp-tree for the money and quickly starts off, laughing with delight. A veiled woman approaches the Lampseller.)

KHADIJAH: Greetings, Mohammed! I have need of a new lamp. *(She shows Lampseller the lamp she is carrying.)* This one is old and tarnished beyond hope.

LAMPSELLER: Then you'll have to speak to the new lampseller, Khadijah. This madman here just bought all my lamps.
(Lampseller exits. Khadijah approaches Sorcerer.)

KHADIJAH: You, sir! How much do you want for a new lamp?

SORCERER: For a new lamp? Your old one will do nicely.

KHADIJAH: What?!

SORCERER: *(With an air of insanity.)* You give me that old and tarnished lamp, and I'll give you a bright and shining new one.

KHADIJAH: Alhamdolillah! The man has lost his senses! New lamps for old?! But what do I care…Here. *(She trades her old lamp for a new one.)* Wait till I tell my friends! You'll do much business!
(She runs off. Lampseller reappears with women and points to Sorcerer with excited whispers. Khadijah reaffirms the news. Sorcerer remains Center and calls.)

SORCERER: New lamps for old! Who will trade with me? A bright new lamp for an old one! New lamps for old!
(People begin to chatter and giggle derisively. Another woman rushes forward, offering a battered lamp to Sorcerer.)

WOMAN: Is this one old enough for you?
(Sorcerer grins and trades. People laugh. More and more people come up and

trade with Sorcerer, who continues his calling and street noise builds with the sound of heckling and laughter. Suddenly, the window Stage Left opens—it is the Princess. A hush falls over the crowd, and they all turn away and hide their eyes.)

SORCERER: New lamps for old!

PRINCESS: What is this? What have you been doing to this poor man?!

SORCERER: Will you trade with me, my lady? New lamps for old? I'll give thee a bright and shining new lamp for an old one...

(Crowd snickers.)

PRINCESS: Silence, all of you! I am ashamed! Making a torment of this poor man's confusion! *(To Sorcerer.)* I am sorry, sir. I cannot help you.

(She begins to shut the window and Sorcerer quietly moans in defeat. Princess stops and opens it again. A thought.)

PRINCESS: No! Wait! Perhaps we *can* help each other.

SORCERER: *(A grin of hope passes over his face.)* Yes, my lady?

PRINCESS: Stay where you are. I shall return. *(Princess leaves the window, a moment, then returns with the Wonderful Lamp.)* I have tried to rid myself of this before. Now my husband will find a new lamp in its place.

SORCERER: I am sure thy lord will be very pleased...

(Sorcerer mounts steps and hands Princess a new lamp; she gives him the magic Lamp.)

PRINCESS: Now all of you depart and leave this man in peace!

(Townspeople bow without looking at Princess and disperse. Princess closes her window. When the stage has cleared, the Sorcerer steps Downstage Center and holds the Lamp above his head with victorious delight. He runs to stairway Stage Right and climbs. Panels part as lights dim to single pool in black void with pedestal Center. Sorcerer sets Lamp on pedestal and rubs the Lamp.)

SORCERER: Jinn of the Lamp, Slave of the Lamp, appear!

(Jet of smoke and Jinn appears.)

JINN OF THE LAMP: Hail to thee, my... *(Jinn sees Sorcerer.)* Where is Aladdin?

SORCERER: Silence! That is no longer any concern of thine! Do not forget that thou art only a slave. As long as I hold the Lamp, thou art mine!

JINN OF THE LAMP: I am the Servant of the Lamp, and him who holds it.

SORCERER: By my teeth, thou art! Now I command: Take up the fine palace which thou hast built, with the Princess Badr-al-Budur and myself, and carry it and us to the sands of Morocco! Lift it up off the earth and fly through the night!

JINN OF THE LAMP: I hear, and I must obey.

SORCERER: Now, I command thee—*Now!*
> (*Lights fade to Blackout. Immediately, the Jinn of the Lamp is seen flying through the sky, his arms outstretched, in his hands the palace. The vision fades. Blackout.*)

SCENE IV

Throne room of the Sultan's palace. Sultan is seated on the throne; Grand Wezir and two Servants standing guard. As lights rise, a female Servant is carrying out a silver breakfast tray.

GRAND WEZIR: Does the Sultan desire a second breakfast?

SULTAN: Possibly, Achmed—possibly. Open the windows—I wish to please myself with looking on my daughter's palace.

GRAND WEZIR: (*Clapping hands.*) It shall be done, O lord of the Age and Tide. (*Servant moves Downstage Center and mimes opening of the large shutters. No blinding light as before. Ominous chord of music.*)

SERVANT: (*Dumbstruck.*) Alhamdollilah! I do not see what I should see!

GRAND WEZIR: Silence!

SULTAN: (*To Servant.*) Stand aside, man, and let me look! (*Servant snaps back to attention and steps away. Sultan rises and slowly begins to descend the stairs.*)

SULTAN: Achmed—what sort of weather do we have today? Is there a heavy fog?

GRAND WEZIR: (*Who has not looked out the window.*) No, my lord.

SULTAN: Is there no darkening of the sky? No eclipse of the sun?

GRAND WEZIR: No, I assure thee; I would be the first to know.

SULTAN: (*At the base of the stairs.*) Allah! Allah, have mercy! The palace is gone!

GRAND WEZIR: Gone, my liege? Surely this is not so...

SULTAN: It is not there! The Princess's palace is gone!

GRAND WEZIR: (*Looking out. Gasps.*) Allah, have mercy on us...

SULTAN: My daughter! *Tell me where my daughter is!*

GRAND WEZIR: (*Undertone.*) Sorcery, trickery, spirits of evil and darkness!

SULTAN: What are you saying? What has happened to my daughter?!

GRAND WEZIR: O, my Sultan! This is the work of Aladdin! Did I not warn thee that he was steeped in sorcery? Evil sorcery and deceit! Did I not tell thee?! He built the palace through the power of evil things, in order to capture the Princess, and now through sorcery, he has taken her and it where we will never find them!

SULTAN: Aladdin? O, treachery! This is treachery, indeed! My adopted son, I was wont to call him…Scoundrel! Villain! Filth! I want his head!

GRAND WEZIR: Alas, I fear we shall never have that pleasure. If he has made off with the Princess, he will not return.

SULTAN: *(Collapsing to his knees.)* O, my daughter! Badr-al-Budur, my child! Black. Drape me in black. From this day forth, let no man sing or laugh. Put out every light and live in darkness.

(Sultan remains at bottom of staircase, his head in his hands. From Offstage Right, the sound of trumpets and young men laughing and shouting. Careem and Hassan appear on horseback, Abdo and Ali carry a wild boar on a spit. Aladdin follows leading his horse. All are splendidly dressed. They cavort for a moment, then present the spitted boar to the Sultan, who has risen to his feet.)

ALADDIN: O, my lord and Sultan—the hunt was successful!

SULTAN: *(To the two Servants.)* Bind him. Bind him tightly, hand and foot.

(Servants advance on Aladdin, drawing their swords. Careem and Hassan maneuver their horses and draw swords to protect Aladdin.)

ALADDIN: My lord, what is this?!

SULTAN: Today thou shalt die. Thou hast used the devices of sorcery and evil to capture my Princess and spirit her away.

ALADDIN: My Sultan, this is not true! The Princess? Where is she?

GRAND WEZIR: We think you know well the answer, Aladdin.

ALADDIN: No! Has any harm come to my bride?

GRAND WEZIR: Look out the windows and tell us what you see.

(Aladdin and his friends turn and look.)

ALADDIN: The palace! The palace of my Princess is gone!

SULTAN: Treachery and evil, Aladdin. I demand thy head.

ALADDIN: *(Still looking out the window.)* This is a mystery. But I will gladly die if I do not find my Princess and her palace.

GRAND WEZIR: Enough of talk! Let him be taken away to the place of execution, and there, beheaded.

(Careem and Hassan again brandish their weapons and prevent Servants from taking Aladdin.)

CAREEM: Stop where you are! Aladdin will not be harmed while the four of us are still alive!

SULTAN: First treachery, and now treason against my court!

HASSAN: No, my lord. We remain thy loyal servants. But Aladdin is our Prince and he has done no wrong.

ALADDIN: I beg you all, put down your weapons and listen.

(Pause. All relax slightly.)

ALADDIN: My Sultan, I ask of you but three days time in which to seek out my Princess and return her safely. If I fail in that, then take me to the place of execution.

SULTAN: Three days time. Since I seem to have no choice, three days grace I grant thee. Find her, Aladdin—for both our sakes, find Badr-al-Budur. *(The Sultan turns, ascends the stairs, and exits.)*

ALADDIN: Farewell, my lord.

(Servants strike throne. All others but Aladdin exit as Aladdin stands and looks out the window for a moment. Music. Aladdin turns and slowly ascends the staircase as lights dim, to a single pool on him. Aladdin falls to his knees in despair. He touches his forehead to the floor, remains on his knees and places his hands over his stomach.)

ALADDIN: The palace...my Princess...the Lamp. The Lamp is gone. O Allah, Lord, Master of the Day of Doom...

(He rubs his hands together in anguish. A circle of flame and the Jinn of the Ring appears.)

JINN OF THE RING: You have rubbed the ring on your hand. Command me.

ALADDIN: The ring! I had forgotten that I even wore the ring!

JINN OF THE RING: I know it well, Aladdin. I have waited for you to call on me since first we met. Do you recall the cavern, and how surprised you were? *(She laughs gently.)* All this time you wore the ring and me. I would have been so pleased to serve a prince. Command me now, Aladdin. Command your servant!

ALADDIN: My need is very great. Bring her back! Bring back the Princess and her palace!

JINN OF THE RING: Alas, my Prince. I cannot obey your command. The palace was removed by the power of the Jinn of the Lamp. There is nothing I can do.

ALADDIN: My Princess is in the hands of the Sorcerer!

JINN OF THE RING: It is forbidden for Jinn to struggle with Jinn.

ALADDIN: Then carry me wherever my Princess might be, to whatever land, unto the ends of the earth.

JINN OF THE RING: This I can do. I hear and I obey!

(Aladdin and Jinn of the Ring are each surrounded by a circle of flame. Blackout.)

SCENE V

The Princess's palace in Morocco. The sky behind the ornate, open lattice-work walls is lit with a harsh, reddish light. The Princess stands, weeping, Downstage Right. Sorcerer exits from chamber Upstage Center, closes panels, and mimes locking the doors.

SORCERER: *(Crosses to Princess.)* Silence! Stop that sniveling and listen to me! By now your Aladdin is long since dead. Did you think your father would reward him when he returned? His reward was the short march and the long blade. He is dead! But you are a princess still. Would you not wish to marry with a king?

PRINCESS: O, Aladdin…what have I done to you?

SORCERER: Speak not that name again! He is dead!

(Aladdin appears at window Upstage Center and listens.)

SORCERER: But I am a king of power—and my kingdom is growing. You could be *my* princess and share in my realm. Of course, if you do not consent to marriage, you will surely join your Aladdin in death. *Your* death, however, will not be so quick and merciful.

PRINCESS: Go away, hateful man! Leave me!

SORCERER: Yes, I shall go. But only for a time. When I return, make certain you have your answer.

(Aladdin steps away from the window opening and hides on the outside ledge as Sorcerer looks about and exits Stage Right. Princess continues weeping. Aladdin steps through window.)

ALADDIN: *(Softly.)* The stars of her sky…

(Princess lifts her head up.)

ALADDIN: Moon of the moons…

(She turns and sees him.)

ALADDIN: The night of her eyes…

PRINCESS: Aladdin!

(They embrace.)

PRINCESS: *(Sinking to her knees.)* O, Aladdin…

ALADDIN: *(Kneeling beside her, dabbing at her eyes.)* Dry your eyes, my Princess.

PRINCESS: Aladdin, it was all my fault—I gave him the Lamp. Now I know its worth—the whole palace was lifted up and brought to Africa!

ALADDIN: *(Standing, leading Princess toward Stage Right stairs.)* Do not trouble yourself, Badr-al-Budur.

PRINCESS: But no! It is still hopeless, Aladdin. This man—the Sorcerer—he would have me marry him! And since he has the Lamp, he has the power.

ALADDIN: There are other powers than magic lamps. There is the power of our own wit and courage. *(He turns her to him, takes her hands.)*

PRINCESS: *(With a tiny laugh through her tears.)* You are sweet, Aladdin…but *lacking* in wit, as I have often told thee.

ALADDIN: I know it well. But listen! When the evil Sorcerer returns, you must tell him that you will marry him.

PRINCESS: Aladdin! No!

ALADDIN: Trust me, lady. Say you'll gladly marry him on one condition…that he will give to you one most special gift.

PRINCESS: What should that be?

ALADDIN: Ask the Sorcerer for this… *(Aladdin whispers into Princess's ear.)*

PRINCESS: *(After a moment.)* But why would I want such a thing?

ALADDIN: You don't, my Princess. But you must make the Sorcerer believe you do, with all your heart.

SORCERER: *(Offstage.)* Badr-al-Budur!

ALADDIN: Quick! Where may I hide?

PRINCESS: Here!

(She quickly leads him t Upstage Right staircase; Aladdin hides behind it.)

PRINCESS: O, Aladdin, I am so very frightened…

(Sorcerer calls again. Aladdin gives Princess a kiss. Princess runs back.)

PRINCESS: Please come in, my Master.

(Sorcerer enters.)

SORCERER: Who is here? I heard whispered speech.

PRINCESS: No one, my lord, but you may have heard me speaking with myself. I used the time you so graciously gave me to think, and what you say about Aladdin is doubtless true. He must be dead—and I am husbandless. I begin to look with favor on your offer of marriage.

SORCERER: Well spoken, my Princess. You have come to your senses.

PRINCESS: But remember, my lord, that I am of royal blood. I require for my marriage a royal gift.

SORCERER: Name it—anything between the heaven and the earth.

PRINCESS: To fetch this gift may not be so easy as you think…

SORCERER: *(Angry.)* Do you doubt my powers?! I can have anything!

PRINCESS: Then give me, my master, for my wedding gift, a single egg.

SORCERER: What!? Do you mock me?

PRINCESS: No, my lord. This egg is precious beyond measure. I require a single egg of the Great Bird Rokh.

SORCERER: *(A laugh.)* A royal gift, indeed! It is nothing! An egg! *(Another laugh.)* Stay where you are. I shall bring your wedding gift immediately.

(Sorcerer goes to chamber. Princess goes to Aladdin.)

ALADDIN: *(Whispers.)* Where does he keep the Lamp?

PRINCESS: In a chamber beneath us.

(Sorcerer parts the two panels. The Lamp rests on a pedestal. Sorcerer rubs the Lamp and Jinn of the Lamp appears.)

ALADDIN: Keep very still. Even *we* may be in danger.

JINN OF THE LAMP: Your wish is my command.

SORCERER: Go from here and find the Great Bird Rokh. Kill the bird and steal one of her eggs. Go now! I have spoken!

JINN OF THE LAMP: Wretched man! *(Rumblings of thunder.)* You command me to kill my ancient mother? Death! Death on your house and death in your heart!

(Loud thunder. The Sorcerer hastily closes the screens of the chamber and runs up the Stage Left staircase.)

SORCERER: Treacherous girl! You set a trap for me! Where are you? You will pay dearly for your treachery!

(Aladdin steps Center and halts the Sorcerer.)

ALADDIN: Stay away! Already you are doomed!

SORCERER: You! Dog! Cause of all my troubles!

(Sorcerer advances toward Aladdin, but just then there is a burst of lightning and smoke from the floor and the Jinn of the Lamp appears Stage Right and faces the Sorcerer. Jinn of the Lamp opens his mouth and the roar of a tiger comes forth. Sorcerer responds with the bellow of an elephant. Thunder and flashes of many-colored lights. Sorcerer conjures two wild mythical beasts with his staff. With a gesture, Jinn causes the beasts to freeze. Jinn advances on Sorcerer and breaks Sorcerer's staff in two. Sorcerer retreats, backing up to window. With a deafening tiger's roar, Jinn thrusts one of the pieces of the staff at the Sorcerer and from its end a burst of flame shoots out. Sorcerer screams, recoiling from the flame, and falls backward out the window. A long, terrible scream. Silence. Aladdin and Princess stand by window, holding one another, trembling.)

JINN OF THE LAMP: *(In his normal, imperturbable voice.)* Does my master desire anything of me?

ALADDIN: *(Somewhat weakly.)* Yes, O Jinn. Please—take us home.

JINN OF THE LAMP: I hear, Master Aladdin, and I obey.

(Jinn of the Lamp bows, raises his arms. The sky is filled with traveling light and shifts in color from red to a gentle blue. Music. Fatmaa and Sultan rush in and embrace their children. Aladdin's friends, Grand Wezir, Abdel-A-Teef, Eunuch also enter with other members of the cast who form tableau. All bow to Aladdin, Jinn, and Princess. Cast bows to audience. Act Scrim slowly falls. When the Act Scrim is down, a single light burns through to reveal Jinn of the Lamp. Jinn raises his arms to audience, bows. Music crescendo. Image of Jinn of the Lamp fades.)

(Curtain.)

END OF PLAY

Beauty and the Beast

First produced by The Children's Theatre Company
of Minneapolis in January, 1978.

Directed by John C. Donahue
Music Composed by Steven M. Rydberg
Set Design by Dahl Delu

CHARACTERS

* Beauty, 14–17 years old
* Merchant, Beauty's father
* Wynne, 12–16 years old, Beauty's brother
* Geoff, 9–15, Beauty's brother
* Iris, 19–22, Beauty's sister
* Lilly, 18–20, Beauty's sister
  Old Woman
  Squire Gregory
  Hector
* The Beast
  Beast's Servants (the number of servants is flexible)
  The Prince (may double as the Beast)

* *Denotes principal roles.*

SETTING

A series of vignettes is employed to tell this story. If the design is not fluid and flexible, it can be slow going. Ideally, the principal design element should be lighting.

Beauty and the Beast has a running time of one hour, forty-five minutes, including intermission.

For information concerning the original score by Steven Rydberg, contact The Children's Theatre Company of Minneapolis.

Beauty and the Beast

ACT I
SCENE I

The Merchant's home, interior. A cold February dawn. The house is bare and grey. Coals burn on a grate. There are two doors in the Upstage wall, black rectangular openings lending to sleeping rooms and the outside, respectively. A small window in the Right end of the stone wall. Very little furniture besides a couple of wooden stools and possibly a low bench. Beauty enters the room from the interior door. She goes to the grate and lights a tinder from the coals. With the tinder, she goes about the room lighting the tallow candles. Then, she pulls a cloak about her, picks up two wooden buckets and goes to the outside door. Just as she is about to exit, her father enters through the door. Beauty stands on tiptoe to kiss his forehead.

MERCHANT: Beauty.
   (Beauty exits, and her two brothers come clambering into the house after their father. The boys have just returned from a hunt in the woods, and they still carry their bows and quivers of arrows on their backs. Geoff has a brace of pheasants on a string over his shoulder.)
WYNNE: But Father, it's *true!*
MERCHANT: Well, tell me what happened, Wynne—tell me what happened.
   (The Merchant sits on a low stool, his two sons gathered excitedly around him.)
WYNNE: Never before have I seen such strange things in the forest. Have *you,* Geoff?
GEOFF: I have not, Wynne.
WYNNE: There were *lights,* Father—about an hour before dawn—like the lights of many torches moving among the trees. Weren't there, Geoff.
GEOFF: That there were, Wynne.
WYNNE: Only there was no one there! Not a soul. And the lights would flicker and go out, and then burst up again from another place!
GEOFF: Tell about the noises, Wynne. There were noises, Father.
WYNNE: Noises like growling and groaning—wild animals, what Geoff?
GEOFF: Right, Wynne.
MERCHANT: Well, that's what they were then. Wild animals...wolves, per-

haps. You boys should not go into the forest before daylight or after dusk. I've told you before, it's dangerous.

WYNNE: But Father, these were not wolves—not unless wolves can talk and laugh!

GEOFF: Talking, they were, Dad.

MERCHANT: Boys—you let your fancy run away with you.

GEOFF: Tell about the old woman, Wynne. There was an old woman, Dad.

WYNNE: Well, we followed the noises, and the lights, and the footprints that just popped into the snow without anyone there to make 'em, and finally I told Geoff to string an arrow, just in case.

GEOFF: And I did that.

WYNNE: And he did that. And then what do you think! Standing there in front of us was an old woman—from out of nowhere, there in the middle of the wood.

MERCHANT: Wynne your story is growing with the telling...

GEOFF: Tell what she said, Wynne.

WYNNE: She said that we'd come the wrong way. That we should put up our bows and leave by the nearest path. She said that...

GEOFF: She said that we were *making things up!*

(*Iris enters, yawning noisily and pulling a comb through her hair. She is followed by Lilly, who holds a looking glass.*)

IRIS: (*Counting the strokes of the comb.*) Yaaaaawwwnnn...One hundred and twenty-six, one hundred and twenty-seven, one hundred and twenty-eight, hello Father, one hundred and twenty-nine...

WYNNE: Talk about waking things up.

(*Iris sits on a stool and Lilly stands before here, holding up the mirror for her to see.*)

IRIS: That's right, Lilly...No—higher dear. There. Now don't fidget. One hundred and thirty-two, one hundred and thirty-three...

WYNNE: And then, Father—just like that—the old woman was gone! Geoff and I, we turned and ran, didn't we, Geoff.

GEOFF: Did we! We run like anything!

IRIS: (*Mimicking Geoff.*) "We run like anything! Geoffrey, *must* you hang dead birds around your neck?

LILLY: Oh, Iris...! (*Lilly breaks into a long simpering giggle.*)

IRIS: Honestly, Father, look at what your sons have become! It's bad enough that you let them *hunt,* like common peasants with their silly arrows. But now they're beginning to *talk* like peasants. It's a disgrace. Lilly, don't fidget with that thing.

WYNNE: *(To Iris.)* You don't complain when it comes to eating what we've hunted, do you, sister.

GEOFF: Good one, Wynne.

WYNNE: No—put a nice roast quail in front of her face and it's all gobble and slobber.

MERCHANT: That'll be enough of that, Wynne.

IRIS: Do you *hear* the way they *talk!* Only two months living in the country and already they've forgotten what they used to be!

LILLY: Forgotten their manners, they have.

IRIS: Keep *still*, Lilly. *(To her father.) And*, as to our little *Beauty*...It seems like the moment you lost your wealth, Father, our little Beauty lost her pride. No sense of pride left at all! She's probably out in the barn this minute, hobnobbing with the cow!

MERCHANT: And that's just where you two should be—helping her!

GEOFF: Good one, Dad.

MERCHANT: We've *all* got to be patient and work hard. When my ships were lost at sea, I lost my fortune—yes. But not my children, and each one of you is more important to me than all my former wealth.

LILLY: But I don't understand why you can't just make some *more* money, Father. We need our dowries, Iris and me. What man would want to marry us now, without a penny to our names?

WYNNE: *(Soberly.)* I can't think of a one. Can you, Geoff?

GEOFF: Can't think of nobody'd want to marry those two.

WYNNE: Good one, Geoff.

IRIS: Father, would you please ask the boys not to stand so close. They *smell*.

MERCHANT: *(Getting up and leaving.)* I think you all owe each other apologies. I want you to do so by the time I get back from the barn. *(The Merchant exits out the outside door.)*

WYNNE: And I think Father's right. Geoff—go ahead. Apologize.

GEOFF: *What?*

WYNNE: That little present you picked up for the girls. Now's the time to give it to them.

GEOFF: *(Undertone to Wynne.)* I don't know about no present...

WYNNE: The one you picked up in the forest, Geoff. You've got it in your bag, there.

GEOFF: Ohhh, *that* present. *(He unbuckles the leather pouch at his side.)*

WYNNE: Oh, you'll like it, girls. It's green, and it's got warts all over it, and it hops when you poke it with a stick.

LILLY: *(Wail of apprehension.)* Aaaaaaww!

IRIS: It's a toad, I know it! It's a toad! Don't you *dare* take that thing out! Don't you *dare!*

(Geoff holds the toad cupped in his hands.)

LILLY: Father! Help! Keep it away!

(Geoff thrusts his cupped hands out to the girls, who jump up and shriek. The Merchant re-enters, carrying coals for the grate.)

MERCHANT: Children!

(The children fall silent, except for little gasps which Lilly continues to emit.)

MERCHANT: I must say that you girls hardly behave as though you were *ready* to be married, for all your talk. And you *boys* act like a couple of ninnies.

LILLY: But Father, I do so want to be married…

IRIS: Married and out of this place! I hate it here in the country! Hate it!

(Beauty enters, carrying the wooden buckets which are now full of steaming milk. She sets them down and takes off her cloak.)

MERCHANT: *(As he stokes the grate with the new coals.)* What about you, Beauty? Are you in a hurry to marry and leave your father, too? Your sisters are.

BEAUTY: Well…yes. I mean, no. I would someday like to be married, very much. I think it would be grand to be married…But I want to stay with you, Father, for a few more years. I don't think I could bear to leave.

IRIS: *(Mocking Beauty.)* "I don't think I could *bear* to leave." Don't worry about it, little sister. No one's going to marry you while you have that odor of the barn about you. *(To her father.)* You've been calling her "Beauty" for too many years, Father. She's beginning to think it's her real name. *(To Beauty.)* Well, it's not! It's just plain old *Rose,* and you'd better get used to it!

LILLY: *(Taunting.)* Rose, Rose, Rose! *(Lilly sticks her tongue out at Beauty.)*

WYNNE: Geoff.

GEOFF: What, Wynne?

WYNNE: Get the toad out.

GEOFF: Right, Wynne.

(Geoff takes the toad out of his pouch again, and the two older sisters jump up and run shrieking from the room. The Merchant follows them.)

MERCHANT: Stop it, boys! Girls! I want you to do some work today! Lilly! Iris!

(The Merchant is out. Geoff turns to Beauty with the toad.)

GEOFF: *You're* not afraid, *are* you, Beauty.

BEAUTY: Oh, but I am! I can't stand it when you boys bring your frogs and lizards and such into the house.

GEOFF: *(Holding out the toad.)* But there's nothing to be afraid of. He's really quite a nice fellow, once you get to know him.

BEAUTY: *(Recoiling.)* Please, Geoff...don't...

WYNNE: Go ahead, Beauty...hold him. But don't let him hop away.

BEAUTY: No...

WYNNE: He won't bite you. Go ahead, sister.

(Geoff's closed hand outstretched to Beauty. Beauty hesitantly stretches her own hand out to touch the toad. Just at that moment, there is a brief and sudden rise in the sound of the wind outside. It dies down a moment later, but there, standing in the doorway, is an Old Woman.)

OLD WOMAN: Beauty.

BEAUTY: *(A cry of surprise.)* Oh! *(She turns to face the woman.)*

OLD WOMAN: That is what you are called, isn't it? Beauty?

BEAUTY: Well, yes...it's not my name, but my mother called me that, and my father and brothers do still. But forgive me...who are you? I mean, do come in out of the cold.

OLD WOMAN: *(Laughs a little at Beauty's confusion.)* Your mother called you Beauty because that's what you are.

BEAUTY: My mother died when the youngest boy was born. That's Geoff.

(Beauty turns to her brother, who is still holding out the toad.)

BEAUTY: Geoff, say good morning to the lady. Geoff?

(Geoff and Wynne do not speak or move.)

OLD WOMAN: Beauty.

(Beauty turns back to the woman.)

OLD WOMAN: I bring a message for your father. Will you give him this letter? *(She gives a letter to Beauty.)*

BEAUTY: Oh, but you can speak to him yourself. I'll just call him. *(Beauty turns to fetch her father, but stops when she sees how still and silent her brothers are standing.)*

BEAUTY: Geoff? Wynne?

(The wind rises again and dies, the lights in the room shift, and the Old Woman is gone. The boys are suddenly animated again.)

GEOFF: *(Still holding the toad out to her.)* Go ahead, Beauty—take him.

BEAUTY: Geoff!

WYNNE: He's a very friendly toad. His name is Arthur.

BEAUTY: But the Old Woman... *(Beauty turns and sees that she is gone.)* Where...?

WYNNE: Old woman?

BEAUTY: She's gone.

GEOFF: Who's gone?

(Beauty looks at them for a moment in confusion. Then she runs to the inside door.)

BEAUTY: Father! Father, come here, please. I have a letter for you.

(The Merchant appears in the doorway.)

MERCHANT: What is it, daughter?

BEAUTY: There was an old woman here with a message for you, Father. But she's gone now…

WYNNE: She's just teasing, Father.

BEAUTY: She was here! An old woman!

MERCHANT: *Another* old woman. I have enough trouble with the two old women I've got in there.

(Iris enters carrying the looking glass, followed by Lilly with the comb.)

IRIS: I heard that, Father.

BEAUTY: You must believe me…Here! Here's the letter she gave me.

(Beauty gives her father the letter. Lilly sits and combs her hair while Iris holds the mirror for her.)

MERCHANT: Well, who *was* she? Where did she say she *came* from? Why would she be bringing messages to me?

LILLY: For goodness' sake, Father. Open it! Read it!

(The Merchant breaks the seal on the letter.)

LILLY: Sixty-two, sixty-three, *out loud,* Father, sixty-four, sixty-five…

MERCHANT: *(Reading.)* "Good sir. Your ship has come in."

IRIS: What! The ship!

MERCHANT: "You may either gain great fortune, or lose the fortune you now have…"

LILLY: I can't believe it! We're going to be rich again!

IRIS: Lilly—hush!

MERCHANT: "The journey which you must undertake is perilous…"

BEAUTY: Oh, Father! What can it mean?

WYNNE: Don't worry, sister. Geoff and I will guard Father on his journey, won't we, Geoff?

GEOFF: That we will.

MERCHANT: I'm afraid you won't, Geoff. It says here that I am to travel alone. It's all quite strange. Not like a business letter at all. "Your ship has come in," it says. That's one ship—there's no mention of the other two. "Take the Southern Road." Very strange, indeed.

LILLY: Oh, *money,* Iris! Money!

IRIS: Dowries!

LILLY: Husbands!

IRIS: Squire Gregory—do you think he remembers me?

LILLY: Of course he does, dear.

IRIS: Now that we're wealthy again, he'll certainly come to call, don't you think?

LILLY: No *question.* Oh, Iris! Maybe he'll bring his cousin, Hector! Ooooo!

IRIS: *(Sudden alarm.)* But whatever will we *wear?* We can't receive gentlemen dressed like this! Father—on your way back from the harbor, you *must* buy Lilly and me some new gowns.

LILLY: And ribbons! Don't forget the ribbons, Father.

IRIS: And maybe a little tiara, what do *you* think, Lilly?

MERCHANT: Girls! Peace—please! You've already dressed yourselves in gowns and captured three husbands apiece and I haven't even saddled my horse.

LILLY: Father, if Iris gets a tiara, *I* get a tiara. It's only fair.

MERCHANT: You girls are hopeless, hopeless. Geoff—go out to the barn and give old Ben a good brushing down.

GEOFF: Right, Dad.

MERCHANT: Wynne—get my saddle and kit together.

WYNNE: Yes, Father.

(Geoff and Wynne exit.)

LILLY: Oh, and *rings,* Father! We must have *rings,* of course. Golden rings!

MERCHANT: Yes, yes, yes… Don't *you* have any requests, Beauty? What would you like me to bring you?

BEAUTY: Really, Father…I don't know…

IRIS: Of course not. She won't ask for anything—just to be different. No— Beauty doesn't want a thing.

BEAUTY: Yes, I do! I mean…let me think. A rose. I want a rose. Several roses. I do miss the sight of them—please, Father?

LILLY: A *rose!*

MERCHANT: I'm afraid, Beauty, that it would be simpler to bring you new gowns or golden rings than a rose. It's the dead of winter, daughter.

BEAUTY: Oh, of course. How stupid of me. Only I couldn't think.

IRIS: A *rose.* We're going to be rich again, and the girl asks for a *rose.*

(Iris and Lilly put their heads together and laugh, long and loud. The curtain falls.)

SCENE II

From the darkness come the sounds of a high wind and the frantic neighing of a horse. The curtain rises on a dark and swirling nighttime snowstorm. We see the Merchant with his lantern lying on the ground. We are able to see little else, except for a few dim shafts filled with eddying snow. The Merchant struggles to his feet.

MERCHANT: Ben! Ben! Oh, my head…
(We hear a horse's whinny.)
MERCHANT: Ben, come back! Come here, old boy! *(The Merchant whistles.)* Whatever got into that horse. Never thrown me before. Ben!
(The whinnying fades into the distance.)
MERCHANT: Cold. And my head fit to crack…Ben!
(Just the sound of the wind.)
MERCHANT: Freeze to death in a hurry. *(The Merchant looks about, but he— and we—can see very little. The Merchant walks painfully Upstage a little casting about with the dim light from his lantern.)* Must keep moving, must keep moving…Sleepy…Suddenly so…Sleepy. Lights? Lights! There in the distance…But I'm so…sleepy…So very…
(From out of the darkness there steps a dim shape. It approaches the fallen Merchant, picks up the Merchant's lantern, and from the light of the lantern we see the creature: something caught midway between the bestial and the human. The creature examines the Merchant, then makes a beckoning gesture back to the darkness. The first creature is joined by a second. The two of them quickly lift up the Merchant and carry him Upstage. The darkness quickly envelopes them, as the lights fade.)

SCENE III

The lights of a chandelier flicker on, revealing a massive organic structure, growing as it were out of the forest itself. A long and winding staircase, stonework overgrown with enormous roots. A massive tree trunk, bent and forming a sloping arch across the stage. Within the arch, an opening suggestive of a grotto, and somewhere in its depths there is a fire burning that sends quivering shafts of red light out onto the walls of stone and wood.

One of the Servants of the Beast—half-human, half-bestial—enters by the base of the staircase carrying a pewter dinner service. Servant One climbs the stairs to the second level—the tree trunk—and is joined there by Servant Two. This creature throws a white tablecloth over what had appeared to be nothing more than a stump on the trunk. Suddenly it is a small dinner table, on which the first Servant lays out a single place setting: covered dishes, a large flagon, a stone carafe of wine, etc. Servants One and Two are aided in this by Servants Three and Four, who have joined them. Servant Five enters bearing warm robes and furs, which he lays out over a stool by the table. Servants Six and Seven enter, carrying the still unconscious Merchant. Servant Three pulls out the large chair that sits by the table and Servants Six and Seven settle the Merchant into it.

Then, all seven Servants go to various positions in the castle and suddenly become part of the "molding," freezing into shadowy corners and niches, and resembling sculptural ornamentations.

All of the above has been accompanied by music, and the Servants all move in a type of dance. Now the music takes up a beckoning sort of call, which seems to awaken the Merchant. He sits up slowly and painfully at the table, and then starts in confusion at his surroundings.

MERCHANT: What? Where… *(Clutches his head.)* Oh, my head. Must have fallen. But what is this place…? Hello! *(He rises from the table.)* Hello? Is anyone there? *(He walks slowly, inspecting his surroundings.)* Fine plate… *(He lifts the cover off one of the dishes.)* Such food!…Hello?…I begin to remember…a castle, the lights…But how did I get here? *(Shouting offstage.)* Hello! Do you hear me? Anyone? *(To himself.)* No servants, no master…Cold and wet…must have fallen in the snow…Starving… *(Lifts the lid off the dish again.)* Steaming hot and just waiting…So hungry…But I must not give offense. *(Shouting.)* Hello? Hello! *(Over-enunciating as he shouts.)* I've had an accident in the road…Horse threw me… I was wondering if you'd mind terribly…Just a bit of food…Perhaps I might stay the night if nobody minds…? *(To himself again.)* You're making a fool of yourself, talking like that. *(The Merchant walks to a shadowed niche.)* The place is deserted…But it can't be—the Master must be out, he'll soon be coming back… *(The Merchant is standing before one of the "frozen" Servants. He reaches out a hand to touch it.)* Now what sort of fellow lives here…A hunter, perhaps. *(He turns around, sees the clothing.)* Look there. Furs and robes…and I am so very cold… *(He goes to the furs, takes off his outer garments and pulls on the warm clothing.)* Nothing else to do…Return these in the morning…That's better. And now—if nobody minds—I'll have dinner! *(He seats himself at the table, takes the covers off the dishes, pours himself a flagon of wine and drinks.)* Ahh. *(Picks up a piece of fowl as the lights on the scene fade.)*

SCENE IV

As the lights fade on the previous scene, moonlight floods the castle room in window-shaped patterns. The Merchant can be vaguely made out, sleeping at his place at the table. The red light of the fire within the grotto flames up and makes the shadows move. The Servants of the Beast drop their statuary poses and emerge. Some of them whisk away the dinner service and the Merchant's old clothing. Others dance together. Suddenly we see the silhouette of a man-shape standing in the mouth of the grotto. He raises his arms and bellows: a mournful guttural bestial cry. The smallest of the Servants runs down the staircase to the figure in the grotto. The small Servant bows before the Beast, takes him by the hand and leads him back up into the depths of the cave. The lights fade.

SCENE V

The lights rise with the light of dawn. The Merchant, asleep at the table, awakens. He stretches and yawns, and then with a shock realizes where he is. There is a bowl of milk set before him.

MERCHANT: What? What? Oh…oh, yes. Now I remember. What a strange night…What a strange *journey* this has become…Didn't trust it from the start. First the letter…and then the storm, and now…*this. (He sees the bowl of milk before him.)* Look there. Milk. A bowl of milk, and last night's dinner all cleared away…Someone or some thing is here, that's for certain. Hello? *(Getting no response, he takes a tentative sip from the bowl.)* Fresh milk…Surely it is the den of some kindly spirit I have stumbled into. *(He lifts the bowl again.)* To the spirit of this place…wherever you might be. *(He drinks the milk, sets down the bowl and rises from the table.)* Dreaming all the night through. Strange dreams…I don't think I shall be staying here long…Shouldn't have set out in the first place, not in such a hurry. Should have looked into it all. *(He is descending the staircase.)* But how am I to get away from here? No horse…Perhaps there is a creature in the stables, if there *are* stables…So warm here…as though it weren't winter at all. *(Down the steps, and into the rose arbor—vines of roses twining among the rock.)* Roses! Blossoms in the deep of winter! *Very* strange…Well—my Beauty shall have *her* gift, at least… *(The Merchant draws a small knife.)* Amazing they are. Each one of them so very alive…like small faces, looking and listening. Almost a shame to cut them… *(He cuts one rose stem.)* For Beauty!

(Immediately, there is a terrible bellow echoing from the grotto. The Merchant turns and falls to his knees in terror. From out of the cave walks the Beast, until he stands over the Merchant.)

MERCHANT: God help me…

BEAST: *(With grief.)* My rose… *(The Beast takes the cut rose from the Merchant's hands. He touches the rose to his face. Then, enraged.)* Ungrateful man! I saved your life. I took you into my castle. I ordered my Servants to give you food and drink and clothing. And you repay me by killing my roses! You cut them with knives!

(The Merchant automatically lets the knife drop from his hands.)

BEAST: My roses, which I value beyond all else…Cruel man! You shall die for this rose!

MERCHANT: My lord, I beg you to forgive me!

BEAST: *(Fury.)* My name is not "My Lord!" My name is Beast! You have eyes, don't you? You can see me, and what I am?

(The Merchant does not answer.)

BEAST: Can't you!

MERCHANT: *(Feebly.)* Yes.

BEAST: Then don't try to flatter me! Lies do not live long in my house—and neither shall you. *(The Beast moves apart, sits, and holds his head in his hands. After a pause, he lifts his head. With grief.)* Why did you cut my rose?

MERCHANT: One of my daughters asked me to bring her one. A gift for her.

BEAST: A costly gift, for which you must pay with your life. You would wish to see your daughters once more, to bid them farewell?

MERCHANT: Very much, my daughters and my sons, yes, I would.

BEAST: Then, I say this: Go to your family, and let the daughter who brought this upon you return in your stead. If she will not freely offer herself to save you from your doom, then you must make your farewells and return to me within a single week.

MERCHANT: My daughter! Send Beauty to *you!* Never.

BEAST: Her name is Beauty…? She will not be harmed, but she must come willingly.

MERCHANT: She will not come at all, sir!

BEAST: *(Standing.)* I am no "Sir!" I am Beast! Go now! You will find a fresh horse saddled for you in the stables. My Servants have placed a quantity of gold in your kit. You have gained a fortune in coming here, and lost another. Go!

MERCHANT: *(Recognizing the words.)* Gain one fortune and lose another… The words of the letter. *(To the Beast.)* Are you the one who sent me on this journey? Are you the one who sent me that accursed letter!

BEAST: Letter. *(The Beast looks at his own hands, and then holds them up to the Merchant and laughs bitterly.)* Letter! I know nothing of letters! I am Beast! Go now. Return within a week, you or your daughter. Go. My Servants and I shall mourn the death of this my rose. Begone!

(The Merchant backs away from the Beast, and then turns and runs off.)

BEAST: This my rose…

(The Servants slowly appear, gathering around the Beast. One of them kneels before the Beast with a small white box. The Servant opens the lid and gently takes the rose from the Beast. He places the rose into the little white casket and rises. The other Servants form a solemn line behind the Servant with the rose, and together they slowly process into the mouth of the grotto and out of sight. The Beast sinks to his knees among the vines of roses and weeps. The curtain falls.)

SCENE VI

The Merchant's home interior. Iris alone, with a small chest of gold coins.

IRIS: *(With wonder, tinged with greed.)* Gold…A whole chest full of gold… from a *beast*…

(Beauty enters the room, and Iris guiltily drops the lid of the chest and whirls around to hide the fact she's been looking in it. Beauty is dressed in a travelling cloak and is carrying a small tied bundle. She is followed closely by the Merchant, and then the boys, and finally Lilly.)

BEAUTY: It's no use, Father. I will not let you suffer on my account.

MERCHANT: And I refuse to let you do this thing!

WYNNE: Father! Geoff and I have been talking, and we've decided to go and find this Beast, or whatever he is, and kill him!

GEOFF: Tell him why, Wynne. *(And then loudly to his father.)* Because we're not afraid of no monster, that's why!

WYNNE: Good one, Geoff.

GEOFF: I mean, we've got our arrows, haven't we, Dad.

MERCHANT: Do not even think of such a thing, my sons. The Beast's power is so great that you would have no hope of overcoming him. But your sister is not going to that castle. Beauty—listen to me. I have lived a *life*-time—it is no great loss for *me*. But you are *young*...

IRIS: What's the use, Father. Anyway, it was her fault you picked the rose. She couldn't ask for clothes or any common gifts like Lilly and me.

LILLY: No—she had to be different and ask for a rose. *(To Beauty.)* And now Father's going to be killed for it, and you don't even shed a *tear!*

BEAUTY: Because there is no need. Father will not come to harm. *(To her father.)* I am like my brothers..."I'm not afraid of no Beast." And I'm that stubborn—you can go to the castle, Father, but you can't stop me from following you, now can you.

MERCHANT: Beauty, you grieve me more than I can say.

BEAUTY: Do not be aggrieved...I am not. Please take me, Father...otherwise I shall have to follow behind on foot... *(She breaks into a sob.)* Oh, Father...

(She runs to him and they embrace.)

SCENE VII

The curtain is down for as few seconds as possible before it rises on the castle of the Beast. Beauty and her father are climbing the staircase to the second level. The candelabra is flickering and the table is laid with a single delicate place setting of crystal and gold. When Beauty and the Merchant reach the second level, one of the Beast's Servants appears before the girl and bows. Beauty gasps and clings to her father.

BEAUTY: Ahh! Is this the Beast?

MERCHANT: No, daughter.

(The creature elaborately shakes his head and bows again several times.)

MERCHANT: It seems to be a servant, by its manner. The Beast told me it was his servants who fed and clothed me on the night of the storm.

(The creature nods and claps in approval.)

BEAUTY: How...how do you do.

(Another Servant appears from behind and gently lifts Beauty's cloak from her shoulders.)

BEAUTY: Oh!

(The first Servant makes motions indicating that he will take Beauty's traveling bag. She gives it to him, he bows again, and gestures for her to follow him. The creature leads Beauty and the Merchant down a terrace of steps to a chamber in which one of the stone outcroppings is laid over with a featherbed and coverings. The Servant places the bundle next to Beauty's new bed.)

BEAUTY: He's showing me that this is to be my room...

(The Servant nods and bows.)

BEAUTY: Father, I do not think this Beast means to kill me. *(She gives a little nervous laugh.)* In any case, not today...

(The Servant leads the way back to the dining table.)

BEAUTY: *(To the Servant.)* Hello...?

(The Servant turns to her.)

BEAUTY: Your master...is he nearby?

(The Servant cocks his head quizzically at her, and then seeming to understand, he makes a sweeping gesture with his arms. Immediately, all of the Servants of the Beast emerge from various locations, assemble, and then perform a dance, welcoming Beauty to the castle.)

BEAUTY: Oh, Father—look at them all!

(When the Servants have finished their dance, they bow to Beauty. Beauty speaks to them hesitantly.)

BEAUTY: Thank you...thank you very much...I think that you are all very... courteous.

(She makes a curtsy to them and they show their delight with her. There is a terrible bellow from above. Suddenly the Servants of the Beast are no longer there, having whisked themselves away in an instant. Beauty and the Merchant look at each other with fear.)

MERCHANT: Daughter, now that the time is come, I cannot let this happen. I cannot leave you here. Let us both escape, while we have the chance.

BEAUTY: My dear Father...I love you so very much. Please go now, before it is too hard to take our leave of each other...

(Another bestial cry.)

BEAUTY: *(Embracing her father.)* Good-bye, Father...

(The Beast appears at the top of the staircase. Beauty sees him.)

BEAUTY: *(Faintly.)* Oh...

(The Beast slowly descends the staircase to the second level. Before he has

reached Beauty and her father, Beauty swoons and drops to her knees, still supported by the Merchant. Instantly, the Beast rushes down the remaining stairs to assist the girl, but as he reaches out to her he remembers himself and draws back.)

MERCHANT: Beauty!

(With her father's help, she gets to her feet.)

BEAUTY: I'm sorry. I'm all right now.

BEAST: *(After a small pause.)* Does the girl come willingly?

BEAUTY: Yes...Yes, I do.

BEAST: You are very good. I am...obliged to you. *(To the Merchant.)* And you are an honest man.

BEAUTY: I'm sorry...just now...I don't know what came over me.

BEAST: You are weak from your journey...

BEAUTY: Yes. From my journey.

BEAST: Please, please...you must sit at table and take your meal.

BEAUTY: Thank you...Father? I think I *will* sit down...

(The Merchant helps Beauty into the chair at the table.)

BEAUTY: You must leave now, Father.

MERCHANT: Beauty—no...

BEAST: Honest man: You took one rose from me, and gave me another. Your debt is paid. Go now, and never think of returning.

MERCHANT: *(Quickly embracing Beauty.)* My daughter... *(He turns and exits rapidly.)*

BEAST: Beauty—will you permit me to watch you while you dine?

BEAUTY: *(Trying to wipe away the tears in her voice.)* As you please...I mean, whatever you wish...

BEAST: No, Beauty. You are the mistress of this castle, and it is yours to command. If you find my presence troublesome, you need only bid me go, and I shall leave you.

BEAUTY: No, please—do stay. I wish you to stay. I'm used to goings-on at the dinner table...jokes and shouting...my sisters and brothers, you know. They don't always get along, and then Father has to step in and settle things...

BEAST: You are fond of your father.

BEAUTY: Oh, very! I shall miss him terribly...I don't know what I shall do.

BEAST: *(He throws back his head and cries in bestial grief. —N.B. Throughout the play the Beast, who has the power of speech, also displays vocally his bestial nature through these bellowings, and his instantaneous unmasked displays of sorrow—the unashamed sorrow of a dog, for example, when rebuked*

by its master, as well as a dog's ability to recover instantly from grief.)
Aaaaoowwaaaowww…

(Startled, Beauty rises from the table.)

BEAUTY: My lord, please! Don't cry!

BEAST: Please do not be *too* unhappy here…You *will* try to amuse yourself in your castle, won't you, Beauty? Everything here is yours and I should be very miserable if you were not happy.

BEAUTY: *(Sitting down again.)* I shall try, my lord.

BEAST: I am not 'my lord.' You are Beauty and I am your Beast.

BEAUTY: I see.

BEAST: Beauty, I know what I am! And I know that I am slow in my mind and cannot speak as well as you.

BEAUTY: I think you speak…very gently.

BEAST: Beauty…will you be my wife?

(Beauty covers her face with her hands.)

BEAUTY: *(Through her hands and tears of fright.)* No, Beast! No, no, I won't! No…

(The Beast rises from the table.)

BEAST: I'll leave. *(The Beast takes up a small white box which has been lying on the table and opens it.)* A small gift for you, Beauty. *(He takes the rose out of the rose casket and places it in a crystal vase on the table.)*

BEAUTY: *(Confused.)* A rose…?

BEAST: As you requested. Good night, Beauty.

(The Beast exits down the staircase and into the grotto. As he is exiting, Beauty takes the rose out of the vase and looks at it, then rises from the table and runs to the top of the staircase, looking after the departing figure of the Beast. When he is gone she crosses into her bedroom and collapses on the bed, still holding the rose. She sobs quietly and then lies down, sobbing. The lights dim, and moonlight again comes in through the windows.)

SCENE VIII

Window-shaped patterns of moonlight fall across the contours of the castle, the light from the grotto's hidden fire heightens and dances on the outer walls of the cave. Beauty lies on her bed, sleeping.

From out of the shadows emerge the Servants of the Beast. They dance together. One of them runs up the staircase, across the second level and into Beauty's chamber. He takes Beauty by the hand and helps her out of bed. He bows to her, she curtsies to him. He leads her out of the bedroom and onto the second level where she is met by other Servants. Beauty dances with them. One of them capers to make her laugh.

Below, on the first level, a man stands at the foot of the staircase, facing Upstage. The Servants of the Beast lead Beauty to the staircase, and she sees the figure standing below her. Her face lights up with joy.

Beauty descends the staircase to the standing figure, beaming and radiant. The figure reaches his hand up to take Beauty's hand, swings her around and embraces her. Beauty laughs. Beauty takes the man by the hand and leads the way up the stairs, but stops suddenly when she sees the Beast at the top of the stairs, standing in a shaft of moonlight and holding out to her a single rose. Beauty cries out in fright and shakes her head, refusing the rose and the Beast. The Beast hangs his head in sorrow, and slowly backs off into the shadows—using the Stage Right second level escape.

Beauty turns back to her partner on the stairs, but when she sees him she puts her hands to her face and screams in terror. He reaches out a grotesque paw to her, which clutches a rose. She pushes the rose and the paw away from her, the figure turns to us and we see that it is now the Beast.

At the top of the stairs on the second level the Old Woman enters. She beckons to Beauty. Beauty runs up the stairs to the Old Woman. The Old Woman embraces Beauty and with her arm around the girl's shoulder, leads her to the bedroom. Beauty gets into her bed and the Old Woman gently tucks her in.)

OLD WOMAN: Go with them, Beauty. It's only a dream. The prince is waiting for you…Dream with them. The Prince is waiting.

(On the staircase, the Beast lifts up his paws and looks at them, back and front. Still looking at his paws, he walks down into the rose arbor, sits and bellows mournfully. The lights fade.)

(After the Dream, three brief vignettes.)

FIRST VIGNETTE.

Morning light rises on Beauty sitting in the chair, sewing. A Servant scurries out from the grotto below her, stops, looks up at Beauty and then scurries off Right. Beauty waves and laughs, and then continues sewing. The Beast enters from the Stage Left tree escape, almost behind Beauty.

BEAST: Beauty.

BEAUTY: *(Startled.)* Oh!

BEAST: Each day you sit here in the light of morning and do that with your hands. What is it you are doing, Beauty?

BEAUTY: What am I doing? Well, can't you see? I'm sewing.

(He does not understand.)

BEAUTY: *Sewing,* Beast. Making clothes. Don't you understand?

BEAST: Is it...work?

BEAUTY: I suppose it is...yes.

BEAST: Beauty, you do not have to do work here. Anything you want—gowns, robes, anything—just tell me what it is and it will be here.

BEAUTY: But I *like* to do this, Beast. It gives me pleasure.

BEAST: *(Not understanding, shaking his head.)* I am slow in my mind...

BEAUTY: Don't say that...I could even teach you to help me—I know I could. That is, if you'd like...

(The Beast lifts up his paws and looks at them. Beauty laughs.)

BEAUTY: Oh, Beast...

(Lights out.)

SECOND VIGNETTE

A game of hide and seek. Lights rise on three Servants, who run on and hide ineptly in three locations on the first level. Beauty enters from the Right tree escape, looks, and then runs down the stairs. She quickly finds each Servant.

BEAUTY: *(Pointing them out.)* There *you* are...and there...and there!

(Each of the Servants emerges from his hiding place.)

BEAUTY: Now it's *my* turn. I'll hide and you find me. Go away now, and don't look!

(They exit. Beauty looks about for a place, then runs up the staircase. She crouches down in the Center hollow of the trunk—or under the table? The Beast at the same time descends the upper staircase and sees Beauty getting into her hiding place. He goes to her but she does not see him approach.)

BEAST: Is something wrong, Beauty?

BEAUTY: *(Giving a cry of fright.)* Oh, Beast! You always frighten me so! Now you've spoiled the game.

(Beauty comes out of her hiding place. The Beast hangs his head in disgrace.)

BEAUTY: I'm sorry. You can't help it. And you didn't *spoil* the game... *(She smiles at him.)* You *won* the game!
(He lifts his head to look at her. The lights fade.)

THIRD VIGNETTE

Lights up on Beauty sitting at the table, second level, the Beast sitting on the stump by her side. Beauty is rolling up a ball of yarn and the Beast is holding a skein to assist her. They continue in silence for a short time.
BEAUTY: *(Looking up at the Beast.)* You see? I *told* you so. Better and better!
(He shrugs sheepishly and drops the skein.)
BEAST: Oh!
(Beauty laughs. Lights fade.)

SCENE IX

Morning in the castle of the Beast. From Stage Left enters one of the Servants, carrying an ink bottle on a little platter with elaborate care. He crosses to Center, then turns back and beckons with his head for another to follow. A second Servant enters Stage Left, carrying a quill. The first Servant turns and continues from Center to the foot of the staircase and up the steps, followed by the second Servant. They cross to the table, where a book is already laid out. Servant One places the ink bottle on the table next to the book, Servant Two places the quill in the bottle with exaggerated precision. Servant One crosses Left down into Beauty's chamber—which is empty— and looks off Left. He tentatively knocks on a piece of the tree trunk.

BEAUTY: *(From offstage, more amused than annoyed.)* Oh, please. Can't you be patient? I'm still dressing!
(The Servant knocks again.)
BEAUTY: You wake me earlier and earlier every morning!
(Servant One looks out at us and then back off Left. He knocks again.)
BEAUTY: Oh, now I *know* you're teasing me! Go away!
(Servant One, pleased with his joke, crosses Right to the dining table. There, Servant Two has somewhat furtively picked up the quill out of the ink bottle and has it poised over a page in the book.)
BEAUTY: *(Shouting from offstage.)* And don't you dare touch my diary!

(Servant Two does a take and then guiltily places the quill into the bottle. The two of them move up of the table to await Beauty. After a moment, she enters from Left, dressed in a lovely new gown.)

BEAUTY: Good morning. You've laid everything out nicely...thank you. *(Beauty sits at the table and takes up the quill. As she writes.)* I find...the days pass...quickly here. Time...does not seem...the same. Only when I think...of Father and...the family...do the minutes...go slowly. I am certain now...the Beast does not...mean to harm me. He is...frightening...but treats me...kindly and gives me...anything I might...want. It seems like he keeps...a great secret...but he is most of the time...very sad. *(Sensing the two creatures looking over her shoulder.)* Now what are you two doing?

(The two of them cock their heads at her and then at each other. Then they move to one side and both of them sit on their haunches and enact a dumbshow: a creature's impersonation of a human in the act of writing—big strokes, a "quill" placed thoughtfully to one's mouth, then more "writing." Beauty laughs.)

BEAUTY: You're making fun of me! Stop it this instant!

(Immediately, the two Servants freeze.)

BEAUTY: No...no. I was not giving you a command...I was only joking...

(Immediately, the two Servants begin "writing" again. Beauty laughs, and then resumes work on her diary.)

BEAUTY: The Servants of the Beast are kind...and when I feel lonely I am...happy they are here. *(She looks over at them in amused exasperation.)* Oh, go away now—both of you.

(The Servants make elaborate show of being hurt, and then exit. Beauty continues writing. During the following, the Beast enters from the grotto, and stands among the roses, listening to Beauty's voice.)

BEAUTY: I have such...dreams here. Some nights the old woman...appears in them...and comforts me. And sometimes...I see in my dreams...a beautiful Prince. He never says a word...but he always chooses me...to be his Princess. Aren't I...foolish...I call him my...Dream Prince.

(The two Servants appear again, and walk with injured dignity past Beauty. Just as they have passed her, one of them turns back and playfully snatches the quill away from Beauty. The two Servants run down the staircase, stopping midway on the steps to see what sort of reaction they have produced.)

BEAUTY: *(Standing and laughing.)* My quill! I am not finished writing yet! Oh, you two are horrid...

(They taunt her with the quill, writing in the air with it, and then continue running down the stairs and offstage. Beauty follows them, running.)

BEAUTY: Come back, you two! Come back or I shall be angry with you! *(As Beauty reaches the lower steps of the staircase, she trips and falls directly into the Beast's arms.)* O!

(She looks up into his face and suddenly recoils from him, abruptly leaving his embrace and backing away. They stand for a moment in silence, Beauty drops her head, shamed and embarrassed by her revulsion at the Beast.)

BEAST: *(After a pause.)* My Servants have been playing their tricks?

BEAUTY: Yes.

BEAST: You are well?

BEAUTY: I tripped on my gown. It's a lovely gift. I thank you for it, and for everything else you have given me.

BEAST: Are you happy here, Beauty?

BEAUTY: You are very good to me…When I think of your kindness, I almost forget… *(She breaks off.)*

BEAST: Tell me, Beauty—do you find me terribly ugly?

BEAUTY: *(She hesitates.)* I think I must not lie to you, Beast. I find you…I find it difficult to look at you. But I believe that your heart must be good.

BEAST: Yes, yes. My heart is good, but still I am a monster.

BEAUTY: No, Beast! Not a monster…There are many in the world who deserve that name more than you. I prefer you just as you are to those who hide a corrupt heart under a handsome form.

BEAST: I am slow in my mind. I cannot think of a fine compliment to thank you. I can only say that I am obliged to you. Beauty…

BEAUTY: Yes, Beast?

BEAST: Will you be my wife?

BEAUTY: *(Kindly.)* No, Beast. I will not.

BEAST: *(He turns from her and walks among the roses, stretching his hands above his head toward them.)* These roses of mine are possessed of secret power and virtue. They are gifted with voice, Beauty—voices. But they will not sing whenever I take it in my head to ask them. Oh no. I ask them and ask them…Please, my roses, sing for me. And they are silent. They only sing when *they* desire to share their beauty. *(He bows to Beauty.)* I must go into the forest now and hunt. Do I have your leave to go.

BEAUTY: Yes, of course…my Beast.

(He looks at her, then turns and exits. Beauty looks after him until the lights fade.)

SCENE X

In the darkness, the candles of a candelabra light themselves, one by one by one, and Beauty's bedroom is gently illuminated by them. We see her standing at the door of the room, observing the candles. Next to the candelabra lies a book. We are not yet aware of the Old Woman, who sits very still and dim on Beauty's bed.

Beauty slowly enters the room and goes to the candelabra. She stretches her fingers out behind the flames in wonder. She takes the book and it opens to a page marked by a dried rose. She lifts the rose and puts it to her cheek as she reads from the book.

BEAUTY: 'Gentle Beauty...' Someone has written in my diary! *(She looks up, bewildered, then resumes reading.)*
'Gentle Beauty, put aside your fear.
You are chosen to be Princess here.
Let your wishes with your will unite,
Take your Prince from darkness into light...'
OLD WOMAN: Beauty. I am pleased with you.
(Beauty turns to the Old Woman, startled.)
OLD WOMAN: The kindness you have shown the Prince shall not go unrewarded.
BEAUTY: Am I dreaming? The candles...the message in the book...This is all a dream. And I know no Prince.
OLD WOMAN: The Prince does not know me, though I have labored long in his behalf. But he is young, Beauty—younger than you think, and noble. Your kindness to him shall not go unrewarded. Push aside the draperies, Beauty—open the window. *(The Old Woman backs into darkness.)* Do as I say, girl!
(She laughs and is gone. Beauty turns out and mimes the drawing back of heavy draperies. A brilliant shaft of light falls on Beauty and illumines the set. The sunlight blows out the candles. At the very top of the staircase stands the Beast, noble and upright in bearing. Beauty sees him and calls to him.)
BEAUTY: Beast!
(At this word, the Beast seems to shrink in dignity. He looks at Beauty, turns, and exits off the top of the staircase.)
BEAUTY: Beast! *(Beauty runs out of the bedroom and up the upper staircase, looking for the Beast.)* Beast, have I offended you? Please! *(At the top of the stairs she finds no one.)* Gone. *(As she descends the upper staircase.)* I have

not treated him kindly. He *is* noble and good. *(One last hope of finding him.)* Beast…? *(She realizes that he will not come, and sadly descends the lower staircase to the first level. She stops at the rose arbor, seeing the Beast in the mouth of the grotto with his back to her. She runs up to him.)* My lord…?

(The Beast turns to her, as if caught in some furtive act. In one hand he clutches the torn carcass of a hare, and in the other a piece of its flesh which he has been eating. A stone pitcher and a bowl are at his feet. Beauty recoils with revulsion.)

BEAUTY: *(With dread.)* Oh, no…No. It's horrible!

BEAST: I hunt and kill and eat. It is my nature…I am sorry you found me.

(She turns her back to him, her hands covering her face. The Beast stands helpless in his disgrace. There is a pause. Beauty seems to steel herself. She turns back to the Beast.)

BEAUTY: Would you like to drink, my lord?

(Beauty kneels, picking up the pitcher. She pours water from the pitcher into the bowl. The Beast kneels, Beauty puts the bowl of water to his lips and he drinks from it, lapping the water. A faint, strange, lyrical music begins.)

BEAST: The roses. The roses are signing. Listen, Beauty…can you hear them?

BEAUTY: *(Rising.)* Yes…Yes, I can!

(The Beast rises, puts out his arm for Beauty to take, and she does so. They walk into the arbor of roses, looking up at them.)

BEAUTY: Such a strange music…So distant and so full of things that have been.

BEAST: Tell me quickly, Beauty: What would you most like to see at this moment?

BEAUTY: I'd like to see my father, of course. And my brothers and sisters, my family, my home…

BEAST: Then come with me…Quickly, Beauty.

(The Beast, with Beauty holding his arm, climbs the stairs to a balustrade. There, they stop and look over the railing down onto the rose arbor.)

BEAST: The roses will show you these things in their song.

BEAUTY: Show me my father and family? Oh, Beast…I feel as though my heart were torn in pieces…

(The song of the roses takes over, Beauty and the Beast standing motionless at the balustrade. Finally, the curtain falls.)

ACT II
SCENE I

The Merchant's home. Wynne, wearing an apron, sits on a stool with a pot in his lap, cutting up potatoes into it.

WYNNE: One potato, two potato, three potato, *four…* five potato, six potato, seven potato… *ouch! (He sucks at his newly cut finger. Then, he resumes peeling.)* Keel the pot and stir the lot and…
(Lilly enters through the outside door, dressed in a fine new gown.)
WYNNE: *(Glancing up at her.)* …and throw it on the floor.
LILLY: Hurry up with that stew, Wynnie. Squire Gregory and Master Hector will be here any minute, and they'll want their supper.
WYNNE: Do you think they'll like the stew so much they'll marry you?
LILLY: If Master Hector proposes to me, it will have nothing to do with the stew!
WYNNE: I'm glad to hear that. Cause I put beetles in it.
LILLY: You what! You…Ooooo, Iris!… *(Lilly runs out the outside door.)*
WYNNE: *(Shouting after her.)* And don't call me *Wynnie!*
(A portion of the Merchant's home backdrop is scrim. It now burns through, dimly revealing Beauty and the Beast at the balustrade, watching and listening.)
(Enter the Merchant through the interior door, closely followed by Geoff.)
GEOFF: Come on, Dad. Go back to bed, now. You're not well enough to be up and about…You know that, Dad…
MERCHANT: Beauty…? Wynne, has Beauty finished with the milking? Where is she?
WYNNE: Beauty's not here, Father. Beauty's gone. Remember?
MERCHANT: She shouldn't have to do such hard work. Such a pretty little girl. Your mother called her Beauty. Where is she?
(Wynne gets up and assists Geoff, each of them taking hold of their father's arms and gently turning him back to the door.)
GEOFF: That's right, Dad. What you need is a little rest, that's all. You'll be up again in no time, and we'll go hunting together—the three of us, won't we, Wynne.
WYNNE: Right, Geoff.
MERCHANT: *(Just before he exits, he turns Downstage.)* I remember…the Beast. He gave me a chest full of gold. One fortune for another, he said. Where is she? Where is Beauty, do you know?

(The boys turn him back around and usher him out.)

GEOFF: Don't you worry, Dad. We'll take care of you…

(They are offstage.)

(The image of Beauty and the Beast behind the scrim fades.)

(As they exit, Iris enters with Squire Gregory.)

IRIS: Oh, Squire Gregory, you have such a way with words!

SQUIRE: *(In his habitually rapid, jerky manner.)* Yes, I do, don't I? Amazing, isn't it? Well always a pleasure to look up old friends, meaning you, not *too* old though, ha ha, lovely young lady, just come into an inheritance of some sort, if I heard correctly…?

IRIS: Well, yes… *(Deprecatingly.)* Some messy old *gold…you* know, nothing much… *(Like a broker.)* …about a chest full as a matter of face.

SQUIRE: Chest full of gold, you don't say, so the rumors *were* true, will you marry me?

IRIS: Why, Squire Gregory, this is so sudden…

SQUIRE: Well, lovely lady, if it's all too sudden, I'd be more than happy to *extend* my proposal, lengthen it, so to speak.

IRIS: *(Hastening to intercept his tongue.)* No! No, thank you. I…accept.

SQUIRE: Well, that's settled then—we'll get married, let's have a look at the stable, shall we? A chest full of gold, did you say?

(He careens out, Iris in his wake. A beat later, Lilly enters with Hector, an unusually well-favored young man.)

LILLY: Tell me, Hector, do you like my gown? I dressed myself especially for you… *(She models her gown.)*

HECTOR: I've got one just like it. Not a gown, of course…tunic and a matching cape, same shade, roughly, I think it suits *my* coloring rather better than it does yours. You should pay more attention to the way you dress, Lilly.

LILLY: *(Crestfallen.)* Yes, yes, of course.

HECTOR: Add your hair, girl! Just look at it, and then look at mine. You see how I've shaped it to fit the contours of my face?

LILLY: Yes, yes, I can see that.

HECTOR: You should try it, it would do your looks a world of good. Promise you'll try?

LILLY: I promise.

HECTOR: Good. Then perhaps I'll marry you.

LILLY: You *will?* And you didn't even *try* the stew…Oh, Hector, you've made me the happiest girl in the whole world!

HECTOR: Well! I should think *so*. I mean, just *look* at me. Not every girl gets a chance at *that*.

LILLY: No, no, of course not. Oh, I must tell Iris!

(At that moment, Iris rushes in, followed by Squire Gregory.)

IRIS: Lilly, you'll never guess!

IRIS: Squire Gregory has proposed to me!

LILLY: Master Hector has proposed to me!

IRIS: What?

LILLY: What?

IRIS: Squire Gregory has proposed to me!

LILLY: Master Hector has proposed to me!

IRIS: What?

LILLY: What?

SQUIRE: Ha ha *Ha*. Look at them, Hector. Tickled pink, ain't they?

IRIS AND LILLY: We're going to be married!

(The two girls pull each other's hair in jubilation. Wynne enters from the interior door.)

WYNNE: *(In a hushed, strident tone.)* Quiet down, you two! Don't you know that Father's sick in there?

LILLY: Oh, Wynnie—we're going to be married!

WYNNE: Hush!

IRIS: They've accepted our dowries and we're finally going to be married!

SQUIRE: Hello, little fellow. Wynnie, is it? Tell me, old man, where d'you keep this chest of gold I've heard so much about?

WYNNE: Gold? The gold from the Beast? Beauty's ransom? You girls are using *that* for your dowries?

IRIS: Well, honestly now, Wynne. *Beauty's* not likely to need it, now is she?

SQUIRE: *(To Wynne.)* Perhaps you haven't met my cousin, Hector. Wynne, Hector, Hector, Wynne.

(Wynne angrily tears off his apron and throws it over Hector's head, then spits on the floor.)

WYNNE: *(Shouting.)* Geoff, come out here! *(To the girls.)* Go ahead and use Beauty's ransom. Get married!—you all deserve each other. *(Calling.)* Geoff!

(Geoff enters. The image of Beauty and the Beast again appears behind scrim.)

WYNNE: Geoff, I can't stand it anymore. Get your bow. We're going to go and hunt the Beast, and when we find him we'll slay him!

GEOFF: Good one, Wynne! That's what we should've done in the first place! We'll kill the Beast and save Beauty.

SQUIRE: What's all this about a beast...?

(The Merchant appears in the doorway.)

MERCHANT: Boys. Do not do this thing. Please, do not do it. I have lost one child already to the Beast. I could not bear to lose you boys as well.

WYNNE: Father, I'm sorry, but we must disobey you. The Beast is the cause of your sickness and our sorrow. When we have destroyed him, everything will be like it used to be.

MERCHANT: Please...*boys*...

WYNNE: Come on, Geoff.

GEOFF: Right, Wynne.

(They start Offstage. The image of Beauty and the Beast behind scrim fades.)

SCENE II

The castle of the Beast. Beauty and the Beast standing at the balustrade where we Left them at the end of Act I. The song of the roses is just coming to its end. The castle throughout the scene is wreathed in mists and fog.

BEAUTY: *(As the song ends, still lost in the vision.)* No! No! You must not harm my Beast! Wynne? Geoff... *(Coming to herself.)* Oh, Beast...what have I seen? What have I *heard*? It seemed to me that in the song the roses sang, I could *see* my family. My brothers said they would kill you with arrows! And my father—he looked so very ill. What did I see?

BEAST: You asked to see your family again, and the roses obeyed.

BEAUTY: Then—my sisters really *are* going to be married?

BEAST: They have been married for some time now. While you and I stood here, listening to this song, two seasons of the world passed by...Spring turned to summer, and summer to autumn, in the world inhabited by your family.

BEAUTY: But we have only been here listening for a few moments.

BEAST: Time flows as it will in my realm.

BEAUTY: But my brothers—what of them?

BEAST: My castle is hard to find for those who wish to harm me. But they have traveled long, and even now have crossed into the borders of my domain. They mean to kill me.

BEAUTY: They must not!

BEAST: You do not wish to be saved from me?

BEAUTY: No!...I don't know.

BEAST: Beauty—you give me hope. Will you be my wife?

BEAUTY: Beast, please…I *cannot*. And I cannot let you believe that I ever will. You must never ask me again.

BEAST: I understand. I shall never ask you again.

BEAUTY: But please—take care of yourself, and do not harm my brothers?

BEAST: I won't harm them, though they put me in great danger.

BEAUTY: Danger? From Wynne and Geoff? No—they are only boys. I will talk to them. I will tell them not to hurt my Beast.

(A hunting horn sounds from below.)

BEAUTY: Oh! What was that?

(Through the mists, we see Wynne and Geoff, stalking with drawn bows. Fog seeps out of the earth, the flames in the grotto rise up and steam comes out of it.)

BEAST: Hide yourself, Beauty! Quickly! Go to your chamber!

(An arrow flies past their heads and sticks into the tree trunk near them.)

BEAUTY: My brothers! Stop! They must stop! *(Beauty runs to the staircase and down the steps.)*

WYNNE: *(Pointing to the Beast.)* There it is, Geoff! Shoot!

(Geoff shoots his arrow and it strikes the Beast in the chest. The Beast staggers. Beauty has not seen the arrow strike. She is now at the foot of the staircase.)

BEAUTY: Wynne! Geoff! Stop! *(Beauty runs to the boys.)*

GEOFF: Beauty! Don't worry, we're here now, we won't let it hurt you!

BEAUTY: Put down your bows! Put them down, I say!

(The boys lower their bows.)

BEAUTY: You must not harm my Beast!

(On the upper level, the Beast pulls the arrow from his chest. Servants of the Beast appear and gather solemnly.)

WYNNE: *Your* Beast? What are you saying, Beauty! We've come to save you!

BEAUTY: I am sorry, Wynne, but I don't need saving! I am only thankful that I have reached you before you did any harm. Now, please…I love you dearly, and I have wanted to see you for such a long time, but you must go. You…you don't belong here.

WYNNE: I don't understand…

GEOFF: I just know one thing—Dad is terrible sick since you want away and we traveled all this way to bring you home! Right, Wynne?

WYNNE: I'm afraid it's true, Beauty.

GEOFF: If only he could just *see* you again…

BEAUTY: So it's true…my poor Father… *(Hesitates a moment.)* Please…wait here. *(Beauty turns and runs up the staircase to the Beast.)*

BEAST: Beauty…

BEAUTY: Beast, I am so very troubled. My brothers say that Father needs me. I don't know what to do…

BEAST: I would rather die myself, than cause you any sorrow, Beauty. Go to your Father, and live with him in happiness. Beast will stay here and die alone.

BEAUTY: Why do you talk of dying? You will not die…and I'll return to you within a single week. I promise you.

BEAST: You will come back?

BEAUTY: In one week's time. I care for you too much to leave you alone.

BEAST: My gentle Beauty…I shall live in the hope of your return. Take this ring.

(He gives her a ring on a chain which she puts around her neck.)

BEAST: It will bring you and your brothers to your home. At the end of the week, if you still wish to return, you need only put it on again. Good-bye…Beauty.

BEAUTY: Farewell, Beast. *(Beauty turns and runs down the staircase.)* Wynne! Geoff! We're going home!

(As she runs down the steps, the curtain falls.)

SCENE III

The following scene is a composite of seven brief vignette blackouts, marking the passage of the week that Beauty spends away from the Beast. They might flow with the rhythm of a slowly striking clock. Perhaps there is a corresponding musical punctuation, such as a low chime or deep string chord marking the passage of the days.

FIRST VIGNETTE

The lights rise on the Merchant's home. Beauty and Wynne are standing just inside the door. Beauty looks about her in wonder at being home again, and then Geoff enters from the interior door, leading the Merchant. The Merchant is stooped and feeble. Beauty's face lights up, she stretches out her arms to him. He looks up slowly, sees her uncomprehendingly for a moment, and then recognizes his daughter. He seems to straighten up and his face breaks into a smile as Beauty moves very slowly to him. Father and daughter embrace with tears. Slow fadeout.

SECOND VIGNETTE

Iris and Lilly seated on stools, talking in irritated tones to each other. Lilly is sewing a garment and Iris helps by holding the unraveling spool of thread on her lap.

LILLY: I *still* can't believe it. I thought we had seen the last of Miss Perfect, but oh, no...

IRIS: ...no...in she trots, just as pleased with herself as she always was...

LILLY: ...just to spite us! Just like she always did...

IRIS: ...with that smile of hers spread from ear to ear, you'd think her face would break...

LILY: ...and don't I wish it would. Happy! She actually...

IRIS: ...she actually seems to be *happy,* can you believe it? I don't think it's *natural,* I don't think it's one bit natural...

LILLY: It's *un*natural, that's what it is...And us, married and respectable...

IRIS: ...happily married young women with respectable husbands, *we're* the ones who're *supposed* to be happy...

LILLY: ...and that's just what we are, *happy*...

IRIS: ...*very* happy.

(Enter Hector and Squire Gregory.)

HECTOR: *(To Lilly.)* Woman, haven't you finished my new waistcoat *yet!* You *know* I *need* it tonight, I can't wear *anything* else...

SQUIRE: So...Iris. Your little sister's back. Lovely little thing she is, such a winning *smile* she's got, don't you think?

IRIS: Gregory?

SQUIRE: Yes, dear?

IRIS: Stop talking.

(Blackout.)

THIRD VIGNETTE

Beauty seated on a stool, her two brothers seated on the floor at her feet. Iris and Lilly stand apart, both of them unconsciously but identically chewing at respective fingernails as they listen in.

GEOFF: But aren't you *scared* of him, Beauty?

BEAUTY: Oh, no, Geoff. He's so gentle, there's nothing to be frightened of. I was at first, of course—yes, quite scared. But that was before I learned how kind and good his heart was. And Geoff—he's quite a hunter.

WYNNE: Can he talk?

BEAUTY: Of course he can, Wynne. He would say that he doesn't speak as well as you or I do…but I think it's just that he doesn't say anything unless there's something to say.

WYNNE: Then Squire Gregory should take lessons from him.

IRIS: I heard that, Wynne.

GEOFF: *(Whispering to Wynne.)* Hsst. Wynne. *(Geoff pulls Wynne's ear to his mouth.)*

LILLY: And no whispering! Secrets aren't allowed.

GEOFF: I was only going to say I hope I didn't hurt the Beast with my arrows.

BEAUTY: *(Sudden alarm.)* You didn't hit him, did you?

GEOFF: *(Uncertain.)* I don't think so…

BEAUTY: *(Reassured.)* No…No, of course you didn't. I would have known.

GEOFF: Can I see the ring, Beauty? The magic one?

BEAUTY: *(Unclasping the chain from around her neck.)* Of course… *(Giving it to him.)* But be careful…

WYNNE: Don't be trying it on for size, now Geoff—or…poof!…no Geoff!
(They laugh, Geoff scratches his head and grins, lights fade.)

FOURTH VIGNETTE

Dusk. The Merchant sitting in his chair, Beauty standing behind the chair with her arms around her father's chest, rocking him gently back and forth. The Merchant looks up at Beauty and smiles and she kisses his cheek. Then they go on rocking slowly as the lights fade.

FIFTH VIGNETTE

Morning. The two sisters together.

LILLY: It's not fair! Things just haven't turned out the way they were supposed to…

IRIS: No, but I've got a plan to fix that. We're not going to let Beauty go back to her precious Beast!

LILLY: What? You mean you *want* her to stay here?

IRIS: No, no, of course not! I can't stand the girl. But we're going to *pretend* to be broken-hearted. We're going to *cry* and carry *on* and *beg* her to stay. We'll rub onions beneath our eyes to make us cry.

LILLY: Why?

IRIS: Oh, don't you *see*, stupid! She promised that Beast-thing that she would return within a week. When she *doesn't*, well…Perhaps the Beast will stop being so *gentle* and kind-*hearted*…

LILLY: *(Catching on.)* If Beauty breaks her promise…the Beast will be *enraged!*

IRIS: Oh, Lilly. You're *slow*…but *fun*.

(Lights fade.)

SIXTH VIGNETTE

Beauty, the Merchant, Wynne, Geoff and, standing apart from them, Iris and Lilly, the Squire and Hector.

MERCHANT: It is another painful parting that we face, Beauty. Are you still determined to leave us in the morning?

BEAUTY: It will be just as hard for me, Father—I love you all so much. But I gave my word…

MERCHANT: I understand, daughter.

IRIS: Oh, Sister…how *can* you go back to that *monster!* How can you leave your loving family?

LILLY: I think you're very cruel, Beauty. We missed you for so long, and now you want to break our hearts all over again.

BEAUTY: Why, Lilly…I had no idea you felt this way…

(Lilly turns her back on the gathering.)

LILLY: *(Undertone to Iris.)* Hss. Iris, give me one of those onions.

(Iris covertly hands Lilly an onion. We can see her rubbing it under her eyes.)

IRIS: You're not being fair to Lilly, Sister. She's been sobbing her eyes out all this day.

(Lilly turns back to face Beauty, her face running with tears, she bursts into loud crying.)

LILLY: *(Crying.)* Awwwwaaawawawa!

BEAUTY: Lilly—please…

(Iris wheels around rubs onion beneath her eyes, and wheels back.)

IRIS: *(A burst of crying.)* Ooooohwawawwaa!

BEAUTY: Sisters…I beg you…don't cry on my account…Please…

IRIS: I can't bear it if you go, Beauty…I just won't be able to bear it!

BEAUTY: Please, Iris...Lilly... *(Hesitates.)* Perhaps...if you feel this way...I might stay just *one* day longer...

LILLY: Oh, thank you, Sister! Thank you!

IRIS: *Two* days longer—please...

BEAUTY: Well...

IRIS: Bless you, Sister! Bless you!

(Lights fade.)

SEVENTH VIGNETTE

Night in the Merchant's home. Just the glow of the grate illumines the empty room, until Beauty enters, takes a tinder and lights two candles. She sits. A moment later she stands and paces up and down the length of the room, pausing at the outside door, looking out and listening. She goes back to the chair and sits.

From out of the night comes a long despairing cry. Beauty jumps up and runs to the door. She can see nothing. She paces the length of the room again and sits. She looks up and sees a woman warming her hands at the grate.

BEAUTY: Lilly? Is that you...Iris?

(The Old Woman straightens up and looks at Beauty. The flames in the grate flare up and then flicker and suddenly die. The grate is dark and the Old Woman is no longer visible. Beauty stands, takes one of the candles and goes to the grate, but there is no one there. After a pause.)

BEAUTY: I broke my word to him. I broke my word and he is dying, just as he said he would. What day is it? Why did I stay so long? I must go back! I must go *now!* *(She feels about her neck.)* The ring! The ring is gone! Geoff... *(Calling through the interior door.)* Geoff! Wake up! Come here, quickly! Geoff! Please! Geoff, the *ring!*

(Geoff, dressed in nightshirt, staggers sleepily into the room, rubbing his eyes. He is followed by Wynne.)

GEOFF: Hello, Beauty. Is it morning?

BEAUTY: Geoff—the Beast's ring! Please, give it to me.

GEOFF: Hmm?

WYNNE: That *ring*, Geoff. The one Beauty was wearing. Give it back to her.

GEOFF: Oh, that, I don't got it.

BEAUTY: *Quickly,* Geoff! Where is it?

GEOFF: Ask Iris. She asked me to give it to her. Can I go back to sleep now?

BEAUTY: *(Turning to the interior door.)* Iris?

(She finds Iris standing just within the doorway.)

BEAUTY: *Iris!* Wake up please. Iris come out here! I need my ring.

IRIS: Your ring? Why such a hurry, sister? For a *ring*, at *this* time of night…?

WYNNE: Do as she says, Sister!

IRIS: *(After a hesitation.)* Oh, have your old ring! I've got dozens nicer. *(She takes the chain holding the ring from around her neck and throws it at Beauty. Iris turns and stalks out of the room.)*

BEAUTY: Wynne, Geoff. The Beast is dying, I broke my word to him and he's dying. I must return to him…Please, tell Father not to worry. I love you both…and I know I shall see each of you again…Good-bye…

WYNNE: *(Running to her.)* Beauty!

(But she puts the ring on her finger. Blackout.)

SCENE IV

The Castle of the Beast. The Servants of the Beast lined up in the mouth of the grotto, looking Upstage at the approaching Beast. The Beast emerges through the Servants, staggers into the rose arbor. He turns and addresses his Servants.

BEAST: My…beloved Servants. Go now. The end has come. You have served me well. Go back to the wood. The Beast is dead.

(He motions them away and they exit. He collapses in the arbor and lies still.)

BEAUTY: Beast? *(The castle seems empty and still to her.)* Hello? Beast, I've come back! *(After a beat, she runs down the upper staircase.)* Where are you? *(She runs along the second level, into her chamber, sees no one, runs back out.)* Please! I'm sorry I broke my promise…Beast! *(Her panic rising, she runs down the lower staircase, pausing midway to call.)* Why don't you answer? What has happened?! *(She continues down the staircase, where she sees the huddled body of the Beast lying in the rose arbor.)* Oh, my Beast!

(She runs to him. He does not stir.)

BEAUTY: Not *dead*…Oh, please, not *dead*… *(She throws herself on him, and feels how lifeless his body is. There is a stone bowl of water nearby, and Beauty fetches it to the Beast. She lifts his head up and tries to give him a drink.)* My Beast, please drink…please…it's Beauty…

(The Beast stirs feebly, and then laps at the water. Then he looks up at Beauty.)

BEAST: *(A hoarse whisper.)* Beauty…

BEAUTY: Oh, my dear Beast...

BEAST: I counted the days...I counted the days and when you did not return...I let my wound take me... *(He gives her the arrow.)*

BEAUTY: This arrow...You were struck!

BEAST: That was not the killing wound...But now that I have seen you once more, I can die...

BEAUTY: No! You must not die! Live! Please, live to be my husband!

BEAST: Beauty?

BEAUTY: I give you my hand...I thought it was only friendship that I bore toward you...But this grief tells me that isn't so...If you should die, I would die...Please...I love you...
(Music, light change.)

BEAST: I promised I would not ask you again...

BEAUTY: Please, Beast...please...

BEAST: Will you be my wife?

BEAUTY: Yes, Beast, yes, I will, yes...

BEAST: Beauty.

(She helps him to his feet, and then he stands strong and well. He pulls her to his chest and holds her. Then, they turn and approach the staircase. Music rising. The Servants of the Beast enter from various locations and then stand, motionless and watching. Beauty and the Beast climb the lower staircase. When they reach the second level, the Old Woman appears at the top of the upper staircase, dressed resplendently and beaming.)

OLD WOMAN: Gentle Beauty, you have chosen well.

You of all the world had purest sense.

Your virtue and your kindness broke the spell

That lay like death and doom upon your Prince.

When next you look upon my noble son,

You will not see the Beast you learned to love,

Do not grieve—his gentle kindness lingers on,

But now he lives as Prince—the Beast is gone.

(The music swells, the Servants of the Beast leap and vanish off. Beauty and the Beast continue up the upper staircase. The Old Woman stands there beckoning them on, and then turns and exits. As Beauty and the Beast reach the summit of the stairs, they both turn out to us for a moment, radiant and beautiful, the Beast transformed into a noble Prince. Then, they are gone. Music up. Curtain down.)

END OF PLAY

Mark Twain's
The Adventures of Huckleberry Finn

The Adventures of Huckleberry Finn was commissioned and first presented by The Children's Theatre Company and School on September 20, 1980.

Directed by Israel Hicks
Produced by John Clark Donahue
Music Composed and Arranged by Roberta Carlson
Scenery Designed by Kristine Haugan
Lighting Designed by Robert S. Hutchins, Jr.
Choreography by Geol Weirs

LIST OF CHARACTERS

* White-suited Gentleman
  Aunt Polly
* Tom Sawyer, 11–13
* Huckleberry Finn, 12–14
* Widow Douglas
* Miss Watson
* Jim
  Ben Rogers, 10–13
  Joe Harper, 10–13
  Tommy Barnes, 9–12
* Pap
  Mrs. Loftus
* The Duke
* The Dauphin
  Jake
  Mrs. Hobson
  Reverend Hobson
  Levi Bell
  Abner Shackleford
  Mary Jane Wilks, 15–17
  Susan Wilks, 13–16
  Joanna Wilks, 12–13
  Aunt Sally
  George
  Silas Phelps

Denotes principal roles.

The cast list is large, but many of the roles can be doubled to include Townspeople, Slaves, Gospel Singers, and Musicians.

The Adventures of Huckleberry Finn has a running time of one hour fifty-five minutes, including intermission.

The original production featured rough-hewn wooden platforms that could be suggestive of many locations, and a wooden raft on quiet casters. This, combined with lighting effects, produced a real feeling of traveling on a broad river.

For information concerning the original score by Roberta Carlson, contact The Children's Theatre Company of Minneapolis.

The Adventures of Huckleberry Finn

PROLOGUE

Stage preset: patterned light on rough-wood set, suggestive of a Mississippi River wharf. Orchestra pit area serves as river. Black void Upstage of platforms. Solo harmonica and gentle lapping water. White-suited gentleman wanders onstage, carrying a folded newspaper under his arm, smoking a cigar. He slowly ascends steps Stage Right, dusts off the platform, takes his newspaper and begins to read. Lights fade to Blackout.

SCENE I

Steamboat whistle. Orchestra strikes up a tune of the period: mid-Southern U.S.A. in the early 1840s. Lights rise on set teeming with activity. Huck Finn, Tom Sawyer, Ben Rogers, Joe Harper, and Tommy Barnes enter from Upstage Left with a whoop and run Downstage and leap into the river, while a small gathering of women remonstrate. The five boys continue to climb out of the orchestra pit, dripping wet in their long underwear, and dive back in.

Sailors and Blacks carry cargo up riverboat ramp at Stage Right. Townsfolk gather to observe activity, passengers embark with farewells and waves. Children—ranging in dress and demeanor from the ragged to the prim—gawk and play about the docks. Once the riverboat is loaded, it blows three blasts of its whistle and the ramp rises up and out of sight. People wave and call good-bye, then gradually begin to disperse.

Tom Sawyer and Huck Finn are about to take another plunge, when an angry Aunt Polly appears and charges down to Tom. She grabs him by the ear. Orchestra fades out.

TOM: Honest, Aunt Polly, I never once touched that firecracker! It was Sid set it off, I swear. And it were Sid's idear to toss it beneath your rockin' chair when you was settin' in it, rockin'. It were Sid all the way…
(Aunt Polly twists his ear.)
TOM: …Owww!

AUNT POLLY: *(Leading Tom offstage.)* You hesh up, Tom Sawyer. Good afternoon, Huckleberry.

HUCK: How do, Miz Polly. See you, Tom...

(They are gone; so, too, the other boys. Other townspeople wander off leaving Huck and White-suited gentleman who is staring after the departing steamboat and tentatively raises an arm in farewell, then lets it fall to his side. Huck looks around, moves toward platform Stage Right, turns his back to audience and relieves himself. Gentleman notices Huck and coughs as a signal; Huck looks over his shoulder, sees audience, and hurriedly buttons up his underwear.)

HUCK: *(To audience.)* You don't know about me without you've read a book by the name of *The Adventures of Tom Sawyer,* but that ain't no matter. That book was made by Mr. Mark Twain and there *was* things he stretched...

WHITE-SUITED GENTLEMAN: Huckleberry...

(Huck turns and sees the man's dark expression.)

HUCK: ...but mainly he told the truth.

WHITE-SUITED GENTLEMAN: Hmmm.

HUCK: *(To Gentleman.)* That ain't nothin'. I never seen anybody but lied one time or another...

WHITE-SUITED GENTLEMAN: The point is *taken,* Huckleberry. *(Gentleman sits back down again and resumes reading his newspaper.)*

HUCK: *(To audience.)* So it were mostly a true book he wrote, with some stretchers, as I said before.

(Gentleman glances up, rolls his eyes in exasperation, and returns to his reading.)

HUCK: Now the way it winds up is this: Tom Sawyer and me, we found the money that the robbers hid in the cave and it made us rich. Tom and me, we got six thousand dollars apiece—all gold! Well, Judge Thatcher, he took it and put it out at interest, which fetched us a dollar a day all the year 'round—more'n a body could tell what to do with.

(Widow Douglas enters from Downstage Left.)

HUCK: And then it started.

WIDOW DOUGLAS: *(Calling.)* Huckleberry?

HUCK: The Widow Douglas, she took me for her son, 'cause of I didn't have no folks proper, 'ceptin' my Pap who beat me considerable when he was sober and more when he warn't.

WIDOW DOUGLAS: *(Seeing Huck and moving to him.)* Huckleberry. You poor lamb, you.

HUCK: She called me that, and she called me a lot of other names, too, but she never meant no harm by it. *(To Widow.)* Yes'm, Widow Douglas.

WIDOW DOUGLAS: *(With an evangelical fervor.)* I'm a-goin' to civilize you, Huckleberry Finn! Yes, I'm a-goin' to civilize you with the help of the Good Lord and my good sister Miss Watson!

HUCK: That's a regular *team* you got lined up there. *(To audience.)* Now Miz Watson, she was a tolerable slim old maid…

(Miss Watson enters.)

HUCK: …with goggles on.

(Miss Watson peers about through her thick spectacles, sees Huck and her sister, and approaches.)

MISS WATSON: But first you've got to change your ways, Huckleberry. When you die you want to go to the Good Place, don't you?

(No response; Huck considers his options.)

MISS WATSON: Well, *don't* you?

HUCK: Mebbe. But I don't think I stand a chance on it. I was brung up wrong.

WIDOW DOUGLAS: Nonsense, Huckleberry.

MISS WATSON: All you have to do is pray, Huckleberry. "Whatsoever ye ask for, that shall ye get."

HUCK: Anything?

MISS WATSON: Anything.

HUCK: *(Innocently.)* Well, if you kin get anythin' you pray for, Miz Watson, how come you cain't get fatted up some?

(Pause as Miss Watson studies the boy through her spectacles; Widow stifles a giggle.)

MISS WATSON: *(Grimly.)* The boy needs a bath, sister. I'll get us some water. *Cold* water. *Ice* cold water, so beneficial to the circulation of the blood. *(Turns Stage Right and calls.)* Jim! You, Jim!

HUCK: I feel fine just like I is…

WIDOW DOUGLAS: *(Kindly.)* Oh, we'll get you all cleaned up and dressed in the finest new clothes…

JIM: *(Entering.)* Yes'm, Miz Watson?

MISS WATSON: Fetch some water for Huckleberry's bath. And Jim—send the bucket *way* down into the well, *way* down.

HUCK: Don't do it, Jim!

(Jim sizes up the situation and chuckles; it grows into full laughter as he exits.)

MISS WATSON: *(Following Jim Offstage Right.)* And get a move on, you lazy thing!

(Widow Douglas has been sorting Huck's old clothes.)

WIDOW DOUGLAS: How *do* you rip your clothes so, Huckleberry?

HUCK: I ain't sartin. I goes one way an' they goes the other, seemin'ly.

WIDOW DOUGLAS: Well, these are a dead loss. Climb into the tub, now, boy.

(Huck obeys, climbing into large wooden tub Center.)

HUCK: I don't understand about this prayin', Widow Douglas. Shoot, *I* prayed once an' got a fishline without any hooks. Well, it warn't no *good* to me without hooks…

WIDOW DOUGLAS: You must pray for spiritual gifts, Huckleberry. Take off them rags, now.

(Huck removes his long underwear and hands them over the side of the tub.)

WIDOW DOUGLAS: You must pray for the will to help other people, and do everything you can for other people…

HUCK: Includin' Miz Watson?

WIDOW DOUGLAS: Certainly!

(Miss Watson enters, carrying a blanket.)

MISS WATSON: *(Shouting behind her.)* Jim? Jim! *(To Widow Douglas.)* I tell you, that boy has got two speeds: slow and slower.

WIDOW DOUGLAS: You bring the towel, sister?

MISS WATSON: I brought better'n a bowel; I brought a fine, rough, horsehair blanket!

HUCK: Oh, Lordy…

MISS WATSON: Just the thing to get the blood moving.

HUCK: Just the thing to skin me alive…

(Jim enters carrying a bucket.)

MISS WATSON: Jim, you old slow-coach, get that water over here!

WIDOW DOUGLAS: Thankee, Jim. *You* pour, will you?

JIM: I sho'ly will, ma'am.

MISS WATSON: *(With relish.)* Now—is everybody ready?

WHITE-SUITED GENTLEMAN: Are *you* ready, Huckleberry?

(Jim pours. Huck yells. Sisters sigh with satisfaction. Widow takes bucket from Jim and Jim holds blanket up to mask Huck in tub. Gentleman stands as others freeze.)

WHITE-SUITED GENTLEMAN: That boy is standin' in the need of prayer. *(Gentleman chuckles and starts Offstage, then stops.)* Oh, yes—just one thing before we begin. By order of the author: persons attempting to find a motive in this narrative will be prosecuted; persons attempting to find a moral in it will be banished. And persons attempting to find a plot…will be shot.

(Sound of pistol shot Offstage. Action. Gentleman exits as Widow Douglas hands Huck fresh clothes and he dresses. Music underscore.)

MISS WATSON: All right, Jim—unveil him!

(Jim drops the blanket. Huck stands in front of tub, stiffly, dressed up dandy in a suit. Sisters go into raptures.)

WIDOW DOUGLAS: Oh, ain't he grand, Jim? The new Huckleberry Finn!

MISS WATSON: Civilized at last! Praise the Lord!

HUCK: *(Feeling his pockets.)* My pipe…my pipe! Miss Watson, you din't throw out my pipe with my old clothes now, did you?

MISS WATSON: I most certainly did! You don't want to go the the Bad Place and the Everlastin' Fire, do you?

HUCK: I wish I was there this minute.

(Miss Watson shrieks and swoons into Widow Douglas's arms.)

WIDOW DOUGLAS: Huckleberry!

HUCK: It appears I done said the wrong thing.

MISS WATSON: *(Miraculously reviving from her "faint.")* You surely did, young man! Let go of me, sister! *(She charges off toward Stage Right.)* Jim, get that tub outta there!

(Jim strikes tub.)

MISS WATSON: *(To herself.)* Never heard such wicked talk in all my born days!

(Huck and Widow follow Miss Watson into living-room area.)

WIDOW DOUGLAS: Please, sister, calm yourself…

HUCK: I din't *mean* nothin' by it, Miz Watson. All I wanted was to go *somewheres,* jist for a *change;* I warn't particular…

MISS WATSON: I wouldn't ever say such a wicked thing for the whole world! *I* want to live so as to go to the Good Place.

HUCK: *(Aside, to audience.)* Well, I couldn't see no advantage in goin' where she was goin', but I never said so.

WIDOW DOUGLAS: I think you had better go to your room now, Huckleberry.

HUCK: Yes'm, Widow Douglas. I'm awful sorry, Miz Watson…

MISS WATSON: Hmmmph!

(Huck turns and ascends stairs to his bed Upstage Left.)

MISS WATSON: Enough to break a body's heart, that boy…

(Widow Douglas puts her hands on her sister to comfort her.)

MISS WATSON: Oh, don't *hang* on me so, sister!

(Miss Watson exits Downstage Right and Widow Douglas follows as afternoon lights rapidly shifts to dusk, then blackout.)

SCENE II

Huck sits on edge of bed and lights a candle. Clear, white stars shine in void. Sounds of the night: owl, whippoorwill, hound howl, and the bogus cry of of nearby Tomcat.

TOM SAWYER: *(Offstage.)* Mee-ow! *(Tom enters and crouches Center Stage beneath Huck's "bedroom.")* Mee-ow!
(Huck springs from his bed and looks out his "window.")
HUCK: *(Jubilant.)* Tom!
TOM: *(Angry whisper.)* Huck Finn, cain't you do *nothin'* right?
HUCK: Sorry, Tom. *(Answers the signal.)* "Mee-*ow!*"
TOM: C'mon!
(Huck flings first one leg, then the other, over the edge of the platform and drops down onto stage level. A sudden gust of wind blows out the bedroom candle as the two boys exit Upstage Left. Orchestra plays light ballad to carry them out. Music fades and candles are lit Downstage Left. Tom Sawyer holding court with Huck, Joe Harper, Ben Rogers, and little Tommy Barnes.)
TOM: Swear!
(The boys hold up their palms.)
JOE HARPER: I, Joe Harper...
BEN ROGERS: Ben Rogers...
HUCK: Huckleberry Finn...
(Pause. Huck nudges Tommy.)
TOMMY BARNES: Tommy Barnes!
TOM: *(Unfolding a piece of paper and reads.)* ...do solemnly swear to join this band of robbers called "Tom Sawyer's Gang," and to stick to the band, and to never tell any of its secrets. And if anybody who belongs to the band tells the secrets, he must have his throat cut, and then have his carcass burnt up, and the ashes scattered all around, and have his name blotted from the list with blood, and never mentioned again by the gang, but have a curse put on it and be forgot forever. Amen.
BEN ROGERS: That's a real beautiful oath, Tom.
JOE HARPER: Did you think it up out o' your own head?
TOM: Some of it. But the rest was out of books. Any gang that's high-toned has got one like it.
JOE HARPER: Hey, Tom—I think it would be good if we killed the *families* of any boy who tells the secrets, too.

TOM: That *is* good, Joe. We'll write that in, too... *(Taking a pencil to his paper.)* ..."families."

BEN ROGERS: Wait a minute—here's Huck Finn. He ain't *got* no family. What you goin' to do 'bout him?

TOM: Well ain't he got a father?

BEN ROGERS: Yes, but he ain't been around for ever so long; some say he's dead.

HUCK: I don't know 'bout that; I just hope he don't never come back. I'm mighty scared of Pap.

TOM: But don't you see, Huck? That means you cain't join the Gang. Every boy's gotta have a family, or someone to kill, or it won't be fair.

HUCK: Aw, shoot, Tom...I *wanna* join...

TOM: Well, I sho'ly wish you could, Huck, but...

HUCK: Jist a minute! You can have Miz Watson! Y'all can kill her, if ya want...

TOM: Oh? Well, she'll do fine! That's settled then; Huck's in. Now, make the sign.

(They all perform a ritual to which they're well-accustomed: They slap their Right thighs, slap their Left thighs, lick their Right thumbs, and press thumbs together all around in percussive unison.)

TOM: There now, that's all there is to it!

BEN ROGERS: Now, what all is this Gang goin' to do, Tom?

TOM: Oh, robbery and murder, mainly. We stop carriages on the road, kill the people, and take their money. Simple.

TOMMY BARNES: Do we always have to kill the people?

TOM: Oh certainly!

HUCK: Do we kill the women, too?

TOM: Huck Finn, if I was as ignorant as you, I wouldn't let folks know about it. Of *course* we don't kill the women! We fetch 'em back here to the cave and we're as polite as pie to 'em. Then they fall in love with us and don't never want to go home.

BEN ROGERS: Sounds like foolishness to me. We'll have the cave so filled up with women there won't be no place for *us*.

TOM: Either we do it by the book or not at all, Ben Rogers! Now let's just get going...

BEN ROGERS: Who we gonna rob this time o' night?!

TOMMY BARNES: I wanna go home...

TOM: *(Suddenly.)* Shhh!

(All drop to the floor and blow out their candles. Faint moonlight.)

TOM: *(Whisper.)* I think I hear a whole caravan of Spanish merchants and rich A-rabs a-comin'! Don't you, Huck?

HUCK: Nope.

TOM: Aw, hesh up and come on!

(The boys rise to their feet and Tom leads them in a "whoop" of a battlecry as they exit Downstage Left. Music.)

SCENE III

Stars fade out. Dim light of dawn. Rooster crow. Huck—his new suit ragged, torn and filthy—quietly makes his way from Upstage Left to Downstage Right. As he enters the house, carrying his shoes in hand, Miss Watson enters from Stage Right, dressed in nightgown and cap, sleepily carrying a covered porcelain chamber pot. When she encounters Huck, she screams.

MISS WATSON: Ahhhhh! Ahhhhhh!

HUCK: Mornin', Miz Watson.

MISS WATSON: Ahhhh!

HUCK: Miz Watson—it's *me*—Huck! I was just…um…out back…

(Widow Douglas enters in her nightclothes.)

WIDOW DOUGLAS: Gracious, sister! What is it?

MISS WATSON: *(Still clutching the chamber pot with one hand while using the other to point with accusation and horror at the boy.)* H…h…h…*him*!

WIDOW DOUGLAS: Huckleberry! Land sakes, child, what's happened to you?

HUCK: Nothin'. I just…I just got up kinda early.

MISS WATSON: *(Recovering her wits, and her rage mounting.)* "Up early," my eye! Why, he's been out all night long! Just you look at him!

WIDOW DOUGLAS: Surely not, sister.

MISS WATSON: *(Indicating Huck's disheveled appearance.)* Well?

WIDOW DOUGLAS: Why, Huckleberry—I could have sworn I heard you moving about upstairs. You weren't out the whole night? *(Pause.)* Were you, Huckleberry?

(Huck cannot lie to the Widow; he hangs his head in shame.)

WIDOW DOUGLAS: Oh, Huckleberry…

MISS WATSON: *(Self-righteous.)* Um-hmmm! Um-hmmm! Now, there's another suit of clothes: ruined! Oh, it's an ungrateful creature! I told you, sister, you can not make a silk purse from a sow's ear, no more than you can civilize a piece of white trash like…

WIDOW DOUGLAS: *(Angry.)* You stop your mouth, sister! I won't have you talking like that!

(She goes to Huck and tearfully embraces him. Miss Watson, offended, finally recalls her errand and starts off.)

MISS WATSON: *(A parting shot.)* That boy is destined to be hanged, you mark my words! Destined to be hanged!

(She stalks Offstage. Widow Douglas releases Huck and turns away.)

WIDOW DOUGLAS: *(Wiping a tear from her eyes.)* Get upstairs to your room now, Huckleberry, and get out of them filthy clothes.

HUCK: I…I don't mean to trouble you so, Widow Douglas. I won't no more…I promise…

WIDOW DOUGLAS: *(Still not looking at him. Softly.)* Go along now, Huckleberry.

(Full of morose, Huck turns and climbs the stairs to his room. Widow exits. Music. A huge figure leaps out at Huck from Offstage, grabs Huck around the neck and whirls him around in a headlock.)

HUCK: Ahhh! *Pap!*

(Pap is about fifty; his face is white, with long mixed-up whiskers, and long, black greasy hair.)

PAP: *(Laughing for his victory.)* His own self! *(He hurls Huck onto the bed.)* Now ain't you a sweet-scented dandy, though? A bed. And bedclothes. And your own father's got to sleep with the hogs. I bet I'll knock some o' those frills out o' you before I'm done.

HUCK: You cain't *be* here, Pap!

(Pap crosses the room in a single step and slaps Huck across the face.)

PAP: You mind how you talk to me, boy! I'm a-standin' about all I can stand now, so don't gimme none o' your sass. You put on consid'rable many airs since I been away. You're educated, too, they say? You can read and write? Who tole you you can meddle with such high-falutin' foolishness, hey? Who tole you you could?!

HUCK: The Widow. She told me.

PAP: An' who tole the Widow she could put in her shovel 'bout a thing that ain't none o' her business?

HUCK: Nobody never told her.

PAP: Well, I'll learn her to meddle…

HUCK: Don't you think you can touch the Widow, Pap—or Miz Watson; I'm a-warnin' you!

PAP: *(Taking Huck up by the hair.)* You warnin' *me?* Your own rightful father?!

(He throws him back down.) Why, there ain't no end to your airs! They say you're rich now, too. How's that?

HUCK: They lie. I ain't...

PAP: *(Grabbing Huck and holding him in a half nelson.)* Don't gimme none o' your lip! I been in town two days, and I hain't heard nothin' *but,* about you bein' rich. I heard 'bout it away down the river, too. That's why I come. You git me that money, 'cause of *I wants it!*

HUCK: *(Strained, in pain.)* You cain't have it. I signed it over to Judge Thatcher, so's if you ever came back you couldn't get at it. He's the trustee, and it's all legal.

PAP: *(Rage.)* Legal?! I'll give you legal! *(Pap throws Huck toward the steps Downstage.)* You comin' with me, boy. I'll git that money or you'll starve. Git up! *(He pushes Huck down into living-room area and follows.)* *(Widow Douglas enters.)*

WIDOW DOUGLAS: Huckleberry? What is all this... *(She sees Pap standing on stairs and raises her hand to her mouth in horror.)*

PAP: You the old hag that ruined my boy? "Legal!"

WIDOW DOUGLAS: *(Screaming off Stage Right.)* Jim! Jim! Come quick!

HUCK: Stay away, Widow Douglas! *Please!*

(Jim enters, running.)

WIDOW DOUGLAS: Jim, stop him!

(Pap grabs Huck by the arm in defiance.)

JIM: Le'go the child, Mister. *(Jim takes a step toward Huck and Pap.)*

PAP: I s'pose *this* is legal, too: a nigger talkin' to me like that! *(Pap suddenly produces a hunting knife with his free hand.)*

HUCK: Don't come near, Jim...

JIM: Le'go the child!

(Jim lunges and Pap's knife flashes out; a line of blood runs down Jim's arm and he doubles over in pain.)

HUCK: Jim!

PAP: *There's* "legal," nigger!

HUCK: Widow Douglas, *please* stay away! He's my Pap; I *want* to go with him! I'm tired of bein' civilized! Just let us go!

PAP: There now—*that's* my Hucky talkin'. Now *git*, boy!

(He shoves Huck toward Center and follows. Jim advances, but Pap whirls on him with the knife, backing off to Upstage Left.)

PAP: "Legal!"

(Pap spits. Huck and Pap exit. Widow Douglas sobs and reaches to help Jim.

They exit Downstage Right as lights shift focus to Downstage Center. Two drunks appear from shadows Upstage.)

DRUNK: Hey! Ephner! Lookee! I got 'em!

EPHNER: Yeah?

DRUNK: *(Holding dead rats on a string.)* Rats, Ephner! Three, nice, fat rats!

EPHNER: Jus' look at 'em!

DRUNK: We gonna eat tonight, eh? We gonna eat tonight!

(They laugh and congratulate one another as they exit Upstage into darkness.)

SCENE IV

Music fades as lights rise on Pap's cabin Downstage Left. It is cluttered with barrels and bags of provisions. There is a ladder from the ground floor up through a trapdoor to upper platform. Huck sits, leaning against a barrel, while Pap, fortified with frequent pulls on a whiskey jug, delivers a lecture on the government.

PAP: You call this a gov'ment?! Oh yes, this is a wonderful gov'ment, wonderful. Why, lookee here: Up in town there was a free nigger, from Ohio, and he had the whitest shirt on you ever did see, and the shiniest hat, an' a gold watch and chain, an' do you know what? They said he was a p'fessor in a college, an' could talk all kinds o' languages, an' knowed ev'rythin'. An' that ain't the wust! They said that, when he was t' home, he could *vote. Vote!!!* Well, that let me out. Thinks I: "What's this country comin' to?" Y'see, Hucky, it was 'lection day, an' I was jus' 'bout to go 'n' vote m'self, only I were too drunk to get there...

(Huck laughs scornfully.)

PAP: ...*but* when I heard that there was a state in this country where that there nigger could vote, that let me right out. Says I: "I'll never vote agin!" Them's the very words I said; they all heard me. The country can rot for all I care—I'll never vote agin as long as I live.

HUCK: You ever vote in your life *before,* Pap?

PAP: No. An' you know why, don't ya? 'Cause of I was too busy and hard-set raisin' you, that's why! And now I done lost my last chance to vote, 'cause o' you and that thievin', prowlin', infernal, white-shirted nigger that they let run 'round *free!* (Pap kicks a barrel in his anger. He clutches *his foot in pain.)* Ow! Dang blast the gov'ment! Dang blast the blasted barrel!

(Pap kicks the barrel with his other foot, injuring that also. Huck doubles up with laughter.)

PAP: You laughin' at me, boy? Oh, you just let me catch you, boy! You just wait! *(Pap makes a grab for Huck and topples down in a drunken heap. He speaks now in a whining, self-pitying tone.)* My jug…where's my jug? Hucky, fetch your ol' Pap his jug. I'm a-hurtin', son; I'm a-hurtin' bad… *(Huck pushes jug toward Pap. Pap whimpers and coaxes Huck to push it closer. Huck does so and Pap lunges, grabbing Huck's wrist and twisting it.)*

HUCK: Pap…don't…

PAP: Laugh at your Pap, will you?!

HUCK: Please…

PAP: *(Still holding Huck, giving the jug a shake with his other hand.)* Nigh on empty. Guess I'll have to pay a visit into town, I reckon. *(He releases Huck.)* Well? Come on, boy—you know what to do when your Pap goes into town.

(Huck steps Downstage away from exit as Pap slowly ascends ladder.)

PAP: Now don't you think you're goin' nowheres, boy, 'cause you ain't. Nowheres! Understand? *(He has reached the upper platform.)* Now, help me with this thing! Hand it up here!

(Huck lifts ladder up to Pap; who sets it beside the trapdoor. Pap takes a final pull from the jug.)

PAP: Whiskey. Gotta get me some whiskey… *(He lets the trapdoor fall shut and starts off.)* …damn the town! Damn the gov'ment! Damn it all!

(Pap exits Upstage Left. Music. Huck steps Downstage and addresses audience.)

HUCK: *(Displaying trickle of blood seeping out between his fingers.)* Musta caught myself on a splinter or somethin', but that gave me the idea to get myself murdered. I couldn't go back to the Widow's, 'cause Pap would just come an' get me agin, *and* make trouble for the Widow more'n likely. I couldn't go home and I couldn't stay, so I figgered I'd let on to people that I was murdered. Who'd follow me then? *(Huck drags barrel beneath trapdoor, climbs on it, leaps and pushes trap open.)* Jackson's Island! I'll find me a canoe and head out for Jackson's Island! It's only 'bout three miles downriver of town, and ain't nobody goes there, mostly. *(He spots Pap's hunting knife, picks it up. He takes a half-plucked turkey that hangs from the rafters, slices it open, and allows it to bleed on the floor. He then slashes some bags of provisions to cause a general mess.)* Gosh, I wish Tom Sawyer could see me now. He'd be right proud o' me! *(He*

throws the turkey up through the trapdoor, cuts a small lock of hair from his head and wraps the hair around the bloodied knife blade.) And there's the murder weapon. *(He drops the knife on the floor.)* Now what did them murderers do with me? Why, shore! They dragged me out to the river. *(Huck hops up onto barrel, leaps to trap opening and, hanging by his hands, kicks the barrel over, then pulls himself up and out. He looks down into the cabin.)* Well, that's it, then. I'm dead! *(He picks up the turkey and quickly exits, leaving trail of blood behind him.)*
(Music up and lights fade.)

SCENE V

Lights rise on bare setting, with river and riverbanks in the background. Huck enters, out of breath.

HUCK: *(Voice-over)* In the moonlight, the river looked miles and miles across. It was late, I could tell—it *smell't* late, and everythin' was so quiet on the island, I could hear people talkin' way over to the ferry landin'. *(Huck climbs to uppermost platform and surveys the scene. He sits and stretches himself out for sleep.)* Anyways, I was pretty tired. It was goin' to be a grand mornin', with them all searchin' the river for my body, so I went right on out to sleep.
(Huck sleeps. Lights rise and sound of birds provide transition into morning. Sound of distant cannon up the river. Huck stirs and sits up. Jim enters, but Huck doesn't recognize him. Huck attempts to find a vantage point to see the stranger, approaching nearer. Jim turns around and sees Huck. Jim is terrified; Huck is relieved.)
HUCK: Jim! Jim—it's *you!* You sho'ly did give me a fright...
JIM: Don't hurt me! I never done you no harm when you was alive, Huck Finn, and I hain't never done no harm to no ghost...
HUCK: Jim...
JIM: I was always your frien' when you was alive, Huck, warn't I?
HUCK: I ain't no *ghost*, dad blame it! Looky here, see for yourself...
(Huck extends his arm out for Jim to touch; he does so, tentatively.)
HUCK: Go on, touch me—ain't no ghost *about* me.
(Jim takes Huck's hand, then the other, he breaks into a big smile and hugs Huck to his chest.)

JIM: I was powerful sorry to hear you was killed, Huck, but I ain't no mo'.
Honey, you is alive as I!

HUCK: Shore is good to see a friendly face, Jim, after all them days stuck in
Pap's shanty.

(Cannon boom.)

JIM: But look here, Huck—who *was* murdered in that shanty if it warn't you?

HUCK: Shucks—*nobody*, Jim! I just fixed things up to look like I was dead, so's
I could get away from 'em all.

(Huck moves Upstage to look upstream at the town. Jim follows.)

JIM: Well, yestiday night the whole town was talkin' bout you bein' dead, and
now they're all out on the river, soundin' a cannon to make your body
rise up from the bottom.

HUCK: *(With a modest grin.)* Yup. Kinder grand, ain't it.

(Cannon boom.)

HUCK: But how do *you* come to be here, Jim?

(Jim takes off his hat and turns away from Huck, looking out over the river.)

JIM: Maybe I better not tell. *(Small pause.)* You wouldn't tell on me if I was
to tell you, would you, Huck?

HUCK: Blamed if I would, Jim.

JIM: *(Sitting.)* Well, it was this way. Some time after yer Pap hauled you off,
there came this nigger trader from New Orleans an' he started to git
mighty thick with Miz Watson. Now that Miz Watson, she treats me
pretty rough, but she always said she wouldn't sell me down to New
Orleans. Well, it were a lie, Huck…

(Cannon boom, louder.)

HUCK: *(Pulling Jim down behind the slope.)* Git down, Jim. They're gettin'
closer.

*(They crouch side by side, glancing out over the river as they speak in more
hushed tones.)*

JIM: One night I creeps to the parlor do', and the do' warn't quite shet, an' I
hear Miz Watson tell the Widow she was a-goin' to sell me, 'cause she
could get eight hundred dollars fo' me. The Widow, she try to git her
not to do it, but I never waited to hear the res'. I hain't Miz Watson's Jim
no more, Huck. I done run off.

(Cannon boom, still louder.)

HUCK: But now you're a runaway nigger, Jim! You know what that means…

JIM: She was a-goin' to *sell* me—away from my wife, Huck…away from my
child'en.

HUCK: *(After a brief pause.)* You got *child'en*, Jim? You got a *fam'ly*?

JIM: Mind…you said you wouldn't tell.

HUCK: And I won't, Jim. People can call me a low-down Abolitionist and a slave-lover, but I said I wouldn't tell, an' I won't.

(Large cannon boom. Jim pulls Huck further down.)

JIM: There they is!

(Musicians strike up a funeral song as riverboat appears on the river, moving closer and closer. Cannon booms continue as we hear the voices of people on the ship.)

RIVERBOAT CAPTAIN: *(Voice-over.)* Look sharp, now—the current sets in the closest about here…

WIDOW DOUGLAS: *(Voice-over.)* Oh, my poor child…! *(Calling.)* Huckleberry! Huckleberry!

RIVERBOAT CAPTAIN: *(Voice-over.)* Maybe he's washed ashore and got tangled among the brush at the water's edge…

WIDOW DOUGLAS: *(Voice-over.)* Oh, Huckleberry…

RIVERBOAT CAPTAIN: *(Voice-over.)* Steady as she goes…Steady!

CREWMAN: *(Voice-over.)* Nothing, Captain. Don't see a thing…

(Riverboat has turned and begins to move back upstream.)

WIDOW DOUGLAS: *(Voice-over.)* Huckleberry…

(Cannon booms fade out. Huck and Jim sit up, dazed. Pause.)

HUCK: Don't that beat all. The grandest day o' my life—and I's dead.

JIM: You ain't dead, Honey.

HUCK: *(Descending to stage level.)* Ain't no one goin' to look for me no more… *(Sudden thought, urgent.)* But they goin' to look for you, Jim! What you gonna do?

JIM: I reckoned I'd head on down the river to Cairo, Illinois. In Cairo, Illinois I's a free man—they ain't no slaves in Cairo. An' then I kin wuk and make me some money and buy my fam'ly. An' I kin bring my fam'ly to Cairo an' we kin live.

HUCK: They ain't nothin' back in St. Petersburg for me, I reckon. I'se dead.

JIM: Don't talk like that, Honey.

HUCK: We're both in a fix now…let's you and me go together, Jim.

JIM: To Cairo?

HUCK: Sho'!

JIM: *(Claps his hands together and laughs.)* Then that's what we a-goin' to do! *(They hug.)*

HUCK: I'm hungry.

JIM: Well then, for the Lawd's sake, chile, we gonna set that to rights! Come on, come *on*…

(Jim exits Stage Left. Huck remains for a moment.)
HUCK: They was cryin' for *me*. They was sad I'm dead. Wait! Jim! Wait for me! *(Huck runs off after Jim.)*
(Lights fade.)

SCENE VI

Sound of river rushing, animal calls of the night. Lights of late evening reveal the two sitting by a campfire: Jim smokes a pipe as Huck finishes his dinner.

HUCK: *(Voice-over.)* Jim an' me spent considerable time on Jackson's Island.
JIM: We cain't stay here forever, chile…
HUCK: *(Voice-over.)* We slept days and woke nights, topsy-turvy like.
JIM: *(Standing and stretching.)* We got to find a way down to Cairo, Illinois, Hucky.
HUCK: *(Voice-over.)* Mostly we didn't show ourselves or make no fires in the daytime.
   (Huck sits. Jim ascends Stage Right steps of platform to look out over river.)
HUCK: *(Voice-over.)* Then one night…
JIM: Huck, there's somethin' out there…
HUCK: *(He wasn't listening.)* How's that, Jim?
JIM: I says there's somethin' on the river…comin' this way.
HUCK: Well, what is it?
JIM: Cain't make it out, but it's mighty big.
   (Huck rises and joins Jim at top of the slope.)
HUCK: *(With a small laugh, not believing his eyes.)* It almost looks like a… house.
JIM: Well, the river's been risin' right along…
HUCK: Mighta swept things off the shore…
JIM: That's jist what it is, Huck! It's a whole, en-tire house a-floatin' down the river!
HUCK: Wonder if they's anybody still in it…
JIM: Not likely, but they's bound to be some truck that there house we could use in Cairo. I's goin' aboard…
   (Jim runs down to stage level; Huck follows.)
HUCK: So'm I!
JIM: No you ain't, chile. Din't you see how sprightly that thing is movin'? I'm goin' aboard; you stan' by.

HUCK: Stand by for what?

JIM: Blamed if I know—jist stan' by. Look now...here she come... *(Jim runs off Stage Left.)*

HUCK: *(Calling.)* Jim! Don't you be too long on that house.

(Music. Vague shapes and shadows appear off Stage Right; sound of rushing water has increased. Huck observes for a bit, then calls again.)

HUCK: Jim?

(No answer.)

HUCK: It's movin' too fast, Jim. Come on back!

(Pause. Suddenly a call.)

JIM: Huck! Here it come—now you catch it!

(A bundle is hurled onto the shore Upstage Right. Huck picks it up.)

HUCK: That's good, Jim—now come on off that thing!

(The house has approached Upstage Center.)

JIM: They's a white man a-sleepin' in here!

HUCK: A white man? He'll make trouble for you, Jim...

JIM: Well, we cain't leave him lie!

HUCK: I know we cain't, but...Jim? Jim!

(The house is moving off Stage Right.)

HUCK: You slippin' away, Jim! *(Pause.)* Jim? *(Another pause. Quieter.)* Jim...

(Huck sinks to his knees, nearly in tears. Long pause and music fades out. Finally Jim appears, wet and dripping, from Stage Right; he carries a bundle.)

JIM: Hucky?

HUCK: *(Whirling around.)* Jim!

(Jim drops the bundle and Huck runs to him, then stops himself from embracing Jim.)

JIM: *(Tousling Huck's hair and laughing.)* You warn't worried 'bout ol' Jim, was you Honey?

HUCK: Nope. *(He wipes his eyes.)* What about the man?

JIM: *(Slight pause.)* He warn't sleepin'. He were dead. Shot in the back.

HUCK: Jiminy! Who was it, you reckon?

(A sound of creaking boards and rushing water. Jim and Huck turn their heads Upstage Right at the sound.)

JIM: Look, Hucky! She's goin' down! She's sinkin'!

HUCK: Bless my soul...

(A huge rush of water and then nothing but the quiet passage of the river. Jim shakes his head, and turns back to Center Stage and the bundles.)

HUCK: I wonder who that man was...

JIM: Bad luck, talkin' 'bout the dead.

HUCK: …wonder who shot him…an' what for…

JIM: *(Angry.)* Talk like that'll fetch nothin' but bad luck, you min' my words! *(Pause.)* Looky here, Huck—a lantern for us. An' a bran'-new Barlow knife…

HUCK: *(Immediately interested, joining Jim in the rummaging.)* A Barlow knife?! Why, that's wuth two bits in any store…you call that bad luck?

JIM: An' a couple o' ol', dirty calico dresses…

HUCK: An' a bonnet… *(Huck puts the bonnet on his head.)* How d'I look, Jim?

JIM: *(Laughs.)* An ol' book…an' here's a fine blanket…Huck, there's some-thin' sewn into the linin'…right here… *(Jim uses the knife on the blanket and silver dollars fall out.)* Huck!

HUCK: Eight dollars silver! Bad *luck?!* Now what did you say, day before yesti-day, when I fetched in that snakeskin I found on the top o' the ridge?

JIM: I said it was the wust luck in the world to touch a snakeskin—worse'n lookin' at the moon over your left shoulder—and it *is.*

HUCK: Well, here's your bad luck: We've rakes in all this truck an' eight dol-lars besides!

JIM: *(Walking away from him.)* Don't you get too pert, Honey…it's a-comin'. Mind you, the bad luck's a-comin'!
(Pause.)

HUCK: Hey, Jim—don't you wish you knew what was goin' on over to town?

JIM: I'd like to know if Miz Watson's done put a reward out on me…

HUCK: How's if I take the canoe an' slip over tomorrow?
(Slight pause as Jim considers.)

JIM: Well, you'll have to go in the dark and look sharp…Say, Hucky—that bonnet don't look half-bad on you. You git yo'self into one o' them cal-ico dresses, an' won't nobody know you's Huck Finn.

HUCK: Hey, Jim, that *is* good. *(Huck holds up one of the dresses to himself.)* Huck Finn? My name's…Sarah.
(Jim laughs.)

HUCK: Sarah Williams to you, Jim.
(Jim's laugh grows as lights fade to Blackout.)

SCENE VII

Table with sewing basket, candlestick, rocking chair, and stool set Downstage Left. Mrs. Judith Loftus: a woman in her forties, enters from Stage Right fol-lowed by Huck, disguised as a girl.

MRS. LOFTUS: Well come on in, Honey. What did you say your name was?

HUCK: Sarah Williams.

MRS. LOFTUS: Oh? Whereabouts you live, Sarah? In this neighborhood?

HUCK: No'm. In Honkerville. My mother's down sick and out of money, and I come to tell my uncle Abner Moore. He lives at the upper end of town, I think. You know him?

MRS. LOFTUS: No. But me an' my husband only just moved here two weeks ago. But it's a considerable ways to the upper end of town. You better stay here for the night, Honey. Now take off your bonnet.

HUCK: No! *(Pause.)* I'll just rest a while, I reckon, and go on. I ain't afeard of the dark.

MRS. LOFTUS: You ain't? Hmmm. Well, take a chair, Sarah. Sit right there. *(She sits and picks up her sewing and Huck sits: knees sprawled far apart. Mrs. Loftus regards him closely; Huck slams his knees together.)*

MRS. LOFTUS: My husband'll be in by an' by. I'll send him along with you. Sure you don't want to take off your bonnet?

HUCK: Oh, no, ma'am. I jist gener'ly keeps it on, mostly...as a rule...yep...

MRS. LOFTUS: Well, like I say, my husband and me moved here from up river nigh on two weeks ago, an' personally speakin'...jist girl-talk, now...I don't know but what we done made a mistake. Why, there's already been murder done, jist before we got here!

HUCK: Murder? *No!*

MRS. LOFTUS: *Yessss!* A little boy; 'bout your age. O' course, he were a reg'lar no-account, but *still.* Huckleberry Finn his name was, and some say it were his own father what done him in. Old Finn came mighty nigh on gettin' lynched, but then some folks changed around and judged the murder was done by a runaway nigger named Jim.

HUCK: *(Blurts in Jim's defense.)* Jim?! Why, he...
    (Pause.)

MRS. LOFTUS: "He" what, Honey?

HUCK: Uh...why would he a-done it?

MRS. LOFTUS: Well, he done run off, didn't he? There's a reward out on his head for three hund'ed dollars! My husband's out this minute, lookin' for him—but don't you tell nobody.

HUCK: Where's he a-lookin'?

MRS. LOFTUS: Well... *(Conspiratorial and extremely rapid.)* Coupla days ago I was talkin' with an old couple what lives next door and they happened to say hardly nobody ever goes to that island they call Jackson's Island. "Don't anybody live there?" says I. "No, nobody," says they; and I done some thinkin' an' like as not that nigger's hidin' over there. "Anyways," says I, "it's worth the trouble to give the place a hunt." So my husband's goin' over to see; him and another man. What did you say your name was, Honey?

HUCK: Uh…Mary. Mary Williams. Is your husband already set off to that island?

MRS. LOFTUS: *(After a small pause.)* No. Him and his friend are goin' to wait till midnight. Didn't you say your name was Sarah when you first come in, Honey?

HUCK: Oh…yes'm, I did. Sarah Mary Williams. Sarah's my first name. Some calls me Sarah, some calls me Mary. *(He offers a weak smile.)*

MRS. LOFTUS: Oh? Fancy that. *(She returns a somewhat false smile. She picks up needle and thread from her basket.)* Thread this needle for me, will you Sarah Mary? My eyes do ache so…

(Huck takes them and tries laboriously, repeatedly, without success.)

MRS. LOFTUS: Perhaps *your* eyes are tired, too, Sarah Mary…from your journey. Why don't you let me finish that… *(She takes the needle and thread and completes the task in a moment.)* Um-hmmm. Come now, what's your real name? Is it Bill or Tom or what is it?

HUCK: *(Standing and edging for the doorway.)* Please don't poke fun at a poor girl like me, ma'am. If I'm in the way here, I'll go…

MRS. LOFTUS: No, you won't. I won't hurt you. It's plain to see you're a runaway apprentice, that's all. Bless you, child; I wouldn't tell on you. Now what's your real name?

(Long pause.)

HUCK: George Peters, ma'am.

MRS. LOFTUS: Well, try to remember it, George. Don't forget and tell me it's Alexander before you go, and then say it's George Alexander when I catch you at it. *(She laughs.)* And don't go about in that old calico—you do a girl tolerable poor!

HUCK: Yes'm.

MRS. LOFTUS: Now then, you'd better spend the night here.

HUCK: Thankee ma'am, but I really got to get goin'.

MRS. LOFTUS: All right, then—you just trot along then now, Sarah Mary Williams George Alexander Peters. *(She laughs.)* But if you get into any trouble, you send word to Mrs. Judith Loftus, which is me, and I'll do what I can to get you out of it.

HUCK: Thankee, ma'am. G'night.

MRS. LOFTUS: Goodnight.

(Huck exits. Mrs. Loftus steps to doorway and calls.)

MRS. LOFTUS: An' mind you lift your skirt when you run, boy—mind you lift your skirt!

(She laughs and lights fade to Blackout.)

SCENE VIII

In the shift, the slow striking of a town clock: eleven o'clock. Lights rise on Jim outfitting a raft Downstage Center. With the blanket and a couple of sticks, Jim has erected a lean-to; a pole holds the lantern; a rudder is improvised with a long pole and a forked branch, etc.

HUCK: *(Offstage.)* Jim! Jim!

JIM: Huck? That you, chile?

(Huck enters, still in his dress, running. He falls to his knees at Jim's feet and pants with exhaustion.)

JIM: Good news, Huck! Guess what Jim done found while you was in town? A raft, Hucky! Mos' beautiful raft you ever did see...sturdy an' fit...

(Huck stands and moves toward the raft, throwing off his dress.)

JIM: ...an' I done fit it out some whiles you was gone: a lean-to, a rudder...Ain't she pretty?

HUCK: *(Caught up in its beauty.)* Jiminy!

JIM: I reckoned you'd like it...

HUCK: Oh, but Jim, it's past eleven, Jim—*way* past. Pretty soon it'll be *midnight...*

(Sound of dogs barking and men's voices.)

HUCK: They's a-comin' for you, Jim! They's three hund'ed dollars on your head, and they's some what thinks it was *you* who killed me!

JIM: *(Instantly grim.)* Who's a-comin aftah me...

HUCK: Two men—maybe more—we gotta go, an' go *now!*

(Dogs and voices nearer. Jim points to some bundles as he moves Upstage.)

JIM: Get them things on the raft an' I'll unhitch her. Go on, Huck. *(Huck grabs the bundles and leaps on board while Jim unties the rope.)*

JIM: Take the rudder, Huck! Take it!

(Huck takes the rudder; Jim gives the raft a mighty shove. The raft begins to move slowly and majestically Upstage. Jim looks back over his shoulder and two men and two dogs enter on upper platform Stage Right.)

HUCK: Jump!

(Jim leaps aboard the moving raft. The dogs snap and snarl as lights fade to Blackout.)

The Adventures of Huckleberry Finn 327

SCENE IX

Lights rise on raft Downstage. Upper platform Center is gone so that river flows continuously Upstage to Downstage Center. Jim is standing, operating the rudder; Huck sits, a fishing pole in one hand, a book in the other.

HUCK: *(Voice-over.)* Them first few days headed downriver warn't too com-f'table. We kept lookin' over our shoulders, but warn't nobody fol-lowin' us. Every night we passed towns—just shiny little beds o' lights—but the fifth night we passed St. Louis, and it was like the whole world lit up! I never knew there was such a big place till I seed that wonderful spread o' light.
By 'n' by we begun to ease up, and lemme tell you—it's lovely to live on a raft.

JIM: What you doin', Hucky?

HUCK: Jus' readin' one o' them books from off the floatin' house. You wanna have a go, Jim?

JIM: You know I cain't read, chile. What's it say?

HUCK: It's hist'ry. All about French kings an' such.

JIM: Ain't but one king I ever heard 'bout, an' that was ol' King Sollermun. They say Sollermun was the wisest man that ever live, but I don't take no stock in that.

HUCK: But Solomon *was* the wisest man, Jim; the Widow told me so herself.

JIM: He warn't no wise man! You know about that chile he was goin' to chop in two?

HUCK: Why, shore—the Widow read it to me out'n the Bible...

JIM: *Well,* then? You jus' take 'n' look at it a minute. *(Setting up a situation.)* This rudder here: That's one o' the women. Now, you is the other...and I's King Sollermun. And this here book is the chile. Both o' you claims it. Now what do I do? Do I go 'round amongst the neighbors an' find out which one o' you the book *do* belong to? No. I take an' whack the book in two, an' give half to you, an' the other half to the other woman! Dat's the way Sollermun was goin' to do with the chile. Now what's the use o' half a chile?!

HUCK: But hang it, Jim, you've clean missed the point...

JIM: Don't talk to me about "point"! See, the real point is down further—it's down deeper; it's all in the way Sollermun was raised. Now you take a man that's got only one or two chillen: He ain't gonna be wasteful of 'em; he's gonna be mindful of 'em. But you take a man that's got five million chillen runnin' 'round the house, an' it's different. He'd jus' as soon chop a chile in half as a cat!

(Huck looks at Jim for a moment.)

HUCK: Well, let's let Solomon slide. Now this here book tells about other kings, like Louie Sixteen that got his head cut off in France and his young son, the dolphin, that would o' been king, but they took an' shut him up in jail.

JIM: Po' li'l chap...

HUCK: But some says he got out and got away and come to America.

JIM: But they ain't no kings here, Hucky—what's he gonna do? He cain't get no situation.

HUCK: I dunno. Some of 'em gets on the police force, and some of 'em learns people how to talk French.

JIM: Hold on there, Hucky—don't the French people talks the same we does?

HUCK: No, you couldn't understand a word they said.

JIM: Well, I'll be ding-busted! Why?

HUCK: I dunno. But s'pose a man was to come up to you 'n' say: "Parly voo franzy." What would you think?

JIM: I wouldn't think nothin'. I'd take 'n' bust him across't the head.

HUCK: Well, it's only saying: "Do you know how to talk French."

JIM: Why don' he jus' say it?

HUCK: He *is* a-sayin' it; that's a Frenchman's *way* o' sayin' it!

JIM: Well, it's a blame ridic'lous way, an' I don' wanna her no mo' 'bout it!

HUCK: Lookee here, Jim! Does a cat talk like we do?

JIM: No.

HUCK: Does a cow?

JIM: A cow don't neither.

HUCK: Well, then, ain't it natural 'n' right for a Frenchman to talk diff'rent from us?

JIM: Lookee here, Huck: Is a cat a man?

HUCK: No.

JIM: Is a cow a man?

HUCK: No.

JIM: Is a Frenchman a man?

HUCK: O'course!

JIM: Well then? If he *is* a man, why don't he talk like one? You answer me *that!*

HUCK: *(To audience.)* It warn't no use to argue, and besides—I reckoned Jim had a point.

(Huck approaches Jim from the lean-to. Jim waves Huck back. Huck slips and rolls off the edge of the raft and Jim grabs onto the boy's hand.

Jim hauls Huck back onto the raft. The two of them ride the lurching raft: Jim at the rudder, Huck crouched behind him, holding onto Jim's shoulders. Final flash of lightning and everything goes dark. Thunder. Stars fill the sky. The river is tranquil. Evening light on raft. From the darkness of the riverbank comes the voice of a single black man singing a mournful spiritual: "Steal Away." The sound of the song slowly approaches, growing then fading as the raft passes.)

JIM: Listen, Hucky.

(Pause as they listen to the song.)

JIM: He sing to me about Cairo, Illinois! That's what I hear when I hear him sing!

HUCK: How're we gonna know Cairo when we get to it, Jim? I heard they ain't but a dozen houses there.

JIM: I shore ain't gonna miss *that* town, 'cause the minute I sees it, I'll be a free man! I tell you, Hucky, it makes me feel all trembly and fev'rish all over to be so close to freedom... *(Jim enters the lean-to to put away a blanket.)*

HUCK: *(To audience.)* I can tell you, it made *me* all trembly and feverish to hear Jim talk like that, because I begun to get it through my head that he almost *was* free. And who was to blame for it? Me. I couldn't get that off my conscience, not no how. I decided I just *had* to turn Jim in, first chance I got. It was that, or go to the Everlastin' Fire.

JIM: *(Entering from the lean-to.)* What you thinkin' 'bout, Honey? Why don't you say nothin'?

HUCK: *(With guilt.)* I dunno.

JIM: Tell you what *I's* thinkin': I's almos' a free man, an' I owes it all to my frien' Huck—the only white gen'leman that's ever done right by ol' Jim, an' I ain't gonna fo'get it. Not ever!

(A man's voice shouts out from the darkness.)

VOICE I: Who's that? Who is that there?

JIM: *(Crouching.)* Lordy, Huck!

(Jim scrambles into the lean-to. Huck raises the lantern and signals Downstage, as if to another boat.)

VOICE II: You hear the man, now answer!

HUCK: It's...It's George Peters, sir.

VOICE I: That raft belong to you, George Peters?

HUCK: Yes, sir.

VOICE I: Any men on it?

HUCK: Only one, sir.

VOICE II: Well, there's five niggers run off tonight, upriver. Is your man white or black? *(Pause.)* Well?

HUCK: He's...he's white.

VOICE II: I reckon we'll come and see for ourselves.

HUCK: *(Frightened urgency.)* Oh, I...I do wish you would, sir...because o' he's my Pap an'...an' he's mighty sick, gentlemen. Ev'rybody else jus' goes away when I ask them to help me tow the raft ashore...

VOICE I: Say, boy—what's the matter with your father?

HUCK: He's got the...uh...well, it ain't anythin' much...

VOICE I: Boy—that's a lie! Now what's he got?

HUCK: *(Desperate.)* Don't leave us, *please,* gentlemen...you won't have to come too near the raft—only throw us a line an' pull us ashore...

VOICE II: *(Urgent.)* Set her back, John, set her back! Keep away, boy! Confound it; I expect the wind has already blowed it to us! Dang it, boy—your pap has the *smallpox* an' you know it precious well! Keep away, hear? You wanna spread it all over?

HUCK: Please, sir! I jus' cain't manage on my own, an' ever'body always leaves us when they hear what Pap's got...

VOICE II: Let's get outta here! Quick! *(To Huck.)* You'll manage somehow, I reckon.

HUCK: Please...

VOICE I: Come *on,* Parker, we're gettin' too close!

VOICE II: Well back-paddle, dang it! Back-paddle!

(Sound of oars fades. All is quiet for a moment. Jim cautiously emerges from the lean-to, goes to Huck and rests his hands on Huck's shoulders.)

JIM: *(Quietly.)* The only white gen'leman that ever do right by ol' Jim.

(Huck hangs his head in confusion and guilt.)

JIM: An' I ain't ever gonna fo'get it...not ever!

(Lights fade to Blackout.)

SCENE X

In the Blackout, the sounds of fiddle and banjo. Late afternoon lights rise on Huck, sitting Stage Right Center on shore near raft and Jim hiding on raft Center. They are observing a large group of white people on the shore Stage Right, enjoying a country hoedown. Fiddle and banjo begin another up-

tempo dance and eight young couples energetically enter in with much laughter, whoops and calls. Toward the end of the dance, dusk approaches and wispy beginnings of a deep fog roll in from the river. Musicians stop their playing to the disappointment of the dancers.

FIDDLER: Hidy! Hidy, folks! Fog's settin' in!

DANCER: You, there—Betty Jane! Gather up our things, child!

FIDDLER: Fog's a-comin', folks! Quick, now! Fetch your stuff and head for town!

(There is a general scurrying and ad-libbing as people gather up picnic baskets, blankets, etc., and exit quickly Stage Right. Fog increases.)

HUCK: *(Voice-over.)* That fog were the thickest I ever did see. Jim threw me a rope to tie the raft up with, good 'n' safe.

(Jim tosses Huck a rope and Huck moves to post Stage Right and winds rope around.)

HUCK: Well, that were my mistake... *(Huck pulls at the rope to make it taut and it comes away from the raft.)*

(Music. Fog thickens and raft begins to move.)

HUCK: Jim? Jim!

(Huck holds up his lantern. Jim takes the lantern from the pole on the raft and also holds it up as the raft travels Upstage in the ever-deepening fog.)

HUCK: Where are you, Jim?

(The calls echo.)

JIM: Huck? Huck! Where is you, chile?

(The fog begins to swallow up Jim's lantern light as Huck, Downstage with his lantern, turns confused in circles and shouts. Jim calls and bangs on a pot with a spoon—the sound becoming more and more distant.)

HUCK: Jim! *Please*, Jim! Answer me! Jim? Jim!

(Music swells as Huck spins, wild and frightened. The fog covers him and lights fade to Blackout.)

Intermission

ACT II
SCENE I

Lights of dawn rise on the raft, which is in far Downstage position. Jim is sitting with his head down between his knees, asleep, his Right arm hanging over the rudder. Parts of the raft are smashed and it is littered with leaves, branches, general debris. Jim is wet and disheveled. The sounds of birds and lapping water. Huck enters from Stage Right and sees the raft. He is about to call, then stops himself. He slowly tiptoes and delicately hops onto the raft, lies down beside Jim, picks up a twig, snaps it, then pretends to fall asleep. Jim awakens at the sound, looks around, sees Huck.

JIM: Huck? Huck!

HUCK: *(Opens his eyes, yawns and stretches.)* Mornin', Jim. Why'd you wake me up?

JIM: Huck! You ain't dead! *(Jim hugs the boy.)* You's back again—jus' the same ol' Huck—alive 'n' sound, praise God!

HUCK: What're you talkin' 'bout, Jim?

JIM: "Talkin' 'bout?!" Why, I's talkin' 'bout thinkin' I'd never see you again, Honey!

HUCK: Jim—you been drinkin'?

JIM: "Drinkin'?!" Now what fo' and *when!?* Up all night in the fog, holler'n' after you…

HUCK: *(Shaking his head.)* This is too many for me, Jim. I been settin' here talkin' with you all night till you went to sleep 'bout ten minutes ago, and I reckon I did the same. You must o' been dreamin', that's all.
(Jim looks at Huck with a scowl. Long pause.)

JIM: Well…then I reckon I did dream it, if'n you say so.
(Huck stifles a laugh.)

JIM: But that dream must o' been sent to me as a sign!

HUCK: Oh, most likely, Jim—most likely.

JIM: An' I got to interpret that dream or we be in trouble bad. Now…lemme see…the rope: that stands for a man that'll try to do us some good. *(Pause.)* The current: that's another man that'll try to get us away from him. The hollerin's: they's a warnin' that'll come to us ev'ry now and then. An' the fog: that's the slave states and all the trouble we done left behind us…but once we come through the fog, we come into the big clear river, and we won't have no mo' troubles, no mo'!

HUCK: Oh, well…that's all interpreted well enough as far as it goes, Jim, but what does all this truck stand for?

(Huck points to the debris on the raft and subdues a sly smile. Jim looks at the debris, looks at Huck, and picks up a tree branch.)

JIM: *(Grimly.)* "What does they stan' fo'?" I'se goin' to tell you. Aftah I goes to sleep and then wakes up and finds you back again—all safe 'n' sound—the tears come 'n' I coulda got down on my knees, I was so thankful! An' all you was thinkin' 'bout was how you could make a fool out o' ol' Jim with a lie! *(He snaps the branch and throws it down.)* That truck there is *trash*. An' trash is what people is that puts dirt on the heads o' they friends, 'n' makes 'em feel ashamed!

(Jim turns away and starts tossing the debris off the raft and onto the shore. Huck stands and hangs his head.)

HUCK: *(Voice-over.)* It took some time before I could work myself up and go humble myself to Jim, but I done it, and apologized good, and I warn't ever sorry for it afterward neither. *(Huck turns and lends a hand with the trash.)* But soon, Jim and I had other things to think about, 'cause we done took on passengers…

(Sound of dogs Offstage Left.)

JIM: Quick, Hucky! Untie the raft!

(Jim ducks into the lean-to as Huck leaps ashore Stage Left to untie the rope. Duke and Dauphin enter at a run on upper platform. They see raft and Huck and climb down ladder Stage Left.)

DAUPHIN: Say, young man! Young man! If I may interrupt your labors for a moment, I've a small favor to ask of you. Would you kindly save our poor lives?

HUCK: Your lives?

DUKE: Our lives!

DAUPHIN: Say—that weren't a colored man I noticed slip into yonder tent now, was it?

DUKE: He wouldn't be a runaway, would he?

HUCK: Shucks, no! He belongs to me. Jim? Come on out, Jim.

(Jim emerges and joins Huck on shore.)

DAUPHIN: Well, if we might travel with you for a bit, just as far as Pokerville, Arkansas, we'd be most obliged.

HUCK: I'm sorry, gen'lmen, but we ain't goin' to Arkansaw; we're only goin' as far as Cairo, Illinois.

DAUPHIN: "Ain't goin' to Arkansaw?!"

HUCK: No, sir.

DAUPHIN: My friend, you happen to be more'n a hundred miles into that Godforsaken state! You passed up Cairo, Illinois long ago...

(Dauphin leaps onto raft and into lean-to; followed by Duke.)

DUKE: Now cast off, boy! Cast off quick!

(Jim, head hanging, unties the rope. Huck looks at him sadly.)

JIM: Cairo...we missed Cairo...po' nigger cain't have no kind o' luck! I knew that snakeskin warn't done with its work...

HUCK: I'm sorry I ever touched it, Jim.

JIM: It warn't your fault, Hucky. You didn't know.

(The raft is untied and the two board it. Lights begin to fade.)

JIM: Cairo behind us, and we headed south...!

(Blackout.)

SCENE II

Evening. Jim operating rudder, Huck standing by. Dauphin and Duke crawl out of tent.

DAUPHIN: *(To Jim.)* Tie up here, boy.

JIM: Yes, sir.

(Jim goes ashore, followed by Huck. Dauphin waits a moment to make sure they're out of earshot.)

DAUPHIN: *(To Duke.)* So...what got you into trouble, my man?

DUKE: Me? Oh...I been workin' the town...sellin' an article that takes the stain off the teeth. And it *does* take it off, too—and gen'rally the enamel along with it. I stayed about one day longer than I ought to've. *(Pause.)* What's your story?

DAUPHIN: Well...I was runnin' a little temperance revival back there, preachin' 'bout the sin of strong drink. I was the pet of the womenfolk until a report got 'round that I had a way of taking a drink myself now and then. So the womenfolk decided that the menfolk should tar and feather me and ride me out of town on a rail. I didn't wait for breakfast; I warn't hungry. *(A sigh, surveying the little raft.)* Yes, this'll do fine, just fine...

DUKE: Oh...yes...it'll have to do...alas.

DAUPHIN: "Alas?!" What're you "alassin'" about?

DUKE: To think I should have lived to be degraded down into such company...alas...

DAUPHIN: An' just what's wrong with the company?

DUKE: Nothing! Nothing! It's just what I deserve. Alas.

DAUPHIN: *(Cordially.)* You'd best explain yourself, my man… *(Threatening.)* …before I rips your hair out…"alas"…!

DUKE: You would not believe me…the world never believes…the secret of my birth, alas…

DAUPHIN: *(Flatly.)* The secret of your birth alas?

HUCK: *(Approaching.)* What's the secret of your birth, sir?

DUKE: Gentlemen, I will explain it to you…by rights, I am a duke!

JIM: A *duke*, Hucky!

DUKE: Yes…Jim, is it? Hucky? I am the rightful Duke of Bridgewater, and yet, here I am, forlorn, torn from my high estate, and degraded to the companionship of criminals on a raft.

HUCK: I'm awful sorry, sir…

DUKE: I'm sure you are, boy. But if you could just manage to call me "Your Grace" or "Your Lordship" it would do me good.

DAUPHIN: Lookee here, Bilgewater—you ain't the only person that's had troubles like that. *(Brief pause.)* Alas.

DUKE: Alas?

DAUPHIN: Dang right! You ain't the only person that has a "secret of his birth."

DUKE: *(Wryly.)* No?

DAUPHIN: Bilgewater—can I—trust you? *(Dauphin stifles a sob.)*

DUKE: *(Dry.)* To the bitter death. "The secret of your being"—speak!

DAUPHIN: Bilgewater…I am the late Dauphin! Louie the Seventeen! Son of Louie the Sixteen and Mary Ann Tonette!

DUKE: You mean you're the late Charlemagne; you must be six or seven hundred years old, at least.

DAUPHIN: Trouble has done it, Bilgewater; trouble has brung these gray hairs and this premature balditude. Gentlemen: You see before you the wonderin', exiled, trampled-on, rightful King of France!

JIM: Lordy!

(Dauphin bursts into tears.)

HUCK: Oh…please, sir…it don't do no good to cry…

DAUPHIN: No…nothin' does—any good…*except…* *(His tears cease.)* …it would make me feel easier if you treated me according to my rights.

HUCK: Shore thing, King; whatever you say.

DAUPHIN: Small matters, really: You *might* just bend down on one knee when you speak to me, and always call me "Your Majesty" and wait on me first at meals and, of course, never sit down in my presence until I've given you permission.

DUKE: *(Bitterly.)* Alas!

DAUPHIN: You know, Bilgewater, your father and all the other Dukes of Bilgewater were quite good subjects of my Pap. Sure! The late King used to allow them to visit us at the palace...*almost* as often as they wanted to.

DUKE: Right nice o' yer Pap.

(Dauphin takes Duke aside and whispers.)

DAUPHIN: Don't bicker, Bilgey—I think you an' me can work together, don't you see? Small towns in Arkansas—ripe for a pickin'...

DUKE: Mebbe we can at that...Majesty.

(Duke and Dauphin step into lean-to. Jim tosses rope to Huck and hops on board. Raft begins to float.)

HUCK: *(Voice-over.)* It didn't take us long to figure out these kings was just rapscallions, but we didn't let on.

(Lights change.)

HUCK: A few mile downriver, we came across a camp meetin', and them two went to work.

SCENE III

Preacher and Congregation enter Downstage Left singing a fervent, white evangelical hymn: "Lord, I Want to Be a Christian." Duke and Dauphin shoot out of the lean-to.

DAUPHIN: Tie up here, boy.

JIM: Yes, sir, Your Grace.

(Jim does so as Duke and Dauphin leap off the raft and join the gathering congregation who face Downstage toward the Preacher.)

PREACHER: *(When the hymn has ended.)* Ah, Lord! Keep it warm! Praise the Lord, keep it warm! The sinner man—he try to git away, but kin he do it? Kin he do it?

CONGREGATION: No, Lord! No, Lord!

PREACHER: The sinner man—he try to shake loose, but do it loosen? Do it loosen?

CONGREGATION: Glory, no! Glory, no!

PREACHER: The sinner man—he sit and tremble, he shiver and shake, and do it bite him? Do it fight him?

CONGREGATION: Yes, it do! Yes, it do! Glory, halleloo—yes, it do!

DAUPHIN: *(Loudly.)* Praise hallelujia—yes it do!

PREACHER: *(Pointing to Dauphin.)* Thar stands a missuble, old critter, with his head a-bloomin' for the grave!

DAUPHIN: *(Moving Downstage on his knees.)* Oh, Lord, save me from the grave!

PREACHER: A few, short years and he go down to perdition, 'less the Lord have mercy!

DAUPHIN: Oh Lord, have mercy!

CONGREGATION: Mercy, Lord! Mercy, Lord!

PREACHER: Testify!

CONGREGATION: Testify!

DAUPHIN: Save my soul, I'll testify! I'll testify!

(Jim remains on raft. Huck has slipped ashore to observe. Duke makes his way slowly through the crowd, picking an occasional pocket.)

DAUPHIN: Brethren! Brethren! Heed my tale. This is a *sinner* talkin'!

CONGREGATION: Praise the Lord; a sinner man!

DAUPHIN: A pirate, brethren—riverboat pirate, thirty years! Up an' down the Mississip thirty years; thirty years a-stealin' and a-cheatin'. Thirty years a-prowlin' and a-thievin'!

CONGREGATION: Glory hallelujia!

DAUPHIN: But thanks be to Goodness I done seen the light! Thanks be to Goodness I got robbed last night! Thanks be to Goodness I was thrown ashore without a cent, and led to these good people in this great tent! It were the blessedest thing ever happened to me, because I am a changed man now, and—poor as I am—I'm a-goin' right back down the river an' spend the rest o' my life turnin' the *other* pirates into the true path! Oh, yes, it'll take time. Oh, yes, it'll take money—money which I ain't got. But I'll do it anyway, and every time I turn a pirate to the Lord I'll say, "Don't thank me. Thank them dear people in the Pokerville camp meetin': natural brothers and benefactors of the race! An' thank that dear preacher there—the truest friend a pirate ever had!"

PREACHER: Praise the Lord! A sinner saved!

VOICE FROM CONGREGATION: Take up a collection for him! Take up a collection!

VOICE FROM CONGREGATION: Let *him* pass the hat!

DAUPHIN: That's all right; my friend'll do that.

(Duke steps forward.)

DAUPHIN: He done converted too.

DUKE: *(Slow at picking up his cue.)* Wha…oh, yes…Praise Goodness, I converted too!

(Congregation murmurs in approval. Duke starts to move through crowd.)

PREACHER: Now pay up, brethren; give what's right!

(Congregation reprises hymn "Lord, I Want to Be a Christian" as Preacher coaches. The entire group moves off Stage Left and fades. Huck and Jim stand on the raft, as Duke and Dauphin crouch on shore and empty the hat.)

DAUPHIN: Praise the Lord, they gave what's right! Eighty-seven dollars and forty-two cents!

(They hop onto raft. Thunder. Lights shift to dark, rainy afternoon. Duke pauses on raft only to pick up suitcase, then moves to Stage Right where people pass, carrying umbrellas.)

HUCK: *(Voice-over.)* In Honkerville the Duke tried to cure everybody of anything that ailed 'em…

DUKE: Oh, yes…oh, yes, my friends…I used to be troubled by weather like this, myself—gets in the bones. Rheumatism, lumbago, arthritis, hair loss and arches fallin' left 'n' right. But not no more! Parker's the name *Doctor* Parker—Doctor Alexander T. Robert E. Lee Parker, how do you do!

(Four folks have gathered; three more pass and Duke calls to them.)

DUKE: Who's that there? Come on, come on, don't be afraid! You've got nothin' to lose 'n' the whole world to gain! That's right, come on, come on…

(A few more people enter and assemble.)

DUKE: Nope: troubles of the body and the soul are troubles no more, far as I'm concerned. Could be the same for you, could be the same. No more this, no more that; troubles of the bladder, liver, gut, and spleen: wiped out! Wiped out clean!

WOMAN: How?

DUKE: *(Slow, smug chuckle.)* Heh, heh, heh, heh, *heh*! "How." Simple question, three little letters… *(Suddenly fierce.)* The lady asks "how!" How, she wants to know, can she be free from the miseries of in-di-gestion! *(He points at others as examples.)* How can she find luck in love! How can he git his eldest sister married off! And how… *(Standing face to face with a skeptical looking laborer.)* …how can he cure himself of those disgusting, revolting, unsightly warts which cover his entire face and body! How!

LABORER: *(A growl.)* Yeah, how!

DUKE: *(Stepping back.)* Bless you, sir; bless your inquirin' heart. You ask me how? Lookee here… *(He pulls from his suitcase a small bottle of patent medicine.)* Parker's Potent Patent Potion! That's right, sir! My friends— just a little teaspoon o' this—mornin' an' night, and, by jings, it'll set you right! Fifteen cents a bottle; forty cents for three… *(He moves a few steps Stage Right.)* …the line forms here.

(No one moves.)

DUKE: Now, now—who's gonna be first? Come along…

> *(Suddenly an ancient man with bent posture hobbles toward the Duke: it is the Dauphin, blanket over his body, cane in hand.)*

DAUPHIN: I'll take three, if you please.

DUKE: *(With a tone of pity for the old man.)* Ohh, bless you, sir. Bless you. That'll be forty cents. A downright pleasure doin' business with you, sir…
> *(The Dauphin opens a bottle and tips his head back. Crowd watches. The old man's body starts to quiver. Suddenly, he shoots upright, spine erect, the blanket falling to the ground. His face suggests Sleeping Beauty just-awakened. He strolls away with confidence. Crowd murmurs.)*

WOMAN: I'll take one!

DUKE: "You'll take one." *(Duke puts his arm around the woman and displays her to the others.)* I ask you good people: Does this woman not have a family?

MAN: Well o' course she do!

DUKE: Well, don't she care about 'em? Don't she *love* her husband an' children?

WOMAN: 'Course I do!

DUKE: Then you'll require three bottles, won't you? Three—at the very least? That is…unless you don't care about 'em…then, o' course…

WOMAN: *(With a quick look at her neighbors.)* I'll…take six!

DUKE: Very good, dear lady, you're doin' the right thing…
> *(Crowd gathers around Duke and quickly purchases the medicine.)*

DUKE: …step right up…form a line…get the goods while you got the time. That's right, that's right…
> *(All exit except for Duke and bellicose laborer. Laborer slowly approaches, threatening. Duke smiles uneasily, certain he's been discovered as a fraud. Laborer slowly reaches into his pocket; Duke winces. Laborer quickly pulls out a bill of currency, puts it in the Duke's hand and takes the Duke's suitcase with the other. Laborer exits. Lightning flash, thunderclap. Duke laughs and joins Dauphin at the shore. They move to raft; Huck and Jim have taken refuge from the rain in the lean-to.)*

DAUPHIN: *(Shouting into lean-to.)* Outta there, you two, an' let royalty enter!

DUKE: *(To Dauphin, as Huck and Jim crawl out.)* Say, Royalty—you ever gone in for any play-actin'?

DAUPHIN: Dunno. Haven't seen much of it; I was too young when Pap used to have it at the palace.

DUKE: Well, you a-goin' to now. I got a bag o' costumes in here, an' the next town we hit, you're gonna be Hamlet, Prince of Denmark! I'll learn you the speech right off.

DAUPHIN: *(As he goes into the tent, followed by Duke.)* Well, as long as it's royal…

HUCK: *(Voice-over.)* But the next place we passed was as downright scary for the King and Duke as it was for Jim…*and* me…

(Lights rise Stage Left. Well-dressed whites assemble on lower platform and look to upper platform as Auctioneer enters, cracking a whip, followed by Slaves in chins herded by a couple White Males. Orchestra plays percussive beat as Auctioneer cracks his whip and sings and Whites raise their hands in bids.)

AUCTIONEER: Let's go gentlemen

Sun's gettin' hot

Down to business

Gonna sell the lot

Bid 'em up, Bid 'em up

(Young Black Woman shoved up onto auction block.)

First one up is a breeder that's prime

Make a good maid if you take the time

Quiet and tame, don't take much whip

Grab 'er Jack—let 'em see 'er stripped

(Assistant turns woman around and tears her dress off her back.)

Lean in the flanks but good and sturdy

Damn good buy if you like 'em purty

Bid 'em up, Bid 'em up

Three-Fifty gentlemen do I hear four?

Four-Fifty goin' do I hear more?

Five hundred once—that's a steal

Five hundred twice…

(Spoken, with an evil grin.)

We got a deal!

(Woman is shoved off the block and pulled Offstage. Black Man is put on the block.)

Bid 'em up, Bid 'em up

Next one up's good fieldhand stock

Alright Jack—put him up on the block

Bid 'em up, Bid 'em up

(Lights fade on Auctioneer and cracking whip.)

HUCK: *(Voice-over.)* The sight of them poor folks up on the auction block was enough to chill your blood! Jim tried to make me forget it, but it were a sight I couldn't get off my mind, not no-how!

(Lights shift to Stage Right area. Jim hops off raft and ties it up.)

HUCK: But by the time we reached Gladsburg, them other two rascals had even gotten *me* involved...

(Duke sticks his head out of lean-to and hands a painted sign and pot and spoon to Huck. The boy steps on shore and pounds against the pot; Audience gathers.)

OLD WOMAN: *(Reading Huck's sign.)* Shakespearean Revival. Wonderful Attraction. One Day Only. The World Renowned...

DAUPHIN: *(Bursting out of lean-to and onto shore.)* World renowned tragedians: David Garrick of London, England, and... *(He bows.)* Edmund Kean, of the same town. Presenting their Spectacular Shakespearean Spectacle: Hamlet's Soliloquoy! Special added attraction: the Fair Ophelia, played by...

(Duke emerges from lean-to dressed in makeshift female costume and loosely fitting wig.)

DAUPHIN: Mr. Garrick himself!

(Duke bows and wig drops to ground. Laughter and applause from Audience. Jim takes his place near Huck and holds a tin cup for coins.)

DAUPHIN: Admission: twenty-five cents; children and servants: one thin dime. Pay the man now; you won't never regret it!

(Audience drops coins in cup and seat themselves up stairs on Stage Right slope; they face us—middle level becoming the playing area. Dauphin and Duke move Upstage and Huck clangs on pot to call Audience to attention.)

DAUPHIN: Are you ready, Mr. Garrick?

DUKE: *(Replacing his wig.)* Ready, Mr. Kean!

(Dauphin strikes a dramatic "brooding" pose; he holds a skull in one hand and a dagger in the other.)

DAUPHIN: To be, or not to be; that is the bare bodkin
That makes calamity of so long life.
For who would fardels bear, till Birnam wood
do come to Dunsinane,
But that the fear of something after death
Murders—*murders!*—the innocent sleep.

(Audience gasps. Dauphin holds for applause. Audience obliges.)

DUKE: *("Gliding" on; employing falsetto.)* Oh, wherefore, Hamlet—wherefore? 'Tis not the nightingale you hear, but...

(Someone in audience gives a raspberry.)

DUKE: ...some other bird...

(Audience boos and jeers the Duke's performance.)

DUKE: …put out the light, Hamlet, and then put out the light again! Out, out, damned light!

(Audience reaction has crescendoed; Duke shouts in normal voice.)

DUKE: Put out the damn light!

DAUPHIN: 'Tis a consummation devoutly to be wished.

But soft, you—the Fair Ophelia

Ope not thy ponderous and marble jaws,

But get thee to a nunnery—go!

(Duke tiptoes out of playing area. Dauphin tosses him the skull, then plunges the dagger into his stomach and falls. Audience screams and gasps in reaction. Spontaneous applause. Dauphin rises to his feet, Duke joins him, they bow. Duke's wig falls off again, and the applause is mixed with laughter and catcalls. Audience disperses and exits. Jake, a young countryman, lingers.)

JAKE: Hey! You two ain't the Wilks brothers from over in England, are you?

DAUPHIN: Ah…why do you ask?

JAKE: Well, when I seed you, I nearly ran back to the Wilks' place to tell 'em old Peter Wilks's long-lost brothers had finally got here. Too late, o' course, for poor old Peter…

DAUPHIN: "Too late"…?

JAKE: Well he up an' died yestiday, didn't he?

(Duke cocks his head like a beast smelling prey.)

DUKE: Oh? Yes…oh, yes…may his soul rest in peace…

JAKE: Yep, poor old Peter'd give purty near anythin' to see his brothers afore he died…

DUKE: Tell me, now…uh…was this Mr. Peter Wilks a wealthy gentleman?

JAKE: That's just it. I reckon he left about six thousand in gold hid up there some'eres, but he never made out a will. He just wrote it all down in a letter to his brother Harvey Wilks: tellin' him where the money was, an' sealed it up for when he got here. Ah, no—you two cain't be the Wilks brothers!

DAUPHIN: Why do you say that?

JAKE: I jus' remembered now: one of 'em is deef an' dumb. Old Willy Wilks cain't hear nor speak a word, so they say.

DUKE: Oh, my! Unfortunate fellow…

DAUPHIN: My friend and I take great interest in the plight of our fellow man. So why don't you just tell us a little bit more about the Wilks family?

JAKE: Well, old Peter had three orphan nieces: There's Mary Jane, she's about nineteen; and then there's Susan, she's about fifteen; and little Joanna—she's the youngest in the fam'ly—but she can write poyms real good.

DUKE: Oh, *can* she...!

(The three men shift into silent conversation as Huck and Jim pack away the acting gear in the lean-to.)

HUCK: I guess I can figure what them rapscallions is up to.

JIM: Mmmm.

HUCK: What's wrong, Jim?

JIM: I dunno.

HUCK: *Somethin's* wrong...

JIM: *(Hiding his face in his hands.)* I's so homesick I could almos' die, Hucky...

HUCK: *(To audience.)* I reckon Jim cared jus' as much for his fam'ly as white folks does for their'n. It don't seem natural, but I reckon it's so.

(Focus shifts back to Duke, Dauphin, and Jake.)

DUKE: So now you're off travelin', is that it?

JAKE: Goin' on a ship for Ryo Janeero, where my uncle lives.

DAUPHIN: My, my! And you won't be comin' back?

JAKE: Not for five year, I reckon. *(Lifts his backpack onto his shoulder.)* Well, it's been nice chawin' with ya. What you say yer name was?

DUKE: Uh...Blodgett. Reverend Blodgett. *(Digging in his vest for a business card.)* Here's my card.

(Duke grabs Dauphin and they leap onto raft.)

DUKE: Quick, Jim; cast off!

(Jim unties the raft and shoves off.)

JAKE: *(Reading the card as raft moves Upstage.)* "Parker's Patent Tooth Cleaner?!"

(Lights fade to Blackout.)

SCENE IV

During scene shift, orchestra and Offstage choir sing funeral hymn.

CHOIR: When I can read my title clear to mansions in the skies
I'll bid farewell to ev'ry fear and wipe my weeping eyes
I feel like, I feel like I'm on my journey home
I feel like, I feel like I'm on my journey home
(Lights rise on Wilks's home. A coffin sits Center, lid opened Upstage. Mourners stand in semicircle around coffin: the three nieces Mary Jane, Susan, and Joanna holding one another and sobbing; Abner Shackleford the

undertaker; Reverend Hobson and Mrs. Hobson, and Levi Bell the attorney.
Second verse of hymn is hummed by chorus under dialogue.)

MRS. HOBSON: Ohhh…he looks so *natural!* Abner Shackleford, you done a
wonder with old Peter; why, he looks so *lifelike…!*

ABNER: *(In a perpetual demi-whisper.)* Thank you, Mrs. Hobson…Reverend
Hobson…

MRS. HOBSON: Why, you'd hardly never know that he was…

REV. HOBSON: Passed over, my dear. Peter Wilks has crossed the river at last,
and gone to his eternal reward!
(Girls sob.)

ABNER: And now, if the family of the departed sit over here…Mary
Jane…Susan…little Joanna…
(They sit on bench Upstage Left of coffin.)

ABNER: …and the friends of the deceased, over here…
(They sit Stage Left.)

ABNER: …little Joanna—young though she may be—has composed a fitting
verse for this lamentable occasion. Little Joanna?

SUSAN: Little Joanna?

MARY JANE: Go on, little Joanna; go on, now…
(Joanna Wilks steps forward, next to coffin. She clears her throat.)

JOANNA: Ode to Peter Jacob Wilks.
(Mrs. Hobson smiles and murmurs approvingly at her husband.)

JOANNA: *(Her foot tapping as a metronome.)*
And did dear Peter sicken,
And did old Peter die?
And did the sad hearts thicken,
And did the mourners cry?
No whoopin' cough did rack his frame,
Nor measles drear with welts;
Not these impaired the sacred name
Of Peter Jacob Wilks.

MRS. HOBSON: *(Immediately, thinking the poem has ended.)* How sweet, why…

JOANNA: Despised love struck not with woe
That old head white as silk,
Nor stomach troubles laid him low,
Old Peter Jacob Wilks.

MRS. HOBSON: Oh, little Joa…

JOANNA: Ohhh no!
Then list' with tearful eye,

Whil'st I his fate review.
His soul did from this cold world fly
From catching of the flu!
Amen!

(A smattering of discreet applause from mourners as nieces sob.)

ABNER: Most fittin', little Joanna; most fittin'.

JOANNA: *(A curtsey.)* Thank you, Undertaker Shackleford.

(She joins her sisters in a huddled embrace. It is becoming obvious that the girls are very physical.)

MRS. HOBSON: Now warn't that just the most beautiful thing you ever did hear Levi Bell?

LEVI BELL: I can say, in all honesty, that I've never heard anything like it. *(Stepping forward. Skeptical.)* So, you're the Reverend Harvey Wilks? And that is William Wilks?

DUKE: Indeed, sir.

LEVI BELL: Un-huh. And just what part of England do you come from, sir?

DUKE: Why, uh...Sheffield, of course. And might you be dear Peter's friend, the lawyer whom he done wrote us about so often? "Bell," is it? Levi Bell?

LEVI BELL: Yes, well, that's my name, anyway...

DUKE: *(Seeing the huddled mass of femininity Stage Right.)* And these poor, dear, heavenly creatures...our orphaned nieces?

MARY JANE: Yes, Uncle Harvey... *(Over-articulating her lips to Dauphin.)* Uncle Will-iam...

DUKE: You must be Mary Jane...

(Mary Jane runs to Duke's arms and hugs him with all her might, then the Dauphin, and then Huck, who can hardly bear it.)

DUKE: And Susan...what are you now—fifteen?

(Susan has been unable to take her eyes off Huck; she walks Stage Right, barely touching Duke, Dauphin, then throws herself into Huck's arms and sobs, and hugs, and sobs. She composes herself and—after giving Huck a meaningful look—joins Mary Jane.)

DUKE: And little Joanna: the sweet poetess of the family...

(Joanna gives a polite hug to Duke, Dauphin, then suddenly discovers a shoelace that needs tying to avoid embracing Huck. She joins her sisters and they huddle united.)

MARY JANE: Well, Lawyer Bell, now that the brothers have arrived, we can open Uncle Peter's letter!

LEVI BELL: *(Reluctantly taking the sealed letter from his pocket.)* Yes…I suppose so…

(Duke's eyes glimmer with greed; Levi notices. Duke whirls around and he and Dauphin throw themselves on the coffin in weeping, wailing, and gnashing of teeth. Levi Bell is disgusted with the show of grief; he hands letter to Abner.)

LEVI BELL: Here, Abner—you read it.

ABNER: "I, Peter Wilks, being of sound…etc., etc…. do leave my house and three thousand dollars in gold to my good nieces…"

(They sob.)

ABNER: "Another three thousand I bequeath to my brothers, Harvey and William. The gold is hid beneath a trap in the parlor floor…etc., etc."

(The nieces run into the sitting room Stage Right and look about. Susan lifts a scatter rug and finds the trapdoor.)

SUSAN: Here it is!

(Duke and Dauphin scramble to the trapdoor, followed by the others. Dauphin opens the trap and scrambles down.)

LEVI BELL: I thought *that* one couldn't hear…

DUKE: Him? Well, uh…he reads lips middlin' well…

(Duke calls down to Dauphin, signing as he speaks.)

DUKE: Can…you…find…it? You found it? He found it!

(Dauphin climbs up out of the trap, carrying a heavy bag of gold coins.)

REV. HOBSON: Six thousand in gold, to be divided equally between you three girls and these two gentlemen!

DUKE: No!

(All look in surprise.)

MRS. HOBSON: No?!

DUKE: No. These poor girls is orphans, alone in the world. Therefore, my brother and I do hearby give the entire six thousand to these sweet motherless things!

(The Dauphin had nearly choked in horror, but then realizes what Duke is up to and nods in agreement. "Ahs" and "Ohs" from the mourners.)

MARY JANE: *(She and her sisters giving a hug to Duke and Dauphin.)* You are too good…too good…

DUKE: Now…I imagine, Mr. Shackleford, that the funeral orgies will be held tomorrow?

(Others exchange looks.)

LEVI BELL: "Orgies?" Perhaps you mean "funeral obsequies?"

DUKE: Oh...oh, no...no, I don't. "Obsequies" has gone clear out in England these days; we figure funeral *orgies* is best.

MRS. HOBSON: Oh?

DUKE: Yes, that's *org*, from the Greek "org" meaning open or public, and *gies* from the Hebrew "jees" meaning burial.

(Levi Bell throws his head back in laughter.)

MARY JANE: Levi Bell! How *can* you laugh so?!

LEVI BELL: Because these two are a couple of low-down frauds, that's how! With their idiotic Greek and Hebrew...and that *accent!* Mary Jane, these men are out to get your money, that's all. As your friend, I'm urging you to turn these pitiful rascals out—I'm begging you. Will you do it?

MARY JANE: *(Shocked and defiant.)* Here's my answer! *(She picks up the bag of money and hands it to Duke.)* Take this six thousand dollars and invest it for us girls any way you want to and don't give us no receipt for it neither!

LEVI BELL: *(Stunned.)* I'm very sorry, girls. Truly sorry. There's a day a-coming when you're a-going to feel sick whenever you think of this day. *(He exits quickly Stage Left.)*

REV. HOBSON: *(Calling after him.)* Now, Levi—hold on a minute—listen to reason *(Exiting after Levi.)* Come along, mother...

(Rev. Hobson and Mrs. Hobson exit. Abner moves Center to coffin.)

DUKE: And now, my dears, my brother and I are weary from our journey...

MARY JANE: Of course you are! You can stay in the guest room up yonder...

SUSAN: And Adolphus can sleep in the attic bedroom. I'll take you there. *(She grabs Huck by the hand.)*

ABNER: Ladies—until tomorrow. *(Abner bows and closes the coffin lid.)*

MARY JANE: Abner...

(She moves to Abner and gives him a hug. He exits. Mary Jane and Joanna then lead Duke and Dauphin to bedroom at middle Stage Right platform, Susan leads Huck to ladder Stage Left and climbs.)

SUSAN: Well, come on, Adolphus...it's up this way.

(Huck follows. Duke and Dauphin settle into their bedroom, Mary Jane and Joanna hug them both and exit Stage Right. Duke and Dauphin then hug each other with glee.)

SUSAN: Adolphus...what a funny name!

HUCK: Yes, ma'am. You don't know how funny it is.

SUSAN: *(Moving close to him, standing nose to nose.)* Well, good night...

HUCK: Yes, ma'am.

SUSAN: ...sweetheart.

(She hugs Huck and gives him a big kiss on the lips. She exits. Huck loosens his collar.)

HUCK: *(With conviction, to audience.)* Well, I jus' couldn't do it!

(Duke and Dauphin are undressing for bed.)

DAUPHIN: That lawyer fellow...Levi Bell...he makes me uneasy. Stash the bag under the bed.

DUKE: We got nothin' to worry about. Especially not after I offered to give away the whole six thousand. *(Duke chuckles.)*

HUCK: *(To audience.)* I reckon those two would kill me quick if they knew what I was a-plannin', but that didn't matter.

DAUPHIN: "Nothin' to worry about?!" Listen to me—crack o' dawn, we takes the gold and goes! We won't be waitin' around for the funeral *orgies,* you dang fool!

DUKE: *(Putting the bag under the bed.)* It were an honest mistake...

HUCK: *(To audience.)* I put up with them rascals' other frauds, but I couldn't stand by an' let 'em steal from those poor orphan girls.

DAUPHIN: *(Climbing into bed.)* You ain't never made an *honest* mistake in yer life! Now put out the candle.

(Duke obeys and settles into bed also.)

HUCK: *(To audience.)* Shore, them girls kissed an' slobbered too much, an' I coulda choked that little poet, but Susan—she was right purty. First, I'd get the money away from them Royalty, and then head out for Jim and the raft. I was done with kings, once and for all.

(Music. Huck stealthily descends the ladder, makes his way Stage Right, climbs to bedroom, Duke and Dauphin are snoring. Huck gropes around room, finds bag beneath bed, stoops down to get it just as Dauphin stirs and reaches his hand down to feel if the bag is there. Huck holds it so Dauphin can touch it. Reassured, Dauphin withdraws his hand and rolls over, back to sleep. Huck slowly lifts the bag and descends the stairs through sitting-room. When he reaches Center, there is a loud knocking at "door" Stage Left. Duke and Dauphin sit up in bed. Huck, terrified, caught between the known evil Stage Right and unknown threat Stage Left, quickly opens coffin and drops bag inside, then ducks under the skirt of the table it rests on. Another knock.)

HUCK: Sorry, Uncle Peter...

MARY JANE: *(Entering, carrying candle and dressed in nightclothes.)* Just a moment...Who is it? Who's there?

LEVI BELL: *(Entering Stage Left, carrying a lantern.)* It's Levi Bell and Abner, Mary Jane.

MARY JANE: Why, whatever is it?

LEVI BELL: A message has arrived by steamboat down at the landing.

MARY JANE: Well? What is it?

LEVI BELL: It's from your uncles: Harvey and William Wilks. The *real* Wilks brothers, I'm afraid.

ABNER: Most lamentable…

MARY JANE: I don't believe you!

LEVI BELL: They say they've been delayed. Their coach broke down in Pittsburgh, but they'll be here within a week.

(Duke and Dauphin leap out of bed and throw their clothes on.)

DUKE: Grab the money and let's *git!*

MARY JANE: You mean…those two *are* frauds?

ABNER: Lamentable…

DAUPHIN: The money—it ain't here!

LEVI BELL: That's right. Now, I've sent for the sheriff; he should be along any minute now.

DUKE: What?' Whattya mean, the money ain't here! If you're holdin' out on me, by dang, I'll…

MARY JANE: What's that ruckus?

LEVI BELL: *(Running for the stairs.)* They're getting away!

DAUPHIN: Never mind the money now—we got to git! Quick: the window!

(Duke and Dauphin climb out Upstage edge of platform and drop out into darkness.)

LEVI BELL: Abner—come with me 'round the back of the house! Mary Jane— when the sheriff gets here, send him down toward the river!

(Abner and Levi exit. Mary Jane, alone, begins to sob.)

MARY JANE: The money…they've taken all the money…

HUCK: *(Peering out from beneath the coffin.)* Miss Mary Jane?

MARY JANE: *(Startled.)* What?! Who is it?

HUCK: It's me…Huck.

MARY JANE: *(Seeing him.)* "Huck?!"

HUCK: My real name. An' don't you worry none, 'cause them frauds ain't got yer money. I couldn't let 'em do that to you, so I stole it. Mary Jane— the money's in the coffin. I hid it in the coffin.

MARY JANE: *(Embracing him.)* Oh, you dear, sweet boy…!

(Joanna and Susan enter, rubbing their eyes.)

JOANNA: *(Half-asleep.)* What is it, Mary Jane?

MARY JANE: Joanna, come and give this boy a great big hug!

(Joanna stumbles sleepily toward Huck. Huck holds his arms out and keeps Joanna at a distance.)

HUCK: Uh, thanks all the same, ma'am, but I got to get back to my friend Jim. We got to get away from them rapscallions quick, or it'll be all over for us. Good night, y'all.

(Susan reaches her arms out, but Huck just bows and exits quickly. Susan's lower lip quivers and she turns to her sister. All huddle in sudden burst of tears and lights fade to Blackout.)

SCENE V

During shift, voice-over in the darkness.

HUCK: *(Voice-over.)* What can I say? It were dark as pitch, and I was all mixed up. I knowed Jim was on the raft upriver of the landing, but danged if I didn't git lost two or three times, at least. I reckoned by now Mr. Bell and the sheriff had caught up with them Royalty, but I wanted to git clear o' the neighborhood fast as I could. Anyways, it were nigh on noon o' the next day when I finally caught sight of our good ol' raft.

(Light rises on raft, Downstage. It appears to be deserted. Huck enters.)

HUCK: Jim? Jim! It's Hucky, Jim! Where are you?

(Huck steps onto raft just as Jim—painted and costumed in an outrageous manner—crawls out of the lean-to.)

HUCK: Jim!

JIM: Look what they done to me, Huck…I's disgraced!

HUCK: *Who* done it, Jim? An' what is that truck you got on yourself?

(Duke and Dauphin appear from lean-to and approach Huck menacingly. Huck sinks to his knees in despair.)

DAUPHIN: What's the matter, Huckleberry? You weren't meanin' to leave your ol' friends behind, now were you? *(He grabs Huck by the hair and pulls his head back.)*

HUCK: *(Fighting back the tears.)* No, sir.

DUKE: No…not likely. Now listen here: We just lost ourselves a heap o' gold back there. Now, we don't know just how we lost it, or who got it…

DAUPHIN: *(Glaring at Duke.)* Although some of us has our suspicions…

DUKE: Don't you start that again, dang it! The point is, we a little short o' cash right now, an' we got to make it up, now don't we? So—here's our new attraction…

(Jim has hung his head in shame; Duke pulls his head up by the turban he now wears.)

DUKE: One demented A-rab chieftain! Twenty-five cents to see him; forty cents to git up close. We goin' ashore now, my boy, with our new A-rab, and you got to stay here and guard the raft. There's a little one-horse town over yonder, name of Pikesville, an' I reckon we should git us fifty bucks by nightfall.

DAUPHIN: Which is a bit short of six thousand in gold...

DUKE: *(Angrily.)* I *didn't* take that gold, dad blame it! You say I did one more time and I'll drown you, so help me!

JIM: Hucky—do I have to go with 'em?

DUKE: What do you think, nigger?! Now come on!

(Duke and Dauphin push Jim off the raft onto the bank.)

HUCK: Jim...I'm sorry...I'll be waitin'...

(The three men exit, leaving Huck alone on the raft.)

HUCK: *(Voice-over.)* It was a close place. I got to thinkin' it would be a thousand times better for Jim to be a slave at home, where his family was, than out here—disgraced by a couple o' low-down thieves.

(The approaching sound of a Negro spiritual: "Take Me to the Water.")

HUCK: And then it hit me: that my wickedness was bein' watched all the time from up there in heaven, because I was stealin' a poor woman's nigger, and makin' things jus' as bad for him as for her. I shoulda known better. There was Sunday School, an' if I'd a-gone, I'd a-learnt that people who helps runaway niggers escape to freedom goes to the Everlastin' Fire. I tried to pray, but I jus' couldn't. So I got a piece of paper... *(Huck gets a scrap of paper and pencil from the lean-to.)* ...an' I set down an' wrote: "Miz Watson: your runaway Jim is down here in Pikesville, Arkansaw. You kin come an' git him. Huck Finn."

(A small black congregation gathers on the riverbank for a baptism. A young man is led to the water's edge Downstage Right to be baptized, Huck observes.)

PREACHER: I baptize you in the name o' the Father, in the name o' the Son, an' in the name o' the Holy Ghost!

(Preacher and another man hold young man and tip him back into the pit area and up again.)

PREACHER: You a chile o' God, now! Glory, hallelujia!

(Congregation bursts into uptempo hymn of jubilation: "Yes, I'm So Glad" They exit as they clap and sing.)

HUCK: *(Voice-over.)* I felt good and all washed clean o' sin, for the first time. But then I went on thinkin'. And I got to thinkin' over our trip down the river, an' I see Jim before me all the time. I see him in the moonlight, an' us talkin', an' I see him in the storms. I see him how glad he was when I come back out o' the fog. An' I hear him sayin' I was the best friend ol' Jim ever had, an' the *only* one he had now… *(Huck begins to cry.)* It was a close place. I looked at that piece of paper I done wrote, and it trembled in my hands. I'd got to decide forever between two things, and I knowed it. *(Huck slowly tears up the note.)*

HUCK: All right then—I'll *go* to hell!

(He lets the torn pieces of paper drift away from the raft. The drunken voices of Duke and Dauphin are heard. They enter from upper platform Stage Left, crossing over bridge and heading down toward Downstage Right. They carry a couple of jugs of whiskey between them.)

DUKE: *(Laughing.)* An' that undertaker! Wha' wash his name? Shackleford? Abner Shackleford?

(They laugh. Huck rises from raft and moves toward them.)

DAUPHIN: *(Giggling.)* "Oh, no! Noooo—in England these days, we moshtly say 'funeral orgies.' *Org* from the Greek *org,* and *gies* from the Hebrew… *(Noticing Huck.)* …Jeez, what'sha matter with you…*Adolphus.*

(Duke and Dauphin laugh again.)

HUCK: Where's Jim?

DUKE: Jim? Jim who? *(Another laugh.)*

HUCK: Where's Jim!

DAUPHIN: I dunno.

DUKE: He don' b'long to ush no more…

HUCK: He never *did* belong to you! Now where is he! Tell me!

DAUPHIN: I dunno…but we got forty dollars for 'im!

(Laughter.)

DUKE: An' a coupla jugs throwed in on the side…!

HUCK: *(Furious. He grabs Duke by the lapels.)* You *sold* him?!! You sold him for *forty dirty dollars?!!*

(Huck throws Duke to the ground and tosses Dauphin down on top of him. They are too drunk to cause any problem. Huck kneels on Dauphin's chest.)

HUCK: Tell me! Where is he! *Tell me now!*

DAUPHIN: Phelps…Silas and Sally Phelps…a small farm…'bout three miles upriver…

(Huck leaps up, unties the raft and shoves it off. He jumps on as it moves Upstage. Duke and Dauphin hurl insults at him.)

DUKE: Uppity white-trash boy

(They remain sprawled, drunken on the ground. Neither of them sees Levi Bell, Abner Shackleford, and Sheriff enter and stand beside them.)

DUKE: Pass me the jug, Your Grace…

DAUPHIN: Don' mind if I do…

LEVI BELL: Allow me, Your Highnesses…

(Levi Bell pours a jug of whiskey over Duke and Dauphin as lights fade to Blackout.)

SCENE VI

Lights rise on Phelps's farm. Jim is in the shadows, sitting, chained to a post beneath Stage Left platform. Aunt Sally enters from Upstage Left and speaks with George Mathers, a young farmhand, who casually carries a shotgun.

AUNT SALLY: I don't know why that darkie has to be kept chained up like that. I don't like it, and neither do *Mr.* Phelps. Fact is, I don't know why he got to be there a-tall.

GEORGE: Well, them two men what brung him here said he were dangerous—said we got to keep him locked up till his rightful owner come up from Newrleans.

AUNT SALLY: Shoot! Why, he's as dangerous as *you*, George Mathers. Now come on inta the kitchen with me and help git him some food. *(As they exit Downstage Right.)* I'm sick o' the whole business, I don't mind tellin' ya…

(They are off. Huck appears and slips furtively over to Jim.)

HUCK: *Hssst! Jim!*

JIM: Huck!

HUCK: Shhh! I got the raft tied up jus' over the ridge. Come on, while we got a chance…

(Jim lifts up the chain clamped to his ankle for Huck to see. Huck drops to his knees in despair.)

JIM: *(Grim.)* Ain't no more chances for Jim. Ain't no more runnin'; no more raft. We traveled a far piece together, boy, but that's done with now. It's the auction block for me now, Huck…

HUCK: Jim!

JIM: *(Fierce.)* Now git outta here, boy, before they find you!

(Huck shakes his head. Aunt Sally enters, followed by George carrying a tray of food along with his shotgun.)

AUNT SALLY: Why, lookee there!

(*Huck leaps guiltily to his feet and moves away from Jim.*)

AUNT SALLY: It's you at last!

(*Huck looks about him in bewilderment.*)

AUNT SALLY: *Ain't* it?

HUCK: (*Quietly.*) Yes'm. Is you Mrs. Phelps?

(*Aunt Sally goes to Huck and hugs and kisses him; Huck doesn't know what is going on.*)

AUNT SALLY: Don't call me "Mrs. Phelps" Honey—call me Aunt Sally.

(*She hugs him again and squeals with delight. George watches. Aunt Sally signals for him to give the tray to Jim. Huck observes.*)

AUNT SALLY: That's jus' a poor runaway we got to keep here for a spell.

(*Aunt Sally leads Huck Stage Right to bench and they sit.*)

AUNT SALLY: Now we been expectin' you for days, Tom. What kept you? Did your boat go aground?

HUCK: Yes'm, she did.

AUNT SALLY: Whereabouts?

HUCK: Well, it warn't really the groundin'—that didn't keep us back more'n a little. We blowed out a cylinder head.

AUNT SALLY: Gracious! Anybody hurt?

HUCK: No, ma'am.

AUNT SALLY: Well, that's lucky, because sometimes folks do get hurt. Two years ago last Christmas, your Uncle Silas was comin' up from Newrleans on the ol' *Lally Rook*. She blowed out a cylinder head and crippled a man. And I think he died afterwards. He was a Baptist. Yes, I remember now, he *did* die. Mortification set in, and they had to amputate him. But it didn't save him. Yes—it was mortification—that was it; he turned blue all over and died in the hope of a glorious resurrection. Where's your luggage?

HUCK: Hmm? Oh, I, ah, left it at the riverboat landin'.

AUNT SALLY: Well, didn't you see your Uncle Silas there? He's been a-goin' ever day to look for you…

HUCK: No, ma'am.

AUNT SALLY: (*Laughing at herself.*) Oh, o' course! You ain't seed him or me since you was but a little'un! Well, now, jus' set here and tell me *all* about the family.

(*Huck gulps, scratches his head, and hopes for the earth to open.*)

HUCK: Well…they's fine, mostly, I reckon.

AUNT SALLY: Nooo—I want to hear about *each 'n' ev'ry one* of 'em, Tom Sawyer!

(Huck's eyes bulge and he mouths the name: "Tom Sawyer".)

AUNT SALLY: How's Mary gettin' on? An' Sid—do you two fight an' carry on as much as your dear Aunt Polly writes?

HUCK: Excuse me, ma'am; do you reckon I could have a cup o' water...Aunt Sally?

AUNT SALLY: Well, o' course, chile. *(She stands and steps over to George who sits on stool by Jim, asleep.)* George Mathers! Fetch my nephew a cup o' water! *(George rouses himself from the stool and ambles off Upstage Left. Silas Phelps enters from Upstage Right, followed by Tom Sawyer, who carries a traveling case.)*

AUNT SALLY: Why, Silas...!

SILAS: Look who's here, Mother; the Sawyer boy!

(Huck and Tom stare at each other.)

AUNT SALLY: *(Pointing at Tom.)* Well, if *that's* Tom Sawyer, who's that? *(She points at a petrified Huck. Pause. Tom suddenly steps forward.)*

TOM: Well, shoot! *I* ain't Tom Sawyer; *that's* Tom Sawyer!

SILAS: If he's Tom Sawyer...who are *you?*

TOM: Why, I'm *Sid* Sawyer, Uncle Silas—Tom's half-brother. Howdy... Tom...

(They exchange polite waves.)

TOM: We was jus' funnin' with you, Aunt Sally. We planned it all on the boat.

(George enters with tin cup of water.)

GEORGE: Here's that cup o' water you asked for...

SILAS: *(Thoroughly confused.)* I'll take that.

(He takes the cup and sits on bench, drinking and mopping his brow. George resumes his seat by Jim and promptly dozes off.)

AUNT SALLY: Well, I've a good mind to whup you both! But I guess I'll fix supper for you instead. *(She kisses Tom and exits Downstage Right.)* Come along, Silas—give me a hand in the kitchen will you...?

(Silas stands wearily and follows. Tom and Huck regard each other.)

TOM: You ain't dead then.

HUCK: Not hardly, but the last five minutes coulda killed me easy. These your kin, huh?

TOM: Yep. But what you doin' here, Huck?

HUCK: I don't care what you think o' me, Tom Sawyer, but I'm helpin' Miz Watson's Jim run away.

TOM: *Jim?!* He here too?

(Huck points to Stage Left.)

HUCK: I know you'll say I'm a low-down slave lover, Tom, but Jim's my friend now, an' I jus' got to help him get away.

TOM: Why, shoot! I'll *help* you help him! Tonight—when it's dark—I'll get the keys from Uncle Silas; he don't know where he is half the time anyways. It'll be an adventure!

AUNT SALLY: *(Calling from Offstage.)* Come on, boys! Come on 'n' wash up! *(Tom and Huck shake hands. Tom runs off, laughing. Huck waits for a moment, looking at Jim. Lights fade as Huck runs after Tom and exits. Blackout.)*

SCENE VII

A lantern light appears in the moonlight farmyard. Huck carries the lantern, accompanied by Tom. George sits on stool Downstage Left, asleep.

HUCK: Hssst! Jim!

JIM: *(Whisper.)* Careful, Huck...

TOM: Is that farmhand asleep?

JIM: I think so.

HUCK: We got the key, Jim. We'll head out an' make for the raft. *(Tom unlocks the chain around Jim's ankle. Jim stands and stretches; massages his ankle. Tom begins to drag chain toward George's ankle to lock him in.)*

TOM: Go on, you two! Up that way! *(Huck and Jim move Stage Right and start up the slope to cross the bridge to Stage Left. Tom locks George's ankle, but awakens the man.)*

GEORGE: Hey—who's that? What're you doin'?! *(Tom stands and runs to follow Huck and Jim.)*

GEORGE: Hey, there! You! Stop or I'll shoot! *(Jim and Huck are nearly off when a shotgun rings out with a blast and a flash of powder. Tom falls. George runs to follow, but the ankle chain catches him and he falls flat. Shotgun fires again.)*

HUCK: Tom!

TOM: *(Strained.)* I'm all right, dang it! Go on!

HUCK: Go on, Jim—we'll meet you at the raft!

JIM: *(Business, urgent.)* No, suh! That boy's hurt! *(Jim returns to Tom; voices approach from farmhouse Downstage Right. Jim picks Tom up in his arms and starts to carry him toward the house.)*

JIM: Come on, Tom. We got to get you tended to...

(Silas enters, carrying a lantern, followed by Aunt Sally.)

SILAS: Who's that? What's goin' on here?

JIM: It's the boy, Mistah Phelps. He been shot, an' he need a doctor bad.

TOM: *(Weak now.)* I'm all right, Jim…you coulda *made* it, Jim…you coulda made it to the raft, dad blame it…

JIM: Kin I take him inside, Miz Phelps?

AUNT SALLY: O' course…*Jim*, is it? Bring him right on in.

GEORGE: *(Timidly, from his supine position.)* Mr. Phelps? Help…?

TOM: Here's the key…

(Huck takes the key from Tom and hands it to George. Aunt Sally leads Jim, carrying Tom, Downstage Right and off.)

SILAS: I don't understand a thing…not a blessed thing!

(George limps into the farmhouse, followed by Silas. Huck remains.)

SCENE VIII

Huck steps to edge of stage Center. Single pool of light on Huck.

HUCK: *(To audience.)* Jim stayed by Tom's bed all the night through, even when the doctor came. And Aunt Sally—she cried to see him sittin' there. *(Lights begin to grow to reveal riverboat landing.)*

HUCK: Oh, sure—Tom would be all right, but he'd a-been a lot better if his own Aunt Polly hadn't a-showed up the next mornin'. She said that she had decided she couldn't trust Tom on his own, and had took the next steamboat south from St. Petersburg…

(Aunt Polly enters, followed by Silas, Aunt Sally, and Jim—who assists Tom in walking. Tom's arm is bandaged and in a sling. Tom, Aunt Polly, and Jim are dressed for traveling; Aunt Sally carries a couple of carpet bags for them.)

AUNT POLLY: …and I reckon I was right, too, Tom Sawyer; you just ain't to be trusted, that's all. And no more are *you*, Huckleberry Finn! Although I *am* powerful glad to see you warn't murdered…

(She hugs Huck. Steamboat whistle. People begin to board riverboat.)

AUNT SALLY: Well, I *don't* see why you have to pack up an' go right off, Sister…

AUNT POLLY: When that steamboat leaves, this boy is goin' to be *on* it! *(To Tom.)* Really, Tom Sawyer! Gettin' yourself shot to help Jim escape, when you knowed all along that he was free already!

TOM: It was the *adventure* of it, Aunt Polly…

HUCK: *(To Aunt Polly.)* Jim *is* free?

AUNT POLLY: Why, shore! Miss Watson, she took ill a couple o' months back, poor thing, an' she always regretted havin' tried to sell Jim.

JIM: *(With a hearty laugh.)* Tha's right, Hucky! She put it in her will: my wife, my chill'en, an' myself! We's all free!

(Huck and Jim look at one another for a moment; Jim tousles Huck's hair. Steamboat whistles twice.)

AUNT POLLY: Well, come *on*, Tom

(More travelers arrive and board steamboat.)

SILAS: Such a short visit...I don't understand...

AUNT SALLY: *(Hugging Aunt Polly and Tom.)* Well you never do, Silas, so don't let it trouble you.

(Aunt Polly and Tom move to board steamboat. Huck and Tom wave farewell to one another. Aunt Polly and Tom climb the ramp, and Silas and Aunt Sally follow them off, carrying their bags. More people linger on platforms to see the riverboat off; among them is the White-suited Gentleman who stands on middle platform Stage Right, smoking a cigar with a newspaper under his arm. Jim and Huck move Downstage Center together.)

JIM: How 'bout it, Hucky? Steamboat this time, Honey—got me a real ticket...

HUCK: No...I'm afeard if I go back, there'll be Pap a-waitin' for me.

JIM: *(Putting his arm around Huck.)* Hucky. You remember the floatin' house...an' the dead man in it? Your Pap won't do you no harm no mo', 'cause o' that were him.

(Huck looks into Jim's eyes, and then nods in appreciation and understanding. Aunt Sally and Silas enter from the ramp and move Upstage Left.)

AUNT SALLY: *(To Silas.)* We'll get clean clothes for that Finn boy, and we'll teach him to be a regular little gentleman, that's what we'll do... *(Calling to Jim.)* Jim! Steamboat leavin'! Don't you miss it!

JIM: Hucky...?

HUCK: I dunno, Jim. I come this far; I reckon I'll head out for the Indian territory for a spell.

(Jim looks at Huck, shakes his head and laughs warmly. Huck embraces Jim with great love. Jim turns, laughing more, and runs up the ramp to the steamboat. Huck waves. Steamboat whistle. All but Huck and White-suited Gentleman; Silas and Aunt Sally, and a few others remain. White-suited Gentleman steps down to edge of middle platform and stands above Huck.)

WHITE-SUITED GENTLEMAN: Nothing more to write about, Huckleberry?

HUCK: No, and I'm rotten glad of it! If I'd a-knowed what trouble it was to make a book, I wouldn't a-started it in the first place.

WHITE-SUITED GENTLEMAN: *(Chuckles.)* Well, I've got a boat to catch. You're
certain you don't want to…?
HUCK: Yep. That Aunt Sally, she's goin' to adopt me and civilize me, an' I can't
stand it.
(White-suited Gentleman moves onto ramp, waving his newspaper in farewell.)
HUCK: I been there before.
*(Steamboat whistle. Ramp rises and steamboat moves off. All exit but
Huck—alone—waving. Lights fade to Blackout.)*

CURTAIN CALL

Lights rise on full cast, singing and clapping hands.

ENSEMBLE: Mississippi Belle, I'm bound to leave you
Mississippi Belle, I'm bound to go
Mississippi Belle, I'm bound to leave you
Mississippi Belle, I'm bound to go
(Repeat Chorus.)
BLACK CHOIR: Well my journey is not over
Yes I still have far to go
And I do not fear the river
Or the stormy winds that blow
There's a time before returning
And a time for moving on
Like the bird that flies from winter
In the morning I'll be gone
ENSEMBLE: Mississippi Belle, I'm bound to leave you
Mississippi Belle, I'm bound to go
Mississippi Belle, I'm bound to leave you
Mississippi Belle, I'm bound to go
(Curtain)

END OF PLAY